D1719906

Semitica Viva

Herausgegeben von Otto Jastrow

Band 23

2000

Harrassowitz Verlag · Wiesbaden

Janet C. E. Watson with
ᶜAbd al-Salām al-ᶜAmri

Waṣf Ṣanᶜā:
Texts in Ṣanᶜānī Arabic

2000
Harrassowitz Verlag · Wiesbaden

Publication of this book was supported by a grant from the University of Durham.

Die Deutsche Bibliothek – CIP-Einheitsaufnahme
Ein Titeldatensatz für diese Publikation ist bei Der Deutschen Bibliothek erhältlich

Die Deutsche Bibliothek – CIP Cataloguing-in-Publication-Data
A catalogue record for this publication is available from Die Deutsche Bibliothek

e-mail: cip@dbf.ddb.de

Gedruckt auf alterungsbeständigem Papier.
Druck und Verarbeitung: MZ-Verlagsdruckerei GmbH, Memmingen
Printed in Germany

ISSN 0931-2811
ISBN 3-447-04266-4

This book is dedicated to the memory of Khadija Diana May

CONTENTS

ACKNOWLEDGEMENTS

I would like to thank the following organisations and individuals for help in the funding of this project: the Leverhulme Trust for awarding me a two-year research fellowship for the period 1997–1999 during which time this book was produced; the University of Durham Travel Fund for providing me with the means to return to Yemen in December 1997 to January 1998 to do more recording for the project, and in December 1998 to revise the first draft of the book; the University of Durham Publication Board for a publication subvention of £500; the British Academy for awarding a grant of £1,200 to pay Abd al-Salām's salary expenses in summer 1998; the Leigh Douglas Memorial Fund for awarding a grant of £500 to pay for Abd al-Salām's airfare and travel expenses from Yemen to Durham; His Excellency, Dr Husayn al-Amri, and the Yemeni Embassy in London for a grant of £300 towards proof-reading and production expenses.

I also have a large debt of gratitude to the following people: first and foremost, to Abd al-Salām al-Amri for allowing me to record his story at various times since 1991 and for spending six weeks in Britain during the cold summer of 1998 to go through the transcriptions, their translations and the glossary. Without Abd al-Salām, there would be no book. I would also like to thank Mike Gowman and Debbie Dorman for acting as messengers, through their fax machine, between me and Abd al-Salām before his visit to Britain; Ahmad Luṭfi and, in particular, Abdul Gabbar Al-Sharafi for going through some of the texts and part of the glossary after Abd al-Salām left Britain; the families of Abd al-Raḥmān al-Kibsi and Muḥammad al-Gīni; Abd al-Karīm al-Amri; as always, Tim Mackintosh-Smith for putting me up for three weeks in December 1997 to January 1998 and in December 1998, for suggesting some analyses of texts, for providing references and for pointing out a number of mistakes; Otto Jastrow for encouraging me to produce the book in the first place; Neil Conduit for proof-reading the text; Shelagh Weir for suggesting sources of funding; my husband, James Dickins, for help with some translations and interpretations, for allowing me time to travel to Yemen for three weeks over Christmas for two years running, for looking after our children while Abd al-Salām was in Durham, and for printing out the final camera-ready manuscript. Finally, I want to thank our children, Alistair and Sarah, for helping me to understand the language of children's games, but more especially for their patience and forgiveness over this, and other projects.

INTRODUCTION

This book comprises an introduction, twenty-eight annotated texts of San'ani Arabic (henceforth SA) with translations, and a glossary. The book was originally conceived as I was completing *Ṣbaḥtū! A Course in Ṣanᶜānī Arabic* and cataloguing several hours of SA texts. Together these spontaneous, unrehearsed oral texts told their own story about Yemeni culture, and particularly the culture of San'a; they also told a story about SA. In order that the language of the texts remained maximally homogeneous, I decided to use texts provided by one principal speaker, Abd al-Salām al-ᶜAmrī (referred to in footnotes to the texts as AS), which were recorded on various occasions between 1991 and 1998. In many ways, this story is Abd al-Salām's story.

Abd al-Salām is a native speaker of SA who comes from a well-established San'ani family living in the al-Bawniya area of San'a near the old Jewish quarter of al-Ga'. He was born in Yemen in 1962. He is educated to diploma level and has spent periods of time in Britain. I initially chose him as an informant because of his keen interest and pride in SA, his knowledge of Yemeni, particularly San'ani, culture and his ability to speak fluently, and often at length, on almost any subject relating to Yemen. Because of his relatively young age, his educational level and the fact that he has travelled outside his country, his recordings exhibit a few features which are not found in the speech of older SA speakers, particularly women. These include the use of the phrase *baᶜḍ al-aḥyān* 'sometimes' in place of *zārathīn* which is more common amongst women and older speakers, and the use of *baᶜḍ* generally in place of *zārat*; the use of occasional classicisms (noted below); the periodic use of pan-Yemeni forms such as *ayš* 'what' in place of *mā*; and the periodic use of words and phrases loaned from non-Yemeni dialects of Arabic. His idiolect is representative of the dialect of SA spoken by male natives of the city born before and slightly after the Revolution.

The texts deal with the following topics: the old city, oil presses, the old watercourse, bread, the development of restaurants from the old caravanserai, Yemeni cooking and recipes, travel in Yemen, gat, Yemeni architecture, the water-pipe, changes in al-Bawniya, public bath-houses, lost customs, children's games of yesterday and today, Ramadan, festivals, weddings and births. The texts tell a story of change and of what remains despite the forces of change – the rules of hospitality, fasting, food, the bath-houses – and shows Yemen as a place of change and adaptation, but as a place which has not abandoned the old ways. The texts are principally descriptives, narratives or mixed descriptive-narratives of personal experience. Text 6 on Yemeni recipes and text 21 on hopscotch, which are both recorded by female speakers, are largely instructional texts. Text 15, the addict from San'a, is a joke which falls within the general class of narratives but is distinguished from the other texts in that it has been told on previous occasions and therefore cannot be described as unrehearsed. In addition, the text is not totally fluent since it was recorded by Abd al-Salām in the presence of a group of British undergraduate students of Arabic. This text was included in the collection to illustrate the way in which speakers tend to adapt their speech to the listener by speaking more slowly, by using words which are felt to typify foreigner-speak, by using pan-Yemeni or pan-Arabic terms in place of specific SA terms, by explanatory apposition and by repetition. As the speaker becomes more involved in the telling and feels he gains the confidence of his audience, the speed of delivery increases, the number of non-SA terms begins to drop, and repetition decreases.

In addition to the twenty-five texts by Abd al-Salām, I have included two short texts from two women SA speakers in the age bracket twenty to twenty-five, and one text from a girl in her early teens. These texts deal with hopscotch (text 21), women's wedding and birth parties (text 28), and San'ani recipes (text 6). The text on hopscotch added to Abd al-Salām's texts on children's games and was included because the woman speaker involved had closer knowledge of the game than Abd al-Salām; the final text on the giving of presents at women's wedding and birth parties was included because it elucidated the final, rather elliptical, paragraph of Abd al-Salām's text on men's wedding parties. It was also interesting to note the slightly different meanings attached to the word *ṭarḥ* in men's gatherings ('giving presents of money at a wedding') as opposed to women's gatherings ('giving wedding presents'). The text recorded by the girl in her early teens on San'ani recipes is interesting because it shows the way in which a speaker who is unused to the microphone adapts and stilts her speech to suit the artificial conditions of recording. It also demonstrates how a speaker may begin to drop the non-SA elements shown earlier in the recording as she becomes more accustomed to the microphone.

Each text has ethnographic and linguistic footnotes and is translated into idiomatic English. Rather than imposing an artificial punctuation on spontaneous, unrehearsed oral texts, the texts are divided by slashes (/) into intonation phrases. By contrast, the English translations, which are essentially more artificial and have required more consideration and afterthought, are fully punctuated. For longer sections of text, I have artificially paragraphed the Arabic (and the English translation) to ease comprehension.

The aim of the book is twofold: firstly, to provide the reader with cultural and ethnographic information about San’a past and present through genuine SA texts; and secondly, to consider the linguistic features (particularly the syntax) of SA beyond the sentence and the simple utterance. From the linguistic point of view, the importance of the book hinges on the fact that Arabic linguistics (and indeed linguistics in general) rarely ventures beyond consideration of the often rather ill-defined unit, the sentence. This book also provides a corpus from which dialectologists of Arabic may draw in future comparative studies on aspects of Arabic syntax and morphology.

1. Transcription

Within the translations and commentaries in the book, I use accepted English spellings for proper nouns and words derived from proper nouns: for example, Ṣanᶜā’ is written as San’a which is one of the standard spellings of the city name in English and is used by a number of current specialist writers (e.g. Mackintosh-Smith 1997, Rushby 1998), Ṣanᶜānī as San’ani and correspondingly al-Gāᶜ as al-Ga’. In the transcription of texts and textual examples, the transcription system used is as follows:

1.1. Consonants

The twenty-eight consonants in SA are given in the left-hand column below:

’	glottal stop
b	voiced bilabial stop
t	voiceless dental stop
ṯ	voiceless interdental fricative
j	voiced alveo-palatal affricate
ḥ	voiceless pharyngeal approximant
x	voiceless velar fricative
d	voiced dental stop
ḏ	voiced interdental fricative
r	voiced dental tap
z	voiced dental fricative
s	voiceless dental fricative
š	voiceless alveo-palatal fricative
ṣ	voiceless pharyngealised dental fricative (emphatic)

ḏ̣	voiced pharyngealised interdental fricative (emphatic)
ḍ	voiced pharyngealised dental stop (emphatic)[1]
ṭ	voiceless pharyngealised dental stop (emphatic)
c	voiced pharyngeal approximant
ġ	voiced velar fricative
f	voiceless labio-dental fricative
g	voiced velar stop
k	voiceless velar stop
l	voiced lateral
m	voiced bilabial nasal
n	voiced dental nasal
h	voiceless laryngeal fricative
w	voiced labio-velar approximant
y	voiced palatal approximant

1.2. Vowels

The three short vowels in SA are given in the left-hand column below:

a	open vowel
u	close, back, rounded vowel
i	close, palatal vowel

When unstressed any of these vowels can be pronounced as a shwa as in *a* in English *against* or *about*. The three long vowels in SA are:

ā	open vowel with two possible pronunciations or allophones: an open back sound, as in *ea* in *heart*, and an open front sound, as in *ea* in *bear*.
ū	close, back, rounded vowel.
ī	close, palatal vowel.

In contrast to *Syntax* and *Sbaḥtū!,* the transcription is not maximally phonological in this work. The results of phonological processes are marked as they occur in the oral texts: these include intervocalic and word-initial voicing of obstruents, geminate devoicing, pre-pausal glottalisation, epenthesis within and across words, syncope, assimilation of consonants, labialisation of high vowels in the environment of emphatic consonants,

[1] [ḍ] is a voiced allophone of /ṭ/ and is not a phoneme in its own right in San'ani.

vowel raising in pre-pausal position and in certain other contexts, degemination, and the lengthening of vowels and sonorants for emphasis or as a sign of hesitation. In addition, words are written as strictly phonological words with the result that verbs are given together with their prepositional phrase complements when the annex of the preposition is a dependent pronoun, as in *yibizzalih* 'he takes himself' in place of *yibizz lih* and *daxaltalī* 'I took myself in' in place of *daxalt lī*.

2. List of abbreviations

Grammatical and referential abbreviations used in this book are as follows:

f.	feminine
m.	masculine
s.	singular
adj.	adjective
adjt.	adjunction
adv.	adverb
bot.	botanical
class.	classicism
coll.	collective
conj.	conjunction
esp.	especially
imperf.	imperfect
intr.	intransitive
neg.	negative
o.a.	one another
oft.	often
o.s.	oneself
p.c.	personal communication
perf.	perfect
pl.	plural
s.o.	someone
s.th.	something
s.where	somewhere
usu.	usually

1.	first person (i.e. I/we)
2.	second person (i.e. you)

3.	third person (i.e. he/she/it/they)
AS	Abd al-Salām al-ᶜAmrī
SA	Ṣanᶜānī Arabic

Waṣf	Al-Šahārī, Jamāl al-Dīn ᶜAlī ibn ᶜAbd Allāh ibn al-Qāsim ibn al-Mu'ayyad bi-llāh Muḥammad ibn al-Qāsim ibn Muḥammad al-Šahārī	*Waṣf Ṣanᶜā': mustall min al-manšūrāt al-jalīyah* (ed. ᶜAbd Allāh Muḥammad al-Hibšī). San'a, 1993.
Syntax	Watson, Janet C.E.	*A Syntax of Ṣanᶜānī Arabic*. Wiesbaden, 1993.
Ṣbaḥtū!	Watson, Janet C.E.	*Ṣbaḥtū! A Course in Ṣanᶜānī Arabic*. Wiesbaden, 1996.

3. Footnotes

Footnotes to the texts are used to elucidate cultural aspects of the texts, to indicate where the speaker deviates from what San'ani speakers would agree is typical San'ani speech, to indicate certain features of the pronunciation, to indicate interesting aspects of the syntax, to indicate idioms and to supplement the translation of a word or phrase where this is felt to be necessary. Where appropriate, reference is made to *A Syntax of Ṣanᶜānī Arabic* (Harrassowitz: Wiesbaden, 1993) and, less frequently, to *Ṣbaḥtū! A Course in Ṣanᶜānī Arabic* (Harrassowitz: Wiesbaden, 1996). Notes relating to the translation and to cultural aspects of the material are placed at the bottom of the right-hand page, below the English translation. Notes relating to linguistic aspects of the material are placed at the bottom of the left-hand page, below the Arabic text. In this Introduction, I will discuss the major types of linguistic features which occur in the texts.

3.1. Deviations from SA

Most of the texts exhibit some deviations from what is considered to be typical SA. For example, Abd al-Salām sometimes uses the Egyptian, possibly from Turkish *bir de* (Hinds and Badawi 1986: 66), *barḍū* 'also' in place of SA *ᶜād bih, ᶜād* or *zid*. He also occasionally uses what I term here classicisms. This includes certain adverbs ending in *–an*, such as *fiᶜlan* 'in fact', *ayḏ̣an* 'also', *jiddan* 'very' and *mubāšaratan* 'directly; straight away', and, rarely, supplementary phrases such as *li-ḏālik* 'therefore; because of that'.

3.2. Pronunciation

Pronunciation features which are noted by footnote, particularly in the earlier texts, include the following: voicing of certain stop consonants (particularly *ṭ*, also *t*,[2] and occasionally *k*) in intervocalic and word-initial position, word-final glottalisation and subsequent devoicing of sonorants and voiced stops, geminate devoicing and anticipatory voicing or devoicing of stops in word-internal consonant clusters. In observing the phenomenon of geminate devoicing, it is seen that the geminate velar *gg* devoices to *kk* far more frequently than geminate coronal (e.g. *dd* to *tt*) or labial (*bb* to *pp*). The degree of devoicing probably depends additionally on the degree of emphasis the preceding syllable receives.

Additional pronunciation notes are provided for the phenomenon of degemination together with syncope within, predominantly, form II verbs. This usually takes place when the verb takes a vowel-initial subject pronoun, as in *ṭal*^{c}*ū* from *ṭalla*^{c}*ū* 'they m. lifted up', *tiḏakrī* from *tiḏakkirī* 'you f.s. remember' and *rag*^{c}*ū* from *ragga*^{c}*ū* 'they m. sewed'.[3] Word-initial syncope is a frequent phenomenon in SA, particularly where sibilants are involved, and is only noted in the earlier texts or where misunderstandings may ensue. Instances of syncope tend to increase in a text with the speed of delivery. Examples of syncope include: *tštī* for *tištī* 'you m.s./she want(s)' and *tjī* for *tijī* 'she/you m.s. comes'. In comparison to many other dialects of Arabic, such as Cairene and Sudanese, syncope is not restricted to one specific vowel phoneme (in the former dialects, *i*). In the appropriate phonological environment and depending on the speed of delivery, any of the vowel phonemes *a*, *i* or *u* may be subject to syncope.

In most Arabic dialects, syncope is restricted to unstressed vowels, however in SA (as in several other conservative bedouin-type dialects) stressed vowels may also be subject to syncope which then results in stress migration. This is particularly the case with words comprising, or ending in, the syllables CVCVC. Much of the stress fluctuation for which Yemeni Arabic in general is well known results from deletion of a stressed vowel

---

[2] Originally noted in a paper by Jastrow (1984).

[3] Noted also by Naïm-Sanbar (1994) for SA and by Johnstone (1967: 45) for Eastern Arabian dialects (e.g. *yjassimūn* > *yjassmūn* > *yjasmūn* 'they distribute').

and stress migration. Examples of syncope and stress migration include *x*raj* in place of **xaraj* 'he went out', *m*rih* in place of **marih* 'woman', *x*šabih* in place of **xašabih* 'piece of wood', *yift*hin* in place of *yif*tahin* 'he relaxes' and *yikt*sir* in place of *yik*tasir* 'it m. breaks'. For further details of syncope in SA, the reader is referred to Watson (1999b). Watson (forthcoming) presents a metrical stress analysis of syncope and stress migration in SA.

As in many other dialects of Arabic, epenthesis is a common phenomenon in SA. However, the degree to which epenthesis is used within a text also depends on the speed of delivery: in contrast to syncope, the slower the speed of delivery, the more examples of epenthesis are found in a text. Where epenthesis occurs within the word, as in *absartuhum* 'I saw them m.' and *ba^{c}dahā* 'after her', this is transcribed but not noted by footnote; by contrast, epenthesis across words is noted in earlier texts as in *jamba jamb* 'side-by-side', *kulla wāḥid* 'everyone' and *ṣaḥna bint* 'a plate of 'daughter [of the plate]''.

One striking aspect of the phonology of SA is the labialisation of short high vowels (including that of the feminine ending and the third masculine singular object and possessive pronoun *–ih*) following any of the emphatic phonemes *ṭ*, *ṣ* and *ḍ*, and also of final long *–ā* once the raising of low vowels in pre-pausal position (*imāla)* has taken place. In the early texts in the present work, I have noted post-emphatic labialisation, but not in later texts. For more details on the labialisation effects of the emphatics in SA, the acoustic and perceptual effects of labialisation and the directionality of labialisation spread, the reader is referred to (Watson 1995, 1996b, 1999a).

Another pronunciation feature noted by footnote in the earlier texts is the optional gemination of *l* of definite article before vowel-initial (original glottal-stop-initial) words, as in *al-lahl* from *al-ahl* 'the family', *al-lumm* from *al-umm* 'the mother' and *al-lawlād* from *al-awlād* 'the boys'.

3.3. Aspects of syntax

The majority of linguistic features footnoted in the texts concern the syntax. Syntactic features noted include: the use of the apophonic or internal passive; the use of the annexion phrase as opposed to, or as a stylistic variant of, a phrase involving a genitive exponent (in SA *ḥagg*); types of apposition; parenthetical phrases; tag phrases and clauses; lack of gender or number agreement; feminine plural agreement for collectives such as *xubz* 'bread' and *ḥaṭab* 'wood' when the collective is viewed as a plural entity by the speaker; use of verbal (i.e. verb-initial) clauses; use of asyndetic linkage, particularly between clauses; use of the conjoin *fa-*; and repetition. Here I shall look in more detail at the use of verbal clauses and repetition.

3.3.1. Verbal clauses

A number of scholars have claimed that the preferred verb-subject-object (VSO) word order of Classical Arabic has been largely overridden by the word order subject-verb-object (SVO) in modern dialects of Arabic (e.g. Agius 1991: 42, Versteegh 1984: 24, 79, 1998: 797). A recent study of word order in Arabic by Dahlgren (1998) shows through a study of modern eastern colloquial Arabic texts that this is a false conclusion 'based ... on the assumption that the loss of case markings in earlier times precipitated the ... order [SVO] in order to avoid ambiguity in the syntax' (Dahlgren 1998: 15). Dahlgren demonstrates that basic word order in Arabic is related to other areas in linguistics including tense, aspect, foreground, background and pragmatic information (ibid: 225).[4] With the exception of Anatolia and certain dialects spoken in Egypt, Dahlgren shows that VSO is the dominant word order in foreground clauses in modern eastern colloquial Arabic and SVO the dominant word order in background clauses (ibid: 219).

In SA, word order often depends on a combination of syntactic, stylistic, rhythmic and semantic factors. When an element in the clause is stressed or is felt to convey new information, this element will tend to be in clause-final position. Thus, where the subject is a single indefinite noun, the verb almost invariably precedes the subject,[5] as in the majority of Arabic dialects (cf. Holes 1995: 210). Accordingly, existential sentences with a verb are almost invariably verb initial. However, depending on the text type and the dynamism of the verb, the verb may also precede a definite subject. Narrative texts with a predominance of dynamic verbs have a higher number of verb-initial clauses, while descriptive texts in which stative verbs tend to predominate have a higher number of subject-initial clauses.[6] In narrative

4 In narratives, foreground clauses describe events which happen in sequence and express a time relative to the narrator, while background clauses describe events which occur out of sequence and express a time which is relative to the time of the foreground.

5 Where subject is an indefinite pronoun such as *man*, *mā* or *wāḥid* (incl. syntactially definite phrases such as *an-nās* and *al-wāḥid* which function as indefinite pronouns) however, it usu. precedes the verb even in cases where a definite noun would not. This is probably because indefinite pronouns do not tend to convey new information. Cf. *Syntax* p. 117-118.

6 Cf. Dahlgren (1998: 224) for modern colloquial Arabic in general.

texts, verbal clauses with an initial main verb tend to detract focus from a following definite subject and to emphasise the sequentiality of events (*Syntax* p. 118). A linking or translocative verb will also precede a definite subject, but in this case the emphasis will either be placed on a following complement or on a clause-final subject (cf. below). The subject often appears in clause-final position when the verb takes an object pronoun as opposed to an independent noun object. In addition, verbal clauses occur quite frequently in the texts in this book when the definite subject is inanimate.

Examples of verbal clauses with a dynamic verb include:

yaᶜnī misik al-gāḏ̣ī yad axī wa-yad ḏayyik
'I mean, the judge took hold of my brother's hand and the hand of the other one'

yaᶜnī bi-twassaḏū al-lahl bi-nās ṯāniyīn
'that is to say, the family get other people to act on their behalf'

wa-ysīr yiḏbilū al-gāt akṯarathum ... wa-yijissū yitgahwaw šwayyih wa-yijtamaᶜū an-nās kulluhum
'Most of them go and spit out their gat ... then they sit and have tea and all the people gather together'

yiḏ̣rubū bi-ṭāsuh wa-yūṣalū an-nās
'They beat the plates and people arrive'

wa-baᶜdā yijirr al-fannān al-ᶜūd wa-yiddī 'uġniyih ḥāliyih
'Then the singer takes the oud and sings a nice song'

yilᶜabu l-banāt wa-l-ᶜiyyāl
'Girls and boys play'

Verbal clauses are more common than nominal clauses when the verb is repeated and the subjects contrast. By placing the subject in clause-final position, the contrasting subjects attract emphasis, as in:

fa-jaw aṣḥāb az-zīnih rakkabū zīnathum, wa-jā' ṣāḥub al-mikrafūn rakkab al-makrafūnāt ... yijaw xubrat axī
'Then the people with the lights came and set up their lights; the man with the microphone came and set up the microphones ... and my brother's friends came'

jaw al-xubrih ^{c}alā wāḥid wāḥid, imtala l-makān wa-jaw nās xayrāt
'Friends came one by one, the place filled up and lots of people came'

tijlis ^{c}induhum wa-yjayn xawāthā wa-yijī 'axwathā
'She stays with them and her sisters come and her brothers come'

daxalna l-mafraj hānāk, daxalu n-nās kulluhum, daxalū hū wa-xubratih kulluhum wa-l-mad^{c}ūwīn wa-l-hāḏā
'We went into the reception room there, everyone went in, he went in with his friends and the people who had been invited and the lot'

ammā yiwaṣṣuluh axūh ... aw yiwaṣṣuluh ṣāḥubuh
'Either his brother takes him or his friend takes him'

Verbal clauses with initial translocative or linking verbs such as *jā'* 'to come [to do...]', *wuga^{c}* 'to become', *ṣār* 'to become', *jarr* 'to take up, to start [doing]', *bigī* 'to remain', *bada'* 'to begin' and *kān* 'to be' often have emphasis placed on the following (verbal, nominal, adjectival or locative) complement. Examples include:

wa-jaw al-fannānīn yiġannaw, bad'ū al-fannānīn yiġannaw
'The singers came to sing, and the singers began to sing'

an-nišārih hāḏā kānū 'ahl as-sūg mā yibālūš bihā
'These shavings, the people of the market didn't care about them'

wa-bad'aw an-nās yihtammū bi-d-dūlār
'People began to be interested in the dollar'

bada'at al-maḏā^{c}um diftaḥ
'Restaurants began to open'

yūga^{c} *al-faḍūr ḥāmuḍuh wallā salaḍuh*
'Breaking the fast will consist of soured fenugreek or salad'

wa-kān al-yawm awwal yawm ibnī brāhīm ṣām
'Today was the first day that my son, Ibrahim, fasted'

bigī al-fannān hānāk wa-l-fannānīn wa-l-hāḏā
'The singer and the singers and the lot stayed there'

wa-yūga^{c} *al-gāt hānāk arxaṣ min hānā*
'Gat there is cheaper than [it is] here'

Examples of verbal clauses in which the verb takes an object pronoun suffix include:

u-gad ista^{c}*malih abraha l-ḥabašī hāḏā fī zamān*
'It was used by Abraha, the Ethiopian, a long time ago'

wa-l-malūj nilgāhin fī s-sūg yisabbirannahin an-niswān
'We can find *malūj* in the market. It is made by women'

w-innu ṣtara^{c} / *ṣara*^{c}*ah duxxān ibb*
'He suddenly became dizzy; he was made dizzy by the smoke from Ibb'

Examples of verbal clauses in which the verbal subject is inanimate include (cf. also above):

hāh w-inthā al-^{c}*iris ḥakkanā hākaḏā*
'Okay, and our wedding came to an end like that'

yūga^{c} *al-ġunā wa-yiġannayn wa-yurguṣayn*
'There is singing and they f. sing and dance'

wa-jā' wakt al-gāt
'The time for gat came'

Verbal sentences are also found where a string of verbs share the same subject. This is probably stylistically motivated in order to split the first verb from the following verbs, as in:

wa-jalasū an-nās akalū yitsāmarū wa-l-ḥarīw baynahum
'The people stayed, they ate chatting with the groom amongst them'

3.3.2. Repetition

Repetition is a common phenomenon in Arabic, and a number of instances of repetition in the texts are noted through footnotes. All repetition tends to indicate emphasis of some type. In the case of verbs, repetition usually indicates repeated action or continuous action: the description of the camel in text 2 on oil presses as *yidūr yidūr yidūr* 'he goes round and round and round' gives the sense of continued, unabated turning, just as *yišrab yišrab yišrab* 'he smoked and smoked and smoked' in text 15 provides a sense of continuous smoking. In other examples, the repetition of a verb may indicate that an action is completed separately several times, as in *yibizzalih al-ḥawlī wa-yibizzalih ṣābūn wa-yibizzalih aš-šambū* 'he takes a towel and he takes soap and he takes shampoo'.

Other syntactic entities which are commonly repeated include prepositions (e.g. *min* 'from'), prepositional phrases (e.g. *bih* 'there is', *ma^cih* 'with him; he has') and, less commonly, nouns (e.g. *sūg* 'market', *jāmi^c* 'mosque'). Where nouns are repeated, the noun may either refer to a single referent which the speaker wishes to emphasise and often describe from separate angles, or it may refer to different referents. As an example of the first type, consider the word *jāmi^c* 'mosque' in:

> *fi ṭ-ṭarīg ḥagg sūg al-milḥ bih al-jāmi^c al-kabīr, jāmi^c ḥālī kabīr gawī 'ismih al-jāmi^c al-kabīr wa-gadīm jiddan*
> 'On the way to Sug al-Milh, there is the large mosque. [It is] a very large beautiful mosque which they call the large mosque, and [it is] very old'

As an example of the second type, consider the word *sūg* 'market; market area' where different types of markets are being described:

> *li-kulla ḥājih mawjūd fīhā sūg, sūg al-janābī, sūg al-^cuswab, sūg al-kawāfī*
> 'For every thing, there is a market there: the curved dagger market; the sheath market; the hat [or kaffiya] market'

And the repetition of *jambiyih* 'dagger; jambiya' in the following passage:

> *bih al-jambiyi l-ġāliyih bih al-jambiyih ar-raxīṣuh bih al-jambiyih al-mudwassaḍuh bih al-janābī min kulla ^{c}aynih*
> 'There are expensive jambiyas; there are cheap jambiyas; there are reasonably [priced] jambiyas; there are all types of jambiyas'

Extended repetition of all types often indicates that the speaker is describing a large number of objects, actions or facts and that the number of these in the real world exceeds the number mentioned. There is a sense that the speaker is providing an incomplete list.[7] This is particularly the case when entities are coordinated asyndetically – i.e. without a conjunction such as *wa-* or *fa-* or *aw*. Consider the following set of repeated instances of the verb *yištī* 'he wants':

> *yiṣallaḥū ayyi šay tištīhā min ^{c}ind al-ibrih lā ^{c}ind ad-dast ma štā al-wāḥid fās yištī mikḥif yištī brih yištī mulgāḍ yištī madfal yištī mā yisammawh mawgad la-n-nār ayyi ḥājih yištī mawjūd fī sūg al-ḥadīd hāḏā yisammawh*
> 'They can make anything you want from a needle to a cauldron, whatever you want, an axe, you may want a shovel, you may want tongs, you may want a spittoon, you may want, what do they call it, a stove for charcoal, anything you want is there in the iron market, [as] they call it'

The sense of a list being incomplete is often enhanced by a final incomplete grammatical entity – often an incomplete clause or annexion phrase. This incomplete listing is well exemplified in Abd al-Salām's walk through the market when he describes the different market areas:

> *bih sūg al-bazz bih sūg al-xšab bih sūg al-ḥadīd bih sūg an-naḥās bih sūg az-zabīb bih sūg al-^{c}inab bih sūg al-bagar bih sūg al-^{c}irj bih sūg …*
> 'There is the cloth market. There is the wood market. There is the iron market. There is the copper market. There is the raisin market. There is the grape market. There is the cattle market. There is the lame [donkey] market. There is the market for …'

Finally, repetition of numbers[8] or single adjectives and occasionally nouns

---

[7] This is described as emphatic listing in *Syntax*. Cf. *Syntax* pp. 316-17.

[8] For numbers, cf. also Mörth (1997: 126, 147).

describing smallness often conveys a distributive sense. These phrases usually function adverbially (cf. *Syntax* p. 252). A large number of phrases of this type are found in text 4 on bread. They are also a common feature of instructional texts:

wa-yigassimannih fī 'akyās zuġayrih zuġayrih
'They divide it up into lots of small bags'

yigassimannih ᶜalā šwayyih šwayyih
'They divide it up bit by bit'

nagaṭṭaᶜhā ġayr zuġār zuġār
'We cut it up into lots of small pieces'

al-aswāg hī jamba jamb
'The markets are next to each other'

nuskubhā guṭrah guṭrah
'We pour it drop by drop'

4. The glossary

The glossary comprises nouns, adjectives, verbs, prepositions, circumstants, independent pronouns, demonstratives, locatives, other independent particles and some set phrases. Nouns are given in the singular and plural, where relevant. The plural form follows the abbreviation pl. The gender of the singular noun is noted only for feminine nouns by the abbreviation f. Thus, the full entries for the masculine noun *bašmag* 'shoe' and the feminine noun *sikkīnih* 'knife' are as follows:

bašmag pl. *bašāmig* 'shoe'

sikkīnih f., pl. *sakākīn* 'knife'

Where a noun takes a regular plural ending (*–īn* or *–āt*), only the ending (not the complete plural form) is given following the abbreviation pl., as in:

dūlār pl. *–āt* 'dollar'

Where a noun takes a collective rather than (or in addition to) a plural form, this is indicated by the abbreviation coll., as in:

dawmih f., coll. *dawm* 'doum fruit'

xayl coll., pl. *xiyūl* 'horses'

Adjectives are given in the unmarked masculine singular form. Feminine adjectives can be identified in the texts by the feminine ending *–ih* (*–uh* after non-pharyngeal emphatics and *–ah* after pharyngeals).[9] Where an adjective takes the sound plural ending *–īn* (*–āt* for feminine plural) the plural of the adjective is not listed. Thus an adjective such as *jāwi*^{c} 'hungry' which takes the sound plural *–īn* ending to denote masculine plural is listed in the glossary simply as *jāwi*^{c}. An adjective such as *ṭawīl* 'tall', however, which takes a broken plural pattern, is listed in its masculine singular and plural form, as in:

ṭawīl pl. *ṭuwāl* 'tall'

Verbs are given in the third masculine singular (he) form in the perfect aspect and the imperfect aspect, as in:

btā^{c} *– yibtā*^{c} 'to buy; to sell'

Transitive verbs are indicated by the abbreviation s.th. (or s.o.) following the gloss, as in:

absar – yibsir 'to see s.th.'

Where a verb takes a following preposition, the preposition is added after the plus sign (+), as in:

bālā – yibālī + bi- 'to care about s.th.'

Alternative pronunciations are given after slashes (/), as in:

ḏalḥīn / ḏaḥḥīn / ḏaḥḥīnih 'now'

---

9 Unless they are colour or defect adjectives of the form *af*^{c}*al* in which case they take the *fa*^{c}*lā* pattern (e.g. *abyaḍ* 'white' *bayḍā* f. 'white').

No notes are supplied in the current reader relating to morphological inflection: for the inflection of verbs in the perfect and imperfect aspects, for negation of verbs and nouns, for details about broken and sound plural formation, and for the defining of nouns and adjectives, the reader is referred to *Ṣbaḥtū!* and *Syntax*. Independent pronouns, demonstratives and uninflected numerals are listed in the glossary. Since they can be best considered in sets, they are also listed here below along with the dependent pronouns for ease of reference:

Independent pronouns

	singular	plural
1.	*anā*	*iḥnā*
2.m.	*ant*	*antū*
2.f.	*antī*	*antayn*
3.m.	*hū*	*hum*
3.f.	*hī*	*hin*

Dependent pronouns

	singular	plural
1.	*–ī* (*–nī* as object to verb)	*–nā*
2.m.	*–ak*	*–kum*
2.f.	*–iš*	*–kin*
3.m.	*–ih*	*–hum*
3.f.	*–hā*	*–hin*

The complete list of demonstratives is as follows:

Proximal demonstratives

hāḏā / ḏayyā	'this m.'	*hāḏawlā / ḏawlayya / hawlā*	'these'
hāḏī / tayyih	'this f.'		

Distal demonstratives

hāḏāk / *hāḏ̣āk* / *ḏayyik* / *ḏāk*	'that m.'	*hāḏawlāk* / *ḏawlayyak* /	
			'these'
		ḏawlāk / *awlāk* / *awlā'ik*	
hāḏīk / *hāḏ̣īk* / *tayyik* / *tāk*	'that f.'		

The numbers from one to ten are as follows:

1	*wāḥid*	6	*sittih*
2	*iṯnayn*	7	*sab^{c}ah*
3	*ṯalāṯih*	8	*ṯamāniyih*
4	*arba^{c}ah*	9	*tis^{c}ah*
5	*xamsih*	10	*^{c}ašarih*

The tens are as follows:

20	*^{c}išrīn*	60	*sittīn*
30	*ṯalāṯīn*	70	*sab^{c}īn*
40	*arba^{c}īn*	80	*ṯamānīn*
50	*xamsīn*	90	*tis^{c}īn*

4.1. Lexical items which are not listed in the glossary

Two types of word are not included in the glossary: firstly, dependent pronouns and verbal prefixes – dependent pronouns are listed along with independent pronouns and demonstratives above, verbal prefixes are given below; and secondly, certain regularly occurring set phrases and words which have a number of different meanings depending on the context. These latter are predominantly closed-list items (*Syntax* p. 21) and include the particles *gad* and *^{c}ād*, the particle *hāh*, the form *ḥagg* which is used predominantly in periphrastic annexion to indicate possession, amongst other relationships (*Syntax* p. 177), the definite article *al-* 'the', and a few set phrases (such as *^{c}ād bih* 'also; there is also'). The use and possible meanings of *hāh* are described below. Set phrases are often referred to by footnote. For the use and possible meanings of *ḥagg* cf. *Syntax* pp. 220-4 and *Ṣbaḥtū!* pp. 119-20, 149 and 174. For the use and possible meanings of *gad* and *^{c}ād* cf. *Ṣbaḥtū!* pp. 57-9.

4.1.1. Verbal prefixes

There are two sets of verbal prefixes: those which indicate future tense, and those which indicate habituality or continuity of action. The future prefixes are *šā-* or *ᶜad-* for the first person singular 'I' and *ᶜa-* for all other persons. The habitual/continuous prefixes are *bayn-* for the first person singular and *bi-* for all other persons.

4.1.2. The particle *hāh*

The particle *hāh*, which I do not mention in my previous books, is a discourse marker which crops up quite frequently in the texts recorded by Abd al-Salām. It is probably related etymologically to the *hā* of the demonstrative pronouns (*hāḏā*, etc.) and may originally have been used in the sense of 'see!' With slightly different senses, the particle *hāh* or *hā* is found in other modern Arabic dialects including some Saudi Arabian dialects (al-Azragi 1998), dialects of north-east Arabia (Johnstone 1967: 92, 108), dialects of the Gulf (Holes 1990: 282), and the eastern Sudanese dialect of the Shukrīyah (Reichmuth 1983: 123), as well as other dialects of Sudanese (J. Dickins p.c.).

According to Abd al-Salām, *hāh* in SA is a feature of men's speech more than of women's speech.[10] Depending on the intonation and context it can be used in four different senses: in the texts in this book, it is most commonly used to involve the listener in the sense of *tamām* 'okay?' or *dirītī* 'do you f.s. understand?' Unlike *tamām*, however, when *hāh* is used in this sense by the speaker the addressee cannot repeat the word *hāh* for confirmation but has to use a word such as *tamām* or *aywih* 'yes'. Secondly, it can be used as an imperative in the sense of *xuḏ* 'take!' Thirdly, it can be used in place of the vocative *yā* 'hey!' in order to attract someone's attention. Fourthly, it can be used by the addressee to ask the speaker for further information, or to ask him to repeat what he has just said.

The ending *–hā* suffixed for emphasis to demonstratives is probably also derived from the *hā* particle of the demonstratives. Examples include: *hākaḏahā* and *kaḏayyahā* 'like that!' The presentational particle *hā* (*Syntax* p. 423) is also almost definitely related to *hāh* differing only in the latter's wider semantic range and in the fact that *hāh* occurs independently.

[10] Women are more likely to use the word *tamām* 'okay?' or an inflected verb such as *dirītī* 'do you f.s. know?' *hāh* is, however, used frequently in women's speech (and probably also in men's speech) in Ibb and many other dialects spoken in the southern regions of erstwhile North Yemen.

Texts

1 *Min al-gā^{c} lā bāb al-yaman*

anā ^{c}ad-asajjil d̲alḥīnih / kayf yuxṭā wāḥid[1] */ fī ṣan^{c}ā / yitmaššā / mat̲alan law axruj min al-bayt ḥagganā / gult šā-sīr atmaššā / awwal-mā 'axruj / axruj min al-bayt w-axṭā aš-šāri^{c} ^{c}alā ḍūl / baytanā*[2] *hū fī bīr al-^{c}azab / w-anā šā-sīr atmaššā d̲alḥīn lā bāb al-yaman / sūg al-milḥ*[3] */ id̲ā ša-mšī rijl amšī min ^{c}ind al-bayt w-a^{c}ṣur min šāri^{c} hand̲al / ba^{c}d-ma xṭā min šāri^{c} hand̲al axṭā ṣalā šāri^{c} jamāl / šāri^{c} jamāl hād̲ā hū sūg / kabīr / ṭawīl hākad̲ā lākin anā ša-xṭā minnih ġayr xaḍiyuh*[4] */ ṣalā bāb as-sabaḥ / wa-min bāb as-sabaḥ adxul ṣala s-sāyilih /*

as-sāyilih hād̲ā hī wasṭ ṣan^{c}a l-gadīmih / yisammūhā as-sāyilih / hī ṭarīg sayl gadīm / d̲alḥīnih mā ^{c}ād biš sayl / ya^{c}nī mā ^{c}ābiš[5] *fīhā mā' xayrāt bi-mšī / illā lā šī*[6] *sayl / bī-ṣallaḥūhā hāda l-iyyām min šān yif^{c}alūhā yixallaw as-sayl yimšī:*[7] */ al-awwal kānat ḥijar wa-turāb wa-wasax wa-d̲ayyā / d̲aḥḥīn gad bī-naḍḍumūhā wa-gadī munaḍḍamuh wa-gadī ^{c}amalūhā bi-l-ḥajar / bi-ḍarīguh ṣan^{c}ānīyuh / bi-ḥabaš / sawdā / miš ḥabaš it̲iyūbī / ḥabaš sawdā / ba^{c}d-ma xṭā min as-sāyilih aḍla^{c}*[8] *min ^{c}ind barrūm / barrūm hād̲ā manḍuguh min manāḍug ṣan^{c}ā yisammūhā barrūm / manḍaguh jamīlih / fīhā / 'awwal-ma ḍla^{c} al-wāḥid fīhā yibsir al-bistān wa-l-mikšāmih*[9] */ wa-biyūt ṣan^{c}a l-jamīlih al-gadīmi l-ḥāliyih*[10] */ yixṭa l-wāḥid minnahā min barrūm hād̲ā yiṭla^{c} / ^{c}alā ḍūl / al-biyūt ^{c}alā yamīnih / wa-^{c}alā šimālih /*

---

1 *wāḥid / al-wāḥid* often used pronominally in the sense of impersonal 'you'. Cf. *Syntax* p. 385. *al-wāḥid* usu. has a more general sense than *wāḥid* (cf. Mörth 1997: 123-4).

2 Note annexion phrase *baytanā* while attribution phrase *al-bayt ḥagganā* used when house is first mentioned. An annexion phrase is often used before or after attribution phrase with *ḥagg* for stylistic purposes. Here, more emphatic attribution phrase introduces house and more concise annexion phrase *baytanā* used shortly afterwards (cf. Eksell 1980: 74-82).

3 Reformulative apposition. Cf. *Syntax* pp. 244-6.

4 Intervocalic voicing of *ṭ* to *ḍ*. Cf. *Syntax* p. 9. Labialisation of final *-i-* due to preceding emphatic (cf. Watson 1995, 1996b, 1999a). Cf. examples below.

5 From *mā ^{c}ād biš* with deletion of *d*.

6 *šī* used existentially in conditional clauses and questions. Cf. *Ṣbaḥtū!* pp. 61, 139.

7 Lengthening of vowel in stressed syllable of intonation phrase for added emphasis.

8 Anticipatory voicing of *ṭ* to *ḍ*.

9 Anticipatory devoicing of *g* to *k*.

10 Synonym of *l-jamīlih*.

1 From al-Ga' to Bab al-Yaman

I am now going to record how you walk in San'a, how you go for a walk. For example, if I go out of our house and said I would be going for a walk, when I first go out, I go out of the house and walk straight down the street. Our house is in Bir al-Azab[11] and I am now going to walk to Bab al-Yaman,[12] Sug al-Milh.[13] If I am going to go by foot, I walk from the house and turn down Handhal Street. After going down Handhal Street, I walk towards Jamal Street. Jamal Street is a big, long row of shops,[14] but I shall just walk down there towards Bab al-Sabah, and from Bab al-Sabah I shall go towards the old watercourse.

This old watercourse[15] is in the centre of the old city of San'a. They call it the Sayila. It is the old path of a watercourse, but now there is no longer any water. I mean, there is no longer a lot of water running in it unless there is rain. These days, they are fixing it so that they can allow the water to run down. In the past, there were stones and dust and dirt and the lot. Now they are tidying it up and it is neater. They have done it in stone in the San'ani way, with black stone [called *ḥabaš*].[16] Not the *ḥabaš* [which means] Ethiopian. Black stone. After I leave the old watercourse, I go up though Barrum. Barrum is an area in San'a which they call Barrum. [This is] a beautiful area. When you first go up into it you can see the garden, and the vegetable garden, and the lovely, beautiful old houses of San'a. You walk from there, from Barrum, and go straight up from there with houses on your right and on your left.

---

[11] Bir al-Azab is described in *Waṣf* as one of the three main parts of San'a. Together with *gā^c al-yahūd* it formed the quarter to which Jews were confined before their migration to Israel (*Waṣf* pp. 50-1, note 7, p. 60, note 4, cf. also Serjeant and Lewcock 1983: 496).

[12] Bab al-Yaman used to be called *bāb ^{c}adan* in the eleventh century AH (*Waṣf* p. 61).

[13] The terms Bab al-Yaman and Sug al-Milḥ are commonly interchanged in reference to the main market area.

[14] Lit: 'a long, large marketplace'.

[15] A description of the old watercourse is given below in text 3.

[16] This stone has been used traditionally in the construction of houses up to the third floor. From this level, baked brick is used (cf. *Waṣf* p. 74).

kullahā biyūt gadīmih / yitfarrajhā wāḥid wa-yibsir al-manāḏug al-jamīlih / ḥawlih / yibsir al-manāḏur / yibsir al-^{c}ugūd fī l-biyūt / yitfarraj al-biyūt al-gadīmih wa-'aškālhā ar-rāyi^{c}ah / yiṭla^{c} min barrūm ^{c}alā l-abhar / hāḏā wa-hū xāḏī rijl / ṭab^{c}an aṭ-ṭarīg hī rijl / allī ša-xḏā minnahā hāḏā / hī rijl / wa-barḏu[17] *s-sayyārāt tuxṭā minnahā / yuxṭā wāḥid yuwāṣul yūṣal al-abhar / al-abhar hāḏā fīhā as-sarḥah / yisammūhā sarḥah / sā^{c} al-maydān hākaḏā ṭawīl / wa-ywaggifū fīhā sayyārāt / wa-n-nās bi-yixṭaw rijl / wa-bih hānāk gad bih fī biyūt ṣan^{c}a l-gadīmih hāḏā / gad bih ba^{c}ḏahā fanādig la-s-siyyāḥ / fi^{c}ilūhā ḏalḥīn /*

^{c}ala ṭ-ṭarīg absir maḥallāt muftaḥah[18] *jadīdih / ba^{c}ḏahā yibī^{c}ū fīhā / hāḏa l-ḥājāt al-gadīmih / ad-dukkih*[19] *wallā l-labbih / wallā l-fuḏḏuh / walla l-janābī ayyi ḥājih tištīhā hānāk mawjūdāt ḥakk al-ašyā al-gadīmih hāḏ allaḏī yibī^{c}ūhā li-s-siyyāḥ / wa-makātib siyyāḥ / lā ḥadd*[20] *yištī yis'al hānāk yiwarrawh wa-bih hānāk / tilgā maktab illī hum ... yixarrijūk bi-s-siyāḥah fī ṣan^{c}ā fī xārij ṣan^{c}ā / ^{c}alā-mā yištī al-wāḥid / wa-ba^{c}d-ma xṭā min al-abhar / aṭla^{c} ṣalā sūg al-milḥ /*

fī ṭ-ṭarīg ḥakk sūg al-milḥ bih / al-jāmi^{c} al-kabīr[21] */ jāmi^{c} ḥālī kabīr gawī / bī-sammūh al-jāmi^{c} al-kabīr wa-gadīm jiddan / wa-ba^{c}d-ma dxul min al-jāmi^{c} al-kabīr ^{c}ind al-jāmi^{c} al-kabīr bih hānāk / aswāg ^{c}adīdih fī ṣan^{c}a l-gadīmih / fīh*[22] *sūg al-milḥ / iḥna nsammīh sūg al-milḥ / aw bāb al-yaman / wa-hāḏā sūg al-milḥ / ya^{c}nī fīh aswāg ^{c}adīdih minnahā hāḏa llī yisammūh sūg al-milḥ / bih sūg al-bazz / bih sūg al-xšab / bih sūg al-ḥadīd / bih sūg an-naḥās / bih sūg az-zabīb / bih sūg al-^{c}inab / bih sūg al-bagar / bih sūg al-^{c}irj*[23] */ bih sūg ... / li-kulla ḥājih mawjūd fīhā sūg / sūg al-janābī / sūg al-^{c}uswab / sūg al-kawāfī / li-kulla šī yištī al-insān hānāk sūg /*

---

[17] Non-SA. Loan from Egyptian.

[18] Syncope of stressed vowel and degemination of *tt*. From *mufattaḥah*.

[19] Devoicing of geminate *gg*. Cf. *Syntax* p. 10.

[20] *ḥadd* is used pronominally in all types of conditional clauses, in negative clauses and in questions (cf. Mörth 1997: 134-7). In SA, *wāḥid* is also used in conditional clauses.

[21] Here and below use of existential *bih* with following definite noun. Cp. *Syntax* pp. 121-2 where it is incorrectly claimed that *bih* occurs only with following indefinite noun.

[22] Use of non-SA existential *fīh*.

[23] Nine asyndetically linked clauses with repetition of *bih sūg* ... and last clause ending on incomplete annexion phrase. Conveys the sense of emphatic listing. Cf. *Syntax* p. 317.

They are all old houses which you can see and you can look at the lovely areas around you. You can look at the top-floor rooms [called *manḍaruh*].[24] You can see the coloured arched windows in the houses. You can look at the old houses with their wonderful shapes. You go up from Barrum towards al-Abhar. This is if you are going by foot. Of course, the route is for walking, the way I am going is by foot, but cars can also go that way. You walk on and continue until you reach al-Abhar. Al-Abhar has a large open courtyard which they call a *sarḥah*. [It is] like a square. It is long. Cars are parked there[25] and people continue on foot. In the houses of the old city of San'a, there are also some hotels for tourists which they have done up now.

On the way, I can see shops which have opened recently. Some of them sell old things [such as] necklaces with large silver spheres, or necklaces which cover the chest, or silver, or curved daggers, anything old you want there can be found. These are the things they sell to tourists. [There are also] tourist offices, if anyone wants to ask there, they will show him. There, you will also find an office where they can take you within San'a or outside San'a on a tourist trip, wherever you want. After leaving al-Abhar, I go up towards Sug al-Milh.

On the way to Sug al-Milh, there is the large mosque. [It is] a very beautiful large mosque which they call the large mosque, and very old. After I go by the large mosque, at the large mosque, there are a number of markets in the old city of San'a. There is Sug al-Milh. We call it Sug al-Milh or Bab al-Yaman. This Sug al-Milh comprises a number of market [areas] including that which they call the salt market. There is the cloth market. There is the wood market. There is the iron market. There is the copper market. There is the raisin market. There is the grape market. There is the cattle market. There is the lame [donkey] market. There is the market for .... For everything, there is a market there: the curved dagger market; the sheath market; the hat [or kaffiya] market. For anything anyone could want, there is a market there.

---

[24] These are top-floor rooms which enjoy a good view, hence the name *manḍaruh*.

[25] Lit: 'they park cars there'.

hāḏā hū as-sūg ar-ra'īsī ḥakk al-yaman kānat ḥakk ṣanᶜā maṯalan kull an-nās yudxulū min al-gurā min kulla bugᶜah yudxulū yitbaḏḏaᶜū / yaᶜnī māhu s-sūg illī 'aštī 'anā sīr layh / ayyi sūg aštī 'asīr layh maᶜrūf awṣal ilayh lā maᶜrafīhš[26] */ allī fi š-šāriᶜ man kān*[27] *as'alih ᶜa-ywarrīnī ᶜalā ḏūl /*

ᶜinda-mā 'awṣal min ᶜind al-jāmiᶜ al-kabīr / txul ᶜala š-šimāl iḏ an aštī sūg al-xšab / atxul atfarraj sūg al-xšab mā bī-sabbirū fīh / bī-sabbiru l-labwāb[28] *al-gadīmih / bī-sabbiru ṭ-ṭīgān / xāṣṣ bi-l-xšab / yaᶜnī māhī al-ḥāji l-xašab*[29] *illī yištī hānā min bāb aw ḏāguh aw šabk aw ayyi ḥājih min xašab hāḏā yisammawh sūg al-xašab /*

lā daxalt sūg al-ḥadīd / sūg al-ḥadīd hāḏā fīh yiṣallaḥū / ayyi šay tištīhā min ᶜind al-ibrih / lā ᶜind ad-dast[30] */ ma štā al-wāḥid*[31] */ fās yištī mikḥif*[32] */ yištī brih yištī mulgāḍ / yištī madfal / yištī mā yisammawh mawgad la-n-nār*[33] */ ayyi ḥājih yištī mawjūd fi sūg al-ḥadīd hāḏā yisammawh /*

wa-min hānāk sa[34]*-'axruj ilā sūg an-naḥās / sūg an-naḥās fīh kull anwāᶜ an-naḥās al-yamanīyih / al-madāfil al-maᶜāšir / al-mazāhir an-naḥās / kulla ḥājih mawjūd / al-mabāxir / allī tištī / min ḥājāt naḥās mawjūd fi hāḏā sūg an-naḥās /*

axṭā min ᶜind sūg an-naḥās awṣal lā sūg as-salab / sūg as-salab hāḏā hī as-salabih illī hī xiyūṭ / ṭawīluh / yisammūh sūg as-salab / fīh al-ḥibāl yaᶜnī as-salab hī al-ḥibāl al-ān / bass iḥna nsammīh sūg as-salab / tilgā fīhā salabih ṭawīluh ᶜala l-mitr allī tištīh / yaᶜni s-salabih ḥabl / al-ḥabl allī tištī 'ant bi-ḏūl allī tištī tilgā fi as-sūg hāḏā / ġalīḏ / salabih ġalīḏuh / aw salabih ḏaᶜīfuh yaᶜnī / wa-s-salabih hāḏā hī 'akṯarat-mā yijī hī salabih ġalīḏuh / yisammūhā salabih /

---

[26] *-h* of 3 m.s. object pronoun usu. not realised when followed by negative suffix *-š*.

[27] Universal-conditional-concession clause. 'Whoever there is'. Cf. *Syntax* pp. 352-3.

[28] Gemination of *l* of definite article before vowel-initial noun. Cf. *Ṣbaḥtū!* pp. 18-19.

[29] Identificatory apposition. 'The wood thing'. Cf. *Syntax* pp. 241-3.

[30] A common saying. 'From a needle to a cauldron'.

[31] Universal-conditional-concession clause. 'Whatever you want'. Cf. *Syntax* p. 353.

[32] Anticipatory devoicing of *g* before *ḥ*.

[33] Five asyndetically linked clauses with repetition in each case of *yištī*. Combination of asyndesis and repetition conveys sense of emphatic listing. Cf. *Syntax* p. 317.

[34] Classicism. *sa-* used in place of SA *šā-*.

This is the main market for Yemen in San'a. For instance, everyone comes in from the villages from everywhere, they come in to purchase things. So, which is the market that I want to go to? Any market I want to go to that I know I can get to, but if I don't know it, I can ask whoever is on the street and they will show me straight away.

When I go from the great mosque, I go left if I want the wood market. I go in to see what they are doing in the wood market. They are making old doors; they are making windows specially from wood, I mean anything you need out of wood whether it be a door or a window or a screen or anything that is made of wood. They call this the wood market.

If I go into the iron market, in the iron market they make anything you would want from a needle to a cauldron, whatever you may want, an axe, or you may want a scoop, you may want a needle, you may want a pair of tongs, you may want a spittoon, you may want, what do they call it, a stove for charcoal, anything you could want is there in the iron market, [as] they call it.

From there, I will go to the copper market. The copper market has every type of Yemeni copper [product]: spittoons, large trays, copper vases, everything is there, incense burners. Whatever you want in the way of copper objects is there in the copper market.

I go from the copper market and come to the rope market. The rope market [deals in] rope which is long fibres. They call it the rope market. There are ropes [*ḥibāl*], I mean ropes [*salab*] are [called] *ḥibāl* today,[35] but we [still] call it *sūg as-salab*.[36] There you will find long rope at the number of metres you want. I mean *salabih* is *ḥabl*. The rope that you want at the length that you want you will find in that market: thick, thick rope or thin rope. Rope is mainly thick rope [there]. They call it *salabih*.

[35] i.e. *salabih* 'rope' is described using *ḥibāl* today except when reference is made to the rope market.

[36] A number of markets are described using terms which are otherwise not used in everyday speech. These include *sūg as-salab, sūg al-muxlāṣ* 'the silver market' and *sūg al-bašāmig* 'the shoe market'. These latter two markets are mentioned below.

wa-ba^{c}d sūg as-salab asīr sūg al-janābī / sūg al-janābī / ṭawīl ^{c}arīḍ[37] */ kull: ya^{c}nī malān dakākīn / dakākīn kullahum bī-sabbirū janābī / w-ant tūṣal lā ^{c}ind man ištayt*[38] */ tibāyi^{c} fī l-jambiyih / tštī jambiyih / tibāyi^{c} fī l-jambiyih / bih al-jambīyi l-ġāliyih / bih al-jambiyih ar-raxīṣuh / bih al-jambiyih al-mutwassaḍuh / bih al-janābī min kulla ^{c}aynih*[39] */ al-janābī hāḏawlā hin akṯarathin min rūs min ya^{c}nī / ar-rās ḥakk al-jambiyih al-jambiyih hī zayy as-sikkīnih yisammawhā jambiyih / wa-hāḏa l-jambiyih fīhā rās allī yizgamūbih / ar-rās hāḏā / hū 'aṣluh*[40] *min waḥīd al-garn / yisammūh min waḥīd al-garn / yisammūh al-garn ḥakk al-waḥīd al-garn hāḏā / hū gadū mamnū^{c} fī l-^{c}ālam ḏalḥīnih bass al-yamanīyīn yistaxdimūh fī l-janābī / kull-mā ya^{c}nī yisīr*[41] *yugtulū waḥīd al-garn wa-yijaw yiddawlana r-rūs lā wasṭ ṣan^{c}ā yif^{c}alūhin janābī / rūs la-l-janābī / rās al-jambiyih hāḏā / min rās waḥīd al-garn / yugūlū 'innahum yugtulūh / aw iḏā hū ḥayy yib^{c}adū ar-rās ḥakkih / wa-yijaw yiddaw hānā yisabbirū / ṭab^{c}an ar-rās hāḏā kulla-mā gidim / kulla-mā kān aġlā / bih janābī yisammawha ṣ-ṣayfānī / aṣ-ṣayfānī hāḏā ya^{c}nī gadī mṣayfanuh / miṣayfanuh ya^{c}nī / bih naw^{c} allī yišūf al-jambiyih hāḏā yišūf al-… / fī r-rās ḥakkahā hākaḏā ḥājih / ya^{c}nī nigūl miṣayfanuh / wa-ṣ-ṣayfānī hāḏā ya^{c}nī 'innū / ṣayfānī ya^{c}nī gadū bi-šakl jamīl min ḥājih raw^{c}ah / kulla-mā gad ar-rās miṣayfan / ^{c}īs kulla-mā ġilī fī ṯamanih / wa-kulla-mā gidim kulla-mā ġilī 'akṯar w-akṯar*[42] */ bih janābī ġāliyāt jiddan ya^{c}nī mabāliġ bāhiḍuh*[43] */ hāḏā fī sūg al-janābī /*

wa-^{c}ād bih fī sūg al-janābī hāḏā 'aḏkur anā / kān min awwal yijirrū ar-rās hāḏā ḥakk al-gurūn / yijirrūh yugḍa^{c}ūh ya^{c}nī ^{c}inda-mā yijaw yisabbirū al-jambiyih bi-šakl / al-jambiyih hū yijī rās ^{c}ādī murabba^{c} aw muṯallaṯ aw mā kān / lākin yinḥatūh bi-šakl bī-xallaw ^{c}alā yad mamsak li-l-jambiyih /

---

[37] Lit: 'Long and wide'. Idiomatic phrase to describe large areas/entities. Phrase used several times to describe different markets. Also used in text 27 to describe women's party.

[38] Universal-conditional-concession clause. Cf. *Syntax* pp. 352-3.

[39] Four asyndetically linked clauses with repetition in each case of *bih al-jambiyih* (*al-janābī* in the last instance) conveys sense of emphatic listing. Cf. *Syntax* p. 317.

[40] Labialisation of *-i-* of *-ih* 'his' due to preceding emphatic *ṣ* (cf. Watson 1995, 1999a).

[41] Lack of number agreement on the translocative verb. Cf. *Syntax* p. 154.

[42] Repetition of *akṯar* for emphasis. Cp. English 'more and more' versus 'more'.

[43] Reformulative appositive preceded by filler *ya^{c}nī*. Cf. *Syntax* p. 246.

After the rope market, I go to the curved dagger [or jambiya] market. The jambiya market is long and wide. It is full of shops, shops [where] they all make jambiyas. You go to whoever you want to and ask the price of a jambiya. If you want a jambiya you bargain for it. There are expensive jambiyas; there are cheap jambiyas; there are reasonably [priced] jambiyas; there are all types of jambiya. Most of these jambiyas are from heads, I mean, the top of the jambiya – jambiyas are like knifes, they call them jambiyas. This jambiya has a top which they take hold of. This top comes from the rhinoceros. They say it is from the rhinoceros. They call it the horn from the rhinoceros. This is prohibited throughout the world now, but Yemenis use it in jambiyas. Whenever they go and kill a rhinoceros, they bring us the heads[44] to San'a to make them into jambiyas, the top of the jambiyas. The top of the jambiya is from the head of the rhinoceros. They say that they kill it, or if it is alive they remove its head[45] and bring it here to make [it into the handle of the jambiya]. Of course, this top, the older it is, the more expensive it is. There are jambiyas they describe as well patinated [*ṣayfānī*]. Well patinated means that it has yellowed and adopted a shine with age. There is something you can see in the jambiya, in the top of it, there is something we call well patinated [*miṣayfanuh*]. Well patinated means that it has become beautiful and lovely. The more the jambiya can be said to be well patinated, the higher its price, and the older it is, the more expensive it will be still. There are some very expensive jambiyas, that is [for] exhorbitant amounts. This is in the jambiya market.

There is something else about the jambiya market that I can remember. In the past, they used to take top of the horns. They would take it and cut it, I mean when they were making the jambiyas, the top would be made square or triangular or whatever, but they would carve it in such a way that it would fit the hand as a handle for the jambiya.

44 The horn is probably meant here.

45 i.e. horn.

ᶜinda-mā yinḥatūh / yuxruj[46] *minnih nišārih / an-nišārih hāḏā kānū 'ahl as-sūg hāḏawlā / mā yibālūš bihā / nišārih bi-tsīr lā hānāk la-l-gāᶜ / kān bih wāḥid yijī yilaflifhā / fi s-sūg yijī yišillahā la'annū marrih ligī ṣīnī wa-gāllih ō ništī min hāḏā / gāl xalāṣ šā-kūn addīlukum / kān yisīr yilaflifhā fi s-sūg / an-nišārih hāḏā / wa-yisīr yibīᶜhā fi ṣ-ṣīn / tiddīlih zalaṭ xayrāt / wa-ṣ-ṣīnīyīn yistaxdimūhā ᶜilāj māniš ᶜārif māhu l-ᶜilāj / hāḏā ḥakk ar-rūs ḥakk al-janābī /*

fa:[47]*-baᶜd fatrih ahl as-sūg ᶜarafū 'inn hāḏa š-šaxṣ yijī yišill an-nišārih hāḏā ᶜalayhum / diriyū 'innah bi-ddī bi-zalaṭ / daxalū hū wayh*[48] *fī mašākil / yištaw minnih gīmat an-nišārih bi-kam / bi-raġm innahum kān*[49] *yurājimūhā miš hum dāriyīn mā yisawwaw bihā / wa-daxalū hū wayh fi š-šarīᶜah wa-min aš-šarīᶜah midrī mā zit*[50] *fiᶜilū / al-muhimm inni l-guṣṣuh ḥagīgīyih / innū kān yilaggiḍ an-nišārih wa-yisīr yibīᶜhā fi ṣ-ṣīn / wa-ṣ-ṣīnīyīn yistaxdimūhā duwā / li-'ayš*[51] *midrī 'ayš / li'ayš yistaxdimūhā / hāḏā fi sūg al-janābī / sūg al-janābī ṭawīl ᶜariḍ /*

wa-baᶜd-ma txulī min sūg al-janābī jambih sūg al-ᶜuswab / al-ᶜuswab hāḏawlā hin ḥakk al-janābī / 'allī ydaxxilū fīha l-jambiyih / yisammawh ᶜasīb / tilgay bi-l-aškāl al-jamīlih / wa-tilgay bi-l-aškāl al-ġāliyih / wa-tilgay bi-l-aškāl ar-raxīṣuh / allī lā kull: wāḥid gadr / yistir yilga l-ᶜasīb allī yištīh lā ḥakkih[52] *al-jambiyih / wa-bih / jambih / aw fī nafs ad-dakākīn yibīᶜū / maḥāzim / al-ḥizām ḥakk al-ᶜasīb / barḍū / al-ḥizām hāḏā hū 'allī yurbuṭūh bi-l-ᶜasīb wa-l-ᶜasīb yidxul fīh al-jambiyih / yisammawh ḥizām / al-aḥzamih hāḏā aškālhā jamīlih / yijaw yaᶜmalūhā*[53] *baᶜḍ an-niswān wallā baᶜḍ ar-rijāl / yirsimūhā bi-'aydīhum /*

---

46 Lack of gender agreement with following feminine singular subject *nišārih*.

47 Sequential use of *fa-*. Cf. *Syntax* pp. 298-9.

48 Cf. *Ṣbaḥtū!* pp. 217-18.

49 Lack of number agreement on linking verb. Cf. *Syntax* p. 154. *kān* is linking/translocative verb most likely to fail to inflect when followed by main verb; however, all linking verbs may fail to inflect. These verbs are probably in the process of becoming grammaticalised as particles (cf. Versteegh 1998).

50 Anticipatory devoicing across word boundary of *d* to *t*.

51 Use of pan-Yemeni *ayš* 'what'.

52 Inversion of attributed term–attribute to emphasise attribute. Cf. *Syntax* p. 224.

53 Lack of gender agreement with following feminine plural noun.

When they carved it, shavings would come out. The people of the market didn't bother about these [horn] shavings. The shavings[54] would fall onto the ground. There was someone who used to come and collect them in the market. He would come and take them because he had once met a Chinese [person] who said to him, 'Oh, we want that!' He said, 'Okay, I will get it for you.' He used to go and collect them from the market, these [horn] shavings, and go and sell them in China. They[55] would bring him a lot of money, and the Chinese would use them as a medicine, but I don't know what type of medicine. This is from the tops of the jambiyas.

Then after a while, the people of the market came to realise that this person was coming to take the shavings from them, and they knew that he was giving them [away] for money. They got into problems with him. They wanted him to give them what he got for the shavings, even though they used to throw them away and didn't know what to do with them. They went to court with him and from the court I don't know what else they did. Anyway, the story is true. He used to gather the shavings and go and sell them in China, and the Chinese use them as a medicine, but for what I don't know, for what they use them. This is in the jambiya market. The jambiya market is long and wide.

After you go from the jambiya market, next to it is the sheath market. These sheaths are for the jambiyas, the thing they put the jambiya in is called a sheath. You can find beautiful ones, you can find expensive ones, and you can find cheap ones. Everyone can find the sheath they want for their own jambiya. Beside it, or rather in the same shops, they sell belts. Belts for the sheath also. These belts are what they bind to the sheath, and the jambiya goes into the sheath. They call it a *ḥizām*. These belts have beautiful patterns. Some women or men make them. They draw on them by hand.

[54] Indefinite in Arabic.

[55] i.e. the shavings.

yijissū yixayyuṭūhā wa-yifᶜalū 'aškāl jamīlih fī l-ᶜasīb / fī l-ḥizām hāḏā[56] / *akṯarat-mā yifᶜalannahā niswān wallā yifᶜalū ḏalḥīn an-nās*[57] *fī s-sijn*[58] / *wa-hum jālisīn masjūnīn hānāk / yijissū yidwālahū*[59] *yisabbirū ᶜuswab yixarrijūha*[60] *s-sūg yibīᶜūhā ᶜuswab jamīlih / wa-baᶜḏahā gad bi-ddawhā mustawradih / bi-tjī gadī ġarr aškāl gadī ġarr maṭbūᶜah ṭabᶜ min wasṭ al-hind / yiddaw min hānāk / bass yaᶜnī ᶜādanā bayn-atḥākā ᶜan al-ḥizām ḥakk al-ᶜasīb / wa-fīh aškāl ġālī / wa-fīh raxīṣuh wa-fīh ᶜalā gadr al-wāḥid yaᶜnī mā hīš ġālī gawī 'inna-mā tilgā bi-xamsih alf tilgā bi-ᶜašarih alf tilgā bi-'alf tilgā bi-xamsamiyih / tilgā bi-hāḏa l-ḥudūd*[61] / *kull wāḥid yilgā ᶜalā gadra ḥālih yilga l-ᶜasīb allī yištīh wa-l-jamīl wa-kull šay / hāḏā fī sūg al-ᶜuswab / wa-baᶜd txul sūg al-bazz /*

fī sūg al-bazz jamīᶜ anwāᶜ aškāl[62] *al-bazz / akṯarathā al-bazz ḥakk an-niswān / ma štat al-marih*[63] *min bazz / tištī bazz amraykanī tištī … baṣmuh / tištī … 'asāmī kaṯīrih la-l-bazz masturš aᶜaddidhin /*

wa-jamb sūg al-bazz bih sūg aṣ-ṣarf / sūg aṣ-ṣarf hāḏā hū sūg ṣarf al-ᶜumlih / kān yisammawh min awwal sūg aḏ-ḏahab / mā yibīᶜu lla ḏahab wa-yištaraw ḏahab / mā kānš yiṣrafū 'ayyi šay fīh / miṯl ad-dūlārāt wallā r-riyālāt wallā šī mā yiṣrafūš fīh / mā yibīᶜū fīh illa ḏ-ḏahab / wa-baᶜdā daxal ad-dūlār[64] / *bad'aw yiṣrafū ad-dūlār mā biš ṣarf dūlār illā fī hāḏa s-sūg / ḥayṯ-mā sūg aḏ-ḏahab yiṣrafu d-dūlār / hāḏā min awwal / mā kānš yitᶜāmalū bihā*[65] *fī 'ayyi maḥall illā lā hū al-bank wallā fī s-sūg / hāḏā fagaṭ / hāḏā min awwal /*

---

[56] Corrective reformulative apposition. Cf. *Syntax* p. 246.

[57] *nās* is often used in the sense of 'men' in Yemeni Arabic.

[58] Verbal clause with emphasis on definite animate subject *an-nās fī s-sijn* which contrasts with subject in preceding clause.

[59] Anticipatory voicing of *t* before *w*.

[60] Impersonal referent. Cp. *yisabbirū* which refers specifically to men in prison.

[61] String of five asyndetically linked clauses with repetition of *tilgā bi-*. Conveys sense of emphatic or incomplete listing. Cf. *Syntax* p. 317.

[62] Reformulative apposition. Cf. *Syntax* pp. 244-5.

[63] Universal-conditional-concession clause. Cf. *Syntax* p. 353.

[64] Verbal clause with dynamic verb.

[65] The pronoun *-hā* refers back to *ᶜumlih* 'currency'.

Then they sew them and make lovely patterns on the sheaths,[66] on these belts.[67] They are mostly done by women, but now people in prison [also] do [them] while they are imprisoned there. They spend their time making sheaths and then they are taken to the market to be sold, beautiful sheaths. Some of them are now imported. These are just machine-made from India. They bring them over from there, but I am still talking about belts for the sheaths. There are expensive ones, there are cheap ones, and there are ones you can afford. I mean, they aren't very expensive, but you can find them for 5,000, you can find them for 10,000, you can find them for 1,000, you can find them for 500, you can find [them] in that region. Everyone can find a nice sheath that he wants which is within his means. This is in the sheath market. Then I go into the cloth market.

In the cloth market, there are all types of cloth. Most of it is cloth for women. Whatever type of cloth women want: whether she wants Amraykani cloth or whether she wants ... Basma[68] cloth, whether she wants ... [There are] a lot of names for cloth. I can't count them [all].

Next to the cloth market, there is the money-changing market. This money-changing market is the market for changing currency. They used to call it the gold market in the past. They only sold and bought gold. They didn't exchange anything there such as dollars or riyals or whatever. They didn't exchange there. They only sold gold there. Then the dollar came in, and they began to exchange the dollar and you could only exchange the dollar in that market. Where the gold market was they exchanged dollars. This was in the past when they didn't deal with it[69] anywhere other than in the bank or in the market. Only there. This was in the past.

---

66 Singular in Arabic.

67 Singular in Arabic.

68 Basma is a striped cloth with marks like finger prints (Piamenta 1990-1).

69 i.e. currency.

ḏaḥḥīn gad intašarayn / baᶜd-ma rtafaᶜ ad-dūlār wa-ṭuluᶜ ad-dūlār[70] *wa-bad'aw an-nās / yihtammū bi-d-dūlār*[71] */ bada'at bih 'aswāg ṯānī fī ṣanᶜā / dāxil as-sūg šāriᶜ jamāl dāxil / nāzil yaᶜnī xarajat / wallā hāḏā hū al-aṣl la-s-sūg al-ḥagīgī la-ḏ-ḏahab wa-la-ṣ-ṣarf / hāḏā fī sūg aḏ-ḏahab /*

wa-tuxrujī min hāḏa l-aswāg tūṣalī lā sūg al-milḥ / allī hū 'ismih sūg al-milḥ / iḥna bi-nsammīh sūg al-milḥ wa-kull:ih sūg al-milḥ lākin sūg al-milḥ al-ḥagīgī hū mawjūd / ḥayṯ-mā yibīᶜū al-ḥabb / wa-yibīᶜū al-milḥ / bi-kaṯrih / yisammawh sūg al-milḥ / wa-saᶜtar / wa-kull al-bahārāt mawjūdih fī hāḏa s-sūg / sūg al-ḥabb wa-sūg al-milḥ wa-sūg al-... / kullahin sūg wāḥid majmūᶜ jamba jamb / mawjūd fīh kull anwāᶜ al-bahārāt wa-kull anwāᶜ al-ḥubūb wa-l-... / kull al-ḥubūb / allī yiḏlubha l-insān /

wa-tuxrujī minnahā lā sūg al-gišr / xāṣṣ bi-l-gišr[72] */ al-gišr hāḏā hū al-gahwih allī yistaxdimhā fī l-yaman / wa-hī al-gišrih allī yikūn dāxilhā al-binn / al-yamanīyīn yistaxdimū al-gahwih gahwat al-gišr*[73] *akṯar min ayyi maḥall / yaᶜnī 'akṯar mimmā yistaxdimū al-binn / yistaxdimū gahwat al-gišr / wa-hī al-gišrih / ḥakk al-binn / as-sūg hāḏā tutxul ilayh wa-yitxayyal innū sāᶜ al-amkinih hākaḏā kabīr / wa-fīhā dakak al-... wa-l-mayāzīn wa-'ašyā hāḏā / mayāzīn gadīm*[74] *yūzinū fīhā aš-šuwālāt ḥakk al-gišr / law-mā yiddaw al-gišr hānāk yugūlū 'išṭāṭū gišr / yiddawhā lā hānāk / wa-yiwazzinū fīhā bi-mayāzin kabīrih / wa-tilgay allī hum bi-ṣlaḥū*[75] */ w-allī bi-btāᶜū / w-allī bi-štaraw / w-allī...*[76] */ tilgay mawjūdīn fī hāḏa s-sūg / li'ann nās xayrāt bi-gṣudu llāh lā hānāk mā hūš*[77] *illī yibīᶜū al-gišr fagaṭ / bih hāḏa llī bī-bīᶜ al-gišr / wa-bih allaḏī bi-yuṣluḥ / allī bi-ṣluḥ hāḏā allī yitdaxxal bayn al-mištarī wa-l-bāyiᶜ / tamām /*

---

70 Reformulative apposition of clauses. Cf. *Syntax* pp. 245.

71 Verbal clause with initial linking verb and definite animate subject.

72 Predicandless predicate. Cf. *Syntax* p. 124.

73 Reformulative apposition. Cf. *Syntax* pp. 244-5.

74 Lack of gender agreement with preceding (feminine) noun.

75 From here, string of definite clauses which function exophorically and pronominally. Cf. *Syntax* pp. 416-17. Definite clauses are often used to refer pronominally to unidentified animate (i.e. human) or inanimate objects. They may have sing. or pl. reference.

76 String of four syndetically linked phrases with repetition in each case of *allī bi-* + verb. Incompleteness of final clause adds to sense of incomplete list. Cf. above.

77 Dummy pronoun. Cf. *Syntax* p. 413.

Now they have spread out after the [value of the] dollar went up, the dollar rose, and people began to become interested in dollars. There began to be other markets in San'a within the [main] market, in Jamal Street. I mean they[78] expanded. This was the origin of the real market for gold and for money-changing. This was in the gold market.

When you go out of these markets you come to the salt market, which is called Sug al-Milh. We call it Sug al-Milh and it is all Sug al-Milh, but the real salt market is there where they sell grain and sell salt in large quantities – they call it the salt market – and wild thyme, and all the spices are there in that market, the grain market, and the salt market, and the market for .... They all form a single market next to each other. There are all types of spices and all types of grains there, all the grains anyone could require.

You come out of there to the coffee husk market. [This is] specially for coffee husk. The coffee husk is the coffee that is used in Yemen. It is the husk that has the coffee bean inside. Yemenis use coffee husk coffee more than any other place, I mean more than they use coffee from the coffee bean they use coffee from the coffee husk. It is the husk of the coffee bean. You go into this market and it seems like it is large like rooms. They have stone seats ... and scales and things like that. Old scales which they weigh the sacks of coffee husk in. When they bring the coffee husks there, they say they sell coffee husks, they bring them there and weigh them on large scales. You find some [people] acting between the buyer and seller, some [people] selling, and some buying, and some ..., you find [them] there in that market because lots of people make their living there. It isn't just those who sell the coffee husks. There are those who sell the husks, and there are those who negotiate. Those who negotiate are the ones who go between the buyer and seller, okay?

[78] i.e. the markets.

wa-bih allī bi-yitḥammalih / wa-bih allī bi-ḥfuḏuh fi l-maxzan ḥakkih / yaᶜnī kullum[79] *an-nās hāḏawlāk bi-gṣudu llāh / wasṭ as-sūg hāḏāk /*

wa-tuxrujī min hāḏa s-sūg wa-tūṣalī lā sūg al-bazz ṯānī ġayr al-bazz ḥakk an-niswān allī hū / yifᶜalū fīh al-malābis al-jāhizih / xiyyāṭ maḥallī hānāk yisammūh sūg al-bazz wa-l-kull[80] */ tištaray minnih / yijaw kulluhum ahl al-gurā 'allī xārij ṣanᶜā*[81] *yijaw yištaraw min hāḏa s-sūg / l-awlādum fi l-aᶜyād wa-l-hāḏā*[82] *yištaraw min sūg al-bazz hāḏā badalāt jāhizih / zinnih / wallā kūt / wallā strih / yisammaw / wallā sarāwīl / wallā 'ayyi šay min hāḏa s-sūg / hāḏā fi l-sābig*[83] */*

wa-bih sūg al-bašāmig[84] */ sūg al-bašāmig hāḏā yaᶜnī al-jazamāt yisammawh sūg al-bašāmig / mawjūd hānāk / sūg ṭawīl ᶜarīḍ barḏū li-kulla šay /*

yitmaššā wāḥid min sūg lā sūg / yaᶜnī al-aswāg hī jamba jamb / bass yuxruj min ḏayya s-sūg yudxul as-sūg aṯ-ṯānī / yuxruj min ḏayya s-sūg yudxul as-sūg aṯ-ṯānī / jamb sūg al-bazz barḏū hāḏā sūg al-ᶜagīg / al-ᶜagīg al-yamānī / minnih barḏū hāḏa l-fuḍḍuh / wa-l-afṣāṣ al-jamīlih / hāḏa llī yjī aš-šakl al-ḥajarī llī hī al-ḥajarīyih / al-ḥajarīyih hāḏā / yiddaw ḥajar min al-jibāl wa-yijissū yifḥaṣūhā / yifḥaṣūhā wa-tilgay fīhā / yifḥaṣūh yixallawh ᶜalā šakla faṣāṣ / wa-l-afṣāṣ hāḏā tibayyin fīhā aškāl / jamīlih / aškāl ṭuyūr / aškāl nās / aškāl ḥayawānāt / ḥinšān / aškāl jamīlih[85] */ al-ᶜagīg al-yamānī / al-ᶜagīg al-yamanī hāḏā hū mašhūr / l-antī ᶜārifih ᶜannih / fa-hū mašhūr /*

wa-bih / jamb sūg al-ᶜagīg hāḏā / sūg al-muxlāṣ / al-muxlāṣ allī hū fuḍḍuh yisammūh al-muxlāṣ / ᶜindanā / hāḏa s-sūg barḏū sūg ṭawīl ᶜarīḍ / dukkān jamb dukkān[86] */ wa-kullum bi-štaġilū /*

---

[79] From *kulluhum*.

[80] Tag phrase. 'Also'. i.e. 'they also call it the cloth market'.

[81] Verbal clause with dynamic verb and definite subject. Here *ahl al-gurā 'allī xārij ṣanᶜā* acts as a designatory appositive to *kulluhum*. Cf. *Syntax* p. 240.

[82] Tag phrase. Note the demonstrative pronoun takes the definite article. Cf. *Syntax* p. 384.

[83] Hesitation produces the unassimilated definite article.

[84] The orig. Turkish word *bašmag* pl. *bašāmig* is not used in general speech today: now shoes are referred to as *jazmih* pl. *jazamāt* / *gunṭuruh* pl. *ganāṭur*.

[85] Fivefold repetition of *aškāl* in asyndetically linked annexion phrases conveys sense of incomplete listing. Cf. *Syntax* pp. 316-17.

[86] Repetition of singular noun *dukkān* to convey distributive sense. Cf. above.

There are those who carry it and there are those who store it in their stores. All of these people make their living in this market.

You go from that market and come to another cloth market which is different from the cloth market for women; they make ready-made clothes there. There is local tailoring there, they also call this the cloth market. You can buy from there. All the people from the villages which are outside San'a come and buy from that market for their children at festival time and the like, from this cloth market they buy ready-made suits, dresses,[87] coats,[88] coats[89] as they call them, or undertrousers or anything from that market. This was in the past.

There is also the shoe market. The market for shoes [*bašāmig*], I mean, shoes [*jazamāt*].[90] They call it the shoe market. It is there. [It is] also a long, wide market for everything.

You can walk from one market to the other. The markets are all next to each other: you just leave one market and you come into the next market; you leave that market, then go into the next market. Next to the cloth market, there is also the market for gem stones. Yemeni gem stones and also silver and beautiful gem stones [for rings]. This is stonework. For this stonework, they bring stone from the mountains and sit and burnish it. They burnish it and you find in it, they burnish it to make it into the shape of gem stones. In these gem stones, you can see beautiful images – images of birds, images of people, images of animals, snakes, beautiful shapes. Yemeni gem stones, Yemeni gem stones are famous. You know about them, because they are famous.

Beside the market for gem stones, there is the silver market. *Muxlāṣ* is silver [*fuḍḍuh*][91] which they call *muxlāṣ* here. This is also a long, wide market with one shop next to the other, and they are all working.

---

[87] Singular in Arabic.

[88] Singular in Arabic.

[89] Singular in Arabic.

[90] Cf. note on *sūg as-salab* above.

[91] Cf. note on *sūg as-salab* above.

kull an-nās fī hāḏa l-aswāg bi-tigṣud allāh bi-tištaġil wa-bi-tibtā^{c} wa-bi-tištarī[92] */ ya^{c}nī as-sūg mā hūš ġarr / bī-bī^{c}ū fīh / sūg la-l-^{c}arḍ wa-ṭ-ṭalab / wa-sūg an-nās yijaw yibī^{c}ū fīh wa-bi-štaraw minnih / allī ma^{c}ih ḥājih*[93] *yibī^{c}hā w-allī m^{c}ih ḥājih yištī yištarīhā ištarāhā*[94] */ hāḏa s-sūg /*

tixrujī min as-sūg hāḏā / txulī sūg at-tamr / hāḏā sūg ṭawīl kabīr / fīhā tamr mawjūd min kull: ^{c}ayyinih / tamr ṭab^{c}an yijī fī tinīk / wa-tamr yijī fī šwālāt lā hū baladī / wallā yijī fī sallāt / sūg kabīr[95] */ akṯarat-mā titwājid at-tumūr / mawjūd hū fīh at-tamr ^{c}alā ḍūl lākin akṯarat-mā titwājid at-tumūr bi-kaṯrih / ayyāmāt*[96] *ramaḍān yixarrijū at-tumūr hāḏā /*

tuxrujī min sūg at-tamr / lā sūg ad-dawm / sūg ad-dawm hāḏā hū ḥubūb / hākaḏā zuġār[97] *yākulūha n-nās / yisammawh sūg ad-dawm / sūg kabīr lahā / tilgā fīh at-tawm*[98] *al-kabīr wa-ṣ-ṣaġīr ya^{c}nī hin zuġār*[99] *yijayn / bass ġarr šaklahā ṭa^{c}īm ḥālī / yisammawh sūg ad-dawm / ya'kulūhā wa-yirjamu l-ḥabbih allī wasṭhā / ḥubūb zaġīrih / zayy al-libb bass hū yākulūh zayy al-gišr al-xārijī fagaṭ / yākulu l-gišr allī xārij / wa-yirjimu l-ḥabb allī dāxil ad-dawmih /*

wa-bih aswāg ^{c}adīdih / sūg at-titin / dā:xil hāḏā ^{c}ādū fī l-jiha ṯ-ṯāniyih / fī l-jiha ṯ-ṯāniyih hāḏā iḏā lawayt fī l-aswāg kullahā 'arja^{c} adxul min nafs al-aswāg awṣal lā sūg at-titin / at-titin hāḏā an-nās yišrabu l-madā^{c}ah kaṯīr / fa[100]*-bih sūg xāṣṣ hānāk yisammawh sūg at-titin / tilgay titin min kulla ^{c}ayyinih / at-titin al-ḥumamī / at-titin as-sirrāt / wa-t-titin as-safanih / ya^{c}nī at-titin min kulla ^{c}ayyinih wa-dakākīn jamba jamb kulla wāḥid yibī^{c} titin / titin ^{c}adanī / titin ġaylī /*

---

92 Optional fem. sing. agreement for *nās* 'people'.

93 Exophoric pronominal function of definite clause. Cf. *Syntax* pp. 416-17.

94 Where action described in main clause is dependent on fulfillment of that described in subordinate clause, the verb may be in the perfect, as here. Cf. *Syntax* p. 64.

95 Predicandless predicate. Cf. *Syntax* pp. 123-5.

96 The plural *ayyāmāt* 'days' as opposed to *ayyām* / *iyyām* used only where days are defined in terms of a specific time period, as in 'the days of Ramadan', 'the days of summer'.

97 Split of attribute from attributed term by indefinite demonstrative. Cf. *Syntax* p. 217.

98 Geminate devoicing of *dd* to *tt*. Cf. above. Devoicing of geminate dental *dd* is considerably less common in SA than devoicing of geminate velar *gg*. Cf. Introduction.

99 Verb–complement inversion to emphasise the complement. Cf. *Syntax* pp. 143-4.

100 Consequential use of *fa-*. Cf. *Syntax* p. 299-300.

Everyone in these markets is making their living, working, selling and buying. I mean the market isn't just for selling; [it is] a market for displaying [wares] and demand, and a market to which people come to sell in and buy from.[101] If you have something you sell it, and if you have something you want to buy you buy it. This is the market.

You leave this market and come into the date market. This is a long, large market with every kind of date. Of course, [there are] dates which are in tins, and dates which come in sacks if they are local, or come in baskets. [It is] a large market. Dates are mainly available – there are always dates – but there are mostly a lot of dates during Ramadan when they bring out dates.

You come out of the date market into the doum market. [In] the doum market, there are small berries which people eat. They call it the doum market. It has a large market [area] and you can find large and small doum berries there. I mean, they are small but they are very tasty. They call it the doum market. They eat them and throw away the pip which is inside. Small berries like seeds, but they just eat the outer skin. They eat the skin which is on the outside and throw away the pip which is inside the doum fruit.

There are a number of markets. The tobacco market [is] further in on the other side, on the other side. If I walked through all the markets, I would go back by going into the same markets and come to the tobacco market. This tobacco, people smoke the water-pipe a lot, so there is a special market there called the tobacco market. You can find tobacco of every type – Humami tobacco, Sirrat tobacco, Safana[102] tobacco – tobacco of every type with shops one beside the other all selling tobacco – Adeni tobacco, Ghayli[103] tobacco.

[101] Apart from buying and selling, handicraft work is carried on in every shop in the market.

[102] Types of tobacco.

[103] Types of tobacco.

^{c}iddat aškāl min at-titin allī yištī yištarī[104] *yištarī min hāḏa s-sūg / sūg at-titin yisammawh /*

wa-jamb sūg at-titin sūg al-^{c}inab / hāḏā ṭab^{c}an sūg al-^{c}inab / mawāsim al-^{c}inab tikūn / kull al-^{c}inab yijī lā hāḏa s-sūg / lā ḥadd yištī yištarī ^{c}inab yisīr lā hinayyih / mā yisīrš ayyi maḥall yijī la s-sūg ḏayyā lā sūg al-^{c}inab /

fī s-sūg amākin ḥāliyih kaṯīrih / samāsir / mumkin anā 'azūrahā la-na štī[105] */ as-samāsir hāḏā / ba^{c}ḍahā ^{c}ādī gadīmih wa-ba^{c}ḍahā jadīdih / as-samāsir hāḏā ba^{c}ḍahā yistaxdimūhā sā^{c} al-gahāwī wa-sā^{c} al-majālis yijlisū an-nās yiḍḍallalū*[106] *fīhā / wa-ba^{c}ḍahā ḏalḥīn gadī / ma^{c}mūlih min gabil ad-dawlih zayy al-matāḥif / min gabil ad-dawlih zayy al-matāḥif / yitxul al-wāḥid*[107] *yilgā fīhā / al-ḥiraf al-yadawīyih / kullahā mawjūdih / allī hānāk zayy al-^{c}agīg al-fuḍḍuh al-... wa-hāḏā yilgā šabāb bi-ya^{c}malūhā fī s-sūg / an-nijārih / yilgā wasṭ hāḏa s-samāsir / gālū yiḥāfiḍū / wa-bī-^{c}allimū fīhā*[108] */ yiḥāfiḍū ^{c}ala l-ḥājāt al-gadīmih /*

ṭab^{c}an al-aswāg allī šaraḥtališ fīhā kullahin hāḏa llī xuḏīnā min ^{c}indahā[109] *kullahā / kullahā 'akṯarathā*[110] *yadawīyih / miṯl sūg al-ḥadīd / miṯl sūg al-xšab / miṯl sūg an-naḥās / al-janābī / hāḏā kullahā yadawīyih / ḥiraf yadawīyih / mā hīš bi-'ālāt wallā hī bi-šī / kullahā ġarr bi-l-yad / naḥt bi-l-aydī / ḥāliyih / jamīlih gawī /*

sūg al-madāyi^{c} / bih sūg xāṣṣ bi-l-madāyi^{c} / al-madā^{c}ah hāḏa llī yišrabu[111] *n-nās / yilga l-wāḥid sūg ṭawīl ^{c}arīḍ la-l-madāyi^{c} / min wāḥid lā wāḥid tilgay al-madāyi^{c} allī tištay an-nafīsih wa-l-ġāliyih wa-r-raxīṣuh*[112] *wa-kulla šī / wa-sūg al-gaṣīb / gaṣīb al-madāyi^{c} / ya^{c}nī / as-sūg fīh yimkin ṯalāṯih wa-ṯalāṯīn sūg aw xamsih wa-xamsīn sūg m-aniš muta'akkid /*

---

104 Exophoric pronominal use of definite clause. Cf. *Syntax* pp. 416-17.

105 From *lā 'anā 'aštī* 'if I want'.

106 Complete anticipatory assimilation of *t* to *ḍ*.

107 Verbal clause with syntactically definite subject and dynamic verb.

108 The phrase *wa-bī-^{c}allimū fīhā* 'and they teach there' acts parenthetically here.

109 Switch to fem. sing. agreement for *aswāg*. Cf. *Syntax* p. 101.

110 Corrective reformulative apposition. Cf. *Syntax* p. 246.

111 No anaphoric pronoun in the attributive clause. Cf. *Syntax* pp. 234-5.

112 Single attributed term with four attributes. Last three describe separate types of *al-madāyi^{c} allī tištay*, and are thus linked syndetically. Cf. *Syntax* p. 216.

[There are] a number of types of tobacco. Those who want to buy, can buy from that market which is called the tobacco market.

Next to the tobacco market is the grape market. Of course, the grape market, during the grape seasons all the grapes come to that market. If anyone wants to buy grapes they come here, they don't go to any place, they come to this market, to the grape market.

There are many beautiful places in the market. [There are] caravanserais. I could visit them if I wanted. Some of these caravanserais are old and some are new. Some of the caravanserais are used as coffee houses and for sitting in. People sit and take shade there. Some have now been made like museums by the State, like museums by the State. When you go in you can find all types of craftwork there such as [work in] gem stones, silver ... and the like. You can find youths doing this in the market, [such as] carpentry, you can find [this] in these caravanserais. They said they would preserve, and teach in them, they would preserve the old things.

Of course, all the markets I have described to you which we have walked through, all of them, all of them, most of them, are handicrafts, such as the iron market, such as the wood market, such as the copper market, the jambiya [market], these are all [done] by hand, handicrafts. They aren't [done] by machines or anything, they are all [done] by hand, carving by hand. [It is] very nice.

The water-pipe market. There is a market specially for water-pipes. Water-pipes[113] which people smoke. You can find a long, wide market for water-pipes. [Going] from one to the other you can find the water-pipe you want, precious, expensive, cheap or whatever. Then there is the pipe market. Pipes for the water-pipes. The market[114] has maybe thirty-three markets or fifty-five [different] markets.[115] I'm not sure.

---

113 Singular in Arabic.

114 i.e. the whole market area.

115 The author of *Waṣf* says there are more than fifty or sixty markets (*Waṣf* p. 84). According to the editor, al-Ḥibšī, forty-one markets are mentioned in the San'ani statute (*Waṣf* p. 85).

anā gad simiᶜt ᶜannih kam hin[116] *aswāg*[117] *bass mā ᶜad aḏkurš kam / samāsir jamīlih /*

wa-baᶜdā 'axruj / lā gadanā tāᶜib / axruj min bāb al-yaman / hānāk ᶜala ṭ-ṭarīg bih al-bugᶜah allī yišrab minnaha l-gadīd / walla yišrab minhā zabīb / bih amākin tilgayhā yiḥawwišū ᶜalayha n-nās / yištaw yišrabū gadīd / wallā yišrabū zabīb / wallā yišrabū ayyi šay / mawjūdih xayrāt / lā gad wāḥid ᶜāṭuš[118] *yišrab ᶜala ṭ-ṭarīg / wallā yākul rawānī awlā šuᶜūbīyāt / allī yištī / mawjūdih hāḏā fi ṣ-ṣabāḥ yitwājid bi-kaṯrih /*

anā lā gadanā tāᶜib axrujlī[119] *min bāb al-yaman / w-axruj lā xārij bāb al-yaman / maᶜ kuṯrat at-timiššā hāḏā kull:ih*[120] */ mā ᶜad aḥibš*[121] *innanā 'anzil rijl / arjaᶜ la-l-bayt bi-rijl awlā šī / bih hānāk mawgif bāṣāt / arkablī*[122] *bāṣ / wa-l-bāṣ hāḏā yišillanī la-l-gāᶜ / wa-min al-gāᶜ axṭā lā ᶜind al-bayt / li'annū garīb min al-bayt / hāḏā hū ad-dawrih ḥakkī lā gadanā ša-ṭlaᶜ lā bāb al-yaman / ad-dawrih tūgaᶜ min arwaᶜ ad-dawarāt al-jamīlih / yikfinī bi-kam absart ṣanᶜā al-jamīlih aš-šāhigih*[123] *gad tlawwayt fīhā / wa-s-sūg wa-l-ḥalā wa-n-nās wa-z-zaḥmih / ḥājih ḥāliyih / ah /*

---

[116] Switch back to fem. pl. agreement for *aswāg* when referents are viewed as separate, particular entities. Cf. *Syntax* p. 101.

[117] Lit: 'how many they are [in terms of] markets'. *aswāg* functions here as adverbial noun complement. Cf. *Syntax* pp. 144-5.

[118] Labialisation of *-i-* due to preceding emphatic *ṭ* (Watson 1995, 1999a).

[119] Reflexive verb (verb + *lā* + pronoun). Cf. *Syntax* pp. 202-3.

[120] Sonorant lengthening in the stressed syllable of an intonation phrase.

[121] Degemination of *bb* before the negative suffix *-š* (cf. Watson 1999b: 504).

[122] Reflexive verb. Cf. *Syntax* pp. 202-3.

[123] *aš-šāhigih* here refers to the tall houses of San'a.

I did hear how many markets there were once, but I can no longer remember how many. Beautiful caravanserais.

Then I leave, if I am tired. I leave through Bab al-Yaman and on the way there is a place where you can drink apricot syrup or drink raisin [juice]. There are places where you find people crowding around. They want to drink apricot syrup or drink raisin juice or drink whatever. There are a lot of them.[124] If you are thirsty, you can drink on the way, or you can eat cake or thin pastry with syrup, whatever you want. There is a lot of this in the mornings.

If I am tired, I will leave by Bab al-Yaman and go out of Bab al-Yaman. With all this walking, I no longer want to go back[125] by foot, return home by foot or anything. There is a bus stop there where I can catch a bus, and this bus will take me to al-Ga'. From al-Ga' I will go to the house, because it[126] is near to the house. This is the walk I would do if I were to go up to Bab al-Yaman. This walk would be one of the most beautiful walks. I am satisfied with what I have seen of beautiful San'a that I have walked through with [its] tall [houses] and the market, the beauty, the people, and the crowds. [It's] a wonderful thing.

124 i.e. places where you can drink juice.

125 Lit: 'down'.

126 i.e. al-Ga'.

2 *Al-maᶜāṣur*

ᶜād bih ḥāji štī agulliš[1] */ fī s-sūg / fī s-sūg / ᶜād bih al-maᶜāṣur / hāḏā maᶜāṣur az-zayt / yuᶜṣurū fīha z-zayt / al-jiljilān*[2] *hāḏā / fa-l-maᶜāṣur hāḏā hī zayy-mā tigūlī samsarāt gadīmih / bass taḥt al-biyūt dāxil ṣanᶜā l-gadīmih / awwal-mā tūṣalī la-l-bāb hākaḏā tibsirī / ḥājih fī l-wasaṭ hākaḏā sāᶜ al-ḥawḍ aw miš ᶜārif ayš*[3] */ kabīrih*[4] */ wa-bih jamal hānāk / al-jamal hāḏā hū 'allī bi-yuᶜṣur / kayf bi-yuᶜṣur / yuṭraḥū al-xardal hāḏā 'aw al-jiljilān wasṭ al-maᶜṣaruh / wa-ᶜalayhā ᶜūdī / wa-l-ᶜūdī hāḏā marbūṭ lā ᶜarḍ al-jamal bi-ᶜūdī ṯānī / al-jamal yiġaṭṭaw ᶜuyūnih / wa-yiddawlih ġarr akl / tijāhih / yijlis ġarr yākul / wa-yuᶜruṭ / wa-yidūr / yijiss ġarr yidūr yidūr yidūr*[5] */ wa-hū hāḏāk ad-dawarān ḥakkih / bī-xalli l-ᶜūdī / yifḥaṣ fī l-jiljilān hāḏā / mijaljal aw al-... / yijiss ġarr yifḥaṣ wa-yifḥaṣuh*[6] *law-mā yuᶜṣuruh wa-yixallīh / zayt /*

al-wāḥid yijiss yitfarraj hāḏa l-ḥājih ḥālī / yaᶜnī 'anā gad sirt atfarrajthā wa-ᶜjabatnī gawī gawī[7] */ ᶜinda-mā šāhadt al-jamal ġarr jiss bī-dūr bī-dūr bī-dūr*[8] *fī maḥallih / wa-yuxrujlak salīṭ / as-salīṭ hāḏā bi-staxdimūh ᶜilāj*[9] *lā saᶜlih / bi-staxdimūh ᶜilāj la-l-jism / bi-staxdimūh ᶜiddat ašyā'*[10] */ hāḏā maᶜāṣur az-zayt mawjūdih xayrāt fī ṣanᶜa l-gadīmih / yimkin fī kull / taḥt bayt kabīr mawjūd maᶜṣaruh / kaṯīrih gawī*[11] */ hāḏā min ḍumn as-sūg / wa:-mā ᶜad bih / hāḏā min ḍumn as-sūg aywih / wa-bass /*

---

1 Lack of anaphoric pronoun referring to *ḥājih* in attributive clause. Cf. *Syntax* pp. 234-5.

2 Nominal apposition in place of annexion phrase. Cf. *Syntax* pp. 193-4.

3 Use of non-SA *ayš* 'what'.

4 Separation of attribute *kabīrih* 'big' from attributed term *ḥājih* 'thing' by phrase *fī l-wasaṭ hākaḏā sāᶜ al-ḥawḍ aw miš ᶜārif ayš*. Cf. *Syntax* p. 217.

5 Asyndetic linkage of repeated verb *yidūr* indicates continuous action. Cp. English translation where the repeated verb is conjoined by 'and'.

6 Repetition of *yifḥaṣ* to indicate repeated action.

7 Repetition of *gawī* for intensity.

8 Asyndetic linkage of repeated verb *bī-dūr* indicates continuous action. Cf. above.

9 Adverbial noun complement. Cf. *Syntax* pp. 144-5.

10 Asyndetic linkage of clauses with repetition of *bi-staxdimūh* 'they use it'. Repetition here emphasises wide range of use of the topic. Asyndetic linkage enhances sense of emphatic or incomplete listing. Cf. *Syntax* pp. 316-17.

11 Predicandless predicate. Cf. *Syntax* pp. 123-4.

2 Oil presses[12]

There is something else I want to tell you about in the market. In the market, there are also presses. These are the oil presses. They press sesame oil in them. These presses are like you would say old caravanserais, but [they are] beneath the houses within the old city of San'a. When you first go to the door you can see something big in the middle like a trough or I don't know what. There is a camel there. This camel is the thing that does the pressing. How does it press? They put the mustard seeds or the sesame seeds in the middle of the press and it has a stick.[13] This stick is attached to the side of the camel by means of another stick. They cover the camel's eyes[14] and just give it [some] food in front of it. It simply keeps eating and chewing and going round. It just keeps going round and round and round, and it is this turning movement which makes the stick grind the sesame seeds .... It[15] just keeps on grinding and grinding it[16] until it has pressed it and made it into oil.

[When] you stay and watch this thing it is lovely. I mean, I have gone to watch it and I really enjoyed it when I saw the camel going round and round and round on the spot and you had oil coming out. This oil is used as a treatment for coughs and as a treatment for the body; it is used for a number of things. There are many oil presses in the old city of San'a. There is probably an oil press beneath every large house. [There are] very many. This is within the market. What else is there? Yes, this is within the market. That's it.

---

[12] A short description of oil presses (sesame mills) is provided in Serjeant and Lewcock (1983: 293).

[13] Placed vertically into the trough.

[14] To prevent the camel from becoming dizzy.

[15] i.e. the camel.

[16] i.e. the seed.

3 *As-sāyilih*

baᶜd al-maᶜṣaruh / aštī ʼasajjilliš ḥājih / al-ḥājih hāḏā hī / as-sāyilih / as-sāyilih hāḏā hī / mawjūdih fī ṣanᶜā / gadīmih / majra s-sayl / kayf bi-jra s-sayl / yaᶜnī / lā šī maḏar xayrāt / tijī siyūl lā ṣanᶜā / gabl-ma tjī as-siyūl lā hānā / gadum yiᶜrafū ᶜanhā yigūlū sāyilat jabal al-lawz / sāyilat banī / b-ismih / xawlān / sāyilāt kaṯīrih / f-[1]*iḏā hī nazalat sāyilih kabīrih / fa-*[2]*gadī tuxṭā / tuxṭā*[3] *min as-sāyilih / as-sāyilih ḥakkanā hāḏā hī fī ṣanᶜā / ʼismahā al-manḏaguh ismaha s-sāyilih / wa-barḏū*[4] *hī makān as-sāyilih / as-sayl yuxṭā min hānāk / mā biš biyūt ᶜalā ṭarīguh / yimšī bi-kaṯrih law bih maḏar*[5] *xayrāt yijiss yawmayn ṯalāṯ*[6] *wa-yiḏlaᶜ / kabīr / lā ᶜind al-biyūt / as-sayl hāḏā yinzil / min jabal al-lawz / yinzil min as-sāyilih / wa-min as-sāyilih yuxṭā ṣalā bāb šuᶜūb / min bāb šuᶜūb yuxruj ṣala r-rawḏuh / wa-min ar-rawḏuh yuxruj ṣalā:*[7] */ bani l-ḥāriṯ / wa-min bani l-ḥāriṯ yinzil wa-yuxṭā … / al-muhimm innū yuxṭā lā mārib lā midrī ʼayn wa-nihāyatih ar-rubᶜ al-xālī / wa-yisīr al-māʼ*[8] *liʼanna*[9] *mā biš sudūd xayrāt tuḥfuḏuh /*

fa-[10]*s-sāyilih hāḏā hī gadīmih / wa-ḏaḥḥīn hum bī-ṣallaḥūhā yixallawhā sayl wa-bī-xallawhā ṭarīg la-n-nās yimšaw bihā bi-dūn xulab bi-dūn wasax bi-dūn šay*[11] */ badʼū yiruṣṣūhā wa-yisabbirūlahā ḥajar / yifᶜalūhā min ḥajar wa-yinaḏḏumūhā min al-jihatayn / wallā ʼaṣlahā hī ġarr turāb wa-xulab / wa-wasax / bass ḏalḥīn gad badʼaw yiṣalluḥūhā wa-bi-yifᶜalū jusūr fawgahā lā nās yigḏaᶜū aṭ-ṭarīg xāṣṣatan*[12] *lā šī siyūl / wa-gadī ṭarīg ḥāliyih / hāḏā hī as-sāyilih /*

---

[1] Consequential use of *fa-*. Cf. *Syntax* pp. 299-300.

[2] *fa-* links apodasis of conditional clause. Cf. *Syntax* p. 300.

[3] Repetition of verb to emphasise continuous movement.

[4] Use of non-SA *barḏū* 'also'.

[5] Intervocalic voicing of *ṭ* to *ḏ*.

[6] Asyndetic linkage of alternative numerical phrases. Cf. *Syntax* p. 312.

[7] Vowel lengthening due to hesitation.

[8] Verbal clause with dynamic verb and definite inanimate subject.

[9] Epenthesis after geminate consonants. Cf. *Syntax* p. 10.

[10] *fa-* is often used to link clauses which partially summarise preceding discussion.

[11] String of three asyndetically coordinated annexion phrases with repetition of *bi-dūn* to indicate intensity. Cf. *Syntax* pp. 316-17.

[12] Classicism.

3 The watercourse

After the oil press, I want to record something [else] for you. This [thing] is the watercourse. This watercourse is in San'a. [It is] old, where the water runs. How does the water run? I mean, if there is a lot of rain, waters come into San'a. Before the waters come here, they[13] know about them. They will talk about the water from Lawz mountain, the water from Bani, what's it called, Xawlan. [There are] a lot of waters.[14] If a large amount of water comes, then it flows on through the watercourse. This watercourse of ours is in San'a, it is called, the area is called the Sayila, and it is also the place where the water runs. The water goes from there, there are no houses in its way. A lot runs if there is a lot of rain and it stays for two or three days, and [it may] flood up[15] to the houses. The water comes down from Lawz mountain and comes down through the watercourse. From the watercourse it goes towards Bab Shu'ub, from Bab Shu'ub[16] it goes out towards Rawda,[17] from Rawda it goes out towards Bani Harith,[18] and from Bani Harith it goes down and goes .... In any case, it goes to Marib, I don't know exactly where, and ends up in the Empty Quarter. The water just flows on because there aren't a lot of barriers to stop it.

The watercourse is old. Now they are repairing it, making it [suitable] for the water and as a road for people to walk along without mud, without dirt, without anything. They have begun to pave it and have laid stones down. They are making it from stone and tidying it up on both sides. Originally it was just dust, mud and dirt, but now they have begun to put it in order and have built a number of bridges over it[19] so that people can cross the road, particularly when there are rains. It is a good road. That is the watercourse.

---

[13] i.e. the people.

[14] i.e. there are a lot of places rain water can come from.

[15] Lit: 'go up'.

[16] The northern gate of the old city which is no longer standing.

[17] A village north of San'a near to the airport.

[18] An area north of Rawda.

[19] In the past, there was only a single bridge across the watercourse. Recently, a number of additional bridges have been built.

4 *Al-xubz*

b-ism illāh ar-raḥmān ar-raḥīm / ḏaḥḥīn hāḏā tištayni tḥākā ᶜan al-xubz / mā gullā[1] *fi l-xubz*[2] */ al-xubz fi l-yaman hū al-ᶜayš / fa-l-xu:bz*[3] *mitᶜaddid al-anwāᶜ fi l-yaman / bih xubz birr / wa-bih xubz ḏirrih / wa-bih xubz šaᶜīr / wa-bih xubz dagīg / bih xubz min kulla ᶜayyinih / wa-bih jamb al-xubz min anwāᶜ al-xubz bih ar-rūtī / wa:-'al-xāṣṣ / wa-ᶜad bih jamb al-xāṣṣ allī hū al-kidam / hāḏa l-kidam min xārij min as-sūg / wa-bih al-kidam barḍū*[4] *fi l-firn / kulla hāḏā 'anwāᶜ al-xubz /*

fa-maṯalan al-xubz allī naᶜmalih fi l-bayt / yijaw yiᶜmalū al-xubz kayfih[5] */ ᶜindanā 'awwal ḥājih yijirrū al-birr / yaᶜnī hāḏā ᶜindanā fi l-bayt / ništarī kīs ḥabb / min as-sūg / nisammīhā kanadih bayḍō*[6] */ wallā birr abyaḍ / f-*[7]*aḥ nagūllih ḥabb / wa-baᶜda-mā yijirrū al-kīs al-ḥabb*[8] */ an-niswān yijirrayn*[9] *yinaggannih / kayf yinaggannih*[10] */ yiṭraḥannuh wasṭ / yuskubannih min*[11] *wasṭ al-kīs / ᶜalā šwayyih šwayyih*[12] */ lā wasṭ al-lajan / wa-wasṭ al-lajan yuskubannih lā hānāk wa-yijirrannih ᶜalā šwayyih šwayyih min wasṭ al-lajan / lā wasṭ al-ġuḍā / wa-fi l-ġuḍā yinaggannih / maᶜnā yinaggannih / yilagguḍayn lā šī fīh ḥijār / lā šī ḥuṣam / lā šī girāš min ḥakk al-ḥabb / lā šī 'ayyi wasax*[13] */ wasṭ al-ḥabb yilaggiḍannuh / wa-hāḏā*[14] *yijlisayn an-niswān wasṭ al-ḥawī wallā wasṭ ad-daymih wallā wasṭ ad-dihlīz ḥakk al-bayt / wa yitjābirayn wa-hin bī-naggayn / bi-tᶜāwanayn maᶜ baᶜḍathun al-baᶜḍ /*

---

1 Elision of *h* of pronoun *hā*. From *agūl lahā*.

2 Rhetorical question.

3 Vowel lengthening due to hesitation.

4 Use of non-SA *barḍū*.

5 Rhetorical question.

6 Labialisation of vowel after pausal *imāla* due to preceding emphatic *ḍ*.

7 *fa-* links summative clause. Cf. text 3.

8 Identificatory apposition. Cf. *Syntax* pp. 241-3.

9 *jarr – yijirr* is used here as a linking verb in the sense of 'to set to' or 'to begin to'.

10 Rhetorical question.

11 Corrective reformulative apposition correcting *yiṭraḥannuh wasṭ*. Cf. *Syntax* p. 246.

12 Repetition of *šwayyih* to convey distributive sense.

13 String of four asyndetically linked subordinate (conditional) clauses.

14 Demonstrative pronoun *hāḏā* acts as clausal anaphoric pronoun and as summariser. It refers back to activity of cleaning grain. *wa-hāḏā / fa-hāḏā* is frequently used in these texts in sense of 'for this'. Cf. *Syntax* pp. 382-4.

4 Bread

In the name of God, the Compassionate, the Merciful, now you want me to talk about bread. What should I tell her about bread? Bread in Yemen is [what is called] *ᶜayš* [elsewhere]. There are a number of types of bread in Yemen. There is wheat bread, there is sorghum bread, there is barley bread, there is white bread. There is bread of every type. Besides [these] types of bread there is roti[15] bread, and round pitta bread. In addition to pitta bread, there are also baps [made from a number of different types of grain]. These baps are from outside, from the market-place. There are also baps which are [baked] in the oven. All of these are types of bread.

So, the bread we make at home, for instance. How do they make the bread? Here the first thing [they do] is get the wheat. This is for us at home. We buy a bag of grain from the market. We call it 'white Canada'[16] or white wheat. We call it grain. After they get the bag of grain, the women begin to clean it. How do they clean it? They put it into, they pour it from the bag, little by little, into a large shallow metal bowl[17] [called a *lajan*]. In the bowl, they pour it into there and take it bit by bit from the bowl into a shallow basket, and in the shallow basket they clean it. What I mean by they clean it is that they pick out any stones or grit or any husks from the grain. If there is any dirt in the grain, they remove it. [To do] this, the women sit in the yard or in the kitchen or in the passageway of the house, and they chat while they are cleaning [it]. They help each other.

---

[15] Small, oblong loaves of imported, refined wheat flour baked in modern bakeries.

[16] Called 'white Canada' because it is felt to come from Canada originally.

[17] Definite in Arabic.

wa-yinaggayn wa-yuskubayn lā wasṭ kīs ṯānī / wa-ba^{c}da-mā yitimmayn yinaggayn al-ḥabb hāḏā kullih / iḏā naggayn la-l-kīs bi-kullih yijirrayn al-kīs / wa-yif^{c}alayn baynih šwayyih milḥ / wa-yigassimannih fī 'akyās zuġayrih zuġayrih[18] */ mišū fī wasṭ nafs al-kīs illī kān fīh al-ḥabb / akyās bayḍā / yigassimannih ^{c}alā šwayyih šwayyih / wa-yif^{c}alayn baynih šwayyih milḥ*[19] */*

wa-ba^{c}d-mā yif^{c}alayn baynih šwayyih milḥ yirbuṭannuh wa-yuṭruḥannuh hinayyik / law-mā yijī wāḥid / min al-^{c}iyyāl / aw ṣāḥub al-bayt / yijirr al-ḥabb hāḏā wa-yišillih aṭ-ṭāḥūn / ^{c}inda-mā yišillih aṭ-ṭāḥūn / yiṭḥanuh / fī ṭ-ṭāḥūn yiṭḥanuh / yixallīh dagīg / ba^{c}d-mā yiṭaḥḥun al-ḥabb / gadū ḏayyik ṣāḥub aṭ-ṭāḥūn yigullanā jawlih maṯalan ba^{c}d al-ġadā / wallā jawlih ġudwih / al-muhimm yiddīlanā maw^{c}id ayyaḥīn nijī la-l-ḥabb / la-ṭ-ṭaḥīn / šallaynāh wa-hū ḥabb / wa-^{c}a-nsīr nijirrih wa-hū ṭaḥīn / ba^{c}d-ma nsīr nijirr aṭ-ṭaḥīn niḏawwīh al-bayt / wa-fi l-bayt yiṭraḥannuh ammā yixallannih wasṭ al-kīs ḏayyik allī hū ṭaḥanuh fīh / aw yuskubannih lā wasṭ / bawārid kabīrih / wallā dast kabīr wallā ṭīsān kabīrih / ^{c}alā mayd yiġaṭṭannahā /

wa-ba^{c}d-ma njirr al-ḥabb hāḏā ^{c}inda-mā yixbizayn an-niswān / ba^{c}ḍuhun yuxluṭannuh ma^c šwayyih dagīg / abyaḍ / ^{c}alā 'asās yikūn maxlūṭ šwayyih / wa-ba^{c}ḍuhum yixallawh[20] *ṣāfī birr abyaḍ / hū 'aṭ^{c}am / law-mā yikūn ṣāfī mā biš baynih dagīg / lākin hum yixawwilū ma^c ad-dagīg / ba^{c}d-mā yijirrayn*[21] *ad-dagīg hāḏā / law-mā gadhin ^{c}a-yuxbizayn / yijirrayn ad-dagīg / yi^{c}jinannih / bi-šwayyih mā' / wasṭ ṭāsuh ma^{c}janih*[22] */ wa-yšnijannih law-mā yišnijannih gawī / wa-ba^{c}dā yixallannih hinayyik maṭrūḥ min šān yixallannih yitxammir / law-mā: yitxammir / ṭab^{c}an yirja^{c}ayn yuxbizannih /*

wa-l-xubz kān maṯalan fī ṣan^{c}ā / wa-ba^{c}ḍ al-biyūt lā zālat lā ḥatt[23] *al ān / yixbizū fī tanāwīr / at-tanāwīr hāḏā hī ma^{c}mūlih / min aṭ-ṭīn at-turāb*[24]

---

[18] Repetition of attribute to convey distributive sense.

[19] Apposition phrase in place of annexion phrase. Cf. *Syntax* pp. 193-4.

[20] Switch from fem. plural to general masc. plural agreement.

[21] Switch back to feminine plural subject.

[22] Identificatory apposition. Cf. *Syntax* pp. 241-3.

[23] Geminate devoicing of *dd* to *tt*. Cf. *Syntax* p. 10.

[24] Reformulative apposition. Cf. *Syntax* pp. 244-6.

They clean [it] and pour [it] into another bag. After they have finished cleaning all this grain, when they have cleaned the whole bag, they take the bag and put a little salt into it. Then they divide it up into smaller bags. Not into the same bag that the grain was in, white bags. They divide it into small amounts and put some salt into it.

After they have added a little salt, they tie it up and put it there until one of the children or the head of the household comes to take the grain and carry it to the mill. When they[25] take it to the mill, they grind it. They grind it in the mill and make it into flour. After they have ground the grain, the owner of the mill will tell us to come for it, for instance, after lunch or to come for it tomorrow. Anyway, he will give us a time when we can come for the grain, for the flour. We took it as grain and we are going to pick it up as flour. After we go for the flour, we bring it back home. At home, they[26] put it somewhere. They either leave it in the bag in which it was ground, or they pour it into large bins or into a large cauldron or into large bowls so that they can cover them.

After we have brought this grain,[27] when the women begin to bake, some of them mix it with a little white imported flour so that it is a bit mixed, and some of them leave it pure, as white wheat [flour]. It is tastier when it is pure and there is no imported flour in it; however, they can save money with imported flour. After taking this flour, when they are about to bake, they take the flour and knead it with a little water in a kneading trough, and they knead it a lot. Then they leave it on the side to let it rise. After it has risen, of course, they come back to bake it.

Bread in San'a, for instance, used to be, and in some houses still is up until now, baked in clay ovens. These clay ovens are made from clay or dust.

---

[25] Singular in Arabic.

[26] i.e. the women.

[27] i.e. ground flour.

nisīr ništarī tannūr min ^{c}ind wāḥid / wa-yijaw yiṭraḥūhā fī bug^{c}ah / fī d-daymih hānāk fī d-daymih / yiḏbilūhā wa-yiṣallaḥūhā / wa-hinayyik / lākin hāḏa l-iyyām gad bih tanāwīr ġāz / at-tanāwīr al-lawwalih hāḏā / hī min at-turāb / aṭ-ṭīn / kayf yiḥarrigū fīhā / yijirrū al-ḥaḏab / li'annū mā kān[28] yixbizū 'illā bi-ḥaḏab / yijirrū al-ḥaḏab wa-yidaxxilūh / wa-yiṭraḥūh lā wasṭ at-tannūr / ṭab^{c}an mā yimallūš lā ṭālu^{c} / min nāzil yidaxxilūh / ma^{c} at-tannūr xuzgī min nāzil / ṭālu^{c} hī maftūḥah /

al-xuzgi llī min nāzil yiharwisū / al-ḥaḏab fīh ^{c}alā zuġayri zġayrih wasṭahā ^{c}alā mayd yiḥragayn[29] / yilaṣṣaw al-ḥaḏab / wa-tibdā tiḥma t-tannūr[30] / ṭab^{c}an law-mā tiḥma t-tannūr gabl-mā tiḥma t-tannūr ^{c}ād tiṭla^{c} al-luṣwuh tayyik li-wasṭ at-tannūr / wa-yiṭla^{c} ad-duxxān wa-yiṭla^{c} al-^{c}īdān hāḏīk ḥakkaha d-duxxān yija^{c}fir ad-daymih ad-duxxān[31] / al-muhimm šuġlih / hāḏā kullih kān minn awwal ḏaḥḥīn mā ^{c}ād biš illā ba^{c}ḍ an-nās / yuxbizū bi-l-ḥaṭab wallā ka-mā mā ^{c}ād biš ġāz / ^{c}ād ma^{c}āhum at-tanāwīr ^{c}ādum yiḥāfiḏū yuxbizū bi-l-ḥaṭab / wa-gad bī-xallaw ḥakkahum at-tanāwīr hāḏā ḥakk al-ḥaḏab xārij al-bayt / law-mā tiḥmā at-tannūr wa-hī ḥāmī / bi-tiḥmā ^{c}alā 'asās / yūga^{c} al-xubz ḥālī /

ṭab^{c}an ḏayyik al-^{c}ajīn / law-mā gadū xāmir / yibda'ū yisīrū yixbizū / al-xubz yijarrannahā at-tannūr / yijarrannahā an-niswān[32] ^{c}afwan / wa-yijarrannaha n-niswān / wasṭ al-ma^{c}janih[33] / yiḏrubūhā[34] bi-l-yad wasṭ al-ma^{c}janih hāḏā / hī zuġayrih ka-ḏayyahā[35] fī l-yad yizgamūhā / al-maxbazih miš al-ma^{c}janih / al-maxbazih / al-maxbazih hāḏā hī ma^{c}mūlih hākaḏahā midawwirih / wa:-w-allāh manā dārī mā llī dāxilhā / wa-ma^{c}āhā mamsak min gafāhā / yijirrayn[36] al-xubzih an-niswān /

---

28 Uninflected linking verb. Cf. *Syntax* pp. 50-1.

29 Fem. pl. agreement for coll. noun *ḥaḏab* when referent viewed as plural entity. Cp. sing. agreement above. Cf. fem. pl. agreement for coll. nouns *xubz, malūj, gafū^{c}, ḏamūl* below.

30 Verbal clause with initial linking verb. Note subject follows main verb *tiḥmā*.

31 Four sequential verbal clauses with identical verbs and emphasis on contrasting subjects.

32 Corrective reformulative apposition. Cf. *Syntax* p. 246.

33 Mistake. This is later corrected to *maxbazih*.

34 Switch of agreement from fem. plural to to impersonal masc. plural.

35 Suffixation of *-hā* to emphasise the demonstrative pronoun.

36 Switch back to feminine plural agreement.

We go and buy a clay oven from someone, and they come and place it somewhere in the kitchen, there in the kitchen. They put ashes around the spot where it will be placed and set it up there. But these days there are cylindrical gas ovens. The old ovens were [made] from clay. How did they light them? They would fetch wood, because they didn't bake with anything but wood. They would fetch the wood and put it in, and put it into the centre of the clay oven. Of course, they wouldn't fill it to the top, they would put it in at the bottom. Clay ovens have a hole at the bottom and they are open at the top.

They shove the wood in through the hole at the bottom little by little so that it burns. They light the wood and the oven begins to heat up. Of course, when the oven heats up, before the oven heats up the kindling fire rises to the centre of the oven, and the smoke rises, the smoke from the sticks rises and the smoke fills the kitchen. In any case, it is hard work. All this used to be done in the past, but now there are only a few people who bake with wood, or if there is no gas they still have the clay ovens to bake with wood. They leave their clay ovens [which use] wood outside the house. When the oven heats up and gets hot, it gets hot so that the bread will turn out well.

Of course, when the dough has risen they begin to go and bake the bread. The oven, the women take it, excuse me. The women take it on a padded cushion [for shaping bread]. They hit it with their hands onto the centre of the padded cushion. It is small like that and they take it in their hand. [It is called] a *maxbazih* not a *ma*^{c}*janih*, a *maxbazih*. This padded cushion is made like that, round. I have no idea what is inside it, but it has a handle at the back. The women take hold of the bread.

yiḍrubannahā bi-yadhin hākaḏa wa-hākaḏā wa-hākaḏā[37] *min jihah lā jihah law-mā titfattaḥ šwayyih šwayyih / hāḏa l-ᶜajīnih / yijirrayn al-ᶜajīnih wa-yifattaḥannahā min yad lā yad / min yad lā yad*[38] */ wa-baᶜdā yiṭraḥannahā fi l-maxbazih / wa-yiwassaᶜannahā malān tayyik al-maxbazih / allī fī yadhin / wa-yizgamayn al-maxbazih min gafāhā wa-yidaxxilannahā la-t-tannūr / wa-yuḍrubayn / bi-yadhin ᶜarḍ at-tannūr / tibga l-xubzih hinayyik fi t-tannūr lā hī ḥāmiyih / tibdā / tithammar / wa-yijirrayn al-ᶜajīnih aṯ-ṯāniyih / wa-yixbizayn bi-nafs aṭ-ṭarīguh al-lawwalih / wa-yiṭraḥanhā wasṭ at-tannūr jamb tayyik / wa-yidaxxilayn wasṭ at-tannūr ṯalāṯ arbaᶜ*[39] */ yaᶜnī xubz / law-mā gad tayyik al-lawwalih ḥamrā / wa-yijirrayn yifᶜalanbihā bi-l-mulgāṭ ihzir*[40] */ wa-yiṭraḥannahā fi l-guwwārih / awwal ḥājih fī ġuṭā gabl al-guwwārih / wa-yijirrayn ᶜajīnih ṯāniyih / wa-yidaxxilan*[41] *badal tayyik / wa-ma tḥammarat min xubzih*[42] *xarrajannahā*[43] *lā wasṭ al-ġuḍā / hākaḏā hum*[44] *bi-yixbizayn ġarr xubz ᶜalā ᶜadad al-ᶜajīn al-mawjūd /*

wa-ᶜād bih yifᶜalayn malūj / jamb al-xubz / al-malūj hāḏā yixallannahā ġalīḍuh / aġlaḍ min al-xubzih / wa-yizīd[45] *yixallannahā ᶜalā mayd titḥammar yifᶜalanlahā min wuššhā zuġayrih ḥilbih / ᶜalā mayd titḥammar wa-tūgaᶜ ḥāliyih hākaḏā / wa-hī 'aġlaḍ / wa-tūgaᶜ akbar / wa-yidaxxilannaha t-tannūr jamb al-xubz / wa-yibaᶜᶜidannahā ᶜalā wāḥidih wāḥidih / law-mā: yitimmayn yixbizayn / hāḏā*[46] *hū al-xubz /*

baᶜḍ al-aḥyān nijī wa-hin bi-xbizayn / fi l-bayt wallā šī / wa-yixwir wāḥid maᶜ rīḥat al-xubz ad-dāfī al-hāḏā /

---

[37] Repetition of *hākaḏā wa-hākaḏā* to indicate repeated action. Cf. immediately following repetition of *jihah* to indicate distributive sense.

[38] Repetition of *min yad lā yad* to indicate distributive sense and repeated action.

[39] Asyndetic linkage of alternative numerical phrases. Cf. *Syntax* p. 312.

[40] Use of masc. sing. imperative as a nominal. Cp. use of imperatives as nominals in English – e.g. 'come on', 'turn on', 'pull up'.

[41] Diphthong simplification and shortening. From *yidaxxilayn*.

[42] Universal-conditional-concession clause. Cf. *Syntax* p. 353.

[43] Perfect in main clause to universal-conditional-concession clause. Cf. *Syntax* pp. 64-5.

[44] Lack of gender agreement with the following feminine plural verb.

[45] Lack of number and gender agreement in linking verb. Cf. *Syntax* pp. 50-1.

[46] Clausal anaphoric pronoun. Cf. *Syntax* pp. 382-3.

They hit it with their hands[47] like that and like that and like that from side to side until it opens up bit by bit. This is the dough. They take the dough and open it up from hand to hand, from hand to hand. Then they put it on the padded bread cushion and they spread it out over the whole of the bread cushion which is in their hand. They take the bread cushion from the back and put it into the clay oven and hit [it] with their hand onto the side of the oven. The bread stays there in the oven if it is hot, and begins to brown. Then they take the second bit of dough, and bake it in the same way and place it into the oven next to the first. They put three or four into the clay oven, pieces of bread. When the first one is brown, they take it out quickly with the tongs and put it into a bread cloth. The first thing is into the shallow basket before the cloth. Then they take a second piece of dough and put it in place of the first, and whatever piece of bread has browned, they take out and [put it] in the shallow basket. In that way, they make just the amount of bread they have dough for.

There is also *malūj* that they make in addition to bread. They make this *malūj* thick, thicker than bread. They leave it longer so that it browns and they put a little fenugreek on the top of it so that it browns and turns out nicely like that. This is thicker and turns out bigger. They put it into the oven next to the bread, then they remove them one by one until they have finished baking. This is [how they make] bread.

Sometimes we come along while they[48] are baking in the house or whatever, and you get a real craving from the smell of the warm bread.

[47] Singular in Arabic.

[48] i.e. the women.

nisīr nijirrlanā[49] *xubzih / wa-hī ḥāmī gawī / wa-nidhanhā bi-zuġayrih samn wa-nik^{c}at abūhā*[50] *wa-nākulhā / aw nākulhā ^{c}ala z-zaḥāwug / al-muhimm innū d̲īk sā^{c} wāḥid yištī yākul min šamm al-xubz al-ḥālī wa-l-hād̲ā / ṭab^{c}an hād̲a l-xubz yi^{c}milannaha n-niswān / gabl aḍ-ḍuhr wagt al-ġadā hākad̲ā / ba^{c}ḍuhum*[51] *yuxbizū aṣ-ṣubḥ / lākin akt̲arat al-xubz hū mā bi-kūn illā gabl aḍ-ḍuhr / hād̲ā*[52] *bi-nisbih la-l-xubz wa-l-malūj /*

wa-^{c}ād bih aš-ša^{c}ir / hād̲a š-ša^{c}īr hī zayy al-malūjih / bass ^{c}ādī min ši^{c}īr min ḥubūb nisammīhā ši^{c}īr / yiṭḥanūh wa-d̲ayyā / wa-yif^{c}alū minnih nafs aṭ-ṭarīguh ḥakk al-xubz wa-l-malūj / inna-mā hū mišū min ḥabb / zayy-ma l-ḥabb al-^{c}ādī / hū ša^{c}īr iḥ[53] *nisammīh / hād̲a š-ša^{c}īr / wa-hād̲a l-xubz / wa-hād̲ā al-malūj /*

wa-^{c}ād bih fi s-sūg ar-rūtī / hād̲a r-rūtī kayf yif^{c}alūh fi s-sūg / hum yif^{c}alū / nafs aš-šī hū min dagīg abyaḍ / yijirrū yi^{c}jinū nafs al-ṭarīgat al-^{c}ajīnih ḥagg ad-dagīg / wa-ḥakk al-xubz / bass ar-rūtī hum bi-ṣallaḥūh fi l-afrān / al-afrān hād̲ā mawjūdih bi-kaṯrih / d̲aḥḥīnih / yijirrū ar-rūtī wa-yṭraḥūh wasṭ at-tabāsī / wa-t-tabāsī hād̲ā wasṭahā ṣanādīg zuġayrih zuġayrih / hād̲ā bi-nisbih la-r-rūtī / yigaṭṭa^{c}ū al-^{c}ajīnih hāḏīk ḥakk ar-rūtī wa-yidaxxilūhin wasṭ aṣ-ṣanādīg az-zuġayrih az-zuġayrih hād̲ā / wasṭ at-tabsī hād̲a l-kabīr / allī hū ṣaḥn ṭawīl yimallūh ġarr guḍa^{c} zuġīrih min al-ḥadīd wa-yidaxxilū wasṭhā al-xubz / wa-yimallaw al-firn / akt̲arat an-nās hād̲a l-iyyām bi-štaraw / rūtī / ar-rūtī gad bih aškāl wa-nwā^{c} / hād̲a l-iyyām / gad bih ḥattā rūtī yisammūh ar-rūti l-faransī mawjūd /

wa-l-kidam / mawjūdih fi l-afrān / ba^{c}ḍ al-afrān / iḥna l-yawm ništarī kidam / ^{c}ala l-ġadā wa-^{c}ala l-^{c}ašā wa-ṣ-ṣabūḥ gad iḥna ništarī kidam / mā nuxbizš xayrāt / ba^{c}ḍ al-aḥyān nixbiz fi l-bayt ba^{c}ḍ al-aḥyān ništarī min al-firn kidam / wa-l-kidam bi-tjī zayy al-birr / birr wa-dagīg hād̲ā kidam t̲āniyih / wa-^{c}ād bih kidam allī[54] *hī al-kidam al-aṣlīyuh /*

---

[49] Reflexive verb. Cf. *Syntax* pp. 202-3.

[50] 'Rolled up'. This is a predominantly women's saying in San'a.

[51] Switch to impersonal masculine plural subject. The referent is probably the household.

[52] Clausal anaphoric pronoun. Cf. *Syntax* pp. 382-3.

[53] From *iḥnā*.

[54] Use of clausal definite article with preceding indefinite noun. Cf. *Syntax* p. 235.

We go and get ourselves a piece of bread while it is still very hot. We spread a bit of fat on it and roll it up, then eat it. Or we eat it with a spicy dip. Anyway, at that time, you want to eat because of the smell of the lovely bread. Of course, the women make the bread before noon, around lunch-time. Some of them bake in the morning, but most bread is [made] before noon. This is about bread and *malūj*.

Then there is also barley [bread]. Barley bread is like *malūj*, but it is [made out] of barley, from grain we call barley. They grind it and the like and make it in the same way as for bread and *malūj*, but it is not from grain like the usual grain. It is barley, we call it. This is barley [bread], and that was bread and *malūj*.

In the market-place, there is also roti[55] bread. How do they make this roti bread in the market-place? They do the same thing. It is from white imported flour. They set about kneading it in the same way as they do the dough from imported flour and dough for bread, but with roti they make it in baker's ovens. There are a lot of these baker's ovens now. They take the roti [dough] and put it into trays. These trays have a lot of small compartments. This is for roti bread. They cut the dough for the roti bread and put it into the many small compartments in the large tray, which is a long tray that they fill with small bits of metal[56] and put the bread in, and they fill the oven. Most people these days buy roti bread. There are different types of roti these days. Now there is even a type of roti which they call French bread.

There are [also] baps done in ovens, in some ovens. Nowadays, we buy baps for lunch, for supper and for breakfast we buy baps. We don't bake a lot. Sometimes we bake in the house and sometimes we buy baps from the baker's ovens. [Some] baps are made from wheat flour, wheat and imported white flour makes another type of bap. There are also baps which are the original baps.

---

[55] Small white oblong loaves produced in baker's ovens. The word *rōtī* is said to be originally Indian.

[56] i.e. compartments are made in the trays by inserting small strips of metal.

hāḏā ništarīhā min as-sūg / hāḏā al-kidam hum bī-ṣallaḥūhā li-l-ᶜaskar / wa-minnahā bi-tuxruj la s-sūg / yiṣallaḥūh / la s-sūg yibīᶜūhā / al-kidam hāḏā laḏīḏih gawī / wa-maᶜmūlih hāḏa l-kidam[57] */ min jamīᶜ anwāᶜ al-ḥubūb / wa-laḏīḏih jittan*[58] */ anā 'aḏkur wa-ᶜād anā zaġīr kunt ākul arbaᶜ kidam ᶜalā galaṣ aw iṯnayn šahay*[59] */ arbaᶜ ᶜalā mā hin / al-ḥamdu li-llāh wa-šukr li-llāh hāḏā min awwal / ḏalḥīn mā gdurš akammil aṯ-ṯintayn / kān al-wāḥid wa-ᶜādū zaġīr yūgaᶜ hawir /*

hāḏā 'anwāᶜ al-xubz al-mawjūdih fī l-yaman / wa-fī s-sūg yilgā wāḥid ar-rūtī wa-yilga l-kidam wa-yilga l-xāṣṣ / al-xāṣṣ hāḏā hū yiᶜmalūh bi-šakl ṭawīl[60] */ hākaḏā sāᶜ al-midawwir yibīᶜūh / min al-afrān / nisammīh xāṣṣ / wa-ᶜād bih fī s-sūg / nilgā xubz / wa-nilgā malūj / hāḏa l-xubz wa-l-malūj nilgāhin*[61] *fī s-sūg yisabbirannahin an-niswān*[62] */ wa-yisīrayn yibīᶜannahin fī / ḥayṯ-mā yibīᶜū as-saltih / wakt*[63] *aḏ-ḏuhr yijaw an-nās yākulū saltih fī baᶜḍ al-maḍāᶜum fī ṣanᶜā /*

wa-hāḏa l-maḍāᶜum nilgā jambahā niswān yibīᶜayn xubz wa-yibīᶜayn malūj wa-yibīᶜayn šaᶜīr[64] */ al-xubzih / ᶜa-tūgaᶜ bi-ᶜašarih riyāl*[65] *wallā bi-xamsih riyāl / al-malūjih bi-ᶜišrīn / aš-šaᶜīr yibīᶜūh bi-ṯalāṯīn / li'ann aš-šaᶜīr ġālī / wa-kull:ahin mawjūdih jamb kull maḍᶜam saltih yilga l-wāḥid min hāḏawlā / al-xubz wa-l-malūj / wa-š-šaᶜīr / hāḏā 'anwāᶜ al-xubz / al-xubz al-mawjūdih fī l-yaman / ar-rūtī hī mitᶜaddidih aškāl wa-'anwāᶜ*[66] */*

---

57 Inversion of predicand–predicate. Predicand spoken at lower pitch than predicate, as if given as afterthought. Cf. *Syntax* p. 129.

58 Classicism. Note devoicing of geminate *dd*. Cf. *Syntax* p. 10.

59 *šahay*, like many items which indicate measure, value, food or drink which can be ordered, functions as a singular count noun: i.e. it occurs in singular after numbers 2–10 where nouns would usu. occur in the plural (cf. Mörth 1997: 179-85). Cf. *Ṣbaḥtū!* pp. 59-60.

60 Mistake. Later corrected.

61 Fem. pl. agreement for coll. *xubz* and *malūj*. Cf. fem. pl. agreement for *ḥaṭab* above.

62 Verbal clause with emphasis on the subject. Translated here using English *by*-passive which places focal element – *an-niswān* 'women' – in clause-final position.

63 Anticipatory devoicing of *g* to *k*.

64 Threefold repetition of *yibīᶜayn* to indicate repeated action.

65 *riyāl* functions as singular count noun: although it has a plural form (*riyālāt*), it occurs in singular after numbers 2–10 where nouns usu. occur in plural. Cf. above.

66 The coordinated synonyms, *aškāl wa-'anwāᶜ*, serve as a complex adverbial noun complement to *mitᶜaddidih*. Cf. *Syntax* pp. 144-5.

These we buy from the market. These baps are made for the soldiers, and some of them go out to the market-place. They make them to sell in the market-place. These baps are really delicious and the baps are made from all types of grains. [They are] very delicious. I can remember that when I was young, I used to be able to eat four baps with one or two cups of tea. Four just as they were. Praise be to God and thanks be to God this was in the past. Now I can't even finish two. When people are young, they can be greedy.

These are the types of bread that are found in Yemen. In the market-place, you can find roti, you can find baps, and you can find pitta bread. They make pitta bread long, like that. They sell it round from the ovens. We call it *xāṣṣ* [pitta bread]. Also in the market-place, we can find bread and we can find *malūj*. This bread and *malūj* we find in the market. They are made by women who go and sell them wherever *saltih*[67] is sold. At noon time, people come to eat *saltih* in some of the restaurants in San'a.

Beside these restaurants, we find women selling bread and selling *malūj* and selling barley bread. Bread will be for ten riyals or for five riyals, *malūj* for twenty, barley is sold for thirty because barley is expensive. They are all there, next to every *saltih* restaurant you will find these: bread, *malūj* and barley bread. These are the types of bread, bread which is available in Yemen. There are [also] a number of different types of roti.

[67] *Saltih* is perhaps the best-known dish which is eaten in San'a and surrounding areas. Said to have originated with the Turks, it consists of meat broth topped with whipped fenugreek and eaten with bread. In areas where *saltih* is not eaten regularly, jokes are told about the lengths to which San'anis will go to eat it. (Cf. *Waṣf* p. 82 for preparation of *saltih*.)

wa-ᶜad bih xubz nuxbishin[68] *nisammīhin*[69] *gafūᶜ / gafūᶜ bilsin / gafūᶜ / min aḏ-ḏirrih / hāḏawlā yūgaᶜlahin*[70] *xawarāt mā hūš kulla yawm yisabbirūhin*[71] *yisabbirūhin baᶜḏ al-aḥyān lākin fī baᶜḏ al-gurā yisabbirūhin akṯarat al-ayyām / fa-gafūᶜ al-bilsin hāḏā tjī*[72] *ġalīḏuh wa-tjī ḏaᶜīmuh / nitxawwirhā wa-nākulhā ᶜalā š-šahay baᶜd al-ġadā / walla ṣ-ṣubḥ yigūmayn an-niswān yixbizannahin*[73] */ wa-yiṣallaḥannahun*[74] */ yūgaᶜayn ṣabūḥ ᶜalā maḏīṭ / yūgaᶜ fīhin ḏaᶜm ḥālī / hāḏā gafūᶜ al-bilsin / hāh /*

wa-bih aḏ-ḏamūl / aḏ-ḏamūl hāḏā nākulhin[75] */ hin zayy al-kaᶜk / aḏ-ḏamūl hāḏawlā yisabbirūhin / min dagīg wa-ᶜalā bayḏ / yūgaᶜ*[76] *ḥāliyāt nākulhin baᶜd al-ġadā ᶜalā gahwih / wallā yākul wāḥid lā hū jāwiᶜ / yākul ḏamūlih ᶜalā šahay /*

wa-bih al-kubān / hāḏā barḏū min anwāᶜ al-xubz / al-kubān hāḏā bi-tṣallaḥ min ar-rūmī / yaᶜnī ḥubūb ar-rūmī nisammīh rūmī / wa-yitsabbar maᶜa bayḏ / wa-samn / wa-bayḏuh yimsaḥūhā min ṭāluᶜ hākaḏāhā[77] *fawgahā / wa-ydaxxilūha l-firn / wa-tuxruj / kubānih laḏīḏih anā yiᶜjibnī*[78] *gawī / ḥāmī*[79] *nākulhā nigaṭṭaᶜhā w-nākulhā / al-muhimm hāḏā 'anwāᶜ al-xubz / al-mawjūdih fī l-yaman allī 'aᶜraf anā*[80] *wa-bih xārij xayrāt / ahā bass /*

---

68 Anticipatory devoicing of *z* to *s*.

69 Fem. plural agreement for coll. nouns *xubz* and *gafūᶜ*. Cf. above.

70 Lack of gender and number agreement with following fem. plural subject.

71 Use of general masc. plural verb inflection for activities performed by women. Cf. above.

72 Switch to fem. singular agreement for *gafūᶜ*.

73 Switch back to fem. plural agreement for *gafūᶜ*.

74 Partial synonym to *yixbizannahin*. Labialisation of *-i-* of object pronoun due to preceding emphatic *ṣ* (cf. Watson 1995, 1999a).

75 Fem plural agreement for coll. noun *ḏamūl*. Cf. above.

76 Lack of gender and number agreement with feminine plural subject.

77 Suffixation of *-hā* to emphasise demonstrative. Cf. above.

78 Lack of gender agreement with preceding noun subject.

79 Fronting of complement before verb to emphasise complement. Cf. *Syntax* p. 143-4.

80 Post-position of independent pronoun to emphasise subject of verb. Cf. *Syntax* p. 251.

There is another [type of] bread we bake which we call *gafūᶜ*. Lentil bread, bread made from sorghum. People get cravings for *gafūᶜ*. It isn't every day that they make it; they make it sometimes, but in some villages they make it most days. This lentil bread is thick and tasty. We look forward to it and eat it with tea after lunch, or in the morning the women will get up to bake it and make it. It will be for breakfast with barley gruel. It has a nice taste. This is lentil bread. Okay?

There is also *ḏamūl*. This *ḏamūl* we eat is like cake. This *ḏamūl* they make from flour with eggs. It is very nice. We eat it after lunch with coffee, or you can eat it if you are hungry, [you can] eat a piece of *ḏamūl* with tea.

There is [also] *kubān*. This is also a type of bread. This *kubān* is made from corn. The corn grains we call *rūmī*. It is made with eggs and ghee, then they glaze it with an egg like that on the top and put it into the oven. It comes out delicious. I like it a lot. We eat it hot, we cut it up and eat it. Anyway, these are the types of bread in Yemen that I know about. There are a lot outside.[81] That's it.

[81] i.e. in the market-place.

5 *Al-madāᶜum fī ṣanᶜā*

ibsirī fī ṣanᶜā' / al-maḍāᶜum / min awwal mā kān biš maḍāᶜum / tamām / min awwal kān bih samāsir / hāh / antī dārī[1] *māhī samāsir mih*[2] */ aywih hāḏik samsarat an-naḥās / bass as-samāsir zayy-ma tgūlī lūkandih / aw hāḏā / tamām / bih samāsir xayrāt fī ṣanᶜā' / kaṯīr fī kulla bayt samsirih / hāḏā as-samsarih kānayn*[3] *zayy al-fundug / mā biš ᶜindanā fanādig / wa-hāḏā / yaᶜnī yūṣal gabīlī / min xārij ṣanᶜā / ᶜa-yūṣal bi-ḥimārih wa-kulla šī lā waṣṭ as-samsarih / wa-fī s-samsarih hāḏīk tilgay bugᶜah marātib / ᶜālīyih hākaḏā ᶜa-yijlisū ṭāluᶜ / wa-fī ṭaraf as-samsarih yijlisayn al-gurāš / wa-l-ġanam / allī maᶜih jamal w-allī mᶜih ḥuṣān w-allī mᶜih ḥimār w-allī maᶜih ...*[4] */ hāh yijlisayn fī bugᶜah ḏulmīyuh hānakah*[5] */ wa-s-samāsir marātib / tilgay wāḥid ᶜālī hākaḏā wa-wāḥid jālis hānāk wāḥid hānāk / marātib / sāᶜ as-sarī'r*[6] */ bass mabnī bināyih / bi-ṭ-ṭīn wa-l-hāḏā / dirītī*[7] */ sāᶜ-mā fī thāmih / tilgay samāsir xayrāt ḏalḥīn xārij ṣanᶜā fī l-gurā wa-l-hāḏā / ᶜādin mawjūdāt /*

fa-s-samsarih fī ṣanᶜā bi-yūṣal gabīlī lā hānā l-ann ahl ṣanᶜā wālifīn[8] *mā gadumš ᶜārifīn bi-l-maḍāᶜum / hānā mā gad biš maḍāᶜum / lā hū fī baytum / mā biš maḍāᶜum / kān yūṣal gabīlī ḥīn mā yiᶜrafš aḥadd / yutxul as-samsarih / fī s-samsarih yilgā mugahwī / wa-mugahwiyih / yuxbizū / wa-yisabbirū fīhā ᶜaṣīd wa-saltih wa-laḥmih / wa-hāḏā wa-hāḏā li-llī yijaw min al-gabāyil / ḍabᶜan kullih bi-zalaṭ / fa-*[9]*tilgay mā biš ᶜindanā hānā maḍāᶜum illā hāḏā / as-samāsir / gadū yūṣal as-samsarih / yirgud / wa-yijlis wa-yitġaddā wa-yixazzin / hāh /*

---

[1] Adjectives ending in *-ī* often fail to take the fem. ending to agree with a fem. noun, as here, due to underarticulation.

[2] Tag question. 'Don't you?' Cf. *Syntax* pp. 384-5.

[3] i.e. *kānat*. Speaker was probably thinking about a number of caravanserais.

[4] Exophoric use of definite clause. Cf. *Syntax* pp. 416-17. Repetition of *allī maᶜih* ending on incomplete phrase conveys sense of incomplete listing. Cf. *Syntax* pp. 316-7.

[5] Suffixation of *-ah* to *hānāk* to emphasise locative. Same function as *-hā* when suffixed to demonstratives. Cf. text 4.

[6] Pre-pausal glottalisation with devoicing of sonorant. Cf. *Syntax* p. 10.

[7] *dirītī* used here where speaker would more normally use *hāh* or *tamām*. Cp. text 30.

[8] Mistake. Followed by corrective appositive *mā gadumš ᶜārifīn*. Cf. *Syntax* p. 246.

[9] Consequential use of *fa-*. Cf. *Syntax* pp. 299-300.

5 Restaurants in San'a

Look, in San'a, in the past there were no restaurants. Okay? In the past, there were [only] caravanserais. Okay? You know what caravanserais are, don't you? Yes, that is the copper caravanserai, but caravanserais were like hotels. Okay? There [were] a lot of caravanserais in San'a. There was a caravanserai in every house. These caravanserais were like hotels, but we didn't have any hotels or whatever. A tribesman would come from outside San'a. He would arrive with his donkey and everything at the caravanserai. In that caravanserai, you would find a place with high benches. They would sit high up. At the far end of the caravanserai, the cows and sheep would stay. Those who had a camel, and those who had a horse, and those who had a donkey, and those who had ..., okay? They[10] would stay in a dark place over there. Caravanserais had benches. You would find someone high up like that and someone else sitting over there and someone over there. [They were] benches, like beds, but constructed out of clay. Do you understand? Like in the Tihama. Nowadays you find a lot of caravanserais outside San'a in the villages. They are still there.

In San'a, the tribesman would come to the caravanserai because the people of San'a didn't know about restaurants. Here there weren't any restaurants. If he was at his[11] house, there weren't any restaurants. A tribesman would come when he didn't know anyone, he would come into the caravanserai. In the caravanserai, he would find the landlord and landlady[12] baking and making porridge, *saltih*[13] and meat and whatever there. This was for the tribesmen who came. Of course, this was all for money. So you would find there were no restaurants apart from these caravanserais. He[14] would arrive at the caravanserai and sleep and sit up and have lunch and chew. Okay?

---

[10] i.e. the animals.

[11] Lit: 'their'.

[12] Indefinite in Arabic.

[13] Cf. description of *saltih* in footnote 67 to text 4.

[14] i.e. the tribesman.

wa-yibakkir aṣ-ṣubḥ / hū mā yijī ṣanᶜā 'illā ḏā gadlih ᶜamalih / yibakkir aṣ-ṣubḥ yiṭlaᶜ as-sūg / yibakkir aṣ-ṣubḥ yiṭlaᶜ lā mᶜih šakīyih yisīr lā ᶜind al-ḥākim wallā šī / yištikī bi-ḥadd wallā 'ayyi ḥājih /

bi-hāḏa š-šakl / bad'ū yiftaḥū maḍāᶜum mā kān biš maḍāᶜum xayrāt bada'at al-maḍāᶜum fī t-taḥrīr u-fī šāriᶜ jamāl wa-hāḏā / kānat maḍāᶜum ᶜādī zuġayrih / yaᶜnī nā ᶜarafthin fī ṯ-ṯawrih min baᶜd aṯ-ṯawrih[15] *ḍabᶜan / mā biš min gabl aṯ-ṯawrih mā biš / li'ann anā ᶜaraft as-samāsir / kān min awwal bih samāsir w-anā ᶜaraft as-samāsir / fī l-bawniyih ᶜindanā hānā kān bih samsarih / samsarat aḥmad zayd / maᶜrūfih / yaᶜnī as-samāsir maᶜrūfāt an-nās yaᶜrafūhin kulluhum / ḥakk as-samāsir allī yaᶜrafūhin /*

bada'at al-maḍāᶜum diftaḥ[16] */ yijaw yibīᶜū faṣūliyuh wa-fūl / wa-hāḏā / dirītī / wa-hāḏawlā ḥakk al-ḥujarīyih hum bāhirīn fī hāḏā ḍabāxat al-faṣūliyuh wa-l-fūl wa-hāḏā / ayn ᶜa-tsīr gāl asīr al-maḍᶜam / yaᶜnī kān min awwal al-maḍᶜam mā ḥadd yisīr al-maḍᶜam / al-maḍᶜam yaᶜnī sarsarī mā biš maᶜih bayt / maḍāᶜum yifᶜalū fīhā fūl wa-faṣūliyuh wa-miš ᶜārif ayš / bada'at diṭṭawwar / al-maḍāᶜum / mā jā' maḍᶜam illā w-hū 'aḥsan min al-lawwal / yifᶜalū maḍᶜam kabī'r*[17] */ fī ḏ-ḏuhr mā kān biš maḍāᶜum tilgay ḍabīx wa-kulla šay / mā kan billā galī:l*[18] *bass / saltih / maḍᶜam as-saltih hāḏa llī fī l-gāᶜ / wa-fī sūg al-milḥ maḍᶜam saltih / bass mā biš maḍāᶜum innū tilgay dijāj / wa-tilgay al-laḥm wa-tilgay al-hāḏā / mā kān biš / bada'at bi-ṣalṣuh / bi-saltih*[19] */ wa-yuxbizū ḏiksāᶜ / xubz dāfiyāt*[20] *wasṭ al-maḍᶜam /*

fa-[21]*ṭṭawwarat / law-mā iftaḥu l-maḍāᶜum illī mawjūdāt ḏalḥīnih / tūṣalī la-l-maḍᶜam wa-l-maḍᶜam kabīr jiddan / tilgay fīh al-faṣūliyuh tilgay fīh al-fūl / tilgay fīh / al-laḥm / tilgay fīh al-... ar-rizz / aṭ-ṭabīx*[22] */*

---

[15] Corrective reformulative apposition of prepositional phrase. Cf. *Syntax* p. 246.

[16] Verbal clause with initial linking verb and emphasis on verbal complement. Voicing of word-initial *t* to *d*.

[17] Pre-pausal glottalisation and devoicing of sonorant. Cf. *Syntax* p. 10.

[18] Lengthening of vowel in stressed syllable of intonation phrase.

[19] Corrective reformulative apposition. Cf. *Syntax* p. 246.

[20] Fem. plural agreement for coll. noun *xubz*. Cf. text 4.

[21] Consequential and sequential use of *fa-*. Cf. *Syntax* pp. 299-300.

[22] Threefold repetition of *tilgay fīh* with asyndetic linkage of clauses conveys sense of an incomplete list. Cf. *Syntax* pp. 316-17.

Then he would get up early in the morning – he wouldn't come to San'a unless he had work to do. He would get up early in the morning and go to the market. He would get up early in the morning, if he had a complaint he would go to the judge or whatever so he could make a complaint about anyone or anything.

In this way, they began to open restaurants. There weren't many restaurants. Restaurants started in Tahrir and in Jamal Street. They were still small restaurants. I knew them during the Revolution, after the Revolution, of course. There weren't any before the Revolution, because I knew the caravanserais. In the past, there were caravanserais, and I knew the caravanserais. In al-Bawniya here, there was a caravanserai. The caravanserai of Ahmad Zayd. Well known. Caravanserais are well known. Everyone knows about them, about caravanserais.

The restaurants began to open. They began by selling beans and foul and the like. Do you understand? Those [people] from the Hugariyya[23] are experts at cooking beans and foul and the like. 'Where are you going?' He would say, 'I am going to the restaurant.' At first, no one would go to restaurants. Restaurants were [for] tramps who didn't have a house. Restaurants where they made beans and foul and I don't know what. They began to develop, the restaurants. Each [new] restaurant was better than the previous one. They made big restaurants.[24] At midday, there were no restaurants where you could find mixed vegetables and everything. There were only a few things, [such as] *saltih*. The *saltih* restaurant which is in al-Ga' and in Sug al-Milh there is a *saltih* restaurant, but there were no restaurants where you could find chicken, or find meat or find whatever. There were none. They began with sauce, with *saltih*, and they would bake warm bread on the spot in the restaurant.

They developed until they opened the restaurants that are around today. You go to a restaurant and the restaurant is very big. You can find beans there and find foul. You can find meat. You can find rice, mixed vegetables.

---

[23] The Hugariyya is an area to the south of Ta'izz.

[24] Singular in Arabic.

kulla-mā tištay[25] *wa-kulla*[26] *^{c}ala ṭ-ṭalab / li'ann / ibsirī ṣan^{c}ā kānat zuġayrih / wa-'ahlahā galīl / ^{c}alā-mā hī kabīr bass ġayr ahlahā galīlih / mā kānatš bi-hāḏa s-sa^c*[27] *kullih / ahla ṣan^{c}ā ḍab^{c}an iḏā ma^{c}ih bayt mā yi^{c}rafš yākul fī maḍ^{c}am / bad'ū yutxulū 'ahl al-gurā*[28] */ min al-ḥujarīyih min al-… al-ḥaymih / min mārib / min hāḏā / bad'ū yutxulū fī ṣan^{c}ā / fīh*[29] *nās fakkarū fī l-maḍā^{c}um bada'at al-maḍā^{c}um ḍarūrī li-hāḏawlā li'ann mā biš ma^{c}āhum biyūt yidxulū / yuḍbuxū fīhā /*

fa-[30]*l-ġadā ḏalḥīn gadū bi-tsabbir fī l-maḍā^{c}um li'ann nās kaṯīr hānā jālisīn mā biš man yiḍbuxluhum / bī-gūlū al-maḍ^{c}am arxaṣlī / badal-mā 'asīr at^{c}ab nafsī w-ašgā fī l-bayt wa-hāḏā /*

fa-l-maḍā^{c}um gadī kaṯīrih / wa-ḏalḥīn gadum bad'ū yiftaḥū maḍā^{c}um ḥakk al-pītsā[31] */ wa-ḥakk al-brust*[32] */ wa-ḥakk al-… ya^{c}nī al-ašyā' allī mā kānatš mawjūdih hāḏa llī kānat fīh ^{c}ind al-ajānib / hāh / bada'at tudxul ^{c}indanā / hāḏa l-lašyā' mā bi-ti^{c}jibš illa š-šabāb / wa-'anā ddī liš miṯāl / abī lā yi^{c}rif bītsā wa-lā yi^{c}rif brust / hāḏā ḏalḥīnih / ams al-^{c}ašī / 'axī ligī 'abī wa-banāt uxtī wa-'uxtī wa-hāḏawlā' / gāl nisīr nit^{c}aššā / gāl abī hayy*[33] */ ibsirayn gāl abī ma štīš at^{c}aššā fī s-sūg*[34] */ gāl nijī ^{c}a-nḍa^{cc}umak bītsā / šall abī al-pītsā / hāḏa l-pītsā hatt / ma^{c}ānā maḍ^{c}am jadīd gad fadaḥū*[35] *pītsā hott fī ḥaddih / fī s-sab^{c}īn*[36] */ sār abī ma^{c}āhum*[37] */ ḍalabū ṯnayn pītsā min al-kibār / ddalhum iṯnayn bītsā / abī jā' al-^{c}ašī*[38] *bī-ḥākīnī /*

---

[25] Universal-conditional-concession clause. Cf. *Syntax* p. 353.

[26] Epenthesis after geminate consonant. Cf. *Syntax* p. 10.

[27] Underarticulation. From *sa^{c}ah*.

[28] Verbal clause with initial linking verb and main dynamic verb followed by subject.

[29] Use of pan-SA *fīh*.

[30] Consequential use of *fa-*. Cf. *Syntax* pp. 299-300. Cf. further examples below.

[31] Loan word. From *pizza*.

[32] Loan word. From *broast*.

[33] Verbal clause with emphasis on the direct speech object.

[34] Verbal clause with emphasis on the direct speech object.

[35] Intervocalic voicing of *t* to *d*.

[36] From *šāri^c as-sab^{c}īn*. Cf. *Syntax* pp. 184-5.

[37] Verbal clause with dynamic verb.

[38] Nominal clause after several verbal clauses indicates change in narration from events to summary. Cf. *Syntax* p. 119 (cf. peak phenomenon, Dahlgren 1998: 82).

Whatever you want and with everything on demand. Because, you see, San'a was small and it had a small population. Well, it is large, but its population was small. It wasn't this size. The people of San'a wouldn't eat in restaurants if they had a home. People from the villages began to come in from the Hugariyya, from … al-Hayma, from Ma'rib, from wherever. They began to come into San'a. There were people who began to think about restaurants. Restaurants started up as a necessity for these people because they didn't have any houses they could go to and cook.

So lunch was now being prepared in restaurants, because there were a lot of people staying here who had no one to cook for them. They would say, 'Restaurants are cheaper for me, rather than me going tiring myself working in the house and that.'

So, there came to be lots of restaurants. Now they have begun to open restaurants for pizza and for roast chicken and for … I mean, things that were not available, things that foreigners had, okay, began to come in, but only young people liked these things. Let me give you an example. My father doesn't know anything about pizzas or roast chicken and that is now. Yesterday evening, my brother caught up with my father, my nieces and my sister and those, and said, 'Let's go for supper!' My father said, 'Let's go! Look!' My father said, 'I don't want to eat in the market-place.' He[39] said, 'We'll go and let you try pizza.' He took my father to the pizza [restaurant]. This is Pizza Hut. We have a new restaurant here, they opened a Pizza Hut in Hadda[40] on [Street] 70. My father went with them. They ordered two of the large pizzas. He[41] gave them two pizzas. My father came back in the evening and talked to me.

[39] i.e. my brother.

[40] A village on the northern edge of San'a.

[41] i.e. the waiter.

gāl māhū al-lakl hāḏāk / bi-'alfayn wa-xamsamiyih ᶜa-yjī yištarī ḏalī wa-nākulih / sār iddīli ṯnayn xubz āh / fawgahin bisbā's[42] */ wa-ḏamāḏīs / gallī māhī al-ᶜašā hāḏā gāllī pītsā /*

yaᶜnī hāḏā wāgiᶜ yaᶜnī miš mitᶜawwadīn iḥna[43] */ bass aš-šabāb ḥakka hāḏi l-liyyām allī sārū wa-jaw wa-hāḏā / yištaw al-fann hāḏā / iḥna niᶜtabir innū al-fann ar-rāgī u-midrī mā / yištaw al-pītsā / li'annū al-ān šūfī lā mā biš an-nās min hāḏ allī hum mitᶜawwadīn ᶜalayh / yisīrū yākilū zayy al-xawrih / wa-ġaṣb / xawrih / yākulū zayy al-xawrih hākaḏahā*[44] */ mā ᶜinduhumš gudrih lākin bi-txawwarū maᶜ al-pītsā / yištaw yākulū bītsā māhī pītsā wa-law-mā yūṣal lā ᶜinduh hī māhī šī bass gadū yikābir bi-yākul kayf-ma wgaᶜat*[45] *bi-raġm an mišī ḥājih ġiḏā wallā ḥājih kwayyisih / wallā šī yistaḥagg az-zalaṭ / kullahā māšī / hāḏa llī ḥaṣal l-abī 'ams / gāl ū māhū hāḏā sār iddawlī xubzih / ᶜalā šwayyat*[46] *ḏamāḏīs wa-bisbās /*

fa-[47]*bayn-agulliš hāḏā ḥikāyat al-maḏāᶜum / tibsirī 'akṯarat al-maḏāᶜum hānā yisammūhin aš-šaybānī / bih maḏāᶜum xayrāt yisammūhin aš-šaybānī / hāḏā šaybānī 'ism šaxṣ / awwal-ma ftaḥ maḏᶜam fī šāriᶜ jamāl / kān yisammūhin fī ṣanᶜā b-ism aš-šaybānī aš-šaybānī aš-šaybānī*[48] */*

– u-miš maḏᶜam /

– illā maḏᶜam / aš-šaybānī / bass hū 'ism rājul[49] */ ismih aš-šaybānī / li'annū kān mašhūr hāḏīk al-liyyām tibsirī nās kaṯīr ḏaḥḥīnih / yiftaḥū yugūlū aš-šaybānī / b-ism aš-šaxṣ hāḏāk / aš-šaybānī aš-šaybānī / gad rubba-mā yikūnū l-ᶜummāl allī kānū yištaġilū ᶜindih / li'annū mašhūr al-lism*[50] */ yitxayyalū 'inn an-nās ᶜa-yjaw / wa-fiᶜlan*[51] *yaᶜnī bi-yinfaᶜ aṣ-ṣīt hāḏā /*

---

[42] Pre-pausal glottalisation. Cf. *Syntax* p. 10.

[43] Inversion of predicand–predicate to emphasise predicate. Cf. *Syntax* pp. 129-30.

[44] Suffixation of *-hā* to *hākaḏā* for emphasis Cf. suffixation of *-ah* to locative *hānāk* above.

[45] Universal-conditional-concession clause. Cf. *Syntax* pp. 351-3.

[46] Use of *šwayyat* in annexion phrase. Cp. text 4 for appositional use of *šwayyih*.

[47] Consequential and summative use of *fa-*. Cf. *Syntax* pp. 299-300. Cf. text 3.

[48] Word stress placed on definite article in these three repeated instances of *aš-šaybānī*.

[49] Non-SA pronunciation. Cp. SA *rajjāl* 'man'.

[50] *al-lism* functions as afterthought outside the predication (cf. Dahlgren 1998: 42, 44).

[51] Classicism.

He said, 'What is this food?' For 2,500 [riyals], he[52] could have gone and bought a goat and we could have [all] eaten it. 'He went and brought me two pieces of bread with chilli and tomato on.' He said to me, 'What is this supper?' He told me it was pizza.

I mean, this is what really happened. I mean we are not used [to this], but the young people of today who have been around a bit want to have this kind of fun. We consider it to be the high life and I don't know what. They want pizza because now, you see, if people aren't used to this they go and eat it as if it's a craving[53] and from a compulsion, a craving. They eat as if it is a craving. They can't afford it, but they crave pizza. They want to eat pizza, what is pizza, and when they get it, it isn't anything but they strive to outdo each other and eat it however it comes even though it isn't nourishing or anything good, or anything that is worth the money. It is none of this. This is what happened to my father yesterday. He said, 'What is this? They went and brought me a piece of bread with a little bit of tomato and chilli on!'

As I say, this is the story of restaurants. You see, most of the restaurants here they call al-Shaybani. There are a lot of restaurants which they call al-Shaybani. This Shaybani is the name of a person who first opened a restaurant in Jamal Street. In San'a, they used to name them using the name al-Shaybani, al-Shaybani, al-Shaybani.

– And not restaurant?

– Yes, al-Shaybani restaurant, but this is the name of a man. His name was al-Shaybani. Because he was well known, these days you can see lots of people opening [restaurants] and calling [them] al-Shaybani, [using] the name of that person, al-Shaybani, al-Shaybani. Maybe they are people who used to work for him, and because this name is well known they think that people will come, and in fact the reputation [of this name] does work.

---

52 i.e. I.

53 i.e. to find out what it is like.

6 *Aṭ-ṭabāxuh*

al-laḥūḥ

d̲irrah[1] / *ṭaḥīn d̲irrih* / *baᶜdayn*[2] *uᶜjinih* / *nibda' bi-l-laḥūḥ* / *d̲irrih baᶜdayn uᶜjanīh* / *ad̲-d̲irrih* / *uᶜjinīh bi-yadiš* / *awwal-mā bih mā' fāyir* / *fāyir*[3] / *lammā yifūr fawg an-nār* / *baᶜday'n*[4] / *kawb*[5] / *baᶜdayn bi-l-malᶜagih* / *šwayyih min aṭ-ṭaḥīn* / *ᶜalā jamb al-waᶜā w aṭ-ṭāsuh* / *baᶜdayn fa-mā' bārid ᶜašān*[6] *tiᶜjinī al-laḥūḥ* / *ᶜalā šwayyih šwayyih*[7] / *šwayyih baᶜdayn uᶜjanīh uᶜjanīh*[8] *law-mā mā fiš*[9] *barāguṭ* / *baᶜdayn uᶜjanīh* / *baᶜdā šwayyih šwayyih uᶜjanīh ᶜašān yūgaᶜ yukūn*[10] *rāxī* / *aywih yikūn rāxī ᶜašān tuskubīh fī aṣ-ṣaḥn wa-hū yikūn* / *miš gāsī* / *baᶜdayn ifᶜalīlih al-xamīrih* / *ifᶜalī 'aywih* / *al-xamīrih ḥagg al-xubz* / *tifᶜalīlih w-intī bi-tuᶜjanīh* / *wa-ḥuṭṭīh law-mā gadū bi-yuxmar* / *antī taᶜrafī kayf yuxmar* / *wa-xalāṣ* / *baᶜdayn tuskubī la-l-kitlī wa-laḥḥī wa-bass* /

– *wa-kayf tsawway al-laḥūḥ* /

– *fī ṣāj aw ṣullā'* / *aw ṣāj* / *ḥammayh* / *šā'š*[11] / *šāš min al-guḍn* / *wa-fᶜalī galīl min as-samn* / *wa-msaḥī aṣ-ṣullā' aw aṣ-ṣā'j*[12] / *gabla-mā taᶜmalī al-laḥūḥ* / *wa-xallayh law-mā bi-yuḥmā wa-baᶜdā tirjaᶜī timsaḥī wa-laḥḥī* / *wa-law-mā tixarrijī al-laḥūḥah* / *wa-msaḥīhā* / *bi-hād̲ā al-guḍn* / *wa-rjaᶜī laḥḥī* / *kulla-mā tixarrijī laḥūḥah*[13] / *wa-bass* /

---

1 This word is pronounced very carefully and slowly here.

2 Use of non-SA *baᶜdayn*.

3 *fāyir* is often used alone to refer to boiling water.

4 Pre-pausal glottalisation with devoicing of the sonorant. Cf. *Syntax* p. 10.

5 Non-SA word used in place of *bardag* 'cup'.

6 Use of non-SA *ᶜašān*.

7 Repetition of *šwayyih* here conveys a distributive sense. Cf. text 4.

8 Repetition of the verb to emphasise the intensive/repetitive action of kneading.

9 Use of non-SA *mā fiš*.

10 Reformulative apposition. Cf. *Syntax* p. 244.

11 Pre-pausal glottalisation. Cf. *Syntax* p. 10.

12 Pre-pausal glottalisation with devoicing of final obstruent. Cf. *Syntax* p. 10.

13 Universal-conditional-concession clause. Cf. *Syntax* p. 353.

6 Cooking and recipes

Pancakes[14]

Dhura, dhura flour, then knead it. We begin with sour pancakes. [Take] dhura, then knead it. The dhura, knead it with your hand. The first thing is boiling water, boiling [water]. When it boils on the stove, then a cup [of water], then with the spoon a little of the flour next to [into] the container or the bowl. Then, and cold water so that you can knead the pancake [mixture], bit by bit. Then knead it and knead it until there are no lumps left. Then knead it. Then knead it bit by bit so that it becomes smooth. Yes, it should be smooth so you can pour it into the plate and it should be not thick. Then add the yeast to it. Put, yes, the rising agent used for bread. You add it while you are kneading it, and leave it [there], until it rises. You know how it rises. That's it. Then you pour it into the kettle and make pancakes, and that's it.

– And how do you make the pancakes?

– In a frying pan or a stone pot, or a frying pan. Warm it. [Take] a cloth, a cloth of cotton and put on a little ghee, then wipe the stone pot or frying pan before you make the pancakes. Then leave it until it gets hot, then wipe it again and make the pancakes. When you take the pancake out wipe it with that piece of cotton, and make another pancake whenever you take out a pancake. That's it.

---

[14] The speaker is a girl in her early teens living at Bab Shu'ub. Her mother is from a well-established San'ani family, but her father is from a village outside San'a. During recording she spoke quickly, but in staccato style. She often gave single words rather than clauses and repeated words or gave alternative near-synonyms. She pronounced the vowel of the definite article carefully, avoided vowel elision, and used more epenthesis than she did when not being recorded. She inserted a number of Cairene-like phrases and words, although this was not a feature of her speech at home when talking with her parents or siblings, or with the author when the microphone was not present. Cairene-like words incl: *ba^{c}dayn* 'later, then' (v. *ba^{c}dā*); *^{c}ašān* 'so that, because' (v. *^{c}alā mayd, alā sibb* or *^{c}asibb*); *kwayyis* 'good' (v. *nāhī* or *tamām*); *mā fīš* 'there is not' (v. *mā biš*). Despite this, AS considered her speech to be clearly SA. As she becomes used to the microphone, later texts show increasing fluency: she uses SA *ba^{c}dā* in place of earlier *ba^{c}dayn*, *^{c}asibb* is used once in place of *^{c}ašān*, and while in early texts she corrects from an SA word to a standard word, in the final text she goes from standard *wa^{c}ā* 'container' to SA *ṭāsuh*.

aš-šafūṭ

al-ān natakallam ^{c}an aš-šafūṭ[15] */ zabādī wa-ḥalīb / uxḍubī az-zabādī / ^{c}asibb*[16] *lā yūga^{c}š mubargaṭ / aw mufargaš*[17] */ w-uskubī al-ḥalīb / fī al-wa^{c}ā' / aw aṭ-ṭāsuh / w-uxḍubī az-zabādī law-mā gadū / mā ^{c}ad fīš barāguṭ w-uskubīh ilā l-wa^{c}ā 'allaḏī fīh al-ḥalīb / w-if^{c}alī zaḥwagī / zaḥāwug / ṯūmih wa-ni^{c}ni^{c}ah / wa-milḥ / wa-galīl bisbā's*[18] */ wa-zḥagīhin ba^{c}dā 'uskubīhin lā l-wa^{c}ā 'allaḏī fīh az-zabādī wa-l-ḥalīb wa-xḍubīhin bi-l-mal^{c}agih / ba^{c}dayn / xuḏī al-laḥūḥ / w-uḍrahīhin fī ṣaḥn / wa-uskubī ^{c}alayh al-laban / allaḏī ga^{c} al-ḥalīb*[19] */ wa-l-laban / wa-xalāṣ /*

– wa-'ayyahīn tif^{c}alī al-laḥūḥ / aš-šafūṭ /

– kayf /

– yā s^{c}am bi-tif^{c}alī šafūṭ kulla yawm /

– lā / fī ramaḍā'n[20] */ aw kulla yawm iḏa ḥna ništī / fī al-layyām al-^{c}ādiyih / ^{c}ādī niṣallaḥlanā*[21] */ aw iḏā fīh ^{c}indanā ^{c}iris / aw ^{c}indanā ḍuyūf / aw fī al-mawt yiṣallaḥū šafūṭ / w-iḏā maṯalan iḥna maṯalan ma^{c} bayt ^{c}ammī mawt / iḥna nšillulhum šfūṭ / wa-nšillaluhum ṣaḥna*[22] *bint ^{c}ašān hāḏā ya^{c}malū ^{c}indanā hākaḏā / aw gahwih / aywih yišillū ^{c}indanā hākaḏā ^{c}ind al-mawt /*

---

[15] Formal opening sentence.

[16] Use of SA *^{c}asibb*.

[17] Reformulative apposition. Cf. *Syntax* pp. 244-6.

[18] Pre-pausal glottalisation. Cf. *Syntax* p. 10.

[19] Milk is described as *ḥalīb* when it is on its own, but as *laban* when mixed with something else, e.g. tea (Piamenta 1990-1) or yoghurt.

[20] Pre-pausal glottalisation and devoicing of sonorant. Cf. *Syntax* p. 10.

[21] Reflexive verb. Cf. *Syntax* pp. 202-3.

[22] Epenthesis.

Safūṭ

Now we are going to talk about *šafūṭ*. Yoghurt and milk. Beat up the yoghurt, so that it is not lumpy [or lumpy]. Pour the milk into the container or the plate, mix the yoghurt until there are no lumps left and pour it into the container which has the milk in. Then make a spicy dip. Garlic, mint, salt and a little chilli pepper and crush them together. Then pour them into the container which has the yoghurt and milk in and mix them[23] together with a spoon.[24] Then take the pancakes and put them into a dish and pour the milk mixture, which was the milk, on top, and that's it.

– When do you make pancakes, *šafūṭ*?

– What do you mean?

– I mean, do you make *šafūṭ* everyday?

– No, during Ramadan, or everyday if we want, on normal days it is okay to make it, or if we have a wedding or we have guests, or at a funeral they will make *šafūṭ*. If, for instance, we had a death at my uncle's house we would take *šafūṭ* to them, and we would take them a *bint aṣ-ṣaḥn*. They do things like this here, or coffee. Yes, they would bring these sorts of things over to us if there was a death.

[23] i.e. all the ingredients.

[24] Definite in Arabic.

as-sūsī

al-ān natakallam ᶜan as-sūsī[25] */ as-sūsī*[26] */ naḥḍur dagīg / wa-ᶜjanīh*[27] *maᶜ as-samn / wa-milḥ / maᶜ al-milḥ / baᶜdayn / wa-xamīrih / wa-ġaṭṭayh / law-mā yuxmar / wa-ḥḍurī bayḍ / wa-ḥalīb / bayḍ / iḏā ntī ᶜa-taᶜmalī zaġīr / iᶜmalī ṯalāṯ / aw arbaᶜ / aw xams / ka-mā 'antī tištay / tiḥibbī*[28] */ wa-ḥalīb / wa-tuxḍubīhun*[29] *fī al-waᶜā / al-bayḍ wa-l-ḥalīb / wa-ᶜmalī bayḍ wa-ḥalīb ᶜalā-mā tištay antī*[30] */ iḏā ntī tḥibbī kwayyis*[31] */ aᶜmalī kaṯīr bayḍ wa-ḥalīb / la-ntī tḥibbī galīl / ᶜalā-mā 'antī tiḥibbī / liš antī*[32] *wa-sārah wa-zawjiš / iᶜmalī galīl ᶜašān … / wa-zayyidī al-ḥalīb wa-l-bayḍ ᶜašān yikūn ḍaᶜmuh laḏīḏ /*

wa-lammā yuxmar al-ᶜajīn / ixbizīh / gassimīh ᶜalā / miṯl al-kurah / zaġīr zaġīr[33] */ wa-baᶜdayn fī al-maxbazih / taᶜmalī / wa-tinaḍḍujīhun*[34] *ᶜala n-nār / wa-baᶜdayn tiḥuṭṭīhun fī al-waᶜā / aw al-maglā' / uskubī al-bayḍ / bayn al-xubz allaḏī fī al-maglā' / uskubī al-bayḍ wa-l-hāḏā / wa-bi-l-malᶜagih fī al-xubz / baᶜdayn daxxilīhin fī al-firn ᶜašān yunḍuj law-mā gadū 'aḥmar bi-tšūfī 'aḥmar al-xubz*[35] */ xalāṣ gadū jāhiz wa-ykūn ḍaᶜmuh laḏīḏ /*

[25] Formal opening sentence (cf. recipe for *šafūṭ* above).

[26] Noun functions as adverb. Cf. *dawl ar-rijāl* in text 17 and further examples.

[27] Change of person and mood from 1 pl. indicative to 2 f.s. imperative.

[28] Reformulative apposition. Cf. *Syntax* pp. 244-6.

[29] Labialisation of *-i-* of object pronoun *-hin* due to preceding emphatic *ḍ* (cf. Watson 1995, 1999a, etc.).

[30] Post-position of independent pronoun *antī* 'you f.s.' to emphasise the subject. The pronoun serves as an appositive to the subject pronoun of the verb. Cf. *Syntax* p. 251.

[31] Use of non-SA *kwayyis*.

[32] Post-position of the pronoun *antī* to emphasise the subject. Cf. above.

[33] Repetition of *zaġīr* conveys distributive sense here. Cf. *šwayyih šwayyih* above.

[34] Labialisation of *-i-* of object pronoun *-hin* due to preceding emphatic *ḍ* (cf. Watson 1995, 1999a, etc.).

[35] Objective complement, *aḥmar*, precedes complemented term, *al-xubz*. Cf. *Syntax* p. 153.

Wheat bread with eggs

Now we are going to talk about wheat bread with eggs. [For] wheat bread with eggs, we take flour, and knead[36] it with ghee and salt, with salt. Then, and yeast. Then cover it until it rises, and fetch eggs and milk, eggs. If you are going to make a small one, use three, or four, or five, as you want, as you like, and milk. Then you beat them together in a container, the eggs and milk. Use [as many] eggs and milk as you like. If you want it to be good, use a lot of egg and milk. If you want a little, as you like. For you and Sarah and your husband, do a little so that … then add more milk and eggs so that it tastes delicious.

When the dough has risen, make the bread. Divide it into, like a ball, into lots of small pieces. Then put them on the bread pillow and cook them on the fire.[37] Then put them[38] into the container or the stone pot. Pour the egg between the bread which is in the stone pot. Pour the egg and that with a spoon into the bread. Then put it[39] into the oven so that it cooks until it becomes brown, and you can see that the bread is brown. That's it, it is ready and it will taste delicious.

[36] Switch to imperative.

[37] i.e. on the sides of the clay oven.

[38] i.e. the baked rounds of bread.

[39] Lit: 'them'.

al-^{c}aṣīd

al-ān natakallam ^{c}an al-^{c}aṣīd[40] */ if^{c}alī māʾ fī an-nār / wa-^{c}malī galīl milḥ if^{c}alī māʾ / ba^{c}dayn*[41] *iḥḏurī aḏ-ḏirrih / aṭ-ṭaḥīn aḏ-ḏirrih*[42] */ unxulīh / miṯl allaḏī yiḥibb ^{c}alī al-manxul / unxulīh / ba^{c}dayn i^{c}malī bi-l-maxbaših i^{c}malī / al-māʾ wa-hūwa*[43] *yafūr xallay al-māʾ lammā yifūʾr / ba^{c}dayn uskubīh / uskubī galīl fī wa^{c}ā zaġīr fāyir galīl min allaḏī fawwartī / ba^{c}dayn uskubīh la-ṭ-ṭaḥīn / w-axbašīh / aywih / ixbašīh / ba^{c}dayn i^{c}malī galīl māʾ w-ixbašīh fawg an-nār xallay an-nār galīlih / hādiʾih*[44] */*

wa-ba^{c}dā[45] *law-mā gadī mā ^{c}ad fīš barāguḍ fī al-^{c}aṣīduh nazzilīhā ^{c}ala l-larḍ / ḍuffay an-nārih / wa-ḍraḥīhā fī al-larḍ ba^{c}dayn imsakīhā bi-rijliš w-a^{c}malībihā hākaḏā / ^{c}ašān mā tiṭḥass w-intī ta^{c}malī hākaḏā / aw timsakīhā bi-yad ṯānī / bi-gummāš / ^{c}ašān lā taḥragīš / w-imsakīhā ba^{c}dayn ixbašī ixbašī ixbašī*[46] *law-mā mā ^{c}ad fīš*[47] *barāguṭ / ba^{c}dā tikūn laḏīḏih / w-i^{c}malī al-^{c}aṣīd / ^{c}alā marag / iḏ antī tiḥibbī ^{c}alā marag / dijāʾj*[48] */ i^{c}malī dijājih / ba^{c}dayn*[49] *uskubī marag / ungulī al-^{c}aṣīduh ilā wa^{c}ā aw fī al-maglāʾ / wa-ṣallaḥīhā hākaḏā sā^{c}-ma l-jabal tukūn šaklahā jamīl / w-uskubī al-marag / wa-xalāṣ /*

---

40 Formal opening. Cf. above.

41 Use of non-SA *ba^{c}dayn*.

42 Identificatory apposition. Cf. *Syntax* p. 243.

43 Careful, exaggerated pronunciation of the pronoun. Usu. *hū*.

44 Reformulative apposition of adjectives. Cf. *Syntax* pp. 244-5.

45 Use of SA *ba^{c}dā* in place of speaker's previous *ba^{c}dayn*.

46 Repetition of *ixbašī* to emphasise intensive, repetitive action.

47 Use of non-SA *[mā] fīš*.

48 Pre-pausal glottalisation and devoicing of voiced obstruent. Cf. *Syntax* p. 10.

49 Return to non-SA *ba^{c}dayn*.

Dhura porridge

Now we are going to talk about dhura porridge. Put water on the fire,[50] and add a little salt. Do the water and then fetch the dhura, the dhura flour. Sieve [it], like Ali likes sieves. Sieve [it], then stir it with a large wooden spoon. Add the water when it is boiling. Leave the water until it boils. Then pour it. Pour a little into a small container, a little boiling water from that which you have boiled. Then pour [it] into the flour and stir it. Yes, stir it. Then add a little water and stir it on the stove. Turn the heat down low.

Then, when there are no more lumps left in the porridge, put it down onto the floor. Turn off the heat, and put it on the floor, then take hold of it with your feet[51] and do like this with it, so that it doesn't slip while you are doing this, or take hold of it with your other hand, with a cloth so that you don't burn yourself, and hold it, then stir and stir and stir until there are no lumps left. Then it will be delicious. Make the porridge with broth. If you like it with chicken broth, do a chicken, and then pour off the broth.[52] Transfer the porridge into a container or into a stone pot, and make it like that, like a mountain,[53] so that it looks attractive. Then pour in the broth, and that's it.

---

[50] i.e. the stove.

[51] Singular in Arabic.

[52] Indefinite in Arabic.

[53] Definite in Arabic.

al-maṭīṭ

al-ān natakallam ᶜan al-maḍīṭ[54] */ iᶜmalī / skubī / uxḏ̣ubī*[55] *az-zabādī / law-mā mā ᶜad fīš fīh barāguḍ baᶜdayn uskubīh lā waᶜā / aṭ-ṭāsuh*[56] *allaḏī ᶜa-tfawwirī fīha l-maḍīṭ wa-ᶜmalī birr / galīl / birr*[57] */ wa-xḏ̣ubī birr / malᶜagatayn*[58] *iᶜmalī / lā tzayyidīš aṭ-ṭaḥīn / al-birr*[59] */*

baᶜdayn uxḏ̣ubīh maᶜ az-zabādey[60] */ w-aᶜmalī mā' / wa-'uxḏ̣ubīh 'uxḏ̣ubīh*[61] */ law-mā mā ᶜad fīš fīh barāguḍ ᶜašān*[62] *tikūn laḏīḏih / wa-law-mā gadī ragīgih / al-maḍīṭ*[63] */ az-zabādī maᶜ aṭ-ṭaḥīn*[64] *gad xaḏ̣abtīh gawī / iᶜmalīlih galīl milḥ / w-aᶜmalī saᶜtar / wa-galīl bisbās iḏa ntī tiḥibbī bisbā's*[65] */ wa-fawwirīhā ᶜalā an-nār wa-xalāṣ /*

---

54 Formal opening. Cf. above.

55 Threefold apposition of verbs until the speaker finds the word she wants.

56 Reformulative apposition from standard Arabic word to SA word.

57 Identificatory apposition with modified appositive. Cf. *Syntax* p. 243.

58 The dual is usu. restricted to nouns indicating time or measure, as here. Cf. *Ṣbaḥtū!* pp. 93-4.

59 Apposition in place of annexion phrase. Cf. *Syntax* pp. 193-4.

60 Pre-pausal diphthongisation. Cf. *Syntax* p. 10.

61 Repetition of *ixbašī* to emphasise intensive, repetitive action. Cf. above.

62 Use of non-SA *ᶜašān*.

63 *al-maḍīṭ* functions as afterthought outside the predication (cf. Dahlgren 1998: 42, 44).

64 Topicalisation of object of verb. Cf. *Syntax* p. 130.

65 Pre-pausal glottalisation. Cf. *Syntax* p. 10.

Barley gruel

Now we are going to talk about barley gruel. Do, pour, beat the yoghurt until there are no lumps left. Then pour it into a container, the bowl you are going to boil the barley gruel in, and add some wheat, a little wheat [flour], and stir in the wheat. Add two spoonfuls. Don't put in too much wheat flour.

Then beat it up with the yoghurt, and add water, and beat it and beat it, until there are no lumps left so that it is delicious. When it is thin, the barley gruel, [when] you have beaten up the yoghurt with the flour very well, add a little salt to it, add wild thyme and a little chilli pepper, if you like chilli pepper. Then boil it on the stove, and that's it.

7 As-safar bi-t-taks

as-safa:r[1] *fi l-yaman / bih ^{c}ittat*[2] *ṭurug / miṯl aṭ-ṭayyāruh / as-sayyārih / taks / wa-l-bāṣ / aw bi-sayyārih xāṣṣuh ḥakk al-linsān*[3] */ wa-kull / ya^{c}nī wa-t-taksī*[4] */ li-kulla manāḍug manḍuguh ma^{c}āhā firzih / wa-l-firzih ma^{c}nahā mawgif / mawgif at-takāsī / fa-*[5]*maṯalan / firzat ti^{c}izz / wa-firzat al-ḥudaydih / wa-firzat ṣa^{c}duh / wa-firzat ḥajjih / hāḏawlā kullahin fī mawāgi^c muxtalifih / fa-law al-wāḥid yištī yisāfir / lā ta^{c}izz / yisīr lā firzat ta^{c}izz / lā hū yištī yisīr al-ḥudaydih / yisīr lā firzat al-ḥudaydih / lā hū yištī yisāfir lā ḥajjih / yisīr lā firzat ḥajjih /*

ḍab^{c}an kulla wāḥidih min hāḏa l-firaz / fī bug^{c}ah muxtalifih ^{c}an al-bug^{c}ah ḥakk hāḏā / fa-maṯalan firzat ta^{c}izz hāḏā / bi-tijma^c bayn / kull: al-gurā wa-l-manāḍug illī fī tijāh ta^{c}izz / fa-l-wāḥid lā hū yištī yisāfir lā ta^{c}izz / bī-sīr la-l-firzih / ḥīn yūṣal al-firzih / bah hānāk takāsī / li-kulla bug^{c}ah / aw li-kulla gariyih / mā ^{c}alayh illā 'annū yūṣal lā hānāk wa-yiṣīḥ aynī firzat ta^{c}izz / wa-hum ^{c}a-ydarrawh aynī firzat ta^{c}izz / yigullih ayyi wāḥid hānāk / aṭ-ṭāruf[6] */ wa-hāḏawla t-takāsī / gadum*[7] */ musajjilīn aṣḥāb at-takāsī fī l-firzih hāḏā zayy-mā tugūl / innahum ašxāṣ ma^{c}rūfīn min gabil aš-šarigih*[8] */ ḥakkuhum aw mā yisammawhum hāḏawlā nigābat as-sawwāgīn / bi-tnaḏ̣ḏ̣umhum wa-hāḏā / fa-l-wāḥid yūṣal lā hānāk / ^{c}inda-mā yigullih aynī firzat ta^{c}izz / yisīr ^{c}alā ḍūl /*

fa-^{c}ind firzat ta^{c}izz hāḏā / kulla taks bi-trayya^c hinayyik / tirayya^c lā rukkāb / ma mtalit min taks[9] */ tjī at-taks aṯ-ṯāniyih / mā biš inn al-wāḥid yisīr fawg at-taks ḏayyā*[10] *wa-ṯ-ṯānī yisīr fawg at-taks aṯ-ṯānī wa-ṯ-ṯāliṯ yisīr fawg at-taks ar-rābu^c /*

---

[1] Lengthening of final stressed syllable. Lengthening here also indicates hesitation.

[2] Geminate devoicing. Cf. *Syntax* p. 10.

[3] Gemination of *l* of definite article before vowel-initial noun. Cf. *Sbaḥtū!* pp. 18-19.

[4] *taks/taksī* can be fem. or masc. Here, speaker often changes from fem. to masc. agreement.

[5] Consequential use of *fa-*. Cf. *Syntax* pp. 299-300. Cf. further examples of *fa-* below.

[6] Lit: 'the one at the end'. Used to emphasise that anyone can tell you where to go.

[7] Cataphoric pronoun referring to *aṣḥāb at-takāsī*. Cf. *Syntax* pp. 406-7.

[8] Intervocalic voicing of *k* to *g*.

[9] Universal-conditional-concessive clause. Cf. *Syntax* p. 353.

[10] Switch to masc. agreement in demonstrative. Cp. fem. verbal agreement with *taks*.

7 Travel by taxi

There are a number of ways of travelling in Yemen, such as by plane, by taxi and bus, or by private car. For taxis, every region has a place with its own taxi rank. [The word] *firzih* means stop, taxi stop.[11] For instance, the Ta'izz taxi rank, the Hudayda taxi rank, the Sa'da taxi rank, the Hajja taxi rank. All of these are in different places. So, if you want to travel to Ta'izz, you go to the Ta'izz taxi rank. If you want to go to Hudayda, you go to the Hudayda taxi rank. If you want to go to Hajja, you go to the Hajja taxi rank.

Of course, each one of these taxi ranks is in a different place from the other. So, for instance, the Ta'izz taxi rank is for all the villages and regions which are in the direction of Ta'izz. So if you want to go to Ta'izz, you will go to the taxi rank. When you get to the taxi rank, there are taxis going to every place or every village. All you have to do is get there and shout, 'Where is the Ta'izz taxi rank?' and they will tell you where the Ta'izz taxi rank is. Anyone there will tell you. Those taxis, the taxi drivers are registered at the taxi rank; you could say that they are people known by their company or what are called the drivers' union, and [the union] organises them. So you get there, and when you are told where the Ta'izz taxi rank is, you go straight there.

So at the Ta'izz taxi rank, every taxi waits there, waits for passengers. As soon as one taxi fills up, the next taxi comes. It isn't that one person gets into one taxi, and the next person gets into the second taxi, and the third person gets into the fourth[12] taxi.

---

[11] i.e. taxi rank.

[12] i.e. the third taxi.

māšī / at-taks ḏayyik[13] *law-mā timtalī tuxṭō*[14] */ wa-baᶜdayn yimallaw at-taks aṯ-ṯāniyih / wa-mistamirrih hākaḏā / ḥawālī 'arbaᶜ wa-ᶜišrīn sāᶜah /*

fa-maṯalan law aštī 'asāfir / tiᶜizz / awṣal agūl tiᶜizz / yigūlūli ḍlaᶜ / f-aḍlaᶜ / fawg at-taks / at-taks al-wāḥidih bi-trakkib ᶜala l-lagall / mišū ᶜala l-lagall / bi-trakkib tisᶜah yaᶜnī ḥakkaha r-rukkāb[15] *tisᶜah / mā tirkabš agalla min hāḏā / mišū as-sawwāg yigbal innū yiḍalluᶜ ṯamāniyih wallā sabᶜah / yirayyaᶜ law-mā yikūn tisᶜah / bī-rakkib iṯnayn guddām / w-arbaᶜah fī l-wasaṭ / wa-ṯalāṯih warā' /*

yūgaᶜ maᶜih šabk / ṭāluᶜ fawg as-sayyārih wa-xānih zaġīrih wara' / yiḍraḥū lā fīh / šanaḍāt wallā ᶜafš wallā 'ayyi ḥājih gadū yiḍraḥhun / ᶜinda-mā yiḍraḥhun / ṭāluᶜ fawg aš-šabk / bī-rabbaṭ / ᶜalayhin lā yinkaᶜanš[16] */ wa-ḥin*[17] *timtali s-sayyārih*[18] *... / ḍabᶜan fī maṯal ṯaman ar-rākib al-wāḥid yaᶜnī ᶜinda-mā yirkab / ḥudūd arbaᶜmiyih aw xamzamiyat riyāl / anā mā gadlī xayrāt ma rkabš taksī /*

bi-yirkab wāḥid fawg at-taks / ḥattā law hū ġarīb min aṯ-ṯāniyīn wa-hāḏā / li'annum[19] *fī taks / wa-t-taks zuġayrih hākaḏā yaᶜnī mā hīš kabīr wāsiᶜ*[20] *mā ḥadd yistir yibsir aṯ-ṯānī wallā šī / bī-kūn fīhā 'inn*[21] *al-musāfir mā bī-yiḍbaḥš wallā šī / yijābir allī jambih*[22] */ walla llī warāh / wallā llī tijāhih / ayyi wāḥid bi-ftaḥ mawḍūᶜ wa-yitḥākā minnih / yā yitḥākaw min al-ġalā' / yā yitḥākaw min al-jibāl illī bi-bsirūhā / yā yitḥākaw min al-xuḍruh / xuḍrat al-arāḍī llī yitfarrajūhā*[23] */ ayyi ḥājih / kullu wāḥid yaᶜnī bi-ddī xabar min rāsih ma štā*[24] */ baᶜdā yitnāgašū fīh /*

---

13 Masc. agreement in demonstrative. Cp. fem. verbal agreement with *taks*. Cf. above.

14 Post-emphatic labialisation of *-ā* following pausal *imāla* to *-ē*.

15 Inversion of attributed term–attribute to emphasise pronoun. Cf. *Syntax* p. 224.

16 Asyndetic linkage of clause of consequence to main clause. Cf. *Syntax* p. 311.

17 Shortening of long vowel. From *ḥīn*.

18 Digression follows. This is a subordinate clause with no accompanying main clause.

19 From *li'annuhum*.

20 Lack of gender agreement with the feminine subject.

21 Corroborative particle.

22 Exophoric pronominal use of definite clause. Cf. *Syntax* pp. 416-17.

23 Identificatory apposition in which *xuḍrat al-arāḍī llī ...* functions as appositive to *al-xuḍruh*. Cf. *Syntax* p. 243.

24 Universal-conditional-concession clause. Cf. *Syntax* p. 353.

No. The one taxi goes when it is full, then they fill the next taxi, and [it] carries on like that for around twenty-four hours.

So, for instance, if I want to go to Ta'izz, I get there and say, 'Ta'izz!' They tell me to get in,[25] so I get into the taxi. One taxi takes at least, not at least, it takes nine. I mean, it has nine passengers. It won't take any less than that. The driver will not be prepared to put in eight or seven. He will wait until there are nine. He will put two in front, four in the middle, and three behind.

He has a luggage rack on top of the car, and a small boot behind. They put, if there are cases or baggage or anything, he will put them [there]. When he puts them up on the luggage rack, he will tie them on so that they don't fall. When the car is full, ... Of course, a single person's fare when he travels will be around 400 or 500 riyals. I haven't been in a taxi for ages.

Someone gets into the taxi, even if he doesn't know the others, because they are [all] in a taxi. And the taxi is small. It isn't so big and wide that no one can see anyone else or anything. The traveller won't get bored or anything. [He] will talk to the one next to him or the one behind him or the one in front of him. Anyone can start a topic and talk about it: either they will talk about price rises, or they will talk about the mountains which they can see, or they will talk about the greenery – the greenery of the land they are watching. Anything. Everyone can say whatever occurs to them, whatever they like. Then they can talk about it.

[25] Imperative in Arabic.

wa-ḥīn tisāfir lā ta^{c}izz / ḍab^{c}an at-taks bi-tmurr bi-^{c}iddat gurā xayrāt / fa-maṯalan bi-tuxṭā: min ḍarīg ta^{c}izz ya^{c}nī / li'annū hānā bāb al-yaman / bih ḍarīg ta^{c}izz[26] / wa-bih ḍarīg al-ḥudaydih / ya^{c}nī muḥaddadāt ya^{c}nī gad an-nās mā yisammūš aš-šāri^{c} ḥakk ta^{c}izz ^{c}ind al-firzih llā ḍarīg ta^{c}izz / bi-wāṣul[27] at-taks[28] / at-taks bī-wāṣul / bi-yuxṭā min manāḍug ^{c}adīdih / wa-gurā / awwal-mā yibda' hū bih xawlān / ya^{c}nī šāri^{c} xawlān hāḏā / ^{c}aṣrat xawlān wa-sanḥān firzat sanḥān / wa-dārisalm / wa:-ḥuziyaz wa-gaḥāzih / hāḏawlā kullahin gurā / ba^{c}d yūga^{c} hāzib yūṣal lā sumārih / mā miš sumārih ^{c}ādū nagīl yasliḥ / hāḏa n-nagīl ya^{c}nī 'innū murtafa^{c} šwayyih / tūṣal as-sayyārih[29] tinzil minnih / zayy al-jabal hākaḏā / zayy al-ḥayd / yisammū ḥayd awlā … / fa-bi-ybsir taḥtih / jahrān wa-l-xuḏ̣ruh hāḏ̣īk / gā^{c} / kullahā / awwal-mā yinzil li'annū bidāyathā min awwal-mā yibdā min bi-txul[30] lā ḥuziyaz wu-guḥāzih tibdā zayy-mā tigūl ^{c}aṣārāt / wa-jibāl / law-mā yinzil min nagīl yasliḥ / fa-[31]yūṣal ^{c}alā jahrān / wa-jahrān hāḏ̣āk gā^{c} kabī:rih / ya^{c}nī gā^{c} wāsi^{c}ah / zirā^{c}īyih / yibsir al-wāḥid xuḏ̣ruh / tibda' aṭ-ṭarīg sā:nī[32] /

ya^{c}nī at-taks tuxṭā masāfih mi^{c}ayyan tuxṭā duġrī[33] / bi-tūṣal minnahā lā ma^{c}mar[34] / ma^{c}bar / wa-min ma^{c}bar lā ḏamār / ḏamār tu^{c}tabar[35] maḥāfaḏuh / wa-min muḥāfaḏah ḏamār[36] ḍab^{c}an bih tištagg ṣalā ^{c}ans wallā yisīr al-wāḥid al-ḥadā / wallā yisīr wāḥid … /

---

[26] Use of existential *bih* with following definite noun phrase. Cf. text 1.

[27] Change of gender agreement in verb for *taks* to masc.

[28] Verbal clause with dynamic verb and definite verbal subject. The next (nominal) clause picks up the subject as the topic.

[29] Verbal clause with dynamic verb and definite verbal subject.

[30] Devoicing of *d* to *t*.

[31] Sequential use of *fa-*. Cf. *Syntax* p. 299.

[32] Verbal clause with initial linking verb and emphasis on the complement *sānī*.

[33] Borrowed adverb. Probably from Egyptian.

[34] Pronunciation error. For *ma^{c}bar*.

[35] Internal passive still partially productive in SA (cf. Rossi 1939; Retsö 1983: 147-8). More frequently attested in descriptive than in narrative texts, and in imperfect than in perfect, e.g. *yu'kal* 'it is eaten', *tuḥlab* 'she is milked', *yusammā* 'it is called' (cf. Holes 1998 for other dialects). Examples incl. *ḥurim* 'he was out', *kumil* 'it was completed', *ṣulub* 'he was crucified', *wulid* 'he was born', are also found in perfect. Cf. also *Syntax* pp. 91-2.

[36] Apposition in place of more common annexion phrase. Cf. *Syntax* pp. 193-4.

When you go to Ta'izz, of course the taxi goes through a large number of villages. For instance, it goes along the Ta'izz road, because here [from] Bab al-Yaman there is the Ta'izz road, and there is the Hudayda road. [They have] specific [names]. I mean, people don't call the Ta'izz road at the taxi rank anything but the Ta'izz road. The taxi continues. The taxi continues. It goes through a number of places and villages. It comes to Khawlan first, I mean, the Khawlan road, the Khawlan turn and Sanhan, the Sanhan taxi rank, and Darisalm, Huziyaz and Gahazih. These are all villages. Then after Hazib it reaches Sumara. No, not yet Sumara, it is just the Yaslih pass. This pass is fairly high. When the car gets there it goes down [something] like a mountain,[37] like a mountain face – they call it *ḥayd* or .... Beneath you, you can see Jahran and the greenness below. All of it is a plain. [You see it] as soon as you go into Huziyaz and Gahazih because it starts with what you would call hairpin bends and mountains until you go down the Yaslih pass. Then you reach Jahran. Jahran is a large plain, that is to say, a wide, agricultural plain. You can see greenness, then the road begins to go straight.

For a certain distance, the taxi continues straight and from there comes to Ma'mar, Ma'bar, and from Ma'bar to Dhamar. Dhamar is a province. From the province of Dhamar, of course, it[38] branches off to Ans or you can go to al-Hada, or you can go to ....

[37] Definite in Arabic.

[38] i.e. the road.

bih ḍarīg minnahā barḏū lā ma^cbar al-ḥudaydih / wa-ḏamār / wa-hānāk bih sūg ^cala ṭ-ṭarīg / yibsir al-wāḥid sūg lā yištī yinzil yištarī šī 'aw ayyi ḥājih /

wa-timšī at-taks mubāšaratan[39] *ḥinū xaṭṭ ṭawīl ^calā ḍūl / mišu m^caṣwaruh / yuwāṣul at-taks*[40] */ law-mā yūṣalū an-nās hānāk bih bug^cah yištaraw fīhā gāt / al-gāt hāḏā ḏiḥlih yisammawh / ^cānisī wa-ḏḥilih / hāḏa l-gāt / an-nās yiḥibbūh all ^cādū badrī ya^cnī wakt yigaṭṭa^cūh l'annū nās yisāfirū lā swāg al-gāt / iḏā hū*[41] *ṣubḥ gadum yištaraw gāt / mā yūṣal ta^cizz illā wa-yixazzin wallā fawg at-taks lā gad wakt al-gāt wa-tġaddā / yixazzin / fa-mā yištarawš min ṣan^cā / yištaraw min aṭ-tarīg / b-ūga^c raxīṣ / wa-gāt ḥālī / ḍarī /*

at-taks ḍab^can bi-twāṣal / min ḏamār tidxul maḥāfaḏat ibb / awwal-mā yidxul maḥāfaḏat ibb bi-bda' bi-yarīm / yarīm hāḏā manḍuguh / xaḏrō / jamīlih ya^cnī / yibsir wāḥid al-xuḏruh gadū min ḏamār wa-maḍla^c / wāṣalat at-taksī hāḏā min yarīm / wa-kullahā ^calā l-gurā fī ... / mā yisammaw hāḏā / 'ibb / titba^c muḥāfaḏat ibb /

gad ḏā[42] *yiḍla^c at-taks hākaḏāhā*[43] */ ṭal^cah jabalīyih / law-mā yiḍull ^calā nagīl sumārih / nagīl sumārih hāḏā nagīl šā:ḥig / yimkin ann irtifā^cah ^can saṭḥ al-baḥr / fī ḥudū:d alfa:yn wa-ṯalāṯmiyat mitr a^ctagid*[44] */ ḥīn yiḍla^c al-wāḥid an-nagīl / yibda' yibsir ġarr taḥtih al-jibāl hāḏīk / wa-š-šāhigih wa-ybsir al-ḥiyūd / allī yibda' yixāf lākin ma^c xuḏrathā wa-mijābirat an-nās fawg at-taksī / mā yifakkirš / innū*[45] *ftaja^c yibgā ḥissih yō wa-midrī mā lā tiddarib as-sayyārih lā*[46] *yūga^c šī / mā yixtār al-wāḥid illā w-bi-yfakkir fī hāḏa š-šī / ḥīn yibsir at-taks kayf bi-tuxṭō / wa-kayf al-jibāl hāḏīk aš-šāhigih wa-l-xuḏruh / masāfat sā^cah aw nuṣṣ sā^cah w-int ġarr bi-tinzil jabal /*

---

39 Classicism: addition of *-an* ending.

40 String of three syndetically linked verbal clauses with dynamic verbs.

41 Dummy pronoun. Cf. *Syntax* p. 413.

42 Presentational particle. Cf. *Syntax* pp. 421-3.

43 *-hā* suffixed to indefinite demonstrative to emphasise the demonstrative.

44 *a^ctagid* 'I believe' inserted parenthetically.

45 Presentational particle. Cf. *Syntax* p. 425.

46 Corroborative particle.

There is also a road from there to Ma'bar, Hudayda and Dhamar. There is a market there on the road. You can see the market. If you want to get out and buy something or anything, [you can].

Then the taxi goes straight on, because it is a long, straight road. It isn't twisty. The taxi continues until the people come to a place where they can buy gat. This gat is called Dhihla,[47] Anisi and Dhihla. People like this gat because it is still early at the time they cut it[48] because people travel to the gat markets. If it is morning, they buy gat. They arrive in Ta'izz to chew or [chew] in the taxi, if it is the time for gat and they have had lunch, they chew. They don't buy [gat] from San'a. They buy en route, [because] it is cheap and nice, fresh gat.

The taxi goes on from Dhamar, of course, and comes to the province of Ibb. The first place it comes to in the province of Ibb is Yarim. Yarim is a beautiful, green region. You can see the green from Dhamar onwards. The taxi continues from Yarim and they are all villages in ..., what do they call it, Ibb, they belong to Ibb.

Then the taxi suddenly goes up into the mountains until it looks out onto the Sumara pass. The Sumara pass is a towering pass. It is probably around 2,300 metres above sea level, I think. When you go up into the pass, you can just see the mountains below and the vast height and the sheer mountain peaks. You would start to get frightened, but with its greenness and talking to the [other] people in the taxi you don't think [of getting frightened]. You are scared, and your mind is still set [on being scared]. I don't know, if the car fell something would definitely happen. You can't help thinking of these things, when you see how the taxi is travelling and see how steep those mountains are and the greenness. For one hour or half an hour, you are just going down mountains.

[47] This gat may be called *ḏiḥlih* due to presence of rust spots (Tim Mackintosh-Smith p.c.).

[48] And, therefore, it is fresh.

kullih ġarr ḥiyūd / mā: yibda' al-wāḥid yifakkir wa-yigūl al-ḥamdulillāh illā ba^{c}d-mā yinzil ā:xir šī fī l-jabal ḏayyik / li'annū jabal ḏ̣axm hākaḏāhā / ḏ̣arīg fi^{c}ilūhā fīh / šāhigih /

al-ān tūṣal at-taksī lā 'ibb / ibb madīnih xaḏ̣rā / jamīlih / wa-ḥīnī xaḏ̣rā ya^{c}nī al-manāḏ̣ur fīhā kaṯīrih / wa-law-mā yitḥākaw ^{c}alā 'ibb / maṯalan yiddaw miṯāl / yigullak mā ta^{c}rafš ibb / gāl ma ^{c}rafš ibb / gad yigullak ibb ibb al-xaḏ̣rā 'allī yixṭā al-ġurab yisāfir yisāfir al-ġurab law yisāfir min ayn-mā sāfar / mā yūṣal fawg ibb illā w-yigūl yōx ya^{c}nī yinzil / w-innu[49] *ṣtara^{c} / ṣara^{c}ah duxxān ibb / ḥīnī xaḏ̣rā / midrī mā bi-zra^{c}ū fīhā 'allī yixalli l-wāḥid yidawwax / ḥašīš aw midrī māhū /*

wa-ba^{c}d ibb yiṭla^{c} lā jiblih / ḏ̣ab^{c}an / bayn ṣan^{c}ā wa-ti^{c}izz / at-taks bi-twaggif wagafāt xayrāt / bi-ḏāt lā hū gadū wakt al-ġadā bī-waggifū ^{c}ind ayyi wāḥid / ^{c}ind ayyi gariyih / ya^{c}nī gariyih min al-gurā / aw madīnih / li'annū kull: gariyih / fī l-xaṭṭ / yilgā wāḥid dakākīn / lā bih gariyih fī l-xaṭṭ / fī l-xaṭṭ ad-dakākīn hāḏawlā yibī^{c}ū fīhā[50] *bibs yibī^{c}ū fīhā ^{c}aṣīrāt ḥagg al-maḏ̣ā^{c}um / aw gahāwī / al-gahāwī hāḏawlā / lā daxal ya^{c}nī lā hū wakt akl / wajbih min al-wajibāt maṯalan nigūl ġadā / mumkin inn ar-rukkāb yinzilū / yidxulū al-gahwih hāḏā / al-gahwih ^{c}ibārih ^{c}an bayt / wa-l-bayt hāḏā fīh ahlih / al-mugahwī aw al-mugahwiyih / gadum mijahhizīn fī l-biyūt ḥakkuhum hāḏawlā / yiḏ̣buxū / yif^{c}alū as-saltih / yif^{c}alu l-laḥmih / wa-laḥmih baladī / ḏ̣arīyuh / ya^{c}nī ^{c}ādū nafs al-yawm yiḏbaḥū ḏīk sā^{c} ba^{c}dā yiḏ̣buxūh / wa-l-laḥadd law yištī yudxul yitġaddā ^{c}indahum / gadū mā ma^{c}ih illā ḏawlayya / laḥmih / ḥulbih / wa-xubz dāfī / ḏīk sā^{c} yuxbizū ^{c}ala ṭ-ṭalab / yākul wāḥid yitġaddā / yišba^{c} maṯalan wakt al-ġadā / tibda' tisāfir at-taks*[51] */ hāḏā lā hū wakt ġadā / wa-lā mišū wakt ġadā gadū ġarr yiwaggif at-taks wa-yijirrūluhum*[52] *šigārih aw yijirrūluhum mā' / aw yijirrūluhum ayyi ḥājih ḏawlayyik ar-rukkāb*[53] */ wa-yuwāṣul at-taks*[54] */*

---

[49] Presentational particle. Cf. *Syntax* p. 425.

[50] Demonstrative takes plural agreement with *dakākīn*, but following pronominal suffix takes fem. sing. agreement.

[51] Verbal clause with initial linking verb and dynamic main verb.

[52] Reflexive verb. Cf. *Syntax* pp. 202-3.

[53] *ḏawlayyik ar-rukkāb* functions as afterthought (cf. Dahlgren 1998: 42).

[54] Verbal clause with dynamic verb. Note again switch to masc. agreement for *taks*.

It is all just mountains. You don't start thinking of saying, 'Thanks be to God!' until you have completely left that mountain [area], because they are enormous mountains, and the road[55] they have built through it is high.

Now the taxi comes to Ibb. Ibb is a beautiful, green town and because it is green it has a lot of sights. When they talk about Ibb they will give an example, they will say to you, 'Don't you know Ibb?' [and if you] say, 'I don't know Ibb!' they will say to you, 'Ibb, green Ibb, the place where the crows fly, the crows fly from wherever they fly until they come over Ibb, then they cry out, 'Caw!' and come down, because they suddenly become dizzy, they were made dizzy by the smoke of Ibb.' It is green. I don't know what it is they grow there that makes people dizzy,[56] hashish or I don't know what.

After Ibb, you go up to Jibla. Of course, between San'a and Ta'izz the taxi makes a large number of stops, particularly if it is lunchtime they will stop at anyone's house, in any village, I mean any one of the villages, or [any] town. [This is] because [in] every village en route you will find shops, if there is a village en route. These shops en route will sell Pepsi, or they will sell juice from restaurants or cafes. These cafes, if you go in at mealtime, any meal, for instance, let us say lunch, the passengers can get out and go into the cafe. The cafe is really a house, and this house has its proprietors, the landlord or landlady. They prepare [food] in their houses. They cook and make *saltih*.[57] They do meat – fresh, local meat. They slaughter on the same day, at that time, then they cook it. If someone wants to go in and have lunch at their place, he can only have that – meat, fenugreek and warm bread. They bake there and then on demand. When everyone has had lunch and is full, for instance, at lunchtime, the taxi sets off [again]. That is if it is lunchtime. If it is not lunchtime, he will just stop the taxi and the passengers will get themselves cigarettes or get themselves water or get themselves whatever, then the taxi will continue.

[55] Indefinite in Arabic.

[56] This is a reference to cannabis which is reputedly grown and sold in the Ibb province.

[57] Cf. text 4, footnote 67.

ḍabᶜan baᶜd ibb yūṣal jiblih / wu-min jiblih baᶜdhā gadū yudxul taᶜizz / taᶜizz ḥālī jawwahā[58] / *jawwahā mišū bārid gawī wallā hū / ḥāmī gawī jawwahā*[59] *jaww laḏīf ḥālī / at-taks ḥīn yūṣal taᶜizz / lā ḥadd yištī yūgaf fi ṭ-ṭarīg awlā šī yigūl taks ᶜalā jamb yā taksī / yā sawwāg / wa-s-sawwāg / yiwaggif / ayn-ma šta l-wāḥid*[60] / *iḏā mā yištawš yiwaggif hū gadū yuwāṣul ᶜalā ḏūl la-l-firzih / mišū muxāḏab bi-r-rukkāb / ḏayyā r-rākib yiššī*[61] *yišillih maṯalan al-jaḥmalīyih wa-ḏayyā r-rākib yiššī*[62] *yišillih / ṣabur jabal ṣabur / wa-ḏayyā / mā biš / mā billā kullu wāḥid yirkab / as-sawwāg ᶜalayh an yiwaṣṣuluh lā wasṭ al-firzih / illā mā kān fi ṭ-ṭarīg / gadū yiwaggif / yigūl ᶜalā jamb / wa-hū yiwaggiflih / bih nās yigūl ᶜalā jamb iḥna hāna ngūl ᶜalā šigg*[63] */ yaᶜnī gad ... maᶜārif ᶜind at-taksī /*

wa-ḥīn yūṣal at-taks / la-l-firzih / yinzilu r-rukkāb hinayyik / baᶜdā kulla wāḥid yā yišill taksī ṯānī wa-yirkab ayn-mā[64] *yištī al-bayt allī yištī aš-šāriᶜ*[65] *aw yuxṭā rijl l-ayn-ma štā / hā:ḏā ḍarī:guh min ḍurug as-safar fi l-yaman maṯalan / fawg taksī /*

---

[58] Inversion of predicand–predicate to emphasise predicate. Cf. *Syntax* p. 129.

[59] Inversion of predicand–predicate to emphasise predicate. Cf. above.

[60] Universal-conditional-concession clause. Cf. *Syntax* p. 352.

[61] Under articulation of *-h* of 3 m.s. object pronoun.

[62] Under articulation of *-h* of 3 m.s. object pronoun.

[63] *ᶜalā jamb* is a general Yemeni phrase used to ask a taxi driver to stop. In SA, the common phrase is *ᶜalā šigg*.

[64] *ayn-mā* is generally followed by a verb in the perfect. The verb may be in the imperfect, however, particularly the verb 'to want', as here. In most cases, even this verb is placed in the perfect. Cp. above and below where *štā* 'to want' follows in the perfect.

[65] Exophoric pronominal use of definite clause. Cf. *Syntax* pp. 416-17.

Of course, after Ibb, you reach Jibla. And after Jibla, you come into Ta'izz. Ta'izz has a lovely climate – its climate is not very cold nor very hot, its climate is just right. When the taxi reaches Ta'izz, if anyone wants to stop along the way or whatever, they will say, 'Taxi, to the side, taxi! Driver!' And the driver will stop wherever the person wants. If they don't want him to stop, he will just carry straight on to the taxi rank. He is not obliged to the passengers: one passenger wants him to take him to al-Jahmaliya, another passenger wants him to take him to Sabur, Mount Sabur. It is not like that. Everyone just travels [in the taxi] and the driver's job is to get them to the taxi rank unless it is [somewhere] en route, and then he will stop. He[66] will say, 'To the side!' and he[67] will stop for him. Some people say, 'To the side!' [using *jamb*]. Here,[68] we say, 'To the side!' [using *šigg*].

When the taxi reaches the taxi rank, the passengers get off there. Then everyone either takes another taxi and goes to where he wants – home or the street, or they may go where they want by foot. This is one of the ways of travelling in Yemen, for instance, by taxi.

[66] i.e. the passenger.

[67] i.e. the driver.

[68] i.e. in San'a.

8 *As-safar bi-ṭ-ṭayyāruh*

wa:[1]*-maṯalan / nigūl ba-ṭ-ṭayyāruh / bi-ṭ-ṭayyāruh / bī-sīr yijirr al-wāḥid / yisīr maktab min makātib šarikat aṭ-ṭayyāruh al-mawjūdih / wa-ḍabᶜan mā maᶜānā hānā 'illā / lā r-raḥalāt al-maḥallīyih / mā biš ġayr al-yamanīyih / hī 'allī bi-twaṣṣul ar-rukkāb maḥallīyan*[2] */ ḍabᶜan tiᶜizz / aw al-ḥudaydih / aw ᶜadan / aw ar-rayyān / aw ḥaḏramawt / ayn-ma šta l-wāḥid / bī-waṣṣuluh fi l-manāḍug illī mawjūdih fīhā maṭārāt /*

kayf yifᶜal ar-rā:kib / yisī:r lā: maktab min al-makātib ḥakk al-yamanīyih / yugḍaᶜ at-taḏkirih / wa-yaḥjiz / hāḏā kullih gabl as-safar / yaᶜnī ḏā hū yšši[3] *ysāfir mā yistirš yisāfir min al-maḍār mubāšarih bi-dūn ḥajz / lannum ᶜa-yriddūh / illā lā bih kursī fāḏī mumkin yigḍaᶜ taḏkirih min al-maḍār / wa-hāḏā*[4] *bī-sīr yiḥjiz / wa-yigḍaᶜ at-taḏkirih / bih taḏkirih law nigūl maṯalan lā: al-ḥudaydih / allī misāfir la-l-ḥudaydih ᶜa-tkūn fī ḥudū:d alf riyāl / min ṣanᶜā la-l-ḥudaydih / yidfaᶜlih*[5] *at-taḏkirih wa-yiḥjiz li-ḏayyik al-muwaḏḏaf ḥakk al-yamanīyih / wa-yigullih inna bih riḥlah aw mā biš ḏiksāᶜ / iḏā mā biš riḥlah fi l-yawm allī yištī ḏayyā bī-gullih ayyaḥīn ar-raḥlah illī ᶜa-tjī / law-mā yiddīlih at-taḏkirih / wa-gad dafaᶜ gīmatih / mā ᶜād ᶜalayh illā yisīr la-l-maḍār / fi l-yawm allaḏī / ḥaddadūlih innū yisāfir fīh /*

wa-law-mā gad yištī yisāfir fi l-yawm al-muḥaddad maṯalan / bī-sīr la-l-maḍār / ammā yiwaṣṣuluh axūh / la-l-maḍār / aw yiwaṣṣuluh ṣāḥubuh[6] */ wallā ᶜa-yjirra taks / wa-yirkab la-l-maḍār / taks min ayyi ṭaraf ayyi taks fāḏī yigūllih al-maḍār / gāl al-maḍār waṣṣaluh*[7] */*

---

1 Vowel lengthening due to hesitation.

2 Classicism: *-an* ending. Cp. *mubāšarih* below.

3 From *yištī*.

4 *wa-hāḏā* functions summatively here. Cf. text 4. *hāḏā* refers back to preceding clauses from *yaᶜnī ḏā hū*. Cf. *Syntax* pp. 382-4.

5 Reflexive verb. Cf. *Syntax* pp. 202-3.

6 Two syndetically linked verbal clauses with repetition of verb and emphasis on contrasting subjects.

7 Initial subordinate clause takes no adjunction (such as *law-mā, iḏā*, etc.). Use of perfect in asyndetically linked subordinate and main clauses enhances consequential effect of main clause: the main clause depends on fulfillment of action mentioned in subordinate clause. Cf. *Syntax* pp. 64-5. Cf. texts 19 and 22.

8 Travel by plane

For instance, let's talk about [travel] by plane. By plane, you go to fetch, you go to one of the offices of the airline company there. Of course, for local journeys here we only have Yemenia. That is the one which takes passengers to local destinations – of course, Ta'izz, or Hudayda, or Aden, or Rayyan, or the Hadramawt – wherever you want to go, it will take you to places where there are airports.

What does the passenger do? He goes to one of the Yemenia offices; he buys his ticket and makes a reservation. All this is before travelling. I mean, if he wants to travel, he cannot travel from the airport directly without a reservation because they would turn him back, unless there were a spare seat [in which case] he could buy a ticket at the airport. So he goes to make a reservation and buy his ticket. Is there a ticket, let's say, for instance, to Hudayda. To travel to Hudayda, it will be around one thousand riyals, from San'a to Hudayda. He buys himself a ticket and makes a reservation with the Yemenia employee. He[8] will tell him whether there is a flight or not at that time. If there is not a flight on the day he[9] wants, he[10] will tell him when the next flight is. When he gives him the ticket and he[11] has paid for it, the only thing he has left to do is go to the airport on the day they have decided he will fly.

When he wants to fly on the appointed day, he will go to the airport. Either his brother will take him to the airport, or his friend will take him, or he will take a taxi and ride to the airport. A taxi from anywhere. Any taxi which is free, he will say, 'The airport!' When he says, 'The airport!' he[12] will take him.

---

[8] i.e. the Yemenia employee.

[9] i.e. the passenger.

[10] i.e. the Yemenia employee.

[11] i.e. the passenger.

[12] i.e. the taxi driver.

yūṣal la-l-maḍār / yis'al ᶜan ar-riḥlah ayyaḥīn gadī / gadū dārī bih hū yis'al ᶜalā 'ayn bugᶜat ar-riḥlah allī ᶜa-duxṭā / maṯalan al-ḥudaydih / yiwarrawh / yidxul lā ᶜind ḏayya llī bi-jrr[13] *at-taḏākir / yisārib min jayz man sārab*[14] */ wa-yimakkinlih at-taḏkarih ḥakkih / wa-š-šanaḏāt lā maᶜih šanaḏāt / w-inn mā biš maᶜih šanaḏāt / gadū yuxṭā / ᶜādī ymakkinūlih at-taḏkarih /*

fa-r-raḥālāt al-maḥallīyih hū masmūḥ li-l-wāḥid innū yixazzin fawg aṭ-ṭayyāruh / mā yimnaᶜūš / bass gadum hānā mā yixallawš ayyi wāḥid innū yudxul al-maḍār wa-hū muxazzin / mamnūᶜ duxūl al-maḍār[15] *(al-gāt) wa-hū mxazzin / wakt ar-riḥlah / bī-sāfir / al-misāfir fawg aṭ-ṭayyāruh / ḥawālī nuṣṣ sāᶜah / mā drā bi-nafsih*[16] *illā w-gadū fī l-ḥudaydih /*

nazal fī maḍār al-ḥudaydih / wa-min hānāk lā ḥadd mistagbillih ᶜa-ywaṣṣuluh / w-innū mā bih ḥadd mistagbillih / gadū yijirlih[17] *taksī wa-yiriḥlih*[18] */ min al-maḍār / hāḏa ṭ-ṭarīgu ṯ-ṯāniyih min ḍurug as-safar fī l-yaman /*

---

[13] Syncope. From *bī-jirr*.

[14] String of four asyndetically linked clauses conveys sense of speed in the narration. Cf. *Syntax* p. 306.

[15] Inversion of predicand–predicate to emphasise the predicate. Cf. *Syntax* p. 129.

[16] Common expression.

[17] Reflexive verb. Cf. *Syntax* pp. 202-3.

[18] Reflexive verb. Cf. above.

He arrives at the airport. He asks about when the flight is. He knows that. He asks where the flight, for instance, to Hudayda will leave from. They show him. He goes up to someone who takes the tickets. He queues up like everyone else, and hands over his ticket and the cases if he has cases. If he doesn't have any cases, he will just go after they have handed him the ticket.

On local flights, you are permitted to chew on the plane. They don't forbid [it]. But here they don't allow anyone to enter the airport while they are chewing. [It is] prohibited to enter the airport while chewing. When it is time for the flight, the traveller travels on the plane for around half an hour. He hardly has time to think before he is in Hudayda.

He comes down in Hudayda airport and, from there, if someone is meeting him, they will take him [wherever he is going]. If no one is meeting him, he will get himself a taxi and leave the airport. This is the second means of travel in Yemen.

9 *As-safar bi-l-bāṣ*

wa-ᶜād bih … / ḍabᶜan mā biš maᶜānā iḥna[1] *l-gaḍārāt / aṭ-ṭarīg aṯ-ṯāliṯih li-s-safar / fī l-yaman / hū*[2] *ba-l-bāṣ / al-misāfir lā hū yiššī yisāfir / aš-šarikih hāḏa n-nagl ḥakk al-bāṣāt / bi-tgūm bi-riḥlatayn fī l-yawm / ḍabᶜan riḥlatayn ṯalāṯ*[3] */ fī l-yawm bass ġayr waktayn / min as-sāᶜah sitt aṣ-ṣubḥ / badrī / wa-s-sāᶜah / wāḥidih / aw ṯintayn / baᶜd aḍ-ḍuhr / fa-*[4]*maṯalan law ana štī asāfir / aṣ-ṣubḥ lā ᶜadan / bayn-abakkir aṣ-ṣubḥ baḥīn / xamz*[5] *wa-nuṣṣ w-annanā*[6] *ᶜind al-mawgif ḥagg al-bāṣāt / allī hū fī bāb al-yaman / hāḏā bi-nisbih lā hāḏā al-manāḍug kullahā / ḥudaydih / taᶜizz / ᶜadan / min bāb al-yaman / min mawgif aš-šarikih /*

as-sāᶜah xamz wa-nuṣṣ / awṣal lā hānāk / adxul ajirr / taḏkirih asārib min jayz an-nās / lā gadū ḏayyik allī bī-bīᶜ taḏākir gadū 'awṣal ajirr at-taḏkirih / wa-t-taḏkirih / yimkin / lā ᶜadan bi-xamzamiyih / aᶜtagid / lannī mā gad sāfartš ᶜadan fawg bāṣ / bass ġarr anā bayn-agūl hākaḏā maṯalan / xalāṣ agḍaᶜ taḏkirih wa-jiss arayyiᶜ la-s-sāᶜah sitt / an-nās kulluhum xayrāt[7] *bī-sāfirū min fawg al-bāṣāt / fa-ḥīn law-mā gadū*[8] *wakt as-safar / an-nās allī mirayyaᶜin hānāk fī š-šāriᶜ li'annū mā biš maᶜāhum bugᶜah hākaḏā yijlisū an-nās wa-hum miftahinīn / wa-karāsī wa-hāḏā mā biš / gadū*[9] *ġarr fī š-šāriᶜ / jamb aš-šarikih / aš-šarikih maᶜāhā maktab zuġayrī*[10] *u-maᶜāhā šwayyih karāsī / wa-n-nās mā yiḥibbūš yijissū fawg al-karāsī yiᶜjibhum yijissū ġarr fī l-bāb yirayyaᶜū la-l-bāṣ / awwal-mā yibdī bāṣ yiḥmilu n-nās kulluhum / yibsirū fī ṭ-ṭarīg / gadum kullu wāḥid*[11] *bī-ṣīḥ / gāl al-ḥudaydih / taᶜizz / gāl ᶜadan / gāl al-ḥudaydih taᶜizz / wa-hākaḏā /*

---

1 Post-position of pronoun to emphasise annex of preposition. Cf. *Syntax* p. 251.

2 Technically lack of gender agreement with preceding noun referent, *aṭ-ṭarīg aṯ-ṯāliṯih*; however, independent pronoun interpretable here as dummy pronoun. Cf. *Syntax* p. 413.

3 Asyndetic linkage of alternative numerical phrases. Cf. *Syntax* p. 312.

4 Consequential use of *fa-*. Cf. *Syntax* pp. 299-300.

5 Perseverative assimilation of voice. From *xams*.

6 Presentational particle *inn*. Cf. *Syntax* p. 425.

7 Reformulative apposition. Cf. *Syntax* pp. 244-6.

8 Dummy subject pronoun. Cf. *Syntax* p. 413.

9 Dummy subject pronoun. Cf. above.

10 Diminutive.

11 *kullu wāḥid* functions here as emphatic appositive to *(h)um*. Cf. *Syntax* p. 249.

9 Travel by bus

There is also ..., of course, we don't have trains.[12] The third means of travel in Yemen is by bus. If someone wants to travel, the transport company for the buses puts on two trips a day, of course two or three trips a day, but only at two times: at six o'clock in the morning, early, and at one or two o'clock in the afternoon. So, for instance, if I wanted to travel in the morning to Aden, I would get up early in the morning, at five thirty there I would be at the bus stop which is in Bab al-Yaman. This is for all those areas – Hudayda, Ta'izz, Aden – from Bab al-Yaman, from the company bus stop.

At half past five, I arrive there. I go in and take a ticket and queue up like everyone else. If the person who sells tickets has already arrived, I get the ticket. A ticket[13] to Aden will perhaps be 500 [riyals], I think, because I haven't travelled to Aden by bus, but I just say that as an example. Okay, I buy a ticket and sit and wait until six o'clock. Lots of people travel by bus. So when it is time to travel, the people who have been waiting are there on the street – because there isn't a place for them to sit and relax with chairs and the like – it is just in the street next to the company. The company has a small office and it has a few chairs, but people don't like to sit on the chairs. They like to just sit in the doorway and wait for the bus. As soon as a bus appears, all the people rush to look down the road. They are all shouting. [One] says, 'Hudayda! Ta'izz!' [Another] says, 'Aden!' [Another] says, 'Hudayda! Ta'izz!' Like that.

[12] Definite in Arabic.

[13] Definite in Arabic.

kulla wāḥid yiṣayyuḥ / allī ^{c}a-ysīr li-waḥdih[14] *yištī yit^{c}ayyan ayyaḥīn yisīr al-bāṣ / fa*[15]*-s-sawwāg wa-ḏayya al-mu^{c}āwin ḥakkih / gadum yūgafū wa-l-mu^{c}āwin yigūl ^{c}adan maṯalan / an-nās yihibbū / fīh zaḥmih / kulla wāḥid yištī yif^{c}allih*[16] *kursī bāhir / bi-ḏāt fi l-karāsī al-lawwalih / lākin gad aṣḥāb aš-šarikih gadum / awġād / gadum yiḥjizū ḏawlayyik al-karāsī al-lawwalih / ^{c}alā sās lā šī ma^{c}āhum ṣāḥub / wallā ḏayf / wallā 'ayyi ḥājih yidaxxilūh fīhā /*

yiḏla^{c} al-wāḥid fawg al-bāṣ / wa:-fawg al-bāṣ law-mā gadū malān law-mā gadū ^{c}a-tḥarrik / ḏayyik al-mu^{c}āwin allī fawg al-bā'ṣ / yibda' yijirr at-taḏākir / min ar-rukkāb / wa-yi^{c}udd kam bih rukkāb / wa-law-mā gad kulla šī jāhiz / wa-ḏayyā / yibda' bi-t-tiḥirrāk / ḏab^{c}an ḏarīg ^{c}adan hū yuxṭā min ḏarīg ta^{c}izz / wa-yuxṭā min ^{c}abr xayrāt al-gura llī šaraḥt ^{c}anhā 'awwal fī ḥagg at-taksī /

fa-l-bāṣ bi-mšī min at-tijāhayn / yā 'immā mšī min ḏarīg ta^{c}izz law-mā yūṣal ta^{c}izz wa-yu^{c}ṣar min al-ḥawbān ṣalā: ar-rāhidih / wallā min ḏamār / yudxul / ḏarīg al-bayḏuh / min hānāk wa-hī ḏarīg ṯānī / agrab / hāḏa ṭ-ṭarīgayn / wa-ba^{c}dā yuxṭā lā muḥāfaḏat laḥj wa-... / laḥj w-allāh m-ana ^{c}rifhinš gawī hāḏawlā ḥagg al-manāḏug al-janūbī li'ann mā gad sāfartš illā marratayn fawg / taksī ma ^{c}rafhinš gawīyih[17] */*

wa-nafs aš-šī fawg al-bāṣ yilgālih[18] *wāḥid yitjābirū hū w-illī jambih / yitjābirū wa-ḏuḥuk / ba^{c}ḏ al-aḥyān yiftaḥū filim ma^{c}āhum taliviziyūn wa-fidiyū fawg al-bāṣ / yiftaḥū la-l-musāfirīn filim / yitfarrajūh gawlathum*[19] *yiḏayyu^{c}u l-wakt / wa:-sāfar yisāfir al-bāṣ / law-mā yūṣal ^{c}adan / ^{c}adan yimkin fawg al-bāṣ sitt lā sab^{c} sā^{c}āt hākaḏā / hī masāfih ba^{c}īdih / wa-ba^{c}dā yūṣal lā nafs al-... / nafs aṭ-ṭarīg yūṣal ilā ^{c}ind mawgif aš-šarikih / ḥakk al-bāṣat hāḏā / wa-min hānāk kulla wāḥid / yiriḥlih / hāḏā ḏarīg fawg al-bāṣ hāh / anā gadanā šaraḥt kayf as-safar fi l-yaman /*

---

[14] Exophoric pronominal use of definite clause. Cf. *Syntax* pp. 416-17.

[15] Sequential use of *fa-*. Cf. *Syntax* p. 299.

[16] This verb used reflexively in several contexts in these texts. Cf. texts 11, 18, 22, 25, 27.

[17] Suffixation of *-yih* to emphasise adverb. *-yih* acts as emphatic suffix to words which end in *-ī*. Cp. suffixation of *-hā* to demonstratives and *-ah* to distal locative *hānāk*.

[18] Reflexive verb. Cf. *Syntax* pp. 202-3.

[19] Common parenthetical phrase.

Everyone shouts: those who are travelling on their own want to see when the bus is going. Then the driver and his assistant, they stop, and the assistant says, 'Aden!' for instance. The people jump up. There is a sudden rush. Everyone wants to get themselves a good seat, especially the front seats, but the company employees are scoundrels. They reserve those front seats so that if they have a friend or a guest or whoever they can put him there.

You get onto the bus, and on the bus, when it is full and it is about to go, the assistant who is on the bus begins to take the tickets from the passengers, and counts how many passengers there are. When everything is ready, it[20] sets off. Of course, the Aden road goes via the Ta'izz road and passes through many of the villages I described before [when I talked] about taxis.

The bus goes one of two ways: it either goes along the Ta'izz road until it reaches Ta'izz, and then turns off from Hawban towards Rahida, or along the al-Bayda road from Dhamar, and the second route is the shorter. These are the two routes. Then it goes to the province of Lahj and ... Lahj. By God, I don't know them very well, these southern regions, because I have only gone twice, by taxi. I don't know them very well.

It's the same thing on the bus [as in taxis], you find yourself someone beside you to talk to. They talk and laugh. Sometimes they put on a film, they have a television and a video [machine] on the bus. They put on a film for the passengers which they watch, as they say, so that they can use up the time. The bus goes on until it arrives in Aden. Aden by bus is perhaps around six or seven hours. It is a long way. Then it comes to the same ... the same road. It arrives at the company bus station, and from there everyone [gets out and] goes off. This is travel by bus, okay? I have described what travel is like in Yemen.

[20] i.e. the bus.

10 *As-safar gabl aṯ-ṯawrih*

min awwal gabl aṯ-ṯawrih mā kān biš al-muwāṣalāt hāḏā al-mawjūdih ḏalḥīnih / kān an-nās yisāfirū fawg aḥmirih[1] */ wallā fawg / jimāl / xiyūl / lākin akṯarat-mā kān yisāfirū fawg aḥmirih wa-l-jimāl wa-l-baġāl / illā gad kān bih šwayyih mawātir yisāfirū fawgahā / bass mitᶜibih gawī*[2] */ ḥīn tūṣal ᶜind al-jabal yijissū ar-rukkāb ḏawlayyik yinzilū yidalhifūh wa-yiḏalluᶜūh / yisāᶜadūhā / mā ḏalḥīn gadī al-ḥamdulillāh*[3] *niᶜmih / sāᶜatayn ṯalāṯ*[4] *w-innak*[5] *fī tiᶜizz / sāᶜatayn ṯalāṯ w-innak*[6] *fī l-ḥudaydih wallā ᶜadbiš sāᶜah wallā nuṣṣ sāᶜah fawg aṭ-ṭayyāruh /*

fa-[7]*s-safar ḥālī / fī l-yaman / fī l-yaman manāḏug jamīlih / jiddan*[8] *lā ḥadd yiššī yisāfir fīhā / manāḏug tizūrahā siyāḥīyuh / wa-jabalīyih / wa-'aṯarīyih / fī 'ittijāhāt ᶜadīdih min al-yaman / maṯalan mārib / hāḏā fī jihat aš-šamāl / bi-nisbih la-l-yaman / mārib / ṣaᶜṭuh*[9] */ hāḏawlā fi š-šamāl / wa:-mā ᶜad bih / wa-l-ḥudaydih / tihāmih / wa-s-sāḥil wa-l-hāḏā yijawlahā min al-ġarb / ᶜadan / wa-tiᶜizz wa-hāḏā / hin fī l-janūb / wa-l-janū:b / iḥna nisammīh ᶜadanī hānā / aṣḥāb ṣanᶜā yisammūh ᶜadanī / hāḏa ṭ-ṭurug illī yisāfir fīha l-linsān /*

wa-l-manāḏug xayrāt fī l-yaman / siyāḥīyih / ḥāliyih / yisāfir wāḥid wa-ᶜādī / an-nās ᶜāduhum / ᶜādum ḍayyubīn yaᶜnī mišum mutᶜibīn wa-mā yi'ḏawš / as-suwwāḥ xayrāt bī-jaw hānā l-yaman yisāfirū / min bugᶜah lā bugᶜah / wa-yisīrū yišāhidū al-manāḏug al-jamīlih fī l-yaman / kawkabān / šibām / aw wādī ḍ-ḍahr / wallā fī ḥarāz / hāḏā min manāḏug jamīlih / hāḏā llī garībāt min ṣanᶜā ḍabᶜan / fī ḥarāz bih / manḍuguh hānāk jamīlih[10] */ mā yisammawhā / hāḏawlā / yisammawhā l-ḥajarih /*

---

1 Verbal clause with initial (uninflected) linking verb *kān* and emphasis on complement. Cf. *Syntax* p. 154ff. Cf. use of uninflected *kān* in following clause.

2 Predicandless predicate. Cf. *Syntax* p. 123.

3 Islamic phrase used parenthetically. 'Thanks be to God!'

4 Asyndetic linkage of alternative numerical phrases. Cf. *Syntax* p. 312.

5 Presentational particle. Cf. *Syntax* p. 425.

6 Presentational particle. Cf. above.

7 Summative use of *fa-*. Cf. text 4.

8 Classicism.

9 Devoicing and pharyngealisation of *d*. From *ṣaᶜduh*.

10 Attribute split from attributed term by locative *hānāk*. Cf. *Syntax* p. 217.

10 Travel before the Revolution

In the old days, before the Revolution, there weren't the means of communication that are around today. People used to travel on donkeys, or on camels, horses, but mainly they travelled on donkeys, or camels or mules. There were a few motor vehicles they could travel in, but [they were] very inconvenient. Whenever it reached the foot of a mountain, the passengers would have to get out and push it to get it up. They would [have to] help it [up]. Now, thanks be to God, it is much better. Two or three hours, and there you are in Ta'izz. Two or three hours, and there you are in Hudayda, or even less than an hour or half an hour by plane.

It is nice travelling in Yemen. There are a number of very beautiful places in Yemen if you want to go there. [There are] touristic, mountainous and historical places you can visit in a number of different directions in Yemen. For instance, Ma'rib, this is to the north of Yemen. Ma'rib and Sa'dah. They are in the north. What else is there? Hudayda, the Tihama, and the coastal plain etc., which you reach from the west. Aden, Ta'izz, and so on. These are in the south. The south we describe here as Adeni.[11] The people of San'a call it Adeni. These are the routes that people travel by.

There are a large number of beautiful tourist areas in Yemen which you can go to, and the people are still good-natured: they aren't tiresome and they don't bother [you]. There are many tourists who come here to Yemen and travel from place to place. They go to see the lovely places in Yemen [such as] Kawkaban, Shibam or Wadi Dhahr, or Haraz. These are some of the nice places. These are the ones which are close to San'a, of course. In Haraz, there is a beautiful area there. What do they call it? They call it Hajarah.

[11] i.e. in the direction of Aden, which is south from San'a.

hāḏā manḍuguh siyāḥī[12] *jamīlih gawī* / *ᶜiddat manāḍug uxrā*[13] / *wallā masāfāt baᶜīdih miṯl* / *šibām ḥaḏramawt* / *wa-tarīm* / *hāḏā manāḍug* / *ḥālī*[14] *wa-jamīlih jiddan*[15] *wa-l-biyūt fīhā šāhigih kullahā mabnī min aṭ-ṭīn* / *wa-šī ḥajar wa-hāḏā* / *fa-*[16]*l-yaman ġanīyih* / *yaᶜnī bi-l-manāḏur al-xallābih* / *wa-l-gadīmih* / *wa-l-ḥāliyih* / *yaᶜnī lā buh wāḥid yištī yisāfir hānā* / *mumkin yiᶜmal riḥlah min ajmal ar-raḥalāt* / *yaᶜnī ka-sāyiḥ*[17] *aw ayyi ḥājih* /

iḥna mā bi-nsāfirš xayrāt hānā maṯalan / *ḍabᶜan* / *ġala l-maᶜīših* / *wa-l-wāḥid lā hū yištī ysāfir yištī zalaṭ xayrāt* / *li-ḏālik*[18] *mā bi-nsāfir illā lā hū ᶜamal wallā lā gadū aṣ-ṣudg yaᶜnī* / *gad la-l-wāḥid xayrāt mā xaraj min ṣanᶜā gadū yisāfir*[19] *fī rās as-sanih sanatayn*[20] / *ayyaḥīn-mā lafī*[21] / *ammā lā šī ᶜamal wallā lā šī xubrih dᶜawlī ššaw yisāfirū*[22] / *ijtamaᶜū jamᶜah wa-ysāfirū kulluhum* / *fa-*[23]*hāḏā as-safar fī l-yaman* / *ᶜalā-mā 'aᶜtagid* / *ḥayyā ᶜala llāh*[24] *innanī gad sāfart ḥājih basīṭuh* /

---

12 Adjectives ending in *-ī* often fail to take fem. ending to agree with fem. noun, as here, due to underarticulation. Cf. also text 5.

13 Classicism.

14 Cf. note 12.

15 Classicism.

16 Summative use of *fa-*. Cf. text 4. Cf. also below.

17 Use of classical *ka-* 'like'.

18 Classicism.

19 Modal use of *gad* before imperfect verb. Cf. *Syntax* p. 69.

20 Use of dual with noun indicating time. Cf. *Ṣbaḥtū!* pp. 93-4.

21 Universal-conditional-concessive clause. Cf. *Syntax* p. 351. The verb *lafī* is used regularly in various universal-conditional-concession clauses in different inflections.

22 Asyndetic linkage of explanatory clause *yiššaw yisāfirū*. Cf. *Syntax* p. 309.

23 Summative use of *fa-*. Cf. above.

24 Islamic phrase.

This is a very beautiful tourist area. [There are] a number of other places [which are] far [from San'a] such as Shibam in the Hadramawt and Tarim. These are very nice, beautiful areas and the houses there are all very tall and built out of mud and stone. Yemen is rich in fascinating ancient, beautiful sights. If someone wanted to travel around here, he could take the most delightful trip as a tourist or whatever.

We don't travel much here, of course. The high cost of living, and if you want to travel you need a lot of money. Therefore, we only travel if it is for work or if it's necessary. I haven't left San'a for a long time. I may travel once a year or once every two years, whenever I can. If there is work or friends invite me because they want to travel, they get together and all travel. So this is travel inYemen, as I believe it to be. Thanks be to God, I have travelled a little.

11 *Al-gāt*

b-ism illāh ar-raḥmān ar-raḥīm / ana ša-tkallim ᶜan al-gāt / al-gāt hāḏā / hū / bi-zraᶜ[1] *fī l-yaman / w-hū ᶜayyinih min al-ašjār al-xaḏrō' / wuṣul ilā l-yaman hāḏā aᶜtagid ᶜan ḏarīg al-ḥabaših / miš ᶜārif matā wuṣul yimkin fī ᶜahd abrahā 'awlā matā yaᶜnī / al-yaman*[2] *u-gad istaᶜmalih abrahā l-ḥabašī hāḏā fī zamān*[3] */ fa-jā' al-yaman ᶜan ṭarīg iṯiyūbīyā wa-ziriᶜat šijarāt al-gāt / māniš ᶜārif matā / yaᶜnī ziriᶜat / lākin hū šijar xaḏrā' / bi-tizraᶜ hānā fī l-yaman /*

hū ᶜayyināt / ᶜayyināt kaṯīrih / yaᶜnī u-bih lih 'asāmī allī ysammīh as-sawtī[4] */ w-allī ysammīh al-baladī / w-allī ysammīh al-ḥamdānī / yaᶜnī wa-kull ᶜayyinih min al-gāt lahā 'ism / wa-lahā maḏāg yaᶜnī / lammā tgūllih ḥamdānī wallā ḥagg al-gariyih hāḏā gadū al-gāt al-bāhir walla ḏ-ḏulāᶜī / hāḏā gadū al-gāt al-kwayyis / al-ḥālī*[5] */ allī bi-ᶜjib an-nās kulluhum*[6] *al-bāhir /*

fa-hū bī-jī ᶜalā šakl ᶜīdān / ṭawīluh / yaᶜnī hī bi-tizraᶜ ka-'ašjā'r / maṯalan miṯl al-gāt al-baladī hāḏā hū bī-jī ṭawīl zayy aš-šajarih / al-kabīrih / wa-baᶜdayn / yigaṭṭufūh / yaᶜnī yigaṭṭuᶜū š-šijar / iḥna ngūl yigaṭṭufu š-šijar / yigaṭṭuᶜū minhā al-ᶜīdān ḥagg al-gāt yaᶜnī aš-šijnī al-wāḥid[7] *hāḏā bī-jī fīh ᶜīdān kaṯīrih / wa-ḏabᶜan mā bī-galᶜūš*[8] *ġarr ma bsarū min axḏar galᶜūh māšī / al-gāt hāḏā bi-jīlih ar-rās ḥaggih*[9] *bī-jī w-gadū / mizhir waragih*[10] */ sāᶜ al-raḏab hākaḏā / gadū yuᶜraf*[11] *min aṣ-ṣūruh allaḏī bi-lmaᶜ / gad al-mugawwit aw aš-šaxṣ allī bi-zriᶜih / gadū dārī bih / al-gabīlī gadū dārī 'ayyin allī yigḏaᶜūh / wa-yigaṭṭufūh / fī ṣ-ṣabāḥ al-bākir /*

---

[1] Internal passive. Cf. text 7. Cf. *Syntax* pp. 91-2.

[2] Split of object, *al-yaman*, from verb, *wuṣul*.

[3] Verbal clause with emphasis on subject. Translated into English as agentive passive.

[4] Exophoric pronominal use of the clausal definite article *allī*. Cf. *Syntax* pp. 416-17.

[5] Reformulative apposition. Cf. *Syntax* pp. 244-6.

[6] Emphatic apposition. Cf. *Syntax* p. 249.

[7] As attribute, *wāḥid* usu. emphasises singularity of attributed term (cf. Mörth 1997: 117).

[8] From *gallaᶜūš* 'pluck out, pick' by syncope of *a* and degemination of *l*.

[9] *ḥagg* is not used with inalienable parts of body. Cf. *Syntax* p. 223. However, it may be used metaphorically with words such as *rās* 'head'.

[10] Adverbial noun complement. Cf. *Syntax* pp. 144-5.

[11] Internal passive. Cf. text 7. Cf. *Syntax* pp. 91-2.

11 Gat[12]

In the name of God, the Compassionate, the Merciful, I am going to talk about gat. Gat is grown in Yemen, and it is a type of green tree. It came to Yemen, I believe, via Ethiopia. I don't know when it arrived,[13] perhaps in the time of Abraha or whenever, in Yemen. It was used by Abraha the Ethiopian a long time ago. It came to Yemen via Ethiopia and trees of gat were planted. I don't know when they were [first] planted, but it is a green tree which is grown here in Yemen.

There are a number of different types with different names. Some are called Sawti, some are called Baladi,[14] and some are called Hamdani.[15] Every type of gat has its own name and its own taste. When you call it Hamdani or from al-Gariya, this is the best gat along with Dhula'i.[16] This is good, nice gat, the excellent type that everyone likes.

It comes in the form of long sticks – it is grown as trees. For instance, Baladi gat comes as tall as a large tree.[17] Then, they harvest it. I mean, they cut the trees. We say that they harvest [branches from] the trees. They cut off the twigs of gat. I mean, a single branch will have a lot of twigs. Of course, they don't just pull out the green that they can see. Gat has a head which has a soft part, like a tender part; it is recognised from its appearance which shines. The gat-seller, or the one who cultivates it, he knows it. The tribesman[18] knows which are the [parts] they can cut and harvest in the early morning.

---

[12] This text comes in two parts: part one was recorded by AS in December 1994; part two was recorded by AS in January 1998. The beginning of the second part of the text is noted.

[13] Sources do not agree on dates for introduction of gat into Yemen. Dates vary between 1222 and 1429. Gat is not mentioned by Ibn Battuta in 1330 (Rushby 1998: 10-11).

[14] A long type of gat grown north of San'a.

[15] Gat from Hamdan to the north of San'a.

[16] A type of gat grown in Dhulā^c near Shamlān just north of San'a.

[17] Definite in Arabic.

[18] The word *gabīlī* could also be translated as 'farmer' since *gabīlī*s are said to own land which they farm.

fī 'ayyi yawm badrī yaᶜnī min aṣ-ṣabāḥ / yibakkirū yigaṭṭuᶜūh[19] */ yigaṭṭufūh / wa-yjī al-mugawwit yštarī min al-gabīlī / yištarī b-ruxīṣ / wa-yiwaṣṣul lā s-sūg /*

akṯarat al-mugawwitīn gadum maᶜrūfīn ᶜind an-nās / maṯalan / gad al-wāḥid yitᶜāmal ᶜalā mgawwit miᶜayyan / gadū yiᶜrifīh / yisīr ḏayyak lā wagt aḏ-ḏuhr yisīr yištarī l-gāt / min ᶜindih / wa-hāḏā / al-gāt hāḏā bī-xazzinūh al-yamanīyīn yimkin ṯamānīn fī l-miyih / aw akṯar ... / kull al-yamanīyīn aṣbaḥ innum bi-yākulū l-gāt / lannū bī-gūllak mā miᶜiyyā w-anā baᶜd al-ġadā' / mā biš ma fᶜal / ajiss axazzin[20] */ kullu wāḥid bī-gullak mā jiss afᶜal mā biš maᶜī / li'annum mā bi-štaġilu llā ṣ-ṣabāḥ / w-baᶜd aḏ-ḏuhr hāḏā gadum bi-htammū bi-l-gāt /*

fa-kullu wāḥid ᶜind aḏ-ḏuhr hāḏā bī-sīr yištarī l-gāt ḥakkih / allī bī-štari l-baladī[21] */ w-allī bi-štari s-sawtī / w-allī bi-štari l-ᶜānisī / w-allī bi-štari l-ġaylī*[22] */ gad bih asmā' kaṯīrih / mā kān minn awwal mā niᶜraf illā sawtī wa-baladī / lākin maᶜ kuṯrat al-mixazzinīn / uṣbaḥ al-gāt yizraᶜ fī kulla bugᶜah / wallā mā minn awwal allī ᶜa-yxazzin / mā yxazzin illā w-bih gāt sawā' / māšī tibsirī fī ṣanᶜā hānā 'ahl ṣanᶜā hāḏā 'iḏā gad al-gāt bāyit mā raḏāš*[23] *yištaraw / al-mugawwit yidawwirlih man yibīᶜ / yifallitūh / wa-yiftajaᶜ lā gad al-gāt ᶜa-ybīt ᶜalayh / wa-yidawwir man yjī yištarī min ᶜindih / bi-kam-mā kān / mā l-yawm w-allāh innū ybayyitih / yaᶜnī / yibiᶜlak bi-z-zalaṭ / bi-z-zalaṭ allī yištī hū / bi-s-siᶜr allī yišti l-mgawwit / māšī yigullak ᶜa-ybīt hū mā ᶜad yibiᶜš li'ann allī gadum bi-yākulūh akṯar / min al-gāt al-mawjūd /*

fa-gadū yirkan / ann iḏā ma štaraytš ant ᶜa-yjī wāḥid ṯānī yištarī / yištarī minnih / iḏā mā tisturš tidfaᶜ tayyih maṯalan gallak bi-miyatayn girš / w-ant mā ᶜa-tsīr tidfaᶜ illā xamzīn girš / mā yirḏāš / li'annum bī-jawlih nās maᶜāhum zalaṭ hāḏawlāk at-tujjār wallā 'allī bī-jaw yidfaᶜū flūs allī kam-mā gāl al-mugawwit /

---

[19] Asyndetic linkage of purpose clause. Cf. *Syntax* pp. 169-71.

[20] Asyndetic linkage of consequential clause. Cf. *Syntax* p. 311.

[21] Exophoric pronominal use of definite clause . Cf. *Syntax* pp. 416-17. Cf. above.

[22] Fourfold repetition of *allī bi-štarī* ... conveys sense of incomplete list.

[23] Lack of number agreement on linking verb. Cf. *Syntax* p. 50.

Any day early, I mean, in the morning they get up early to cut it, to harvest it. Then the gat-seller comes to buy from the tribesman. He buys [it] cheaply and takes [it] to the market.

Most of the gat-sellers are well known to the people. For example, you [tend to] deal with a certain gat-seller and get to know him. You go around noon to go to buy gat from him. This gat is chewed by possibly eighty per cent of Yemenis or more .... All Yemenis have come to chew gat because they will tell you, 'I haven't anything to do after lunch. There's nothing for me to do, so I will sit and chew.' Everyone will tell you, 'What should I do? I have nothing to do,' because they only work in the morning. After lunch, they are concerned about gat.

So around noon everyone goes to buy his gat. Some buy Baladi, some buy Sawti, some buy Anisi, and some buy Ghayli. There are a lot of names. In the past, though, we only knew of Sawti and Baladi,[24] but with the increase in gat chewers, gat has come to be grown everywhere. In the past, people who chewed would only chew if there was nice gat. Otherwise you see here in San'a, the people of San'a, if the gat was from the previous day they wouldn't agree to buy [it]. The gat-seller would have to look for people he could sell to. They[25] would leave it and he[26] would be concerned that the gat would go off on him, and would have to look for someone to come and buy from him, at whatever price. But today he will leave it until the next day. I mean he will sell to you for money, for the [amount of] money he wants, for the price the gat-seller wants, otherwise he will tell you it can be left until the next day. He won't sell[27] because there are more [people] who eat it than there is gat.

So he can reckon that if you don't buy, someone else will come to buy, to buy from him. If you can't pay that: for example, if he says to you 200 riyals, and you are only prepared to pay 50 riyals, he won't agree [to that] because people will come to him who do have money, those merchants or those who come and pay the amount of money the gat-seller asks.

[24] 'We' refers to San'anis. AS says other types of gat were probably known outside San'a.

[25] i.e. the gat-buyers.

[26] i.e. the gat-seller.

[27] i.e. for less than he wants.

al-gāt hū miškilih hānā fi l-yaman li'annū / al-insān idā hū mwaḍḍaf mā miᶜih illā l-maᶜāš / minayn yiddīh / yiddī fi gāt awlā yiddī fi / fi 'akl wa-širb wa-dayya llī lā jahhālih / gad al-maṯal bī-gūl / kam ad-dīk / wa-kam al-marag[28] / *hādā madal*[29] *yamanī yigullak ayš / kam ad-dīk wa-kam allī marag / yaᶜnī maᶜak dīk / wa-maᶜak ᶜišrīn wāḥid / kam ᶜa-yākulū min ad-dīk / wa-kam ᶜa-yšrabū l-marag ḥakkih / kam ad-dīk wa-kam maragih / inn al-maṯal wa-l-maᶜāš kamū yiswā al-gāt aw mā' / lākin al-yamanīyīn w-allāh kulluhum bī-xazzinū / yaᶜnī mā hūš*[30] *innū wāḥid awla ṯnayn /*

al-muhimm / innū hādā ḥagg al-gāt kull wāḥid bī-sīr yštarī fi ḍ-ḍuhr hādā / fi 'awgāt aḍ-ḍuhr / aswāg al-gāt gadī kaṯīrih dalḥīnih / minn awwal mā kān biš / illā galīlih / yā sawtī yā baladī / wa-mā yijirrū 'illā rūḥ al-gāt / lākin mā daḥḥinih mā gad jā gadū ᶜalā gadr az-zalaṭ / ᶜalā gadr firāšak midd rijlak[31] *yigūlū /*

tijirr al-gāt / wa-txazzin gadak tittafig ant w-aṣḥābak / tugullum[32] *w-allāh al-yawm nixazzin jamᶜah / aw yigullak wāḥid min aṣḥābak ᶜa-tjī l-yawm tixazzin ᶜindī wa-gad ᶜa-yjaw ᶜindī flān wa-flān wa-ᶜa-yjī dayyā / yaᶜnī l-xubrih / gadum ujtamaᶜū fi bayt wāḥid / hādawlāk allī njiss nixazzin iḥna w-iyyāhum / wa-nsīr nixazzin wallā ᶜind wāḥid gadum yijtamiᶜū kullu yawm gad kullu wāḥid yidri' / innū ᶜa-yxazzin fi l-bayt al-flānī / gad kullu wāḥid yiddī gātih / wa-nsīr ᶜind dayyā llī ᶜa-nxazzin ᶜindih /*

baᶜḍ al-aḥyān tilgā dayyā llī ᶜa-txazzin ᶜindih gadū yiddī ṯalājāt ḥagg al-mā' / yimallīhin bi-l-mā' / wa-yiṭruḥ al-barādig wa-ygaddim aṭ-ṭufāyāt wa-yiddī yaᶜnī ḥājāt allī ᶜa-yxazzinū ᶜindih kulluhum / lākin hādi l-iyyām gadī[33] */ bi-tigtalib al-lumūr / mā ᶜād bi-fᶜalūš hādawlā kullahin*[34] */*

---

[28] Yemeni proverb. Lit: 'how much chicken [cockerel] and how much broth' (cp. *kam aš-šugrī wa-kam maragih* in al-Akwaᶜ vol. 2 1984: 884, Muḥammad n.d.: 121).

[29] Intervocalic voicing of *ṯ*. From *maṯal*.

[30] Dummy pronoun. Cf. *Syntax* p. 413. Cf. below.

[31] Yemeni proverb. Lit: 'spread your leg the length of your mattress', i.e. 'only spend what you can afford' (cp. *ᶜalā gadr firāšak wassiḥ* [= *wassiᶜ*] in al-Akwaᶜ vol. 2 1984: 723, and *ᶜalā gadr difāk maddid rijlak* in Muḥammad n.d.: 109).

[32] Elision of initial *h* of the pronoun *hum*. From *tigūl luhum*.

[33] Cataphoric pronoun referring to *al-lumūr*.

[34] Emphatic appositive. Cf. *Syntax* p. 249. Cf. also further examples below.

Gat is a problem here in Yemen, because if someone is employed he has only his wages. Where should he spend it? Should he spend it on gat or on food and drink and whatever for his children? The proverb goes, 'How much is the chicken and how much is the broth?' This is a Yemeni proverb which tells you what, 'How much chicken and how much broth?' That means if you have a chicken and twenty people, how much will they eat from the chicken and how much will they drink from its broth. How much is the chicken and how much is its broth? This is a proverb and how much is your salary and is it enough to buy gat or not? But, by God, Yemenis all chew, it isn't just one or two.

Anyway, with gat, everyone goes to buy at noon, around noon. There are a large number of gat markets now, whereas in the past there were only a few, [selling] either Sawti or Baladi, and they used to take nothing but the best gat. But now whatever it is depends on the amount of money. 'Stretch out your leg the length of your mattress!' they say.

You fetch your gat and chew. You agree with your friends. You say to them, 'By God, let's chew together today!' Or one of your friends will say to you, 'You come to chew at my house today. So-and-so and so-and-so are also coming.' Friends meet up in one house, those who we are going to sit and chew with. We go and chew, or [they go to] the house of someone where they meet everyday and everyone knows that they will be chewing at so-and-so's house. Everyone brings their own gat, and we go to the house of the person we are going to chew with.

Sometimes, you find that the person whose house you are going to chew at brings out thermos flasks for water and fills them with water. He will put out small cups and offer ashtrays and give, that is to say, the things that all those who are going to chew at his house will require. But these days, things have begun to change, and [people] no longer do all of these [things].

gad lā bih wāḥid bī-xazzinū ᶜindih nās kullu yawm kullu yawm kull yawm[35] *gadū zabal / gadū māᶜ hāḏā bī-jī bi-ftaḥ baytih ahla wa-sahla bass ġarr inn mā gad kullu wāḥid bi-ddī gātih yaᶜnī yiddi l-gāt ḥakkih*[36] *wa-yddī l-mā ḥakkih wa-yddī ḥājātih maᶜih / lannū ḏā 'ant bi-txazzin fi l-bayt hāḏā yawmīyih / kam jahd ṣāḥub al-bayt / yiddīlak mā' / wa-yiddīlak / bibs / wa-ᶜād allī yištī madāᶜah / hāḏa llī yijī yišti l-madāᶜah mā ḥakk al-madāᶜah hāḏā šuġlih / yaᶜnī al-madāᶜah tištī nā'r / wa-n-nār tištī man yigūm ywahhiflhā wa-yiṣalluḥū hāḏā lā mā bi-xbizūš fī l-bayt / inn al-ašyā gadī ṣaᶜbuh lākin gadū ḏā*[37] *bayn-agūl hākaḏā innahū / al-ān gadū kullu wāḥid bi-ddī gātih u-māhuh / wa-ṣāḥub al-bayt mā bī-gaṣṣarš illī bi-nxazzin ᶜindih / mā bī-gaṣṣarš bi-ddī kullu šī*[38] */*

hāḏā min nāḥiyih / baᶜdayn nijtamaᶜ mixazzinīn fī bayt wāḥid / nijiss nitjābar / wa-tilgā hāḏāk awwal al-matkā'[39] */ kullu wāḥid ġarr bi-graḥ garīḥah / kullu wāḥid ġarr bi-ddī / yaᶜnī kullu wāḥid yištī yitḥākā ᶜādū fāriḥ mā gad xazzanš kull wāḥid bi-tḥākā min ṣalayh / ḏayyā*[40] *bi-ddī*[41] *guṣṣuh / wa-ḏayyā bi-ddī as-syāsih wa-ḏayyā bi-yiḍḥak / wa-ḏayyā bi-yizbij / al-muhimm kullu wāḥid bi-tkallim tijī an-nušṭuh / la-s-sāᶜah ka-ḏayyāhā*[42] *xams / mā tibsir illā w-gad al-makān ḏayyā ayn jaw hāḏawlā llī gad ṣayyaḥū mā ᶜād biš / gad kulluhum ġarr sākitīn / gadum yiḏannunū maᶜ al-gāt / allī bi-ḥsub*[43] *bi-kam ištarā l-gāt al-yaw'm / w-allī bi-yiḥsub / kayf ᶜa-yifᶜal ġudwuh minayn ᶜa-tjī gīmat al-gāt / w-allī: bī-fakkir fī mašākilih /*

ḏīk sāᶜ maᶜ aḍ-ḍunnānī / gad al-wāḥid ġayr muḍannun / bī-fakkir wa ḏayyā /

---

35 Asyndetic repetition of *kull yawm* to emphasise habituality of action. Cf. *Syntax* p. 316.

36 Annexion phrase *gātih* followed by attribution phrase *al-gāt ḥakkih* for stylistic variation.

37 Presentational particle *ḏā*. Cf. *Syntax* pp. 422-3.

38 Reformulative apposition of clauses. Cf. *Syntax* p. 245.

39 The term *matkā* (lit: arm-rest) used metaphorically to refer to gat party (Weir 1985: 118).

40 *ḏayyā* used pronominally like definite clause; however, while definite clause may refer to undefined number of people/objects, *ḏayyā* refers to single person/ object.

41 *yiddī* 'to give' is often used, as here, in the sense of 'to tell'.

42 Suffixation of *-hā* to emphasise the demonstrative. Cf. texts 4 and 9.

43 Exophoric pronominal use of definite clause (and below). Cf. *Syntax* pp. 416-17. Note *ḏayyā* could replace *allī* in these examples.

If there is someone whose house people chew at day after day after day, it becomes tedious. Despite that he[44] will open up his house [and say,] 'Welcome!' but only if everyone brings their gat, brings their own gat, brings their own water and brings the things they need with them. Because if you chew at that house on a daily basis, how much trouble it will be[45] for the host to supply you with water and Pepsi and there will also be some who want the water-pipe, and for those who come and want the waterpipe, the water-pipe requires effort. I mean, the water-pipe needs charcoal, and the charcoal needs someone to fan it and set it up [which will be difficult] if they don't bake bread [with wood] at the house. These are difficult things, but I am just telling you that now everyone brings their own gat and water. However, the person whose house we chew at won't skimp, he will bring anything [he can].

This is on the one hand. Then we get together chewing in one house. We sit and chat. You find this at the beginning of the chew. Everyone just sparks off talking.[46] Everyone just talks. Everyone wants to talk, they are happy because they haven't yet chewed. Everyone talks from where they are. One tells a story, another talks about politics, another laughs, another tells a joke. Anyway, everyone talks and there is activity until around five o'clock. All you can see is that those who were shouting in that room are no longer doing it. They are all simply silent. They are all contemplative with the gat. Some will be working out how much they bought the gat for today, some will be working out where they will get the money for tomorrow's gat, and some will be thinking about their problems.

Then, with the contemplation, you are just meditating, thinking and that.

---

[44] i.e. the host.

[45] i.e. will it cost.

[46] i.e. everyone is talking at the same time in loud, energetic voices.

gadū tijī[47] law-mā mā bih ḥadd yitḥākā / gadū ġarr bī-xaddir wa-bī-fakkir fī mašākilih / fī 'umūrih[48] / mā ma^{c}ih ġudwuh min ^{c}amal / mā ^{c}a-ysabbir min ġudwuh / wallā ba^{c}d ġudwuh / wallā … / gadū yudxul fī baḥār / min at-tafkīr wa-s-sarayān wa-l-hāḏā gadū yitxul fī l-baḥār yitxayyillak innū / iḥna ngūl innū gadū mxaddar ma^{c} al-gāt / bi-raġm innū 'anā bayn-a^{c}tagid inn al-gāt mišū muxaddir māniš ^{c}ārif ya^{c}nī / maḥna mā nitḥākā kullunā la-ngūl hākaḏā gad ḏā[49] xaddar bih al-gāt gadū mxaddar bi-l-gāt / lākin mā 'a^{c}tagid inn al-gāt mixaddir awlā / inna-mā hū ma^{c} al-jalsih / ma^{c} aṭ-ṭunnānuh / wa-ḍūl al-wagt al-wāḥid ġarr fī lukfih hāḏā bi-yākul bi-yākul bi-yu^{c}raḍ / bi-yu^{c}raḍ[50] al-gāt sā^{c}atayn ṯalāṯ wa-hū bi-yu^{c}raḍ al-gāt / gadū yxallīh yijiss yifakkir law-mā mā ḥadd bī-ḥākīh wa-hū jālis waḥdih / al-bidāyih tišġalih umūr ad-dunyā wa-l-ḥayāh ḥakkih gadū ġarr yifakkir /

wa-njiss nixazzin wa-nitjābar / gadak ġarr tisma^{c} min as-sā^{c}ah xams zā:rat[51] wāḥid / yiddī kalimih / wallā yitḥākā min mawḍū^{c} / lā šī mawḍū^{c} gadum kulluhum yitḥākaw fīh / fī s-syāsih fī l-… / aw igtiṣād ḥagg al-bilād fī: 'ayy xabar yiṭla^{c} fī rās al-wāḥid gadum yitḥākaw minnih ^{c}alā sās innū jadīd miš mawḍū^{c} gadīm wallā šī / wa-ba^{c}dayn min al-maġrib hāḏakā gad kullu wāḥid bī-gūm yiriḥlih / kullu wāḥid yiriḥlih ayyaḥīn-mā štā ya^{c}nī / gad allī bī-riḥlih as-sā^{c}ah sitta wa-nuṣṣ / w-allī b-riḥlih sab^{c}[52] / w-allī ma^{c}ih ^{c}amal bī-gūm badrī / w-allī mā biš ma^{c}ih ^{c}amal yštī yijiss yirinn / iḥna ngūl yirinn ya^{c}nī innū yixiḏḏ yixiḏḏ wa-yirinn lahā ma^{c}nā wāḥid / lākin yijiss yiftahin / mā gadūš ^{c}a-yriḥlih awlā šī / iḥna ngūl yirinn / hāḏā yijlis lā ṯamān / lā tis^{c} / wa-gadū wagt mḥaddad / gad kullu wāḥid ma^{c}ih wakt mḥaddad yigūm yiriḥlih hū la-l-bayt / ba^{c}d al-gāt / wa-hāḏā ḥagg al-gāt / wa-yawmīyih hākaḏā' / min yawm lā yawm /

---

47 Note this common use of *tijī* in sense of 'it gets to the stage; it comes to be'.

48 Reformulative apposition of partially synonymous prep. phrases. Cf. *Syntax* p. 244.

49 Presentational particle. Cf. *Syntax* pp. 422-3.

50 Repetition of *bi-yākul* and then its partial synonym *bi-yu^{c}raḍ* to convey sense of intensive, repetitive action. Cf. also above.

51 *zārat* as annexed term used more by women than men. E.g.s inc. *zārathīn* 'sometimes'.

52 Exophoric pronominal use of definite clause. Cf. *Syntax* pp. 416-17. *ḏayyā* could replace *allī* in these two examples; however, it could not replace *allī* in following two examples where *allī* occurs at head of universal-conditional-concession clause.

It gets to the point that no one is talking. They[53] are just doped and thinking of their problems, of their affairs, what work they have tomorrow, what they will do tomorrow or the day after tomorrow, or .... They fall into seas[54] of thought and that. When they enter these seas [of thought] you could imagine that they are, we say that they are doped on gat despite the fact that I believe gat is not a narcotic, but I don't really know. We all talk like that and say that the gat has had a doping effect on him, that he is doped on gat, but I don't believe that gat is a narcotic. It is just with the sitting and the anxious meditating. The whole time, the chewer has gat in his mouth which he is eating and eating, chewing and chewing. For two or three hours, he will be chewing gat and it makes him keep thinking until no one is talking to him and he is sitting on his own. In the beginning, he will be occupied with worldly matters and things that affect his life, and he just thinks.

We sit and chew and chat. From five o'clock on, you can only hear the odd one say a word or talk about something. If it is something they all want to talk about – politics, ... or the economy of the country, or anything that comes to mind – they talk about it because it is new, it isn't anything old. Then, from around sunset, everyone starts to leave. People[55] leave whenever they want. Some leave at six thirty, some leave at seven. Those who have work [to do] will get up early, while those who do not have work [to do] will want to stay and relax. We say relax [using *yirinn*] and it is [the same as] *yixiḏḏ*. *yixiḏḏ* and *yirinn* have the same meaning, but if someone stays and relaxes and is not about to go or whatever we say *yirinn*. They may stay until eight or nine. It is a set time. Everyone has their own set time when they get up and set off for home after gat. This was about gat. Every day it is like that, from one day to the next.[56]

53 Singular in Arabic.

54 Metaphorical use of *baḥār* 'seas' carried over into English translation.

55 Lit: 'everyone'.

56 End of part one.

athākā ᶜan al-gāt / al-gā:t hū: šijarih xaḏrō / yākulhā[57] *al-yamanīyīn / miš yākulūhā / yixazzinūbihā / awwal-mā jā l-gāt hānā yigūlū 'innū ddawh min al-ḥabaših / innū ddaw aġṣān min al-ḥabaših / kānat fi l-ḥabaših baᶜdā ddaw ġṣān lā hānā / zaraᶜūhā hānā / bad'aw yixazzinūbiha n-nās*[58] */ wa-kayf yixazzinūbihā / yixazzinūbihā yiḍraḥū hānahā*[59] */ taḥt al-miljaᶜ / yixallawhā mwarrimih fi l-fumm / wa-yijissū / yākulūhā yaᶜnī yimḏaġūhā /*

fa-[60]*l-gāt fi l-yaman xayrāt / yaᶜnī mā kān biš gāt xayrāt minn awwal / mā kān bih illā gāt šwayyih / yaᶜnī galīlih / fa-kān al-gāt yiftaxirū bi-ḏ-ḏulāᶜī / bi-l-gariyih / ḏaḥḥīnih gad bih al-gāt min kulla bugᶜah / bih al-gāt al-ḥamdānī*[61] */ bih al-gāt aḏ-ḏulāᶜī / bih al-gāt / al-gariyih / bih al-gāt al-ᶜansī / bih al-gāt al-wahhāsī*[62] */ ᶜiddat aškāl min al-gāt / w-aswāg al-gāt xayrāt / fī kull bugᶜah tilgā sūg la-l-gāt / bih al-gāt al-ġālī / wa-l-gāt ar-raxīṣ / wa-l-gāt al-mudwassaṭ*[63] */ kulla muxazzin bi-yilgā gāt ᶜalā kam-mā štā / ḏabᶜan hānā yixazzinū al-gāt / baᶜd aḏ-ḏuhr / akṯarat-mā yixazzinū / yaᶜnī hū*[64] *gadū baᶜd aḏ-ḏuhr / baᶜd al-ġadā wa-l-hāḏā / ayn ᶜa-tsīr gāl ᶜad-sīr axazzin /*

aswāg al-gāt xayrā:t / fī kulla bugᶜah sūg / fi l-gāᶜ bih sūg / bāb as-sabaḥ sūg / al-ḥaṣabuh sūg / bīr ᶜubayd sūg / fī kull:a[65] *bugᶜah / sūg la-l-gāt / wa-l-gāt hī ᶜayyināt / bih gāt ᶜīdān / wa-bih gāt gaḏal / wa-bih gāt rubaṭ zuġār / yaᶜnī 'aškāl wa-nwāᶜ al-gāt / hāḏa l-iyyām yiddaw gaḏal / fī mušammaᶜāt / yaᶜnī kān awwal yixarrijū ġarr gāt / yiksirū aš-šijar al-ᶜīdān wa-l-hāḏā / wa-yibīᶜū ᶜalā 'asās / mā bilā yaᶜnī ᶜīdān gāt / ḏaḥḥīn gadum / bi-ddaw al-gāt ᶜalā šakl gaḏal wa-ᶜalā šakl rubaṭ zuġār wa-hāḏā /*

---

57 Lack of number agreement on the verb.

58 Verbal clause with initial linking verb. Subject introduced as afterthought after main verb.

59 Suffixation of *-hā* to emphasise the locative pronoun. Cf. texts 4 and 9 in particular.

60 Consequential use of *fa-*. Cf. *Syntax* pp. 299-300. A large number of examples of *fa-* are used in this part of the text. Cf. below.

61 Existential *bih* followed by definite noun. Cf. text 1. Cp. *Syntax* p. 121.

62 Fivefold repetition of *bih al-gāt* with asyndetic linkage conveys sense of incomplete list and emphatic listing. Cf. *Syntax* pp. 316-17.

63 Anticipatory devoicing of *t* to *d*.

64 Dummy subject pronoun. Cf. *Syntax* p. 413.

65 Sonorant lengthening in stressed syllable of intonation phrase.

[66] I am going to talk about gat. Gat is a green tree which the Yemenis eat. They don't eat it, they chew it. When gat first came here, they say it was brought over from Ethiopia. They brought branches over from Ethiopia. It was in Ethiopia, then they brought branches over to here. They planted them here and people began to chew it. How do they chew it? They chew it by putting it here, under the cheek. They leave it bulging in their mouths and keep eating it, I mean chewing it.

There is a lot of gat in Yemen. In the past, there was not much gat. There was only a little gat, just a little. They used to show off with Dhula'i and Gariya gat. Now there is gat from everywhere. There is Hamdani gat; there is Dhula'i gat; there is Gariya gat; there is Anisi gat; there is Wahhasi gat. [There are] a number of types of gat. There are also a large number of gat markets. You can find a gat market anywhere. There is expensive gat, cheap gat and medium-priced gat. Everyone who chews gat will find gat for the price they want. Of course, here they chew gat in the afternoon. They mainly chew gat in the afternoon, after lunch and the like. 'Where are you going?' He will say, 'I'm going to chew.'

There are a lot of gat markets. There is a market everywhere. In al-Ga', there's a market; in Bab al-Sabah, there's a market; in al-Hasaba, there's a market; in Bir Ubayd, there's a market. In every place, there is a market for gat. There are different types of gat too. There is long gat, there are gat pickings [*gaḍal*], and there is gat in small bundles. There are different sorts of gat. Nowadays, they do gat pickings in plastic sheets.[67] At first, they just used to take the gat. They would break the branches from the trees and sell [it] so that there were only branches of gat. Now they give[68] gat in the form of pickings, or in the form of small bunches.

---

[66] This second part of the text was recorded by AS in San'a in January 1998.

[67] i.e. more than any other type of gat.

[68] i.e. sell.

fa-l-gaḍal hāḏā yigūlū yibazzaġūh / bizzāġ / wa-l-bizzāġ hāḏā ya^{c}nī yigḍa^{c}ū ġarr / al-gaflih / ḥagg al-gāt walla l-gāt illī gadū nājuḥ / mā ygaḍ^{c}ūš al-^{c}ūdī bi-kullih / wa-b-yūga^{c} axraj la-l-mugawwit w-aṣḥāb al-gāt /

iḥna ḥīn nixazzin / bi-nxazzin ba^{c}d al-ġadā / wāḥid gadū yisīr yištarī al-gāt yitwājid al-gāt min ḏayyik gabl aḍ-ḍuhr wa-ba^{c}d aḍ-ḍuhr / anā ^{c}ādatī m-aštarī al-gāt illā ba^{c}d al-ġadā / ya^{c}nī ba^{c}da-ma šba^{c} hākaḏā ba^{c}da-ma tġaddā' / abda' afakkir asīr adawwir gāt / bass axbuṭ min sūg lā sūg law-mā lgā gāt ḥālī / wa-njiss nixazzin / al-xizzān illī bi-nxazzin iḥna wa-l-xubrih / anā w-abī 'anā w-axwatī / anā wa-man kān / niġassil al-gāt / wa-nxazzin ba^{c}d al-ġadā / gadū lā maġrib lā ^{c}ašā s-sā^{c}ah ṯamān / ayyaḥīn-mā wāḥid šibi^{c}[69] gadū yiḏbil al-gāt / yisīr yif^{c}allih[70] bardag šāy / ba^{c}d al-gāt / yifsax al-gāt gawlathum / lākinnih yizayyid al-xiddārih /

al-gāt hānā / ya^{c}nī al-yamanīyīn bi-yi^{c}tabirū ka'annū / ḥājih ^{c}ādiyih bi-nisbih luhum / lākin fī ba^{c}ḍ ad-duwal / yi^{c}tabirū 'inn al-gāt / muxaddir / fa-ya^{c}tabar[71] mamnū^{c} / fa-maṯalan fī s-sa^{c}ūdīyih mamnū^{c} / duxūl al-gāt wallā 'akl al-gāt / fa-law wāḥid[72] daxxal gāt walla msakūh u-ma^{c}ih gāt wallā šī fī s-sa^{c}ūdīyih yigūlū yiḥbisūh min ^{c}ašar sinīn lā xamsat^{c}ašar sanih / fī s-sa^{c}ūdīyih ya^{c}tabirūh min al-muḥarramāt al-kabīrih / lākin ba^{c}ḍ ad-duwal mā biš / ^{c}indahum ^{c}ādī yā'kulū / maṯalan fī London bih mawjūd gāt / tilga l-gāt fī Sheffield / tilga l-gāt fī London / tilga l-gāt fī ^{c}iddat amākin fī London / gālū 'innū bi-tjī ḍayyāratayn aw ṯalāṯ ṭayyārāt fī l-lusbū^{c} tūṣal lā London /

wa-hāḏa l-gāt illī bi-yūṣal lā hāḏa l-manāḏug / lā London / bi-yūga^{c} gāt / min ḥagg al-ḥabaših / yisammaw gāt māhū / nisīt al-lism māhū / hararī / 'aywih / gāt hararī / lākin ḥīn kun[73] nixazzin hānāk fī London / al-gāt al-hararī hāḏā mā yijīš ḍarī sā^{c}-mā hānā / hānā hū[74] kulla yawm yigḍufūh / kulla yawm bi-yawmih / fa-yūga^{c} al-gāt ḍarī /

---

69 It is unusual for subject to precede verb after adjunction ending in *-mā*. Where this occurs, the subject is almost invariably *wāḥid*. Cf. *Syntax* pp. 112, 117.

70 Reflexive verb. Cp. use of *yif^{c}allih* in *kullu wāḥid yištī yif^{c}allih kursī bāhir* 'everyone wants to get himself a good seat' in text 9. Cf. also above and texts 9, 18, 22, 25, 27.

71 Internal passive. Cf. text 7. Cf. *Syntax* pp. 91-2.

72 Indefinite pronoun may precede verb after adjunction such as *law*. Cf. *Syntax* p. 117.

73 Simplification. From *kunnā nixazzin*.

74 Dummy pronoun. Cf. *Syntax* p. 413.

For these pickings, they say they pick the tips. Picking the tips involves them just cutting the very top part of the gat or the gat which is ready. They don't cut the whole branch. This is more profitable for the gat-seller and for the people who own the gat.

When we chew, we chew after lunch. When you go to buy gat, gat can be found from before noon and in the afternoon. I usually don't buy gat until after lunch. That is to say, after I am full, after I have had lunch, I begin to think about going to look for gat. I just go around from one market to the other until I can find nice gat, then we sit and chew with friends – me and my father, me and my brothers, me and whoever else there is. We wash the gat[75] and chew after lunch; this will be until sunset or until the evening at around eight o'clock. When you have had enough, you spit out the gat and go to have a glass of tea after gat to remove the taste of the gat, as they say; however, this[76] also increases the effect of the gat.

Here, Yemenis consider gat to be a normal thing for them, but in some countries gat is considered to be a narcotic and so it is prohibited. In Saudi, for example, it is prohibited to import gat or to eat[77] gat. So if someone were to import gat or they caught him with gat or whatever in Saudi they say they would imprison him for between ten and fifteen years. In Saudi, it is considered to be one of the worst forbidden things, but in some [other] countries it is not [like that] and [people] can eat it normally; for example, in London there is gat. You can find gat in Sheffield; you can find gat in London; you can find gat in a number of places in London.[78] They say that two or three planes [of gat] come to London each week.

The gat that comes to these places, to London, is gat from Ethiopia. They call it gat, what is it? I've forgotten what the name is. Harari, yes, Harari gat. But when we used to chew over there in London, the Harari gat wasn't fresh like it is here. Here they cut it every day, every single day so the gat is fresh.

---

[75] Most Yemenis do not wash gat before chewing.

[76] i.e. drinking tea after chewing increases the effect of gat.

[77] i.e. chew.

[78] i.e. in Britain.

hānāk ḥīnū yigḍafūh / wa-bacdā yišḥanūh fi ṭ-ṭayyāruh lā wasṭ London wa-yijiss cal agall yawmayn ṯalāṯ / law-mā yūṣal lā cind al-muxazzin / yacnī yūgac fīh / yūgac gāriḥ / yirḥig al-wāḥid yitxayyal inn al-wāḥid gadū muxaddar awlā midrī māhū / al-muhimm innū yūgac bāyit kulla-mā bāt aš-šī / yūgac gāriḥ / yixaddir al-insān / anā ḥīn kunt axazzin kunt axazzin hānāk / yacnī lā xazzant al-yawm / ma rgattš[79] ṭūl al-layl / mā rugutt illā yawm ṯānī yacnī aḥiss inna jismī tācib wa-hāḏā / ma rgud illā ṯānī yawm / lākin hānā / ḥīnū ḍarī wa-ḥīn iḥna mitcawwadīn calayh / nixazzin bacd al-ġadā / la-l-cašī wa-l-gāt ḍabīcī cādī fa-l-wakt ḥakkanā muḥaddad /

fa-[80]l-gāt hāḏā ya'kulūh al-kabīr wa-ṣ-ṣaġīr / yacnī aṣ-ṣuġār mā hūš[81] muḥabbab innum ya'kulūh / bass hākaḏā min bāb aḍ-ḍuḥk wa-l-hāḏā / al-lab yigūl l-ibnih ca-nxazzin wallā ḏayyā law-mā 'ann ibnī yitcawwad cala l-gāt wa-yirjac yištī yixazzin /

ḍabcan al-gāt cindanā hānā / bih al-ġālī[82] wa-bih ar-raxīṣ wa-bih al-mudwassaḍ wa-bih kulla šī / akṯarat al-yamanīyīn bi-ṣrufū ḥakkuhum az-zalaṭ[83] / fi l-gāt / yisīr yištarī gāt / bi-xamsamiyih / bi-'alf[84] wa-ḏayyā / wa-yisīr yištarī la-l-bayt / wa-fi l-bayt mā yiddīš maṣrūf sawā wa-mā yiddīš ḥājāt al-bayt wallā šī / wa-hāḏā muškilih / fa-ṣarf al-murattab wa-l-hāḏā yijissū yitṣarrafū ġarr fi l-gāt / hāḏā muškilih hānā fi l-yaman ḍabcan / gullih minanlak[85] ḥakk al-gāt yigullak bi-ddī 'allāh /

hāh / wa-l-gāt hāḏā hū šijarih xaḍrō / fa-zirācatih mitwājidih bi-kaṯrih fi l-yaman / w-allī bi-zracūh[86] / māluhum šī / yacnī bī-ḥaṣṣulū flūs kaṯī:rih jiddan / min zirācat al-gāt / wa-hāḏā kull al-kalām can al-gāt min šān ticrafū can al-gāt māhū / wa-tidraw / kayfū al-gāt wa-hāḏā / al-muimm[87] innū šijarih xaḍrā / wa-mazrūc bi-kaṯrih fi l-yaman / salām calaykum /

---

79 Anticipatory devoicing of *d* to *t*. Syncope of initial unstressed vowel.

80 Summative use of *fa-*. Cf. *Syntax* pp. 299-300.

81 Dummy pronoun. Cf. *Syntax* p. 413.

82 Existential *bih* with following definite noun. Cf. text 1. Cp. *Syntax* p. 121.

83 Inversion of attributed term-attribute to emphasise pronoun in attribute. Cf. *Syntax* p. 224.

84 Asyndetic linkage of alternative numerical phrases. Cf. *Syntax* p. 312.

85 Diphthong simplification. From *min ayn lak*.

86 Exophoric pronominal use of definite clause. Cf. *Syntax* pp. 416-17.

87 From *al-muhimm*. *h* deletion.

There, because they cut it and then load it on a plane to London and it stays for at least two or three days until it reaches the chewer, it becomes really strong. It exhausts you,[88] and it seems as if the person [who chews it] is doped or whatever. Anyway, the less fresh it is the stronger it becomes and [the more] people are doped by it. When I used to chew when I chewed there, if I chewed today I would not be able to get to sleep all night. I would not be able to sleep until the next day, I mean I would feel that my body was tired and the like. I would not be able to sleep until the next day. But here, because it is fresh and because we are used to it, chewing after lunch until the evening, gat is normal and our time [for chewing] is limited.

Gat is chewed by old and young [alike]. I mean it isn't considered good for the young to chew it, but as a joke the father will say to his son, 'Are we going to chew or what?' so that my[89] son will get used to [the idea of] gat and will later want to chew.

Of course, [of] the gat we have here, there is expensive gat, there is cheap gat, there is medium-priced gat and there is everything. Most Yemenis spend their money on gat. They will go to buy gat for 500 or 1,000 [riyals], and they will go to buy [things] for the household, but for the household they will not give enough housekeeping money or get the things needed for the house or whatever. And this is a problem. They just keep spending their wages on gat. This is a problem here in Yemen, of course. Ask [anyone] where he gets [his money] for gat and he will say to you, 'God will provide!'

So there it is, gat is a green tree which is cultivated a lot in Yemen. Those who cultivate it are well off. I mean, they receive a lot of money from cultivating gat. All this talk about gat is so that you can get to know what gat is and you can get to know what gat is like. In any case, it is a green tree and is grown a lot in Yemen. Peace be upon you.

---

[88] i.e. the effects of it make the chewer feel exhausted the next day.

[89] i.e. his.

12 *Waṣf al-bayt*

b-ism illāh ar-raḥmān ar-raḥīm / anā ša-šraḥ ḏalḥīnih / al-bayt ḥagganā / allī banitih umm^{wi} fī ᶜām iṯnayn wa-sabᶜī'n / al-bayt hāḏā hū mabnī min al-libn[1] */ wa-fīh ṯalāṯ ġuraf / wa-mistarāḥ / wa-daymih / aṯ-ṯalāṯ al-ġuraf hāḏawlā ġurfih kabīrih / wa-ṯ-ṯānīyih hāḏā mutwassaḍuh wa-ġurfih zuġayrih*[2] *la-l-jahhāl yilᶜabū fīhā / fī al-ġurfi l-kabīrih fīhā ᶜugū'd / wa-ḍīgān / wa-ṣufwaf / wa-l-makān ḥālī mafrūš bi-firiš ḥālī / wa-d-daymih / ᶜādī min an-nawᶜ al-gadī'm / fīhā / 'at-tannū'r / ṯintayn tanāwīr / hāḏā ṭabᶜan at-tanāwīr al-ᶜādih al-yamanī yukūn*[3] *yuxbuzū fīhin / wa-t-tannūr hāḏā bi-tjī mdawwirih / wāḥidih*[4] *kabīrih u-wāḥidih zuġayyirih*[5] */ wa-mdawwirāt*[6] *ṭabᶜan maᶜāhin fatḥah min nāzil min šān li-l-hawā ḥakk an-nār ᶜinda-mā yuxbizū*[7] */*

ḍabᶜan ᶜinda-mā yuxbizū yuḍraḥū l-ḥaḍab / wa-l-ḥaḍab hāḏā yilaṣṣaw wa-yilṣu' / law-mā tiḥma t-tannūr / yixallawhā tiḥmā gawī / wa-baᶜdā yuxbuzū fīhā / māšī mā ᶜād tilsāš al-xubzih ᶜa-dinkaᶜ / law at-tannūr bāridih / tannūr zuġayyirih wa-tannūr kabīrih / wa-hāḏā / wa-yawm yistaxdimū tayyih / wa-yawm tayyih / wa-yiᶜtamid ᶜala l-ḥāji llī yistaxdimu l-kabīrih aw az-zuġayrih / wa-ṭabᶜan iḏā hum bi-yuxbizū fi t-tannūr / ᶜādum bī-sabbiru l-ġadā wasṭ at-tannūr wa-l-biram / yaᶜnī al-laḥm mā tūgaᶜ ḥālī llā wasṭ al-birmih / miš sāᶜ-mā hāḏi l-iyyām / yijirrū aṭ-ṭīsān walla l-bristaw[8] *allī yisammawhin / mā yinfaᶜanš hāḏawlā*[9] */ mā tūgaᶜ ḍaᶜīmu llā wasṭ al-birmih / ᶜinda-mā yḥašwišūhā wa-yṭraḥūhā fi l-birmih / ᶜala n-nār ḥakk at-tannūr yūgaᶜlhā ḍaᶜm /*

---

[1] Pre-pausal aspiration. *libn* differs from *yājūr* (cf. below) in that *libn* are bricks made of clay or mud and left to dry in the sun, whereas *yājūr* are bricks baked in a kiln (cf. Serjeant and Lewcock 1983: 472).

[2] Diminutive.

[3] Lack of number agreement on linking verb. Cf. *Syntax* p. 50.

[4] *wāḥidih* functions here as indefinite anaphoric pronoun to *at-tannūr*. Cf. *Syntax* p. 391.

[5] Diminutive.

[6] Predicandless predicate. Cf. *Syntax* pp. 123-5.

[7] This is a job done by women, but general unmarked (masc.) gender is used here. Cf. also below. Cf. texts 4, 23 and 24. Cf. *Syntax* p. 126.

[8] 'Pressure-cooker'. Loan word from the brand-name *Presto*.

[9] Verbal clause with emphasis on the demonstrative subject.

12 Description of a house

In the name of God, the Merciful, the Compassionate, I am now going to describe our house which my mother had built in the year '72. This house is built of clay bricks and has three rooms, a bathroom and a [traditional] kitchen. These three rooms comprise a large room, the second is medium sized, and a small room for the children to play in. The large room has coloured arched windows, [opening] windows and shelves. The room is beautiful and is furnished nicely. The kitchen is of the old style. It has a clay oven, two clay ovens. Of course, these ovens are the type the Yemenis are used to baking in. The clay oven is round. [There is] a large one and a small one, and [they are] round, of course. They have an opening at the bottom to allow air for the fire when they bake.

Of course, when they bake, they put the wood [in]. They light this wood and it burns until the oven gets hot. They let it get very hot, and then they bake in it. Otherwise the bread wouldn't stick and would fall off, if the oven were cold. A small oven and a large oven. One day they will use this one, and another day that one. It will all depend on the thing [they are cooking] as to whether they use the large one or the small one. Of course, while they are baking in the oven, they will also be preparing lunch in the oven in clay pots. I mean, meat does not turn out nice unless [it is done] in a clay pot. Not like these days when they take these metal pots or pressure-cookers as they call them. These don't work.[10] It only turns out tasty in a clay pot, when they stir it [with tomatoes, onions and oil] and put it in a clay pot on the fire of a clay oven, then it has taste.

[10] i.e. they don't work as well as the clay pots with regard to taste.

wa-l-ḥammām / kān ḥammām min al-lawwalāt al-gadīmāt lākin gad fīh[11] *ḏalḥīnih murḥāḏ / ᶜalā-mā bi-sammawhin hāḏi l-iyyām / iḥna nsammīhin mistarāḥ wa-muṭhār / al-muṭhār hāḏī yṭahhurūbuh fīh / yaᶜnī kalimat muṭhār jāyih min aṭ-ṭahāruh ḥakk al-wuḏū' / wallā hū smih mistarāḥ / al-muhimm hāḏa l-bayt / ḥakki ṭ-ṭarḥah al-lūlā*[12] /

wa-baᶜdā 'ummī baᶜd fatrih banit ṭarḥah ṯāniyih / fawg aṭ-ṭarḥa l-lūlā / al-lawwalih[13] / *ṭarḥah min yājūr / banittā*[14] / *fīhā makān kabī'r / wa-ṯnayn amkinih zġār / al-makān al-kabīr hāḏā fiᶜilnāh sāᶜ ad-dīwān / gadū lā ḥadd jā' ᶜindanā wallā šī / bi-nxallīh la-ḏ-ḏuyūf / wa-fīhā*[15] *mistarāḥ / hāḏi l-iyyām mā ᶜād bi-nsammīš mistarāḥ gadiḥna bi-nsammīh ḥammām / wa-ḥujrih zġayrih / wa-mᶜānā ḥawī / xārij al-bayt / mā lahā šī kaḏayyā ḥīn yijiss wāḥid bayn aš-šams / wa-ᶜalayhā šwayyih šijar wa-hāḏā / mā lahā šī ḥāliyih* /

wa-baᶜdā jalasat ummī fatrih wa-zid fiᶜilat dawr ṯāliṯ / ṭarḥah ṯāliṯih / aṭ-ṭarḥa ṯ-ṯāliṯih fiᶜilat fīha ṯnayn amkinih / wa-daymih / daymih fisaḥ / fisaḥ wāsiᶜah šwayyih / wa-ᶜala ṭ-ṭurāz ḥakk hāḏa l-iyyām / mā biš fīhā tannūr / gadū ġarr al-būtāgāz / wa-l-maxsal[16] *ᶜalā gawlathum mā ᶜad biš ḏayyik as-sāḥil / as-sāḥil hāḏā hū al-maxsal ᶜalā gawlathum hāḏi l-iyyām as-sāḥil fi d-daymih allī nāzil / ᶜalā sās innū daymih gadīmih / gad an-nās bi-ṯṭawwurū mā ᶜad yištawš sāḥil gadum yištaw maxsal abū ḥanafī*[17] */ wa-fīhā ṯalājih / wa-dūlāb / wa-marwaḥah wa-kullahin / wa-bih al-jūbʷā ḥayṯ-mā bī-ḏaḥḥaw fīh al-ladāh / bī-ḏaḥḥaw al-ladāh baᶜd al-ġasīl bī-ṭallaᶜūhun la-l-jubā yḏaḥḥawhun / wa-law-mā yibasayn / yijirrū yinazzilūhin wa-yᶜaṭṭufūhun wa-ykawwawhin / hāḏa l-bayt ḥakkanā llī ḥna jālisīn fīh / anā mā ᶜādanīš jālis fi l-bayt hāḏāk / gadū 'axī ḥāriṯ / allāh yiftaḥ ᶜalayh / w-axī xālid / aṯ-ṯānī az-zġīr / hāh wa-niswānhum w-ummī / al-muhimm* /

---

[11] Use of non-SA *fīh*.

[12] Classicism. Later corrected.

[13] Corrective reformulative apposition. Cf. *Syntax* p. 246.

[14] Complete perseverative assimilation of *-h-* of pronoun to *t*.

[15] The pronoun refers back to *ṭarḥah* 'floor'.

[16] Anticipatory devoicing of *ġ* to *x*.

[17] For use of *abū* to indicate inalienable possession by inanimate object, cf. *Syntax* p. 186.

Then there is the bathroom. There used to be bathrooms of the old type, but now there are lavatories as they call them these days. We call them *mistarāḥ* [latrine] or *muṭhār*.[18] The *muṭhār* is what you use[19] to make yourself clean. The word *muṭhār* comes from [the word] *ṭahāruh* 'ritual purity' for ablutions. It can also be called *mistarāḥ*. In any case, this house had the first floor.

Then, after a little while, my mother had a second floor built, above the first floor. A floor [built] from baked brick which she [had] built with a large room and two small rooms. The large room we made into a sitting room in case anyone came to visit us or anything, we keep it for guests. There is [also] a bathroom. These days we don't call it *mistarāḥ* anymore. Now we call it *ḥammām*. [And there is] a small landing. We have a courtyard outside the house. It is pleasant when you sit outside in the sun; it has a few trees and the like. It is rather nice.

Then, my mother waited a while before she had a third floor built. A third floor. On the third floor she put in two rooms and a kitchen. A big kitchen, quite big, and in the style of these days. It has not got a clay oven, it is just gas, and a sink, as they say. There is no scullery. The scullery is the sink [*maġsal*], as they call it these days. The scullery is in the kitchen which is downstairs, because that is an old kitchen. People have gone forward. They no longer want a scullery, they want a [proper] sink with taps. It has [also] got a fridge, a cupboard, a fan and everything. There is [also] the roof where they hang out the clothes, they hang out the clothes after washing. They take them up to the roof to dry them, and when they are dry they go and take them down, fold them up and iron them. This is our house which we live in. [Actually,] I no longer live in this house. It is my brother Harith, may God grant him success, my youngest brother Khalid, and their wives[20] and my mother, anyway.

---

[18] For details of lexical items used to describe parts of the house, cf. Näim-Sanbar (1987).

[19] i.e. where you go.

[20] Lit: 'women'.

13 *Al-ᶜugūd wa-l-mafraj*

anā ḏaḥḥi:n ša-tḥākā ᶜan al-ᶜugūd al-yamanīyih / al-ᶜugūd al-yamanīyih hāḏā 'ašyā / jamīlih jiddan / mawjūdih fī kulla bayt / yamanī / mawjūd / wa-hī ṭāguh yamanī / ṣanᶜānī bi-ḏāt yaᶜnī mitmayyizih fī ṣanᶜā' / la-l-gadīm wa-l-ḥāḏur / fa-[1]*l-ᶜugūd hāḏā hī / tijī murakkabih fawg aṭ-ṭīgān / yaᶜnī aṭ-ṭāguh aw aš-šubbāk / hāḏa ṭ-ṭāguh yijī fawgaha l-ᶜagd / wa-hū yaᶜtabar*[2] *ḏaww fawg aḏ-ḏaww illī bi-yijī min aṭ-ṭāguh /*

fa-l-ᶜugūd hāḏā bi-tuᶜmal[3] *min al-guṣṣ wa-z-zijāj / bih nās mutxaṣṣīn*[4] *lahā / bi-fᶜalūhā / yaᶜnī li-š-šakl al-handasī 'illī bī-sabburūh / hāḏawlā hum mutxaṣṣaṣīn aw mumkin yaᶜmalhā 'ayyi wāḥid / lākin hāḏa l-ᶜagd gadum nās mutxaṣṣaṣīn fī hāḏa l-lašyā yisabbirūhā bi-stimrār / fa-l-ᶜagd bī-timm / ᶜamalih / min al-guṣṣ / wasṭ al-guṣṣ hākaḏā / miš ᶜārif kayf yifᶜalūhā / wasṭ al-guṣṣ ᶜalā-ma ᶜtagid / wa-ḍabᶜan al-wasṭ al-guṣṣ*[5] *hāḏā yifᶜalū fīhā aškāl handasīyih / wa-l-laškāl*[6] *al-handasīyih hāḏā yiḍruḥū fīhā az-zijājāt / wa-zijājāt / az-zijāj hāḏā yikūn milawwan / aw abyaḏ ṣāfī bass yifaḏḏal*[7] *law yūgaᶜ milawwan aḥmar wa-zrag wa-xḏar wa-ṣfar ḥālī / yiᶜkis / lawn aš-šams hākaḏā tibsirhā tiddī ḏaww ḥālī jamīl gawī gawī*[8] */*

hāḏa l-ᶜagd / bī-kūn fawg aṭ-ṭāguh / al-mawjūdih fī l-makān / fa-fī kulla bayt wa-fī kull: ṭāguh / mawjūd al-ᶜagd hāḏā / al-ᶜagd manḏar jamīl / fī l-bayt / bī-zayyin al-bayt / ḥna maᶜānā ᶜugūd fī l-bayt hāḏā kān ḥakk al-lamkinih ḥakk al-lamkinih / fīh ḥakk al-makān hāḏa d-dīwān yimkin wāḥid iṯnayn ṯalāṯ arbaᶜ xams sitt sabᶜ ṯamān[9] */ ṯamāmiyih ᶜugūd fī ṭ-ṭāguh fī l-makān waḥdih / tijāhāthin muxtalifīh / tijāhāt al-ᶜugūd ḥakk makānanā /*

---

1 Consequential use of *fa-*. Cf. *Syntax* pp. 299-300. Cf. further examples of mainly consequential *fa-* in this descriptive text.

2 Internal passive. Cf. text 7. Cf. *Syntax* pp. 91-2.

3 Internal passive. Cf. above.

4 Simplification. From *mutxaṣṣaṣīn*. Cp. below.

5 Appositive phrase in place of annexion phrase *wasṭ al-guṣṣ* which appears above.

6 Gemination of *l* of definite article before vowel-initial noun. Cf. *Ṣbaḥtū!* pp. 18-19.

7 Internal passive. Cf. text 7. Cf. *Syntax* pp. 91-2. Cf. further examples below.

8 Repetition of adverb to indicate intensity.

9 In this list of numbers, numbers given in their non-suffixed form, as they would occur before noun which is feminine in singular. Suffixed form *ṯamāniyih* used before *ᶜugūd* which is masculine in singular.

13 Arched windows and the reception room

I am now going to talk about Yemeni arched windows. These Yemeni arched windows are very beautiful things and are found in every Yemeni house. They are a [type of] Yemeni window, [which is] particularly San'ani, I mean they have been a San'ani feature both in old and recent times. These arched windows are set up above the opening windows, I mean the *ṭāguh* or *šubbāk*.[10] The [opening] window has the arched window above it. It is a light which comes from above the light which comes through the main window.[11]

Arched windows are made from gypsum and glass.[12] There are people who specialise in this and make them. [They are specialists] in the geometry work they do. They are specialists, otherwise anyone could do this work, but for the arched windows they are people who specialise in these things and who do them all the time. For an arched window, the work is done in gypsum, in gypsum like that. I don't know how they do it. In the middle of the gypsum, I think. Of course, in the middle of this gypsum they make geometrical shapes. Then they set glass in the geometrical shapes. This glass is coloured, or it [can be] pure white, but it is preferred if it is nicely coloured red or blue or green or yellow. It reflects the colour of the sun, you see it give a very nice light.

The arched window is above the main window in the room. In every house and over every main window there is an arched window. Arched windows are a beautiful sight in the house. They decorate the house. We have arched windows in this house, in the main rooms, in the main rooms. In this room, there are maybe one, two, three, four, five, six, seven, eight, eight arched windows above ordinary windows in the one room, facing different directions, the directions of the arched windows in our room.

---

[10] Two different terms for 'window'. *šubbāk* not used in SA to mean an opening window.

[11] i.e. the coloured light coming through the arched window appears above the clear light coming through the main window.

[12] Arched and circular windows used to be made of alabaster (Serjeant and Lewcock 1983: 484); in a few houses, alabaster windows are still found.

wa-kullahin bi-txul minnahin aš-šams bi-ḏāt fī š-šitā' / aš-šams bi-ddī ḍaww / aḍwā' / muxtalifih / wasṭ al-makān hākaḏā milawwanih[13] */ li'annī al-^{c}ugūd ḥakkanā hī ḏā*[14] *milawwanih / wa-jamīlih / hāḏa l-^{c}agd / fa-hī ta^{c}tabar*[15] */ ḥājih jamīlih fī l-makān ^{c}inda-mā yišūfha l-wāḥid wa-yunḏur ^{c}alayhā wa-yibsirli*[16] *ḍ-ḍaww illī yijī minnahā / muxtalif al-lalwān ḥakkih wa-l-laškāl wa-l-hāḏā / hāḏa l-^{c}ugūd / hāḏa l-^{c}ugūd / anā gult ^{c}ad bih al-ḥāji ṯ-ṯānī 'atḥākā ^{c}an al-mafraj /*

ma^{c}ānā hānā mafraj[17] */ mi'ajjirīn lih / al-mafraj dāyiman yikūn wasṭ al-bayt / ya^{c}nī hāḏāk fī l-biyūt / miš kull al-biyūt mawjūd fīhā mafārij / ba^{c}ḍ al-biyūt fagaṭ / fa-ḥna niskun fī bīr al-^{c}azab / bīr al-^{c}azab malān mafārij kullahā mafārij / ya^{c}nī kānat akṯarathā mafārij / ḍab^{c}an bīr al-^{c}azab hāḏā kānat tiskun fī s-sābig / al-latrāk kān yuskunū fīhā / al-latrāk kānū sākinīn fī bīr al-^{c}azab / ayyām al-iḥtilāl at-turkī fī l-yaman / kānat tu^{c}tabar bīr al-^{c}azab / zayy al-ḥayy ad-diblūmāsī*[18] *al-lān ^{c}indanā*[19] */ fī s-sābig /*

f-hī madīnih xārij ṣan^{c}ā / wa:-ya^{c}nī ba^{c}d ṣan^{c}ā / ya^{c}nī xawrij[20] *as-sūr ḥakk madīnat ṣan^{c}ā min bāb as-sabaḥ wa-manzal / wa-hāḏā al-biyūt ḥakk al-atrāk bayt ma^c al-ḥawš / wa-l-mafraj / wa-l-bistān al-jamīl / allī fīh kull al-fawākih wa-l-xuḏruh wa-l-... / ya^{c}nī kullahā kānat bi-hāḏa š-šakl / wa-l-mafraj / hū ^{c}ibārih ^{c}an ġurfih / wasṭ al-bayt / muxarrajih ^{c}an al-bayt / ġurfih fīhā 'abwāb kabīr*[21] *hākaḏā maftūḥah*[22] */ wa-kṯarat-ma tšūfhā ^{c}adanī ṣaḥḥ / ^{c}adanī šūf w-allāh gad šuft ḥakk baytanā / ... ḥakk bayt al-ḥamdānī / ḥakkanā kullahā ^{c}adanīyih / ṣaḥḥ ^{c}adanīyih*[23] */ bī-xallawhā ^{c}adanīyih hāḏa llī kānat fī bayt al-^{c}abbās kānat ^{c}adanīyih /*

---

[13] Attribute *mulawwanih* separated from first attribute by prepositional phrase.

[14] Presentational particle. Cf. *Syntax* pp. 422-3.

[15] Internal passive. Cf. text 7. Cf. *Syntax* pp. 91-2.

[16] Reflexive verb. Cf. *Syntax* pp. 202-3.

[17] Cp. description of *mafārij* provided in *Waṣf* pp. 99-101.

[18] Loan word. From *diplomacy*.

[19] Verbal clause with initial linking verb.

[20] From *xārij*.

[21] Lack of gender agreement with attributed term. Cp. following attribute.

[22] Attribute split from preceding attribute by demonstrative *hākaḏā*. Cf. *Syntax* p. 217.

[23] Corroborative parenthesis.

The sun comes in through each one of them, especially in the winter. The sun brings light, different coloured lights into the centre of the room, because these arched windows of ours are coloured and beautiful. Arched windows are thought to be something beautiful in the room, when you see them and look at them and see the light that comes through them with their different colours and shapes and the like. These are arched windows. These are arched windows. There is something else I said [I would talk about]. I will talk about the *mafraj*.

Here we have a reception room which we are renting out. The reception room is always in the centre of the house. That is in the houses, but not all the houses have reception rooms. Only some of the houses. We live in Bir al-Azab. Bir al-Azab is full of reception rooms. All of them [have] reception rooms. Most of them[24] used to [have] reception rooms. Of course, in the past the Turks used to live in Bir al-Azab. The Turks lived in Bir al-Azab during the time of the Turkish occupation of Yemen. Bir al-Azab was considered to be the diplomatic quarter in the past.

It was a town outside San'a, and beyond San'a, I mean outside the city wall of the old town of San'a from Bab al-Sabah and further down. The houses belonging to the Turks were houses[25] with a courtyard[26] and a reception room[27] and a beautiful garden with all the fruit and greenery and .... All of them were of that type, and the reception room was a room in the centre of the house, an extension to the house. [It is] a room with large, open[28] doors, and you mainly see them south-facing. South-facing, look, I can see that those of our house, ... of the house of al-Hamdani,[29] ours are all south-facing. That's right, south-facing. They make them south-facing. Those which were in the house of Abbas were south-facing.

24 i.e. the houses in Bir al-Azab.

25 Singular in Arabic.

26 Definite in Arabic.

27 which opened out onto the garden. Noun definite in Arabic.

28 i.e. doors which open.

29 This is the house of the neighbours. Slight digression.

hāḏa l-ġurfih bi-tkūn kabīrih / wa-l-labwāb ḥakkahā kabīrih / ba^c^ḍuhā mawjūd ma^c^hā 'abwāb uḏāfīyuh zujāj / min šān ayyāmāt[30] *aš-šitā' yiftaḥū al-labwāb al-xašab*[31] *wa-yxallaw al-labwāb az-zujāj yišūfū minnahā / yibsirū al-jaww kayfuh ya^c^nī yibsirū aš-šaḏarawān / hāḏa l-ġurfih / wa-l-ġurfih jambahā wa-ba^c^dā xārij al-ġurfih hāḏīk zayy al-^c^agd / zayy al-maḏall hākaḏahā / yuḏull min al-maḏar mā yutxulš al-maḏar ilā dāxil / wa-barik / al-barik hāḏā fīha š-šaḏarawān / šaḏarawān yuxruj minnih al-mā lā wasṭ al-barik / anā bayn-absir ḥakkanā hāḏa llī mawjūd ^c^indanā kayf kān yinzil al-mā fīhā / ḍab^c^an al-mirna^c^ / hū ḏak*[32] *al-mirna^c^ hā*[33] *mawjūd / wa-fī l-mirna^c^ ḍālu^c^ fīh aḥwāḏ / aḥwāḏ al-mi'*[34] */ al-laḥwāḏ hāḏā timtalī min wasṭ al-bīr / gālū kān*[35] *yimallawhā bi-yisnaw sani / allī kān yištaġilū fi l-bistān ḥakkanā*[36] */ kān yisnaw sani / wa-yimallū al-laḥwāḏ mā' / wa-ba^c^dā min al-laḥwāḏ yuxruj al-mā yisaggī la-l-barik / wa-min al-barik la-š-šaḏarawān /*

kayf kān yištaġil aš-šaḏarawān / kān yinzil bi-ḍarīgat aḏ-ḏaġḏ / yinzil al-mā' hāḏā bi-ḍarīgat aḏ-ḏaġṭ[37] *min-wasṭ al-laḥwāḏ hāḏi llī mawjūd fi l-mirna^c^ / lannī mirtifa^c^ah wa-tinzil*[38] */ bi-ḏaġṭ / wa-tūṣal wasṭ gaṣīb / bih fi l-barik arba^c^ gaṣīb / mittajahah ila l-wasaṭ / iḏāfuh / ila l-gaṣabu llī fi l-wasaṭ / wa-kullahā tiḏla^c^ / wa-tizaġbir al-mā' zaġbirih / fa-nsammīhā šaḏarawān / hāḏā ḥakk al-mā' ^c^inda-mā yiṭla^c^ wa-yizaġbir hākaḏā / fa-kān al-mā' yinzil / bi-ḍarīgat aḏ-ḏaġṭ / wa-yiṭla^c^ / šaḏarawān yimtalī / wasṭ al-mafraj hākaḏahā / bug^c^ah yif^c^alayn*[39] *fīhā šwayyih ward / wa-zahr wa-kaḏā min šān yūga^c^ manḏarhā jamīl wa-hāḏā / wa-l-jadr ḥakkahā / ma^c^mūr min al-yājūr /*

30 Use of plural *ayyāmāt* when specific season mentioned in narration. Cp. text 1.

31 Identificatory apposition. Cf. *Syntax* pp. 241-3. Cf. also below.

32 Distal presentational particle. Cf. *Syntax* pp. 423-4.

33 Presentational particle. Cf. *Syntax* p. 432. *hā* related to emphatic suffix *-hā*.

34 Pre-pausal *imāla* raising *-a* to *-i*.

35 Lack of number agreement on linking verb. Cf. also below.

36 Exophoric pronominal use of definite clause. Cf. *Syntax* pp. 416-17.

37 Verbal clause with dynamic verb and inanimate subject.

38 Change of gender agreement for *al-mā'*.

39 Change of gender to feminine plural with change of referent.

This room[40] would be large and its doors would also be large. Some of them[41] also have additional glass doors, so that during the winter they can open the wooden doors and leave the glass doors [closed] so that they can look through them. They can see what the weather is like, they can watch the fountain. This is one room, and the next room,[42] or outside that room, there is something like an arch, like a shade, which provides shelter from the rain so that the rain doesn't come inside. And a pool. This pool has the fountain in. The water comes out of the fountain into the middle of the pool. I can see with ours how the water used to come down into it. Of course, the ramp of the irrigation well,[43] there is the well ramp there, and above the well ramp there are troughs, water troughs. These troughs fill up from the centre of the well. They said they used to fill them by drawing up water from the well. Those who used to work in our garden used to draw water up from the well and fill the troughs with water. Then the water would come out of the troughs and irrigate the pool, and [go] from the pool to the fountain.

How did the fountain work? It used to work by gravity. The water would come down through gravity from the troughs which were in the irrigation ramp because they were raised, and it would come down by gravity and come into the pipes. In the pool, there are four pipes facing the middle in addition to the pipe that is in the centre. They all go up and spout forth water. We call it a fountain, that which goes up and spouts forth water like that. The water used to descend by the force of gravity and rise up. The fountain[44] would fill up in the centre of the reception room.[45] [It is] a place that they[46] put a few flowers in and the like so that it looks beautiful. The wall is built of baked brick.

---

40 i.e. the *mafraj*.

41 i.e. some reception rooms.

42 This is not a room, but resembles a porch.

43 For a description of well ramps in San'a, cf. Serjeant and Lewcock (1983: 302).

44 Indefinite in Arabic.

45 i.e. it can be seen from the centre of the reception room.

46 i.e. the women.

wa-l-yājūr al-maᶜmūr bih al-jadr mā hūš / zayy-mā ḥīn yibnaw al-bina l-ᶜādī / māšī / xallawh bi-šakl ᶜugū'd / wa-yxallaw al-yājūr maᶜmūrāt[47] *min wāḥidih lā wāḥidih / ᶜan ḍarīg al-guran ḥakkahin / bi-hāḏa š-šakl / ᶜalā mayd yūgaᶜ fīh xizgān / wasṭ al-jadr hāḏā / wa-min al-xizgān hāḏā bi-tšāhid al-ḥadīgih al-bistān*[48] *al-mawjūd / ᶜindanā hānā / bistānnā ḏalḥīn wa-hū gadū yābis lākin hāḏā kān zamān / bi-tšāhid al-bistān hāḏā kayfū / min xilāl al-xizgān hāḏā bi-tšāhid al-xuḏruh / wa-'ayḏan*[49] *wasṭ al-mafraj bi-tšāhid aš-šaḏarawān wa-l-mā' bi-drib wa-l-hāḏā /*

maᶜānā 'ayḏan[50] *fi l-mafraj hāḏā / makā'n / jambih / gulnā makān / wa-jamb al-makān mistarāḥ zuġayrī ḥālī / wa-gāᶜat al-mafraj hāḏahā al-xārij wa-l-ḥawš yaᶜnī / kullahā / yaᶜnī al-larḏīyuh ḥakkahā mišī turāb wallā ḥājih / kullahā ġayr ḥajar ḥabaš sawdā' / wagīṣ / yaᶜnī al-gāᶜ kullahā muwaggaṣuh bi-l-ḥajar al-ḥabaš / al-muimm*[51] *innahā bugᶜah ḥāliyih / sāᶜ-mā ḥīn yiddaw maṯal hākaḏā jannih / bi-hāḏa l-maṯal / hāḏa l-mafraj ḥakkanā /*

ḍabᶜan al-mafraj yisaᶜ yimkin ᶜišrīn nafar aw akṯar / yūgaᶜ[52] *fīh taxzīnāt al-gāt mā 'aḥlā minnahā / fī 'ayyāmāt*[53] *aṣ-ṣayf wa-l-makān ḥāmī hākaḏā mišū bard wāḥid yirtāḥ wa-ḏayyā / dunyā xaḏrā / lamma l-wāḥid yitfarraj al-xuḏruh wa-l-lašyā hāḏā / kān abī mā yxazzin illā fīh hū wa-xubratih*[54] */ yaᶜnī kān makān ar-rāḥah ḥakk abī / hāḏa l-mafraj / wa-l-ᶜagd allī ḏakarnā*[55] */*

---

47 Change from masc. sing. to fem. pl. agreement for coll. noun *yājūr*. Cf. fem. pl. agreement for collective nouns *xubz* in text 5, and *ḥaṭab*, *xubz*, *malūj* and *gafūᶜ* in text 4, when the referents are considered to be plural entities.

48 Reformulative apposition of synonyms. Cf. *Syntax* p. 244.

49 Classicism.

50 Classicism.

51 From *al-muhimm* with *h* deletion.

52 Lack of gender agreement with following subject.

53 Use of plural *ayyāmāt* when specific season mentioned. Cf. note above. Cf. text 1.

54 Verbal clause with initial linking verb.

55 Lack of anaphoric pronoun in attributive clause. Cf. *Syntax* pp. 234-5.

The baked brick which the wall is constructed from is not like when they build normal buildings. No. They made it like arched windows and they place the baked brick in constructions one next to the other with their corners touching,[56] in that way, so that there are holes in the middle of the wall, and through these holes you can see the garden that's there. Here our garden is dry now, but this was a long time ago. You could see what the garden was like. Through these holes you could see the greenery. Also, in[57] the middle of the reception room, you could see the fountain with the water cascading and the like.

We also have a room next to this reception room. Let's say a *makān*. Next to that room is a rather nice, small toilet room. The floor outside the reception room and the courtyard is all, I mean the ground is not dust or anything, it is all dressed black stone. The whole floor is constructed out of dressed black stone. Anyway, it is a nice place like they would say, it is paradise, in this way. This is our reception room.

Of course, the reception room can hold twenty people or more. The best gat chews are held here during summer days when the place is hot and not cold, then you can relax. [The] world is green. Then, you can look at the greenery and other things. My father always used to chew there with his friends. It was my father's place of relaxation. That is the reception room and the arched windows which I mentioned before.

[56] The square-shaped bricks are laid out in diamond-style with only their corners touching.
[57] i.e. from.

14 *Al-madā^{c}ah*

hāḏa l-makān ḥagganā / makān ya^{c}nī kabīr / mišū zuġayrī / fa-hū ḏ̣ūluh ^{c}arḍuh ṯalāṯih mitr[1] *fī xamsih hākaḏā / ṯalāṯih mitr fī xamsi mtār / fī l-makān ḥagganā / 'arba^c ḏ̣īgān / ṯintayn ḏ̣īgān bī-ḏ̣ullayn ^{c}ala š-šāri^c / wa-ṯintayn ḏ̣īgān bī-ḏ̣ullayn ^{c}ala l-ḥawī / ḏ̣ab^{c}an hāḏa l-makān bi-nij^{c}alih li-l-xizzān / ma^{c}ī fī l-makān hāḏā taliviziyūn / wa-fīdiyū wa-msajjilih / wa-mafrūš bi-mafāriš*[2] */ wa-firiš / ya^{c}nī ^{c}alā šakl aṭ-ṭābu^c al-yamanī ma^c al-wasāyid / wa-fīh al-madāki' / ya^{c}ni llī bi-nxazzin ^{c}alayhin bi-ntkī' ^{c}alayhin / wa-m^{c}ī madā^{c}ah fī l-wasaṭ ṭab^{c}an / wa-l-madā^{c}ah hāḏā / madā^{c}ah la-t-tadxīn / kull wāḥid yi^{c}rafhā fī l-yaman /*

hāḏa l-madā^{c}ah bi-šakl / gaṣabuh hākaḏā ṭawīluh[3] */ wa-min nāzil ^{c}alā šakl kurah / bi-šakl al-jawzih jawz al-hind hāḏā wa-bi-tkūn markūzih ^{c}alā jallās / al-jallās ^{c}a-ykūn ṣaḥn mdawwar / aw yikūn bi-š-šakl allī hū mawjūd ma^{c}ī ma^c al-madā^{c}ah / bi-š-šakl aṯ-ṯulāṯī hākāḏahā*[4] */ zayy al-kursī wa-tijlis ^{c}alayh al-madā^{c}ah*[5] *bi-š-šakl aṯ-ṯulāṯī /*

wa-l-madā^{c}ah maṣnū^{c}ah min al-xšab / wa-fī l-madā^{c}ah ṭab^{c}an hāḏā ^{c}alā-mā gult anā gabl šwayyih innahū / bi-šakl al-jawzih / jawz al-hind / jawz al-hind hāḏā a^{c}tagid innū bi-yiḥfarūhā min dāxil / bi-yiḥfarūhā yixallawhā zayy al-… / zayy al-kurah / bi-hāḏa š-šakl / bass mistadīrih lā mistaḏīluh / wa-min šān taḥwī hāḏa l-kurah hāḏā / 'aw nsammīh iḥna l-jawzih / al-jawzih hāḏā / taḥwī al-mā' / al-mā' allī yikūn fīhā / al-mā' ḥagg al-madā^{c}ah hāḏā /

ṭab^{c}an al-mā ḥna nbaddil kull yawm / kull yawm abaddil al-mā' li'annī bayn-ašrab yawmīyih / bayn-abaddil al-mā' ḍarūrī al-mā' tabdīlih / fī l-madā^{c}ah / lannū law mā baddilš fīhā l-mā' ṭab^{c}an ^{c}a-dības[6] */ ya^{c}nī ^{c}a dības bass bi-sur^{c}ah / u-mā ^{c}a-tkunš kwayyisih / fa-*[7]*tabdīlih ḍarūrī /*

---

1 *mitr* functions as singular count noun here (cf. Mörth 1997: 179ff.). Below, and in discussion about the length of pipe, *mitr* given in plural following a number from 3 – 10.

2 Predicandless predicate. Cf. *Syntax* p. 124.

3 Attribute split from attributed term by indefinite demonstrative. Cf. *Syntax* p. 217.

4 *-hā* suffixed to indefinite demonstrative to emphasise demonstrative. Cf. texts 4, 9, 11.

5 Verbal clause with definite inanimate subject.

6 Intervocalic voicing of *t* to *d*. Change of gender of *al-mā'* to feminine. Cf. text 13.

7 Consequential use of *fa-*. Cf. *Syntax* pp. 299-300. Cf. further examples below.

14 The water-pipe

This room of ours is a large room. It is not small. Its length and its width are around three metres by five metres, three metres by five metres. There are four windows in our room – two windows which look out onto the street and two windows which look out onto the courtyard. Of course, we use this room for chewing. In this room, I have a television, a video and a tape recorder. [It is] furnished with carpets and mattresses in the Yemeni style with back cushions and it has arm-rests – those we chew on and lean against. And, of course, I have a water-pipe in the middle [of the room]. This water-pipe is a water-pipe for smoking. Everyone knows about it in Yemen.

This water-pipe is in the form of a long pipe and at the bottom it is in the shape of a ball, in the shape of a coconut, a coconut, and it stands in the middle of a stand. The stand will be a round plate or it can come in the shape of the one I have for my water-pipe, in a triangular shape like that, like a chair, and the water-pipe rests on it, in a triangular shape.

The water-pipe is made of wood. The water-pipe, of course, as I said just before is in the shape of a coconut, a coconut. This coconut, I believe that they scoop it out from the inside; they scoop it out and make it like a ... like a ball,[8] in that shape, but round and not long, so that this ball, or what we call the *jawzih* [coconut], so that this coconut can take the water, the water that should be in it, the water for the water-pipe.

Of course, I change the water every day. Every day, I change the water because I smoke on a daily basis. I change the water, it is essential to change the water in the water-pipe because if I didn't change the water in it, of course it would dry out. It would dry out quickly and wouldn't be good, so it is essential to change it.

[8] Definite in Arabic.

ṭabᶜan fa-min ᶜind hāḏa l-jawzih mamdūdih zayy al-gaṣabuh / ᶜalā fawg / bass min al-xšab maxzūgih fī l-wasaṭ / wa:-fī rāshā bi-yirtkiz al-būrī / iḥna nsammīh al-būrī hāḏā ḥakk an-nār / ṭabᶜan al-būrī maṣnūᶜ min at-trāb / hāḏa l-būrī zayy-mā: / tigūl innahū ḥājih bi-ntruḥ fīha t-titin /

wa-baᶜdā t-titin hāḏā ṭabᶜan at-titin bi-nbillih wa-nxallīh axḏar[9] *šwayyih / ma nxallīš yābis / wa-lā nxallīh axḏal gawī / fa-bī-kun / titin / mablūl bi-l-mā' / wa-niṭraḥ fawgih an-nār / niṣubb ᶜalayh nār / niġaṭṭīh kullih bi-n-nār min šān yiḏlaᶜ naxs kwayyis*[10] */ ṭabᶜan / wa-baᶜdayn fīh gaṣabuh / al-gaṣabuh mamdūdih yaᶜnī ṭabᶜan al-gaṣabuh / mumkin tijirr gaṣabuh mitr mitrayn*[11] *ṯalāṯih arbaᶜah*[12] */ yaᶜnī mmā ṯalāṯ amtār xams amtār hāḏa l-gaṣabu bi-tkūn gadī l-gaṣabu l-kwayyisih / xams amtār kwayyisih / wa-l-gaṣabuh / bi-tudxul fī xuzgī wasṭ al-jawzih / wasṭ al-jawzih hāḏā / al-jawzih hāḏā / mġallafih bi-n-naḥās / mġallafih bi-n-naḥās / fīhā xuzgī min an-naḥās bi-ṭṭraḥ fīh / al-mišrab ḥagg al-gaṣabuh allī bi-txul lā wasṭ al-madāᶜah / rās min al-mašārab / wa-l-mašrab aṯ-ṯānī fī yadī hāḏā bayn-ašrab fīh / hāḏā ṣawtahā /*

al-gaṣabuh hāḏā maṣnūᶜah / ᶜalā-mā gult innū mumkin wāḥid yijirrahā mitrayn aw ṯalāṯih aw arbaᶜah aw xamsi mtār[13] *kullu ᶜala ṭ-ṭalab / kayf bi-ṣnaᶜūhā*[14] */ yaᶜnī ḥasab aṭ-ṭalab iḏā gulnā arbaᶜ amtār štī*[15] *gaṣabuh arbaᶜ amtār / gaṣabat madāᶜah / allī bi-ᶜmalū l-gaṣīb hāḏā / kayf bi-yiᶜmal*[16] */ bī-jirr xayṭ yirbiṭuh masāfih min maḥall / yaᶜnī ᶜalā masāfat al-amtār al-maṭlūbuh / yixallī muᶜallag fī l-hawā / wa-yidraḥ fawg al-xayṭ hāḏā / jarr / bi-ḏūl al-xayṭ / al-jarr hāḏā ka'annū zayy / yikūn fatḥat al-gaṣabuh / fatḥat al-gaṣabuh hāḏa l-jarr / fawg al-jarra hāḏā bi-ġallafūh*[17] */ bi-jild /*

---

[9] From *axḏar*.

[10] Use of non-SA *kwayyis*. Cf. use of non-SA *baᶜdayn* and *fīh* below.

[11] Dual usu. restricted to nouns denoting time or, as here, measure. Cf. *Ṣbaḥtū!* pp. 93-4.

[12] Asyndetic linkage of alternative numerical phrases. Cf. *Syntax* p. 312.

[13] Unusual syndetic linkage of alternative numerical phrases. Cp. *Syntax* p. 312.

[14] Rhetorical question.

[15] Change of number from first plural to first sing.

[16] Rhetorical question. Change of number from masc. plural to masc. singular.

[17] Change of number back to masc. plural.

Of course, from this coconut, it[18] stretches upwards like a pipe,[19] but the wood is perforated down the centre. At the top of it, is the clay bowl which we call the *būrī* for the burning charcoal. Of course, the bowl is made of clay. This bowl, as you would say, is something for putting the tobacco in.

Then the tobacco; of course, we wet the tobacco and make it a bit moist. We don't allow it to be dry, nor do we make it very wet. So, it is tobacco moistened with water, and we put the burning charcoal on top of it. We put burning charcoal on it. We cover it all with burning charcoal, so that we get a good smoke, of course. Then there is the pipe: the pipe is long, I mean you can, of course, get pipes[20] one, two, three or four metres long. A good pipe will be between three metres and five metres long. Five metres is good. The pipe goes into a hole in the middle of the coconut, in the middle of the coconut. The coconut is covered in brass, covered in brass. There is a hole of brass so that you can insert the mouthpiece of the pipe which goes into the middle of the water-pipe, one of the mouthpieces. The second mouthpiece in my hand is what I smoke through. This is what it sounds like.[21]

The pipe is made, as I said, it is possible to get one of between two, three, four or five metres, as you wish. How do they make it? I mean it depends on what you want. If I said four metres, I wanted a pipe four metres long, a pipe for the water-pipe. Those who make the pipes, how do they make them? They take a string and bind it a certain distance from one spot, I mean the distance of the metres required, they suspend it in the air,[22] then they put a coil on the string, the length of the string. This coil is like the opening of the pipe. The opening of the pipe is the coil. Then they cover this coil with leather.

---

18 i.e. the water-pipe.

19 Definite in Arabic.

20 Singular in Arabic.

21 On the tape, the speaker smokes the pipe to illustrate the noise.

22 AS describes suspension of the string like suspension of a washing line.

bī-ġallafū bi-jild / wa-yragᶜū[23] *ᶜalayh / ma yxallūš xizgān baynih awlā … / min šān mā yxrujš al-hawā / baᶜda-mā yġallafū bi-l-jild aṭ-ṭabagu l-ūlā wa-ṭ-ṭabagu ṯ-ṯānī jild yizayyidū 'innum ayš*[24] */ mā yixallaw al-hawā yibtiᶜid badātan*[25] */ fawg al-jirr /*

wa-fawg al-jild hāḏā / yizīdū yijirrū ftilih / al-ftilih hāḏā yiluffūhā ᶜala l-jarr / ᶜala l-jild hāḏā bi-ḍūl al-jildih / bi-ḍūl al-gaṣabuh kāmilih / yiliffūhā bi-šakl kabīr / mukaṯṯaf / min šān yiḥakkumū / al-hawā 'innū ma yxrujš akṯar / yišiddūh akṯar yaᶜnī / aḥna nigūl at-taḥkīm[26] *hākaḏā yiḥkum al-hawā ma yxrujš / li'annū law yjī wāḥid yišrab fī gaṣabuh / wa-hī mxazzagih / agall hawā yisīr min kulli bugᶜah wa-hū mā bi-šrab šī bi-šrab hawā / lākin law-ma tkūn al-gaṣabuh masdūdih mā yuxrujš minnahā naxs abadan / wa-yjī yišrab madāᶜah / ᶜa-yḥiss inn al-madāᶜah ᶜinda-ma yjī yišrab / ᶜa-yḥiss inn ad-duxxān bī-jī min al-gaṣabu llī mamdūdih la-l-būrī / wa-ydxul / bi-šakl dāyirih hākaḏā yadūr bayn al-mā' / yudxul fi n-nār /*

al-mā yifᶜal yijī bi-ṣawt ġal ġal ġal ġal hākaḏā / al-mā' hū ddī ṣ-ṣawt hāḏā bass allī yuxruj min al-gaṣabuh / hū ad-duxxān fagaṭ / mā yiḍlaᶜš al-mā'[27] */ lann iḥna ᶜinda-ma njī nmallī l-mā' lā wasṭ al-madāᶜah / bi-njī njarrib / yaᶜnī bi-l-gafā nšūf gadī mawzūnih mā b-yuxrujš al-mā' / mā' bi-tjī bi-ṣawt / wa-baᶜḍ al-aḥyān nijī wa-ṣ-ṣawt gadū mā ᶜad b-uxrij ṣudg / gawī gad al-mā' bi-xruj (h)ūw / nuskub al-mā'*[28] */ wa-baᶜḍ al-aḥyān nijī nimuṣṣ / ᶜan al-gaṣabuh hākaḏā nišūf lā hī jayyidih wa-nilgā l-mā mā yābis / yaᶜnī tiᶜraf ant ka-mawlaᶜī tiᶜraf inn al-mā nāgiṣ aw zāyid / bi-tzayyidih*[29] */ baᶜda*[30] *hāḏā bī-sabbirū / baᶜda-mā yġallifū al-jild bi-ftilih / fawg al-ftilih yifᶜalū xirgih / yiragᶜū*[31] *ᶜalayhā / min šān tixallī*[32] *l-gaṣabuh laṭīfuh /*

---

[23] From *yiraggaᶜū* with degemination of *gg* and syncope.

[24] Rhetorical question.

[25] Intervocalic voicing of first *t* to *d*.

[26] According to Ahmad Lutfi, the word *liḥām* is more likely to be used in this context.

[27] Verbal clause with dynamic verb and inanimate subject.

[28] Asyndetic linkage of clause of consequence. Cf. *Syntax* p. 311.

[29] Asyndetic linkage of clause of consequence. Cf. above.

[30] Epenthesis.

[31] From *yiraggaᶜū* with degemination of *gg* and syncope. Cf. also above.

[32] Change of person.

They cover it with leather, then sew over it. They don't leave any holes in it or ... so that the air doesn't escape. After they have covered it with leather on the first layer, they add more leather on the coil on the second layer. Why? So that they don't let the air escape at all.

Then, on top of this leather, they take a thread, and this thread they wrap around the coil on top of the leather, the length of the leather, the whole length of the pipe. They wrap it a lot and thickly, so that they can contain the air and it doesn't escape. They tighten it more. We call it *taḥkīm* [securing]. In that way, the air is secured and doesn't escape, because if someone came to smoke the pipe and it was full of holes, the smallest amount of air would escape from every part and they wouldn't be smoking anything, they would be smoking air. But when the pipe is blocked, no smoke can escape[33] at all and they will be smoking the water-pipe.[34] They would feel that the water-pipe, when they came to smoke, they would feel that the smoke was coming from the pipe which stretched to the clay bowl and went in a circular motion in the water and to the charcoal.

The water makes a gurgling sound gal, gal, gal, gal, like that. The water makes that sort of noise, but the only thing that comes out of the pipe is the smoke. The water doesn't come up, because when we come to fill the water into the water-pipe we try it, I mean we go behind to see that it is correctly proportioned[35] and that water is not coming out. The water[36] makes a noise. Sometimes we come and the noise doesn't sound quite right because the water is coming out, so we pour off [a little of] the water. Sometimes we come and suck on the pipe like that to see if it is all right and we find that the water has dried up. I mean, as a water-pipe addict you know whether there is too little water or too much. So you add some more water. After this, they do, after they cover the leather with thread, they put some cloth on top of the thread and sew over that, so that it makes the pipe attractive.

---

[33] i.e. from any holes in the pipe.

[34] Indefinite in Arabic.

[35] i.e. that the water-pipe is balanced.

[36] Indefinite in Arabic.

baᶜḏ an-nās yaᶜnī akṯarat an-nās kulla n-nās yaᶜnī[37] / *bi-yifᶜalū yizīdū yiġallifūhā bi-šakl alṭaf* / *wa-huwa maᶜmūl min aṣ-ṣūf* / *yiᶜmalannahin an-niswān b-aydīhin*[38] / *ᶜalā ḏūl fatḥat al-gaṣabuh* / *bass bi-tkūn wāsiᶜah hākaḏā* / *tiġaṭṭi l-gaṣabuh lā: ᶜind al-mašārib* /

fa-l-gaṣabuh bī-zīd[39] *yuṭruḥū ṯnayn mašārib* / *al-mašrab allī bi-nišrab fīh aḥna nsammīh mašrab layš*[40] *lann aḥna bi-nišrab minnih* / *ad-duxxān allī bi-yuxruj min al-hāḏā* / *bi-nsammīh mišrab* / *wa-ṯ-ṯānī hum yisammūhā al-guḏb* / *wa-ṯ-ṯānī bī-kūn fī rās* / *fī r-rās fī l-jiha ṯ-ṯāniyih* / *allī bī-daxxulūh wasṭ al-xuzgī ḥakk al-jawzih* / *hāḏā gadū bi-bgā jamb* / *at-titin allī bī-jī min wasṭ al-madāᶜah wa-hāḏā* / *wa-hāḏa l-mašrab bī-jī la l-lukf* /

al-mašrab yaᶜnī maᶜmūl bi-ḏarīguh / *šakl mā hūš ᶜūdī fagaṭ* / *al-mišrab hū ᶜūdī* / *xišabih* / *wa-l-xšibih hāḏa l-ᶜūdī* / *bī-zīdū yuxzugūhā fī l-wasaṭ* / *yixdirūlahā* / *bi-maxdar*[41] / *min dāxil yixallawhā bi-šakl* / *maxzūgih min dāxil wa-mġallafih min xārij bi-xšab* / *bass bi-šakla*[42] *gaṣabuh* / *wa-baᶜdayn bī-zaxrafūhā* / *yixallaw šaklahā laḏīf jamīl*[43] / *bi-yiᶜmalū al-mazgam al-bugᶜah allī azgam fīhā* / *bi-raġm innak mumkin tizgam* / *fī 'ayyi bugᶜah* / *fa-tizgam tišbah*[44] / *tišbaḥ fī 'ayyi maḥall fī l-gaṣabuh wu-timsakhā* / *w-ant bi-tšrab* / *fa-hāḏā bī-xallaw jamīl min al-jihatayn* / *fī jihat al-yad u-fī jihat allī bī-sīr lā wasṭ al-gaṣabuh* / *āh hāḏa l-madāᶜah allī bi-nišrab fīhā* /

---

[37] String of reformulative appositives. Cf. *Syntax* p. 246.

[38] Verbal clause with emphasis on the prepositional phrase complement.

[39] Lack of number agreement on linking verb. Cf. *Syntax* p. 50.

[40] Rhetorical question. Use of non-SA *layš*.

[41] Reformulative apposition of verb phrases. Cf. *Syntax* pp. 244-5.

[42] Epenthesis.

[43] Reformulative apposition of verb phrases. Cf. above.

[44] Reformulative apposition of synonymic verbs. Cf. *Syntax* pp. 244-5.

Some people, I mean most people, all people, cover [the pipe] even more nicely. This is [something] made of wool[45] which the women make by hand for the whole length of the pipe. It should be wide like that so that it covers the pipe up to the [two] end-pieces.

There are two end-pieces in the pipe: the mouthpiece we smoke from which we call a *mašrab*, why? Because through it we smoke the smoke that comes out of it. We call that a *mašrab*. The other they call the *guṭb* [pipe stem]. The other is at the top, at the top of the other end, which they put into the hole of the coconut shell. This is beside the tobacco which comes from the centre of the water-pipe. The [other] mouthpiece goes to the mouth.

The mouthpiece is made in a [certain] way: it is not just a piece of wood. The mouthpiece is a piece of wood, a piece of wood, and this piece of wood they perforate down the centre. They bore a hole through it with a drill from the inside so that there is a [long] hole down the centre and it is wood on the outside, in the shape of a pipe. Then they decorate it to give it a nice appearance. They make the handle the part which I hold, although you could hold it anywhere. [The word] *tizgam* means *tišbaḥ*. You can hold it anywhere along the pipe while you smoke. So in this way, they make it attractive at both ends – at the end for your hand and at the end which goes into the pipe.[46] This is the water-pipe that we smoke from.

---

[45] This is a colourful crocheted cover for the pipe which can be removed for cleaning.

[46] i.e. the water-pipe.

15 *Al-mawlaᶜī min ṣanᶜā*

anā ᶜabd as-salām al-ᶜamrī / addī an-nuktih hāḏī la-l-lustāḏ tīm / mih[1] */ anā bayn-agūllukum / kān fīh*[2] *wāḥid yišrab madāᶜah / mawlaᶜī min ṣanᶜā / ᶜārif al-madāᶜah / hāḏā / wa-baᶜdayn*[3] *rāḥū*[4] *gariyih / ᶜinda*[5] *nās / ḏ̣uyūf / fī ᶜiris hānā law-mā yirūḥū yaᶜnī xārij ṣanᶜā / yūṣalū ᶜinda nās / ka-*[6]*ḏ̣uyūf / hāh*[7] */ yaᶜnī lahum / al-afḏ̣alīyuh / wallā yiraḥḥibūbuhum / wa-yugdimūhum yaᶜnī yiᶜāmilūhum gabl aṣḥāb al-bayt / yaᶜnī maṯalan ḏaḥḥīnih anā wa-tīm / law jaw ᶜind tīm ḏ̣uyūf / anā šā-'akūn zayy-mā tīm yaᶜnī mumkin anā 'axdam bugᶜat tīm mumkin anā 'axdam an-nās mumkin anā 'aᶜmal ayyi šay*[8] */ tamām / wa-ḏ̣-ḏ̣uyūf hum yirtāḥū /*

fa-hāḏawlā sārū al-gariyih hāḏā / fī l-ᶜiris / wa-law-mā wuṣulū hānāk / tġaddaw / wa-bad'aw yixazzinū / wa-fīh[9] *wāḥid yišrab madāᶜah / ᶜammarūli l-būrī / širib naxs / wa-baᶜdayn jāb lā wāḥid gabīlī*[10] */ ḏayyik al-gabīlī yišrab / madāᶜah kaṯīr / yišrab yišrab yišrab*[11] *law-mā šibiᶜ / wa-baᶜdayn yimakkin li-ṣāḥubuh / wa-hāḏ̣āk bi-šrab / yaᶜnī / kaṯīr / wa-hāḏ̣āk mirāᶜī bi-tgarḏ̣aḏ̣ / gadū /*

ᶜārifīn bi-tgarḏ̣aḏ̣ ayš[12] *maᶜnāh / yaᶜnī bi-tgarḏ̣aḏ̣ hāḏā bi-ṣ-ṣanᶜānī / maᶜnā al-garḏ̣aḏ̣uh innū yitḥargag aw ... / yaᶜnī yitgarḏ̣aḏ̣ innū yūgaᶜ mirāᶜī lā šay / wa-hū bi-ḥrag dammih / awlā ... / layš*[13] *mā timakkinūlīš muntaḏ̣ur lā šay mā maᶜnāh / minzᶜij / tamām / layš mā jābūlih al-madāᶜah yišrab / hāḏa š-šaxṣ /*

---

1 Tag clause *mih*, also *mā*. Cf. *Syntax* p. 268.

2 Use of non-SA *fīh*.

3 Use of non-SA *baᶜdayn*.

4 Use of non-SA *rāḥ*.

5 Epenthesis.

6 Classicism.

7 Here *hāh* used in the sense of 'Do you understand?'

8 Threefold repetition of *mumkin*.

9 Use of non-SA *fīh*.

10 When *wāḥid* precedes indefinite noun usu. has sense of 'a certain' (cf. Mörth 1997: 127-9).

11 Asyndetic linkage of repeated verb *yišrab* denotes continuous action. Cf. *yidūr yidūr yidūr* and *bi-dūr bi-dūr bi-dūr* in text 2.

12 Use of pan-Yemeni *ayš*.

13 Use of pan-Yemeni *layš*.

15 The addict from San'a[14]

I am Abd al-Salam al-Amri. I am going to tell this joke to Professor Tim, aren't I? I tell you, there was once someone from San'a who was addicted to smoking the water-pipe. Do you know the water-pipe? [It's] this. Then they went to a village as guests of some people. If there is a wedding here when [people] go outside San'a, they arrive at the other people's house as guests, okay? They are given preferential treatment and they[15] welcome them. They welcome them, that is to say, they put them before the people of the house. For example, now with Tim and me. If guests came to Tim's house. I will be like Tim. I could take Tim's place. I could serve the people. I could do anything. Okay? And the guests would relax.

So these [people] went to this village for the wedding. When they arrived there, they had lunch and began to chew. There was one person smoking the water-pipe. They had prepared the bowl of the water-pipe for him. He smoked. Then he passed [it] to a tribesman, and that tribesman smoked the water-pipe a lot. He smoked and smoked and smoked until he had had enough. Then he handed it to his friend, and he smoked a lot. The other one was waiting and getting really fed up.

Do you know what *bi-tgarṭaṭ* means? This *bi-tgarṭaṭ* is in San'ani. *al-garṭaṭuh* means that he was angry and burning inside, *yitgarṭaṭ* means he is waiting for something and his blood is burning, or ... 'Why don't you give [it to] me?' [He is] waiting for something, what does it mean? Annoyed, okay? Why don't they give him the water-pipe to smoke, this person.

---

[14] This joke was told to a group of British students of Arabic in San'a. The main intention was to help the students understand the joke. As a result, the text is more staccato and less fluent than other texts. AS's pronunciation begins slowly, exhibiting less syncope and more epenthesis than in other texts: e.g. *šā-'akūn* 'I will be' and *anā 'axdam* 'I serve' in place of *šā-kūn* and *ana xdam*. Pan-Arabic *fīh* 'there is' is used in place of *bih*, *rājul* in place of *rajjāl* 'man', *muntaḍur* in place of *murayyi*^{c} or *murā*^{c}*ī* 'waiting', *ba*^{c}*dayn* in place of *ba*^{c}*dā* 'then', *rāḥ* in place of *sār* 'to go', *jāb* in place of *ddā* or *makkan* 'to give' and *šāl* in place of *bazz* or *jarr* 'to take'. Pan-Yemeni *ayš* and *layš* are used in place of *mā* 'what' and *lilmā* 'why'. The words *tamām* 'okay?' and *mumkin* 'possible', felt to typify foreigner-speak and used more often when talking to non-Arabs, are repeated more frequently than in a normal Yemeni setting. AS also spends time explaining the words *yitgarṭaṭ* and *malatt*.

[15] i.e. the hosts.

hāḏā kalimih ṣanᶜānī yidgarḍaḍ / iḥna nigūl hākaḏā / wa-muntaḏur innū yijībūlih al-madāᶜah / tamām / fhimtūhā / mā ḥadd jāblih al-madāᶜah /

ayš gāl hāḏa r-rājul / gāl yā jamāᶜah / jalas šwayyih kaḏayya baᶜdā[16] *gāl uhhuh / gālū mā lak / gāl mā lak / gāl w-allāh mā bilā / ragatt šwayyih naᶜᶜast / wa-law tibsirū mā ḥalimt / gālū mā ḥalimt / gāl tḥallimt ḥulm atxayyilih ḥulm min ᶜind allāh / gālū gullanā / gāl mā ᶜad-agullukumš / gālū gullanā / gāl ḥilimt innanā mutt / wa-ḥīn mutt daxalt al-jannih / wa-fī l-jannih hānāk / xurt naxs titin / yaᶜnī būrī / titin yiᶜammar*[17] */ gālū 'aywih baᶜdā / gāl gaḏḏā*[18] *'ahl al-jannih iddawlī titin fī malatt ḥālī muraṣṣaᶜ bi-l-jawāhir bi-ḏ-ḏahab wa-kulla šay / malatt zayy hāḏāk / hāḏāk nisammīh malatt šūfūh / hāḏa l-xašab tišūfu l-xašab hāḏā / malatt / aywih / malatt ḥilw*[19] *wa-bi-l-jawāhir wa-fīh at-titin / aḥsan titin fī l-jannih / gālū 'aywih / gāl wa-l-madāᶜah hāḏīk illī min al-fuḏḏuh wa-ḏ-ḏahab wa-l-ḥalā' wa-l-būrī 'illī sāᶜ hāḏā / lākin mā gad ᶜammarūš /*

rijiᶜū daᶜawlī mālik / yā mālik ᶜammir / mālik sār yiᶜammir / wuṣul ġarr la-n-nār[20] */ jarr mulgāṭ sāᶜ hāḏā kabīr*[21] */ mulgāṭ / hāḏā yišīl an-nār / mulgāṭ / jarr al-mulgāṭ*[22] */ wa-ḍaraḥ bayn an-nār / fhimtū / bayn an-nār / wa-xarraj gabīlī / ṭaraḥuh wasṭ al-būrī / hāh*[23] *jamb al-būrī*[24] */ gālū 'aywih / gāl wa-jarr al-mulgāṭ marrah ṯāniyih / wa-xirrij gabīlī ṯānī wa-ḍaraḥuh fī l-jamb aṯ-ṯānī / gālū 'aywih / gāl / wa-jarrih marrah ṯānī wa-ḍaraḥ gabīlī gālū 'aywih / gāl wa-ḏayyik al-wasaṭ / ᶜādū ġayr ᶜa-ysīr fa-š-šayx gām gāl makkinūlih al-madāᶜah lā ᶜād yiddī aš-šayx /*

---

16 From this point, the text adopts an increasingly SA style.

17 Internal passive. Cf. text 7. Cf. *Syntax* pp. 91-2.

18 *gad* + *ḏā*. Cf. *Syntax* pp. 422-3. Note assimilation of *d* of *gad* to interdental fricative of presentational particle, and pharyngealisation of interdental fricative. Cp. optional pharyngealisation of *ḏ* of distal demonstrative pronouns *hāḏāk* or *hāḏāk*.

19 Use of non-SA *ḥilw*.

20 The word *nār* is used in three different senses in this text: firstly, to denote Hell; secondly, to denote fire; thirdly, to denote burning charcoal.

21 Attribute separated from attributed term by adverbial phrase *sāᶜ hāḏā*. Cf. *Syntax* p. 217.

22 From *baᶜdā* (cf. note above), string of asyndetically linked clauses conveys sense of speed and brevity. Cf. *Syntax* p. 315.

23 Use of *hāh* to signal correction (from *wasṭ* to *jamb*).

24 *jamb al-būrī* functions as corrective appositive to *wasṭ al-būrī*.

This is a San'ani word, *yitgarṭaṭ*. We say this. [He was] waiting for them to give him the water-pipe, okay? Do you understand now? No one gave him the water-pipe.

What did this man say? He said, 'Friends.' He waited a little while and then he said, 'Ah!' They said, 'What is wrong?' They[25] said, 'What is wrong?' He said, 'By God! I just fell asleep for a short while, I dozed, and if only you could see what I dreamt!' They said, 'What did you dream?' He said, 'I had a dream I thought to be a dream from God.' They said, 'Tell us!' He said, 'I'm not going to tell you!' They said, 'Tell us!' He said, 'I dreamt that I had died, and when I died I went to heaven. In heaven, there I was longing to have a smoke, to have tobacco prepared in the water-pipe bowl.' They said, 'Yes, and then?' He said, 'There the people of heaven gave me some tobacco in a beautiful tobacco-box inlaid with jewels and gold and everything.' A tobacco-box like that one. We call that a *malatt*. Look! That wood. Can you see that wood? A tobacco-box. Yes. A beautiful tobacco-box with jewels and with tobacco inside. The best tobacco in paradise. They said, 'Yes?' He said, 'And the water-pipe made of silver and gold and beautiful things, and the water-pipe bowl which was like that. But they hadn't prepared it.

'They went back and called [an angel called] Malik for me. [They said,] "Malik, prepare the bowl of the water-pipe!" Malik went to prepare the water-pipe. He just went to Hell, and took a pair of tongs as big as that.' Tongs. These are to pick up the burning charcoal. Tongs. 'He took the tongs and put [them] into the fire.' Do you understand? 'Into the fire. And he took out a tribesman, and put him in the middle of the bowl of the water-pipe, okay, on one side of the water-pipe bowl.' They said, 'Yes?' He said, 'He took the tongs once more and took out a second tribesman and put him on the other side.' They said, 'Yes?' He said, 'He took them once more and took a tribesman [for the third time].' They said, 'Yes?' He said, 'And the one in the middle he [Malik] was going to…' Then the Shaikh got up and said, 'Give him the water-pipe, so he doesn't fetch the Shaikh!'

---

[25] Lit: 'he'.

16 *At-taġīr fi l-bawnīyih*

tišti tdrā / māhū at-taġīr / allaḏī ḥaṣal fi l-bawnīyih / mā biš ayyi ḥājih mitġayyar fi l-bawnīyih / al-bawnīyih hāḏīk al-bawnīyih / fa-l-bawnīyih ᶜumurhā / wa-hī al-bawnīyih / ahl al-bawnīyih hum nafshum ahl al-bawnīyih illī fīhā / mā biš taġīr fīhā 'illā šwayyih / nās jidā'd / mista'jirīn / fī dakākīn ḥakk al-bawnīyih aw fī baᶜḏ al-biyūt allī xarajū minnahā 'aṣḥābhā /

fa-[1]*l-bawnīyih kull an-nās allī fīhā / yiᶜrafū baᶜḏathum al-baᶜḏ / wa-t-taġīr illī 'ūgaᶜ fīhā maṯalan / ḏakartih ḏalḥīnih / kān min awwal al-bawnīyih fīhā tuᶜtabar*[2] */ malān dakākīn*[3] */ wa-kullahin aswāg / yaᶜnī kullahin dagākīn*[4] *li-l-bīᶜ ma štayt*[5] *tilgā fīhā / lākin mā biš taḏwīr fīhā / innum*[6] *ahl ad-dakākīn ḏawwarū nfushum wallā yiddaw biḏāᶜah ḥāliyih wallā jadīdih / wa-ḏarīgat bīᶜ wa-širā jadīdih / mā biš ᶜindahum hāḏā / kull allī bi-ᶜmalūh ahl al-bawnīyih*[7] */ ġallagū dakākīnhum illī kān maᶜāhum dakākīn li-'annum itwaḏḏafū / ġallagū dakākīn / law-mā gadin ᶜa-yitxarrabayn /*

ḏaḥḥīnih / bada'ū baᶜḏ an-nās illī bī-jaw min xārij / ṣanᶜā / min al-gurā / wa-maᶜāhum ᶜarabīyāt / jaw bi-sta'jirū ḏayy[8] *allī kānayn ḥawānīt / yista'jirūhin / lahum la-l-ᶜarabīyāt ḥakkuhum allī bi-bda'aw yištaraw fawgahin / allī*[9] *bī-bīᶜ jazamāt fawg ḥakkih al-ᶜarabīyih*[10] */ w-allī bī-bīᶜ šukalātih wallā jaᶜālih la-l-jahhāl / w-allī bī-bīᶜ aṣ-ṣuḥūn wa-l-malāᶜig fawg al-ᶜarabīyih / yijiss yilwī ḏūl al-yawm / f-akṯarat ad-dakākīn illī kānayn fi l-bawnīyih / dakākīn ṣudk*[11] */ gadin / muġallagāt / wa-ḏawlā 'aṣḥāb al-ᶜarabīyāt / yurgudū fīhin /*

---

1 Consequential use of *fa-*. Cf. *Syntax* pp. 299-300. Cf. further examples below.

2 Internal passive. Cf. text 7. Cf. *Syntax* pp. 91-2.

3 Adverbial noun complement. Cf. *Syntax* pp. 144-5.

4 Intervocalic voicing of *k* to *g*.

5 Universal-conditional-concession clause. Cf. *Syntax* p. 353.

6 Simplification from *innahum*. Cf. *annum* from *annahum* below.

7 Exophoric pronominal use of definite clause. Cf. *Syntax* pp. 416-17.

8 From *ḏayyā* with vowel elision.

9 Exophoric pronominal use of definite clause. Cf. *Syntax* pp. 416-17.

10 Inversion of attributed term-attribute to emphasise pronoun of attribute. Cf. *Syntax* p. 224.

11 Utterance-final devoicing of *g* to *k*.

16 Changes in al-Bawniya

You want to know about the changes[12] which have taken place in al-Bawniya. Nothing has changed in al-Bawniya. Al-Bawniya is al-Bawniya. Al-Bawniya has always been [the same] al-Bawniya. The people of al-Bawniya are the same people of al-Bawniya that were. There has only been a little change. A few new people renting the shops of al-Bawniya or some of the houses that their owners have left.

In al-Bawniya, everybody knows everybody else. The change that has taken place, for example, I can remember it now: in the past, al-Bawniya was full of shops and marketplaces, I mean they were all shops for selling [things] where you could find anything you wanted, but there has been no development in them, such as the people developing themselves or bringing nice or new goods, or introducing a new way of selling and buying. None of this has happened. All that the people of al-Bawniya have done is close down their shops, if they had shops, because they have become employees. They closed down the shops, and [these shops] have come to a state of near-collapse.

Now some of these people who came from outside San'a, from the villages, who have barrows, have come to rent what used to be shops, to rent them for their barrows that they[13] have begun to buy things from. Some sell shoes from their barrows, some sell soft, wrapped sweets or other sweets to children, some sell plates and spoons from barrows. They go around all day. Most of the shops that were in al-Bawniya, the real shops, have closed down now, and those people with the barrows [now] sleep in them.

---

[12] Singular in Arabic.

[13] Change of referent, i.e. other people in the area.

wa-ᶜād bih taġīr ṯānī / kān minn[14] *awwal fi l-bawniyih / bih samāsir / samsarat zayd / wa-samsarat anā w-allāh maniš dārī b-ism ḏayyik illī kān fīhā / samsarat zayd hāḏā / gadī muhaddamih / kān min awwal fīhā yūṣal zayy al-fundug hī tuᶜtabar*[15] */ yijaw an-nās al-misāfirīn / min xārij ṣanᶜā*[16] *wa-yijlisū fīhā wa-l-gurāš ḥakkuhum wa-l-laḥmirih wa-l-bahāyim wa-l-hāḏā / wa-ḏayyā ṣāḥub as-samsarih aḥmad zayd / gad yisabbirluhum al-gahwih wallā 'akl mimmā kā'n*[17] */ ḏaḥḥīnih mā ᶜad biš hāḏa s-samsarih gadī muhaddamih*[18] */*

hāḏa s-samsarih / wa-l-ḥāji ṯ-ṯāniyih al-jāmiᶜ ḥakk ᶜaddil / zid fiᶜilūlih ṣawmaᶜah / kabīrih gawī / wa-min arwaᶜ aṣ-ṣawmaᶜāt al-mawjūdih fi l-yaman / yaᶜnī ḍawīluh / wa-kabīrih / wa-ḥāliyih / ihtammū bihā / hāḏa l-ḥājatayn illī tġayyarayn fi l-bawniyih / samsarat zayd mā ᶜad biš / wa-l-ṣawmaᶜah[19] *allī / mawjūdih ḏalḥīnih / ᶜādum banawhā jadīd as-sani l-lawwalih / al-ḥammām ḥakk al-bawniyih mā zāl mawjūd ᶜādū ḏak*[20] *jālis /*

---

[14] Gemination of *-n* of function word before vowel-initial word.

[15] Internal passive. Cf. text 7. Cf. *Syntax* pp. 91-2.

[16] Verbal clause with dynamic verb.

[17] Utterance-final glottalisation and devoicing of sonorant. Cf. *Syntax* p. 10.

[18] Asyndetic linkage of explanatory clause. Cf. *Syntax* p. 309.

[19] Lack of assimilation of *-l-* of definite article to initial *ṣ* of *ṣawmaᶜah*.

[20] Distal presentational particle. Cf. *Syntax* p. 424.

There is another change. In the past in al-Bawniya, there were caravanserais. Zayd's caravanserai and a caravanserai belonging to someone else whose name I can't remember. Zayd's caravanserai has been knocked down. In the old days, it was considered to be like a small hotel, people who were travelling would come from outside San'a and stay there with their animals, their donkeys, their cattle and the like.[21] The owner of this caravanserai, Ahmad Zayd, he would make them coffee or a meal, or whatever there was. Now this caravanserai is no longer there, because it has been pulled down.

That is the caravanserai. Another thing is the mosque of Addil. They have built a very large minaret for it. [It is] one of the most beautiful minarets in Yemen. [It is] tall and large and beautiful. They took care over it. These are the two things that have changed in al-Bawniya: Zayd's caravanserai is no longer there, and the minaret which now is there. They only just built it last year. The public bath-house of al-Bawniya is also still there.

[21] Cf. text 4 which describes the use of caravanserais before the development of restaurants.

17 *Al-ḥammām*

al-ḥammām ḥakk al-bawniyih mā zāl mawjūd / ᶜādū ḏak[1] *jālis / hāḏa l-ḥammām kān minn awwal ... / ᶜād fīh taġīr ᶜādanā ġayr ḏakart*[2] *ḏalḥīn / minn awwal kān yiḥarrigū / fi l-ḥammām ḥirrāg / yiḥarrigū garāṭiṣ ᶜuḏmān / lākin akṯarathā / kānū an-nās hānā fi l-yaman*[3] */ mā kān biš al-ḥammāmāt al-jadīdih wa-l-majārī wa-l-lašyā hāḏā / kānat ḥammāmāt šaᶜbīyih / nugar yisammawhin / fi l-mustarāḥ yisammaw an-nugrih / an-nugrih hāḏā hī ḥakk al-aḏā' / yijlis wāḥid wa-tinzil min xuzgī lā wasṭ ġurgih hākaḏāhā*[4] */ wa-twātā fīh /*

fa-[5]*hāḏa l-aḏā' / kān yijī wāḥid yisammawh al-mujaḥḥif / hāḏa l-mjaḥḥif*[6] *hū yijlis fi l-ḥammām / bī-jī ḏabᶜan bi-zalaṭ yibāᶜ*[7] *li-n-nās lā gadī an-nugrih ḥakkuhum malān / yidᶜawh / yijī bi-majḥaf ṭawīluh / yisḥab al-aḏā' hāḏā wa-yudxul lā dāxil an-nugrih / wa-ydxul yixarrijih / wa-yibuzzih fī šwālāt fawg al-ḥimār ḥakkih /*

wa-l-ḥammām / al-ḥammām hāḏā hū ḥammām šaᶜbī ḏabᶜan yitḥammamū fīh an-nās / ayn yišill hāḏa l-aḏā' yišillih juba l-ḥammām / bī-rišših wa-yiḏaḥḥīh / fawg al-jubā ḥakk al-ḥammām[8] */ al-ḥammām / ḥīn mā kān biš majārī / kān maᶜāhum ġurgih kabīrih wasṭ al-ḥammām / fawg al-ḥammām*[9] *hākaḏā / ġurgih / la-l-mā' / yaᶜnī al-mā' allī fi l-ḥammām yuxruj ilayhā / fa-kān al-mujaḥḥif yisīr yiddī al-aḏā' hāḏā*[10] *wa-yiḏaḥḥīh fī juba l-ḥammām /*

wa-l-ḥammāmī / 'allī hū bi-yūgaᶜlih al-ḥammām / kayf yidaffī al-mā' / maᶜāhum nāzil fi l-ḥammām / dast kabīr / wa-ġurgih zayy al-fīrn hākaḏā /

---

1 Distal presentational particle. Cf. *Syntax* pp. 423-4.

2 Lack of anaphoric (object) pronoun in attributive clause. Cf. *Syntax* pp. 234-5.

3 Verbal clause with initial linking verb.

4 Suffixation of *-hā* to emphasise indefinite demonstrative. Cf. texts 4, 9 and 11. Cf. further examples below.

5 Consequential use of *fa-*. Cf. *Syntax* pp. 299-300. Cf. further examples below.

6 Also *mujaḥḥiṯ* (Piamenta 1990-1, Serjeant and Lewcock 1983: 515).

7 Internal passive. Cf. text 7. Cf. *Syntax* pp. 91-2.

8 Use of attribution phrase *al-jubā ḥakk al-ḥammām* after annexion phrase *juba l-ḥammām* for stylistic variation.

9 Corrective reformulative apposition. Cf. *Syntax* p. 246.

10 Verbal clause with initial linking verb.

17 Public bath-houses

The bath-house of al-Bawniya is still there. There it is still, this bath-house. In the past ..., but there is one change I have just remembered now. In the past, they used to burn [things] in the bath-houses. They burnt paper and bones, but mostly, in earlier times, the people here in Yemen, there were not the modern bathrooms of today with drainage systems and such things. They were old-fashioned bathrooms. Sewers, they call them, in the bathroom, they call [them] a sewer.[11] This sewer was for the excrement. You would sit down and it would fall through a hole into a cistern like that and collect there.

For this excrement, there was someone called a *mujaḥḥif* [lavatory cleaner]. This lavatory cleaner was attached to the bath-house. Of course, he would come to people for money, if their cisterns were full, they would call him. He would bring a long scoop to clear out this excrement and go inside the sewer. He would go in to remove it, then he would take it in sacks on his donkey.

The bath-house, the bath-house was a public bath-house, of course, which people bathed in. Where would he take this excrement? He would take it to the roof of the bath-house and spread it out and dry it in the sun on the roof of the bath-house. The bath-house, because there weren't any drains, they had a large cistern in the middle of the bath-house, on top of the bath-house, a cistern for water, and the water which was in the baths would go into it. So, the lavatory cleaner would go to take the excrement and dry it on the roof of the bath-house.

The bath-man who had the bath-house, how would he heat the water? Downstairs in the bath-house, they had a large boiler and a hole which was like an oven.

---

[11] Definite in Arabic.

ad-dist hāḏā fīh / mā' / wa-l-mā'[12] *bī-ḥammawh / kayf bī-ḥammawh / yijirru l-aḏā' hāḏā 'aw xirag aw mā kān / wa-yiḥarrigūh wa-yūga^{c} al-aḏā' hū / ya^{c}nī yūga^{c} luṣwuh aw lahīb yilhab gawī*[13] */ law-mā 'innahū / yidaffī al-ḥammām wa-yidaffī al-mā' hāḏāk allī fī d-dast /*

hāḏā ya^{c}nī naw^{c} min at-taġīrāt illī ḥaṣalat fī l-ḥammām / ḏaḥḥīn mā ^{c}ābiš / mā ^{c}ad bi-f^{c}alūš al-aḏā' hāḏā / li'ann al-ḥammām gadū ^{c}alā / dayzal / an-nās gad fi^{c}ilūlih gaṣīb wa-dayzal / wa-yiḥarrigū ad-dayzal wa-yuḥammā[14] *zayy al-firn fī l-firn zayy-mā ḥīn yif^{c}alū li-l-firn / yilhib wa-ydaffī al-mā' wa-hāḏā / mā ^{c}adūš sā^{c} awwal / hāḏa*[15] *n-nās yigūlū 'innū / al-aḏā' hāḏā hū 'afḍal wa-ṣoḥḥī / min ad-dayzal ḥakk hāḏi l-liyyām / hāḏā hū at-taġīr fī l-ḥammām / wa-mā ^{c}ad biš hāḏīk al-ġurgih illī fī l-ḥammām al-lawwalih / allī kān al-mā' yisīr layhā / li'annum ḏaḥḥīn gad maddū al-mā' illī bi-yuxruj min al-ḥammām gad maddūh la-l-majārī / al-^{c}āmmih / yuxruj al-mā' la-l-majārī*[16] */ hāḏā / šay min at-taġīr allī ḥaṣal fī l-bawniyih / amma l-bawniyih mā zālat hī al-bawniyih / wa-n-nās allī fī l-bawniyih hum nafs an-nās al-lawwalīn / mā ^{c}adā ba^{c}ḍ an-nās illī hum daxalū jidā'd / mista'jirīn / yista'jirū ba^{c}ḍ al-biyūt wa-gadum / mit'aṣṣalīn hānā fī l-bawniyih / wa-hāḏā ḥakk al-ḥammām aštī agullukum bi-l-ḥammām /*

hāḏa l-ḥammām[17] */ hum yidaffūlih al-mā' min nāzil / ḍab^{c}an yudxul wāḥid al-ḥammām / ḥammām al-bawniyih maṯalan bi-nzil manzal / yikūn hū 'akṯarat-mā tkūn al-ḥammāmāt hānā fī ṣan^{c}ā / hī taḥt al-larḍ / hākaḏā / mabniyih / yudxul wāḥid al-bāb allī hū al-lawwal / wa-ba^{c}dā yinzil daraj / wa-yudxul al-bāb aṯ-ṯānī / wa-ḥīn yudxul lā wasṭ al-ḥammām / yibsir hānāk wāḥid rajjāl*[18] *musannib / nisammīh iḥna al-ḥammāmī / jālis fī dakkih hākaḏahā*[19] *murtafa^{c}ah / wa-jambih aṣ-ṣundūg ḥakkih /*

---

[12] Topicalisation of object. Cf. *Syntax* p. 130.

[13] Verbal clause with initial linking verb and inanimate subject.

[14] Internal passive. Cf. text 7. Cf. *Syntax* pp. 91-2.

[15] Demonstrative pronoun refers back to introduction of diesel as fuel. Cf. *Syntax* pp. 382-4.

[16] Verbal clause with dynamic verb.

[17] Topicalisation of prepositional annex. Cf. *Syntax* pp. 131-2.

[18] *wāḥid* used before indefinite noun in sense of 'a certain' or as emphatic indefinite article (cf. Mörth 1997: 127-9).

[19] *hākaḏahā* separates *dakkih* from its attribute *murtafa^{c}ah*. Cf. *Syntax* p. 217.

This boiler had water in it. The water was heated. How would they heat it? They would take this excrement or rags or whatever there was and burn it, and the excrement would become so hot that it could heat the bath-house and heat the water that was in the boiler.

This is one of the changes which has taken place in the bath-houses. Now, they no longer use this excrement, because the bath-houses are [run] on diesel now. People have laid pipes to them with diesel; they burn the diesel [to heat the water] and it heats up like a [public] oven, in a [public] oven, like they do in ovens. It gets very hot and heats the water. It is no longer like it was in the past. People say that the excrement was better and healthier than the diesel of today. This is the change in the bath-houses. There are no longer the cisterns that were in the old bathrooms that the water went into. [This is] because the water that comes out of the bathrooms now goes into the public drainage system. The water goes out into the drains. This is one type of change that has taken place in al-Bawniya. However, al-Bawniya is still al-Bawniya, and the people who are in al-Bawniya are the same as the old people apart from some people who have come in recently as tenants, renting some of the houses, and they have become established here in al-Bawniya. Now, about the bath-houses, I want to talk to you about the bath-houses.

For the bath-house, they heat the water for it from below. Of course, [when] you go into the bath-house, for example the al-Bawniya bath-house, you go downstairs. Most of the bath-houses here in San'a are built underground. You go in through the first door,[20] then go down some steps and go in through the second door. When you go into the bath-house, you see a man standing there. We call him the bath-man [*ḥammāmī*]. [He] sits on a raised stone seat with his box beside him.

[20] Lit: 'the door which is the first.'

hāḏa ṣ-ṣundūg[21] *yiḍraḥ fīh adawātih / mugaffal bi-gufl / fi^{c}ilū xuzgī zuġayrī min ḍālu^{c} / ^{c}alā sās ^{c}inda-mā yijirr al-ḥisāb ḥakk al-ḥammām yiḍruḥuh wasṭ al-xuzgī ḏayyik /*

f-ḥīn yudxul al-wāḥid la-l-ḥammām / bi-yūṣal / lā wasṭ / ġurfih kabīrih / al-ġurfih hāḏī yuxliṣ al-ladāh ḥakkih / wa-yi^{c}allig al-ladāh bi-ma^{c}ālig wa-ġurag hākaḏahā ḍīgān zuġār / wa-bih sā^{c} ad-dakkih la-n-nās yijlisū fīhā / aṭ-ṭīgān az-zuġār hāḏawlā yiḍruḥū fīhin al-ladāh wa-yi^{c}alligū al-ladāh allī fī bugših / ḍab^{c}an al-bukših[22] *hāḏā tijī ṣurruh*[23] */ tūga^{c} kabīrih / yiluffū fīha l-ladāh / wa-yi^{c}ṣubūhā wa-yiḍruḥḥā*[24] *fī ṭ-ṭāguh /*

allī yiššī yitḥammam[25] */ bī-bizza*[26] *ma^{c}ih / ḥakkih al-ladāh fī l-bukših / aw fī mušamma^{c} hāḏi l-liyyām / wa-ybizza ma^{c}ih al-līfih / al-līfih hāḏa llī yifḥasūbihā ma^{c} aṣ-ṣābūn / wa-ybizza ma^{c}ih aṣ-ṣābūn / wa-ybizza ma^{c}ih aš-šambū*[27] */ yiġsil*[28] *bih ša^{c}rih / min awwal kān yif^{c}alū trāb rūs / hāḏa t-trāb rūs hū min al-jibāl yisammūh tirāb rūs / yiddaw yifḥasu š-ša^{c}r bih / wa-kān ḥālī yisammawh turāb rūs / turāb hū sā^{c} aṣ-ṣābūn midrī kayfū /*

wa-ba^{c}dā yudxul lā dāxil al-ḥammām / yuxliṣ ladātih / yi^{c}allighin aw yiḍraḥḥun fī ṣurruh / wa-yḍraḥḥun hinayyik / yilbas al-fūḍuh ḥakk al-ḥammām / yilbas al-fūḍuh ḥakk al-ḥammām / ḍab^{c}an al-ḥammām ḥakkanā / hāḏa llī fī ṣan^{c}ā / hin ḥammāmāt yif^{c}alū yawm / dawr li-r-rijāl / wa-yawm dawr li-n-niswān / hākaḏā / yawm bi-yawm / f-ḥīn yilbas al-wāḥid al-fūḍuh / wa-gadū jāhiz / gad xallā ladātih hinayk maḍrūḥāt / al-ḥawlī / wa-l-ladāh allī ^{c}a-yxruj bihin /

[29]*al-ḥammāmī yijlis ḍab^{c}an hānāk / ^{c}ind aṣ-ṣundūg ḥakkih / yijirr al-ḥisāb /*

---

[21] Topicalisation of prepositional annex. Cf. *Syntax* pp. 131-2.

[22] Anticipatory devoicing of *g* to *k*.

[23] *ṣurruh* is a synonym for *bugših*.

[24] Change of number in verb from plural to singular.

[25] Exophoric pronominal use of definite clause. Cf. *Syntax* pp. 416-17.

[26] Epenthesis after geminate consonant. Cf. *Syntax* p. 10.

[27] Series of four syndetically linked clauses with repetition of *yibizza ma^{c}ih* ... to emphasise the fact that a number of things are taken into the bath-house.

[28] Degemination of *ss* to *s* and syncope. From *yiġassil*.

[29] Interruption in train of thought.

He puts his things in this box. [It is] locked with a lock. They made a small hole in the top so that when he takes money for the bath, he can put it into that hole.

When you go into the bath-house, you come into the middle of a large room. [In] this room, you take off your clothes, you hang your clothes up on hooks and [there are] holes which are small windows.[30] There is [something] like a stone slab for the people to sit on. These small windows they put their clothes in and hang up their clothes which are in a bundle. Of course, this will be a large bundle. They roll up their clothes in it and wrap them up and put them on the window shelf.

Those who want to bathe will take their clothes with them in a bundle or in a plastic bag these days; they will take a loofa, a loofa is what they use with soap to rub [themselves]; they will take soap; they will take shampoo[31] to wash their hair with. In the past, they used to use hair clay. This hair clay is from the mountains. They call it *trāb rūs*.[32] They rub[bed] their hair with it. It was good. They call it *trāb rūs*. [It is] dust like soap. I don't know what it is like.

Then you go into the bath-house, take off your clothes, and hang them up or put them in a bundle and put them there. You put on a sarong[33] for bathing. You put on a sarong for bathing. Of course, these bath-houses of ours which are in San'a, they are bath-houses which do one day for men and the next day for women. Like that. Day by day. When you put on the sarong and you're ready, you've left your clothes over there, the towel and the clothes you will go out in.

The bath-man stays there beside his box, of course. He takes the money.

---

[30] These windows are built into the wall with a deep shelf. It is this shelf that constitutes the 'hole' or 'cavity'.

[31] Definite in Arabic.

[32] In Serjeant and Lewcock, *trāb rūs* is said to no longer be used by women (Serjeant and Lewcock 1983: 521). In San'a in 1997, however, I saw *trāb rūs* still being used by women prior to using shampoo. As well as cleaning the roots of the hair, it is said to make the hair soft and straight.

[33] Definite in Arabic.

fa-l-ḥammām / bih ya^{c}nī yikūn al-ḥammām šarāgih[34] */ li-nās yista'jirū min al-lawgāf li'annū ḥakk ad-dawlih al-ḥammām*[35] *aṣlan / fa:-tilgā 'innum an-nās illī musta'jirīn lih / yūga^{c}luhum dawl / yisammūh / ad-dawl ya^{c}nī 'innū ḏayyā maṯalan lā hum iṯnayn musta'jirīn / dawl ḏayyā yūga^{c} maṯalan nuṣṣ šahr / wa-dawl ḏayyā ba^{c}dih nuṣṣ šahr / aw dawl ḏayyā ^{c}išrīn yawm / wa-ḏayyā ^{c}ašar iyyām ḥasb al-littifāg illī baynahum / wa-ḍab^{c}an / iṯnā-mā yikūn al-wāḥid hū mistalim al-ḥammām kull ad-daxl lih / mā ^{c}ada llī hum bi-ddawhā lā 'ījār al-ḥammām gadum yifrigūha l-liṯnayn / ya^{c}nī lā hum iṯnayn ḥammāmīn mistalimīn la-l-ḥammām / zayy al-ḥammām illī ^{c}indanā hānā fī l-bawniyih /*

al-ḥammāmī yijlis hānāk / jālis / lā ḥadd[36] *yištīh yinfa^{c} aḥadd / yiddīlih al-ladāh / yiddīlih šambū min xārij / yiddīlih ṣābūn min xārij yi^{c}mal ayyi ḥājih / waḏīfat al-ḥammāmī 'innū yixdam an-nās al-mawjūdīn / ḍab^{c}an fī l-ḥammām al-ḥammāmī mišū ġayr waḥdih illī bi-jlis hinayk ^{c}ala z-zalaṭ / bih axwatih / ^{c}iyyāl ^{c}ammih / nās min aṯ-ṯāniyīn / yijaw yištaġilū fī l-ḥammām / fa-dawl ar-rijāl*[37] *yūga^{c}ū mikayyisīn /*

fa-ba^{c}da-mā yuxliṣ al-linsān ḥakkih al-ladāh kull:ahin / yidxul / yibsir amāmih barik hākaḏahā[38] *^{c}ādū xārij kullih bārid mā gadūš ḥāmī gawī lākin ḍab^{c}an aḥmā min aš-šāri^{c} / bih barik hānāk fīhā mā' bārid / wu-bih / zayy al-karāsī min ḥajar / yisammūhin dikak / yijlisū an-nās*[39] *yuxrujū yibridū fawgahin / fīhin wa-yijlisū ^{c}alayhin / wa-bih fī l-ḥammām dūš*[40] *hākaḏahā / lā gad aḥadd xaraj yiššī yitġassal bārid yitġassal minnih / wallā min al-barik yijirr ad-dalw / wa-yitġassal bih /*

wa-ḥīn yidxul ba^{c}dā al-wāḥid min ^{c}ind al-barik yidxul ^{c}alā ġurfih zuġayrih hānāk maxḍā[41] *ḥakk al-mā' / bih ḥammām zuġayrī li-š-šwāx /*

---

[34] Intervocalic voicing of *k* to *g*.

[35] Inversion of predicand–predicate to emphasise predicate. Cf. *Syntax* pp. 129-30.

[36] Indefinite pronoun precedes verb following adjunction. Cf. *Syntax* pp. 112, 117.

[37] The noun phrase *dawl ar-rijāl* functions here as an adverb.

[38] Suffixation of *-hā* to emphasise indefinite demonstrative. Cf. above and below.

[39] Verbal clause with dynamic verb.

[40] Recent loan. From French *douche*.

[41] This room is called the *maxṭā*. It has channel for water round the outside and pathway for people to walk on. According to AS, both the channel and the pathway are called *maxṭā*.

So the bath-houses,[42] the bath-houses are a partnership concern for people to rent from the *Wakf* [Ministry], because the bath-houses are actually the property of the State. You find that the people who rent it take turns. Taking turns means that if there are two people renting, the turn of one [of them] will be half a month, for instance, and the turn of the other after him half a month. Or the first one's turn will be twenty days and the other one ten days, depending on the agreement between them. Of course, while someone is in charge of the bath-house he will receive all the revenue, apart from what they give as rent of the bath-house. They split it between the two of them, I mean, if there are two bath-men in charge of the bath-house as there are at the bath-house we have here in al-Bawniya.

The bath-man stays there in case anyone wants him to help them by fetching their clothes, or getting them shampoo from outside or soap from outside, or doing anything. The job of the bath-man is to serve the people who are there. Of course, in the bath-house it isn't just the bath-man on his own who sits there over the money. There are his brothers, his [paternal] cousins and other people who come to work there. [When it is] the men's turn, they work as masseurs.

So, after you have removed all of your clothes, you go in and see a pool in front of you in the outer area; it is all cool – it isn't very hot, but of course it is hotter than the street. There is a pool there with cool water in, and there are [things] like seats made of stone which they call *dikak*. People sit on them; they come out to cool off on them, and sit on them. There is also a shower in the bath-house. If someone has come out and wants to wash with cold [water], they get washed there, or from the pool they take a bucket and wash from it.

When you then go in from the pool, you go into a small room where there is a channel for water. There is a small bathroom for urinating.

[42] Singular in Arabic.

wa-ba^c^dā yidxul / ^c^alā bug^c^ah / makān[43] *hākadahā*[44] */ fīh / dakkih / w-iṯnayn aḥwāḍ / ad-dakkih hāḏī yijissū fīhā / an-nās / w-ījī w-yid^c^aw*[45] *ḥammāmī / aw min allī bi-štaġilū fi l-ḥammām / yitkayyasū fīhā / fa-maṯalan law anā 'aštī 'asīr atḥammām ba^c^da-ma lbas wa-xluṣ wa-hāḏā / awṣal lā hāḏa l-bug^c^ah absir an-nās hāḏawlā / hum hinayyik bi-tkayyasū / bi-tṣabbanū /*

wa-buh wāḥid / fi l-ḥammām bi-štaġil / bi-ddī mā' / yisammawh yā bā:rid / yiṣayyaḥūluh wasṭ al-ḥammām / hāḏā fi yadih dalw / ad-dalw hāḏā hū zayy al-maġraf bass kabīr / aw tanak / kabīrih hākaḏā / yisayyib minnahā mā' /

wa-min hāḏa l-ġurfih mitfarra^c^āt ṯintayn ġuraf aw ṯalāṯ ġuraf / ġurfih yidxul fīhā / fīhā ṯnayn aḥwāḍ / lā ḥadd yištī yitḥammam hinayyik min nafsih / tḥammam / wa-ba^c^dā yudxul aṣ-ṣadr / hāḏa ṣ-ṣadr yisammūhā ṣadr li'annū al-bug^c^a l-ḥāmiyih / wa-hū taḥtih an-nār / bī-laṣṣaw taḥtih an-nār / wa-bi-tibgā ḥāmī gawī / yitxul al-wāḥid la ṣ-ṣadr hāḏā[46] */ wa-bih ṯintayn ġuraf / min aṣ-ṣadr / mitfarra^c^āt ṯintayn ġuraf / wāḥid*[47] *yisammawh al-xizānih / wāḥid yisammawh aḏ-ḏulmīyuh / al-xizānih hāḏā ya^c^nī zayy-mā tigūl ġurfih fīhā ṯnayn aḥwāḍ wa-l-kull / al-liṯnayn aḥwāḍ hāḏawlā yitḥammamū fīha l-mā'*[48] */ an-nās*[49] */ yitḥammamū fīha n-nās / gadanā bayn-alaxbuṭ /*

fa-l-laḥwāḍ hāḏawlā[50] */ bih fīhin / xizgān / al-xizgān / ma^c^āhin gaṣīb mā' ya^c^nī yūṣal fīhin / yiḍraḥ al-ḥammāmī / yiddī ḥakkih al-librih / yiftaḥ yifjir*[51] *lana l-ḥawḍ / yuxruj minnih mā' / hāḏā fi l-xizānih maṯalan / wa-ṣ-ṣadr nafsih fīh iṯnayn aḥwāḍ / ḍab^c^an al-laḥwāḍ hāḏā kullahā min ḥajar / wa-l-ḥawḍ / ya^c^nī innahū zayy al-wa^c^ā / yiḍraḥū fīh al-mā' /*

fi ṣ-ṣadr hāḏā / an-nās yitmaddadū / wāḥid yitmaddad / w-allī yištī yijlis/

[43] Reformulative apposition. Cf. *Syntax* pp. 244-6.

[44] Demonstrative separates *makān* from its attributive clause.

[45] Correction from *w-ījī*. 'He comes, they call …'.

[46] Verbal clause with dynamic verb.

[47] Lack of feminine agreement with singular of preceding noun.

[48] *l-mā'* is a mistake, which speaker then corrects.

[49] Corrective reformulative apposition. Cf. *Syntax* p. 246.

[50] Topicalisation of prepositional annex. Cf. *Syntax* pp. 131-2.

[51] Use of partial synonymy.

Then you go into a place, a room, with a stone seat and two tanks. The stone seat is for people to sit on. Then they call the bath-man[52] or one of those who are working in the bath-house and wash with a bath-bag. So, for example, if I want to go and bathe after I have [dressed and] undressed and the like, I go to this place and see these other people cleaning themselves there with a bath-bag and washing themselves with soap.

There is someone in the bath-house who works bringing water. They call him the *bārid* and they shout for him in the middle of the bath-house. He has a bucket in his hand. This bucket is like a scoop[53] but big[ger], or a large tin, which he pours water from.

There are two or three rooms which branch off from this room. [There is] one room you go into which has two tanks; if you want to bathe on your own there, you can. Then you go into the hot room. They call this room the *ṣadr*[54] because it is the hot[test] place, and the furnace[55] is underneath it. They light the fire beneath it, and it becomes very hot. You go into this hot room, and [then] there are two rooms which branch off from the hot room: one is called the *xizānih* and the other is called the *ḍulmīyuh* [dark room]. The *xizānih* is also a room with two tanks in it. These two tanks [water] people bathe from. People bathe there. I'm getting mixed up.

These tanks have holes, the holes have pipes which water comes into. The bath-man has a long rod which he uses to unblock the tank for us so that water comes out. This is in the *xizānih*, for instance, and the hot room also has two tanks. Of course, these tanks are all made from stone. The tanks are like containers which they put water in.

In this hot room, people stretch out: some people stretch out. Some like to sit down.

---

52 Indefinite in Arabic.

53 Definite in Arabic.

54 Lit: 'chest'. AS suggests it may be called this because people tend to lie on their chests in this room.

55 Lit: 'fire'.

w-allī yištī / yisannib / ᶜalā-ma šta l-wāḥid / wa-bih aḍ-ḍulmīyuh[56] */ aḍ-ḍulmīyuh hāḏā / fīhā / iṯnayn aḥwāḍ wa-l-kull / wa-fīhā ḥawḍ kabīr / al-ḥawḍ al-kabīr hāḏā / al-māʼ yudxul layh / gadū maftūḥ layh māʼ ᶜalā ḍūl / fa-l-māʼ allī bi-txul lā hāḏā min xārij ḥāmī ḍabᶜan / al-bārid / yibizz al-māʼ minnih / yiddī li-n-nās bih minnih / bi-dalw / liʼannū kabīr wa-bi-yimtalī yaᶜnī / bī-xallawh yimtalī yikfī an-nās / aḍ-ḍulmīyuh hāḏā / bugᶜah lā ḥadd yištī yitġassal wa-hū xāliṣ al-ladāh mā ḥadd yibsirih min allī xārij yisammawhā ḍ-ḍulmīyuh / yitġassal hinayk bi-sāᶜatih wa-yitwaḍḍā wa-ḏayyā*[57] */*

wa-ᶜad bih ḍabīᶜah fī ʼahl ṣanᶜā hānā / al-ḥammām hāḏā hū yudxul yiᶜragū[58] *fīh / wa-yigūl yifᶜal ᶜargih / fa-fī ṣ-ṣadr / baᶜḍ al-laḥyān baᶜḍ an-nās yiᶜjibhum yirguṣū / fa:-ḥīn yurguṣū yijī wāḥid min allī ᶜirif yurguṣū / yiġannī yiddī ʼuġniyih ḥāliyih / maṯalan wa-hum baᶜdā hāḏawlāk bi-yurguṣū / law-mā yiᶜragū tūgaᶜ ḥāliyih / hizzih ḥāliyih la-l-ᶜargih /*

wa-baᶜd al-ᶜargih l-anā ša-tkayyas gadanā azakkin ᶜalā wāḥid min al-ḥammāmīn al-mawjūdīn hānāk agullih ᶜa-tkayyisnī / yigullī ʼaywih / yigullī ʼiᶜrag / gadanā ʼaᶜrag law-mā yitimmalī fī yadih wa-yidᶜīnī / wa-baᶜdā yidᶜīnī ykayyisnī / ḍabᶜan yikayyisnī hāḏā bi-kīs xirgih sawdih / yidaxxilhā fī yadih wa-yifḥasnī / yifḥas jismī / ʼaydī / ʼarjulī / wa-yifḥas wa-yixarrij al-wasax / al-wasax yixruj baᶜālil[59] */ iḏā gadlī min al-ḥammām xayrāt yuxruj baᶜālil xayrāt / wa-l-kīs hū xārij fī l-… / miš ᶜind aṣ-ṣadr lannī ḥāmī gawī wa-l-ḥammāmī mā yitḥammalš al-ḥamā al-gawī /*

fa-fī tayyi l-bugᶜah yiḥammimnī wa-yikayyisnī / baᶜda-mā yikayyisnī yiġassilnī bi-l-māʼ / wa-baᶜda-mā yiġassilnī bi-l-māʼ yiġassilnī bi-ṣ-ṣābūn / barḍū bi-xirgih / nisammīhā līfih / mā ᶜadīš kīs hāḏā nisammīhā līfih yiḍraḥ fīhā ṣābūn / wa-yifḥas jismī bi-kullih / hāḏa l-ḥammāmī / wa-baᶜdā yifᶜallī aš-šambū wa-yigūm yiṣfīnī / yidaxxilnī lā dāxil lā ᶜind aḍ-ḍulmīyuh[60]*/*

---

[56] Existential *bih* followed by definite noun. Cf. text 1. Cp. *Syntax* p. 121.

[57] *wa-ḏayyā* functions as tag phrase and used here to prevent an abrupt ending on a verb.

[58] Change to plural referent.

[59] Adverbial noun complement. Cf. *Syntax* pp. 144-5.

[60] He is taken into the dark room because this room has large troughs so the bath-man can scoop up the water easily.

Some like to stand up, depending on what they want. Then there is the *ḍulmīyuh* [dark room]. This dark room also has two tanks. There is a large tank in it. Water comes into the large tank, water comes into it constantly, and this water which comes into it from outside is hot, of course. The water-carrier takes water from it in a bucket to give to the people because it[61] is large and it fills up. They let it fill up so that it is enough for the people. The dark room is a place where people can wash having taken off their clothes without anyone from outside seeing them. They call it the dark room. You wash there quickly and do your ablutions and the like.

There is another custom among the people of San'a here. They go into the bath-house to sweat.[62] It is called having a sweat. In the hot room, occasionally some people like to dance. When they dance someone who can dance comes to sing, to sing a nice song, for example, and the others then dance until they sweat. It is nice, shaking yourself is good for sweating.

After sweating, if I'm going to clean myself with a bag, I mention to one of the bathmen there, I say to him, 'Will you clean me with a bag?' He says to me, 'Yes!' [then] he tells me, 'Sweat!' I sweat until he motions to me with his hand and calls me [over]. Then he calls me to clean me with a bag. Of course, when he cleans me, it is with a black cloth bag. He puts his hand into it and rubs me. He rubs my body, my arms, my legs. He rubs the dirt out and the dirt comes out in blobs. If I haven't been to the bath-house for a long time, it comes out in lots of blobs. This goes on outside in ..., not in the hot room because it is very hot and the bath-man cannot tolerate a lot of heat.

So in that place, he washes me and cleans me with a bag. After he has cleaned me with the bag, he washes me with water. And after he has washed me with water, he washes me with soap, again with a cloth which we call a loofa. This isn't a bag now, we call it a loofa which he puts soap on. Then he rubs my whole body. This is the bath-man. Then he puts shampoo on me and begins to rinse me. He takes me inside into the dark room.

---

[61] i.e. the large tank.

[62] Cf. Serjeant and Lewcock (1983: 521) for description of the bath sweat, which is described there as *ᶜarqat al-ḥammām*. In text 25, AS uses apposition phrase *ᶜargih ḥammām*.

wa-hānāk yijirra dalw / wa-yiṣfīnī wallā yixallī ḏayy allī bi-l-bārid hu llī yuṣfī / al-mā’ xārij mā biš fīh ḥanafīyāt yijanlih[63] *al-mā’ mā bilā l-bārid yisayyib / wa-ḥīn yisayyib al-bārid / ba^{c}da-mā nuxruj min al-ḥammām yiddīlih*[64] *^{c}išrīn wallā yiddīlih ṯalāṯīn wallā xamsīn ka-mā yišti l-wāḥid yiddīlih / fa:-ba^{c}da-mā yitimm yiġassilnī bi-š-šambū / wa-ṣ-ṣābūn / wa-l-kīs wa-l-hāḏā / yiṣaffīnī / yiṣalfīnī*[65] */*

ba^{c}ḏ̣ an-nās / yijissū bayn al-ḥamā xayrāt / ba^{c}dā yuxruj yibrid xārij šwayyih / wa-gaḏḏā[66] *yudxul yitġassal min jadīd / wa-yuxruj xārij šwayyih / yibrid / hākaḏā yijissū sā^{c}ah sā^{c}atayn wa-hum yitḥammamū / anā ḥīn asīr atḥammam / anā min allī bi-^{c}jibhum al-ḥammām gawī / yi^{c}jibnī asīr atḥammam w-ajiss ^{c}ašar dagāyig rub^{c}a sā^{c}ah nuṣṣ sā^{c}ah*[67] */ ya^{c}nī mā ḏ̣awwulš xayrāt fī l-ḥammām /*

wa-law-mā yitimm al-wāḥid yiṣṭafī / wa-gadū jāhiz gadū yuxruj maxraj / wa-ḥīn yuxruj lā xārij / yigūl li-l-ḥammāmi ddīlī al-ḥawlī / fa-l-ḥammāmī yigūl ayyin al-ḥawlī / yigūl ḏayyik illī fī z-zuwwih wallā ḏayyik illī fī mušamma^c wallā ḏayyik allaḏī mu^{c}allag / al-ḥammāmī yiddīlih al-ḥawlī / yijirrih yitnaššaf al-wāḥid[68] *wa-^{c}ādū xārij / wa-xalaṣ al-fūḏ̣uh / ^{c}aṣṣab ^{c}alā nafsih wa-daxal / jalas yibrid / hāḏā ḥīn nitḥammam hākaḏā /*

ba^{c}ḏ̣ al-laḥyān lā ništī al-ḥammāmī yirazzimnī aw yiḥammiṣnī[69] */ gadanā d^{c}ih wa-dmaddad / wa-hū yijī yigarraḥ ḏ̣ulā^{c}ī / yirazzim arjulī / ba^{c}dā yirazzim aydī / wa-yirazzimnī fī ṣadrī / yigarraḥ yitgāraḥ yigaḥḥ gaḥḥ hākaḏā / zayy al-masāj*[70] *bass ġarr hū naw^c min at-tarzīm hākaḏā / ba^{c}dā ka-mā gadanā bārid šwayyih wa-gad baradt mā biš al-^{c}arag wa-l-hāḏā ’agūm albas al-ladāh ḥakkī / wa-law-mā lbast ladātī*[71] *wa-gadanā šā-ruḥlī /*

---

63 Diphthong simplification. From *yijayn + lih*.

64 Change of person from 1 pl. to impersonal 3 m.s.

65 Reformulative apposition of synonymic verbs. Cf. *Syntax* pp. 244-5.

66 *gad* plus presentational particle. Cf. *Syntax* pp. 422-3.

67 Asyndetic linkage of alternative numerical phrases. Cf. *Syntax* p. 312.

68 Verbal clause with dynamic verb. Subject follows two asyndetically linked verbs.

69 Syndetically linked partial synonyms.

70 Recent loan. From *massage*. Predicandless predicate. Cf. *Syntax* p. 124.

71 Use of annexion phrase *ladātī* after attribution phrase *al-ladāh ḥakkī* for stylistic variation.

There he brings a bucket and rinses me, or he lets the water-carrier rinse [me]. The water is outside, there aren't any taps to bring the water, it is just the water-carrier who brings [it]. Because the water-carrier brings water, after I come out of the bath-house, you give him 20 or you give him 30 or 50 [riyals], depending on what you want to give him. When he has finished washing me with shampoo, soap and the bag, he rinses me, he rinses me off.

Some people spend a long time in the hot part [of the bath-house], then they go out to cool off a little, and there they are going in to wash again, and then they go out to cool off a bit. In this way, they can spend one or two hours bathing. When I go and bathe, I am one of those who love the bath-house, I like to go to bathe and stay for ten minutes, quarter of an hour or half an hour. I mean, I don't spend a long time in the bath-house.

When you have finished rinsing yourself and you are ready, you go outside. When you go out, you say to the bath-man, 'Give me the towel!' Then the bath-man will say, 'Which towel?' You say, 'The one in the corner!' or 'The one in a plastic bag!' or 'The one which is hanging up!' The bath-man gives you the towel. You take it and dry yourself when you are outside[72] and have taken off the bath sarong. You wrap [it][73] around yourself and go in. You sit to cool off. This is when we bathe, it's like that.

Sometimes, if I want the bath-man to massage me, I call him and lie down. Then he comes and makes my ribs crack and massages my legs then massages my arms and massages me on my chest. He makes a cracking sound, crack, crack, like that. [It is] like a massage,[74] but it is a type of pressing down action. Then, when I am a bit cooler and I have cooled off and there isn't any more sweat or whatever, I get up and put on my clothes. When I have put on my clothes, I am about to go.

[72] i.e. in the changing room.

[73] i.e. the towel.

[74] Definite in Arabic.

ḍabᶜan ḥīn tudxul al-ḥammā:m / hāḏā nisīt mā gullukum minn[75] *awwal hāh / awwal-ma tdxul al-ḥammām / tidxul tigūl salām ᶜalaykum*[76] */ wa-yigullak wa-ᶜalaykum as-salām / tigūl niᶜīman ᶜalaykum yigūl anᶜam allāh ᶜalaykum bi-l-ᶜāfiyih / w-antū naᶜīm / w-ant tigūl anᶜam allāh ᶜalaynā wa-ᶜalaykum bi-l-ᶜāfiyih / wa-tidxul / hāḏā 'awwal-ma tdxul al-ḥammām / wa-man daxal*[77] *yigullak hākaḏā w-ant tijāwiblih bi-nafs al-kalām / wa-ḥīn tuxruj gadak tigūlluhum salām ᶜalaykum naᶜīman ᶜalaykum / wa-hum yigūlū ᶜalaykum salām w-anᶜam allāh ᶜalaykum bi-l-ᶜāfiyih w-antū naᶜīm / wa-hākaḏā ᶜādih /*

fa-baᶜda-mā timm albas al-ladāh ḥakkī / 'agūm aḥāsib al-ḥammāmī ḥakk al-ḥammām / xamsīn miyih / kam-ma šta l-wāḥid yiddīlih / ḍabᶜan ma ykunš galīlih / baᶜdā kam-ma šta yddīlih / iḏa na tkayyast gadana ddī aš-šaxṣ allī kayyasnī / addīlih miyatayn[78] */ ṯalāṯmiyih / miyih wa-xamsīn*[79] */ ḥasb / yaᶜnī kam-ma štayt anā*[80] */ wa-ddī ḥakk al-bārid / addīlih ᶜišrīn ṯalāṯīn / xamsīn*[81] */ mā yigullakš mā hī hāḏā / wallā šī / tiddīlih kam-ma ddayt /*

wa-hākaḏā al-ḥammām fi l-yaman aᶜtagid kullahin hākaḏā ᶜādāt al-yaman / ḍabᶜan gad bih ḥammāmāt jadīdih al-ān[82] */ al-ḥammāmāt al-jadīdi llī bi-fᶜalūhā ḥadīṯih ḏalḥīn gad bi-fᶜalū ḥammām la r-rijāl wa-ḥammām la-n-nisē*[83] */ wa-hāḏā ᶜalā 'asās innū yikūn arbaᶜ wa-ᶜišrīn sāᶜah la-r-rijāl w-arbaᶜ wa-ᶜišrīn sāᶜah la-n-nisē / ḥammām al-bawniyih hāḏā hūh / arbaᶜ wa-ᶜišrīn sāᶜah maftūḥ / ayyi wakt wāḥid yištī yijī yitḥammam jē'*[84] */ mā hūš ġarr awgāt dawām rasmī miᶜayyan wallā šī /*

---

[75] Gemination of *-n* of function word before vowel-initial word. Cf. text 16.

[76] Series of set Islamic greetings (cf. Serjeant and Lewcock 1983: 520).

[77] Universal-conditional-concession clause. Cf. *Syntax* pp. 352-3.

[78] Use of dual with nouns denoting measure (including money, as here). Cf. *Ṣbaḥtū!* p. 93.

[79] Asyndetic linkage of alternative numerical phrases. Cf. *Syntax* p. 312.

[80] Post-position of independent pronoun *anā* to emphasise subject.

[81] Asyndetic linkage of alternative numerical phrases. Cf. *Syntax* p. 312.

[82] Classicism.

[83] Pre-pausal *imāla* raising *-ā* to *-ē*. Cf. also below.

[84] This is a type of universal-conditional-concession structure, hence the use of perfect for the verb in the main clause. Cf. *Syntax* pp. 64-5.

Of course, when you go into the bath-house, I forgot something I should have told you in the beginning. Okay. When you first go into the bath-house, you go in and say, 'Peace be upon you!' They say to you, 'And upon you be peace!' You say, 'Have a pleasant bath!' And they say, 'May God give you the enjoyment of good health!' And you say, 'May God give you and us the enjoyment of good health and happiness!' Then you go in. This is when you first go into the bath-house. Whoever comes in will say this to you, and you will answer him in the same way. When you go out, you will say to them, 'Peace be upon you and the grace [of God] be upon you!' And they will say to you, 'Upon you be peace, and may God give you the enjoyment of good health!' This is the custom.

So, after I have finished putting on my clothes, I go and pay the bath-man for the bath. [I give him] 50 or 100 [riyals], depending on what I want to give him. Of course, it won't be a little. You give however much you want. If I have been cleaned with a bag, then I give some money to the person who cleaned me. I will give him 200, 300 or 150 [riyals], depending on, I mean, however much I want [to give]. I also give for the water-carrier. I give him 20, 30 or 50 [riyals]. He won't say to you, 'What's this?' or anything. You give however much you [are prepared to] give.

This is what the bath-house is like in Yemen. I think that they are all like that according to the customs of Yemen. Of course, there are new bath-houses now [as well]. The new bath-houses that they are doing now they make bath-houses[85] for men and bath-houses for women. This is so that it is 24 hours for men and 24 hours for women. The al-Bawniya bath-house is open for 24 hours. At whatever time you want to bathe, you can go. It isn't just certain official opening hours or whatever.

[85] Singular in Arabic.

al-ḥammāmī lā gadū mistalim / gadū yurgud fi l-ḥammām / wa-yijlis hinayyik ḍūl al-yawm lā hū mustalim / hū walla xūh[86] *wallā man kān / hāḏa l-ḥammām / w-iḥna yiᶜjibna l-ḥammām / al-ḥammām ḥā:lī / yiᶜjibnī 'asīr*[87] *atḥamm:am*[88] */ ayyaḥīnih*[89] */ akṯarat-ma tḥammam gabla-mā xazzin / yimkin kulla yawm / iḏā hū dawr an-niswān asīr lā ḥammām ᶜalī / iḏā hū dawr rijāl fi l-bawniyih*[90] */ ana tḥammam fi l-bawniyih /*

hāḏa l-ḥammām wa-hāḏa l-bawniyih / hāḏā fi l-bawniyih / lākin bayn-atḥākā ᶜan al-bawniyih nagalt la-l-ḥammām / lākin hūw aḥsan / fikrih yaᶜnī wāḥid[91] *bayn-aᶜarrifkum ᶜan al-ḥammāmāt / fi ṣanᶜā 'aw fi l-yaman /*

[86] From *axūh* with initial vowel deletion.

[87] Change of number of subject from first plural to first singular.

[88] Sonorant lengthening in stressed syllable of intonation phrase for emphasis.

[89] Suffixation of *-ih* to add emphasis to the interrogative. Cp. suffixation of *-hā* to demonstrative and locative pronouns and suffixation of *-yih* to words ending in *-ī*.

[90] Cf. *Waṣf* p. 94.

[91] *wāḥid* inserted by mistake.

If the bath-man is in charge of the bath-house, he sleeps at the bath-house and stays there all day, if he is in charge. Either him or his brother or whoever else there is. This is the bath-house. I like the bath-house. The bath-house is really nice. I like to go and bathe whenever. I mainly go and bathe before I chew. This may be every day. If it is the women's turn, I will go to the Ali bath-house. If it is the men's turn in al-Bawniya, I will bathe in al-Bawniya.

That was about the bath-house and that was about al-Bawniya. I was talking about al-Bawniya, then I switched to the bath-house. But it is better this way, I mean I can let you know about the bath-houses in San'a or [and] in Yemen.

18 *Al-baggālāt fi l-bawniyih*

al-baw:niyih / gadī al-bawniyih / al-bawniyih gad fīhā baggālāt hāḏi l-liyyām / mā ᶜādīš ad-dakākīn al-lawwalih hāḏīk ḥagg an-nās al-lawwalīn / gad bih baggālāt jadīdih / ḏalḥīnih / al-baggāl hāḏā bī-bīᶜū fīhā xuḏruh wa-bī-bīᶜū fīhā / ma štayt / mᶜallabāt / jaᶜālih la-l-jahhāl / ma šta l-wāḥid /

ḏabᶜan al-baggālāt hāḏawlā llī mawjūdih fi l-bawniyih al-ān / mā ᶜādūš sāᶜ awwal illī kānū zāgimīn lahin ad-dakākīn ḏawlayyik illī mawjūdīn hinayyik fīhin min aṣḥāb al-bawniyih / gadum nās / muxtalifīn / kulluhum / mir[1] *raymih / wallā min wuṣāb / wallā min tiᶜizz / gadum nās mišum min al-bawniyih / wa-baᶜḏuhum min illī kānū muġtaribīn fi l-xalīj / rijiᶜlih al-yaman / wa-hānā mā ligīš mā yifᶜal / fiᶜillih*[2] *baggālih / wa-mā šā 'allāh bi-yištaġilū / wa-yigṣudu llāh yiddī rizguhum wa-mā biš fīhā šī /*

fa-l-baggālāt hāḏi l-liyyām gadī kull-ma ftaḥ ḥadd dukkān yisammawhā / baggālih / wallā kān min awwal yisammawhā ḥānūt / bih hānāk ḥānūt fi l-bawniyih / ᶜādī nafs al-ḥānūt / ḥakk ibn ᶜāḏuf / ḏayyā 'ibn ᶜāḏuf ḥānūtih[3] *mā yiġallagš*[4] *arbaᶜ wa-ᶜišrīn sāᶜah / mawjūd / fīhā wa-nafs ad-dukkān ḥaggih bugᶜatih / li'annū kān maᶜih dukkān w-abūh dukkān lākin mā hū ma xrajš mā ᶜad bilā hū / min ahl al-bawniyih al-laṣlīyīn / wa-gad bih dukkān hānāk / ṯānī*[5] *li-n-naḥās / bī-bīᶜū fīh an-naḥās / fi l-bawniyih / hāḏā min at-taġīrāt allī ḥaṣalat fi l-bawniyih / bass hāḏā la-l-bawniyih /*

wa-kān bih hānāk fi l-bawniyih barḏū samsarih / ṯānī / yibīᶜū fīhā sawd / as-samsarih hāḏā gad xarrabūhā wa-mā ᶜābiš[6] *allī bī-bīᶜū sawd / gad wasṭahā gad banaw badalhā bināyih jadīdih / wa-l-bināyih hāḏā iftaḥūhā fiᶜilūhā baggālih / hāḏā bugᶜat al-bināyih / hāḏa llī fi l-bawniyih / mā ᶜābiš ḥājih inn aḏakkirhā jadīdih*[7] *agullukum ᶜalayhā / wa-hāḏā ḥikāyat al-bawniyih / wa-mā šā' allāh innanā ddayt mā fi rāsī / wa-lā bih ḥāj ġuluṭṭ wallā: šī sāmiḥūnī /*

---

[1] Total anticipatory assimilation. From *min*.

[2] Reflexive verb. Cf. *Syntax* pp. 202-3. Cf. use of this verb in texts 9, 11, 22, 25, 27.

[3] Use of annexion phrase *ḥānūtih* after *al-ḥānūt ḥakk ibn ᶜāḏuf* for stylistic variation.

[4] Internal passive. Cf. text 7. Cf. *Syntax* pp. 91-2.

[5] Attribute separated from attributed term by locative *hānāk*. Cf. *Syntax* p. 217. Cf. below.

[6] From *mā ᶜād biš* 'there is not'. Note following definite entity.

[7] Attribute separated from attributed term by *inn aḏakkirhā*. Cf. *Syntax* p. 217.

18 Grocer's shops in al-Bawniya

Al-Bawniya is al-Bawniya. There are grocer's shops in al-Bawniya these days. They are no longer the shops of the past belonging to the people of the past. There are new grocer's shops now. In these grocer's shops, they sell vegetables and they sell whatever you want, tinned goods, sweets for children, whatever anyone wants.

Of course, these grocer's shops that are in al-Bawniya now are not like those shops of the past which were owned by the people of al-Bawniya. They are different people. They are all from Rayma or from Wusab or from Ta'izz. They are people who are not from al-Bawniya. Some of them used to be migrant [workers] in the Gulf and came back to Yemen. Here they could find nothing to do, so they got themselves a grocery shop. Goodness, they really do work! They earn their living [by working hard] and God blesses them. There is nothing wrong with that.

The grocer's shops nowadays, whenever someone opens a shop they call it a grocer's shop [*baggālih*]. In the past, they used to call them *ḥānūt*s [shops]. There is a shop [*ḥānūt*] there in al-Bawniya. It is the same shop belonging to Ibn Atuf. That shop of Ibn Atuf's doesn't close [once] in twenty-four hours. It is there and it occupies the same spot as it always did, because he had a shop [there] and his father [also had] a shop, but he did not leave. Now he is the only one left of the original people from al-Bawniya. There is another shop there for copper where they sell copper in al-Bawniya. This is one of the changes which has taken place in al-Bawniya. This is all there is about al-Bawniya.

There was also another caravanserai there in al-Bawniya where charcoal was sold. They demolished that caravanserai and there is no longer anywhere where charcoal is sold. In the middle of it, they have put up a new building in its place, and this new building they opened and made into a grocer's shop. This is the site of the building. So this is about al-Bawniya. There isn't anything else new that I can tell you about. This is the story of al-Bawniya. I have given [you] what is in my head. If I have made any mistake or whatever, forgive me.

19 *Al-ᶜādāt al-awwalih*

al-laylih al-misaḥbalih

hāḏā[1] *yā tīm / law-mā jīt lā ᶜindak / bi-tgullī: / ant wa-jānīt ᶜan al-laylih al-misaḥbalih / anā mā kuntš dārī mā hī al-laylih al-musaḥbalih aw al-lism jālī fujᶜah hākaḏā / al-laylih al-misaḥbalih / law-mā sa'alt abī / w-innū*[2] *bi-šraḥlī mā hī al-laylih al-misaḥbalih / fa-*[3]*fhimt mā bi-tugṣud ant / aw kunt gad nisīt al-lism anā ba-ḏ̣-ḏ̣abṭ / al-laylih al-misaḥbalih / hāḏā hī yawm al-ᶜīd / baᶜd šahr ramaḏ̣ān /*

ḏ̣abᶜan šahr ramaḏ̣ān hū bī-jī šahr / kāmil / wa-n-nās fi š-šahr hāḏā mitᶜawwadīn ᶜala s-sahar / ḏ̣ūl al-layl / yurgudū fajr / wa-fajr yijissū rāgidīn lā: nuṣṣ aṣ-ṣubḥ law-mā yisīru l-waḏ̣āyuf wallā lā baᶜd aḏ̣-ḏ̣uhr / kulla wāḥid ᶜalā ḏ̣abīᶜatuh / allī maᶜih waḏ̣īfuh[4] *gadū bī-bakkir w-allī mā biš maᶜih waḏ̣īfuh gadū bī-wāṣul an-nawm / law-mā yigūm yiṣallī /*

fa-l-laylih al-misaḥbalih / hī: yawm al-ᶜīd aw laylat al-ᶜīd / li'ann al-wāḥid kān laylat al-ᶜīd gadū ᶜādū ramaḏ̣ān kān sāmir / sāhir[5] */ malān naw:m / mā ragatš*[6] *al-ᶜašī li'annū / ᶜādū ṣāḥī*[7] */ fa-bī-jī / al-yawm aṯ-ṯānī wa-ᶜādū ṣāḥī*[8] */ yawm al-ᶜīd maṯalan*[9] *bī-jī wa-hū ṣāḥī tāᶜib / yaᶜnī mā yugaḏḏī mašāwīrih illā w-hū tāᶜib / murhag / yijī al-ᶜašī*[10] *wa-gadū tā:ᶜib / wa-hāḏā at-taᶜab / min kuṯrat-mā kān sāhir ḏ̣ūl al-layl / al-laylih al-lawwalih wa-l-yawm aṯ-ṯānī yištī yizūr al-makālif wa-ysīr yiᶜayyid wa-yisīr / yizūr aṣḥābuh wa-ṣdugā'uh*[11] *wa-baᶜd al-ġadā mā yustirš yurgud li'ann yištī yixazzin / hāh mā ᶜa-ysbirš yurgud wa-hū mā xazzanš /*

---

1 Use of demonstrative pronoun to indicate introduction of new subject.

2 Presentational particle. Cf. *Syntax* p. 425.

3 Consequential and sequential use of *fa-*. Cf. *Syntax* pp. 299-300. Cf. further examples of consequential and/or sequential *fa-* below.

4 Exophoric pronominal use of definite clause. Cf. *Syntax* pp. 416-17. Cf. also below.

5 Reformulative apposition of near-synonymic adjectives. Cf. *Syntax* p. 245.

6 Anticipatory devoicing of *d* to *t*.

7 'He had just woken up'.

8 'He is still awake'.

9 *maṯalan* used here as filler.

10 Verbal clause with inanimate subject.

11 Synonym of *aṣḥābuh*.

19 Lost customs

al-laylih al-misaḥbalih[12]

Tim, when I came to your house, you and Janet mentioned to me *al-laylih al-misaḥbalih*. I didn't know what this *al-laylih al-misaḥbalih* was and the name *al-laylih al-misaḥbalih* came as a surprise, then I asked my father and he explained to me what *al-laylih al-misaḥbalih* was. Then I understood what you meant even though I had forgotten the actual name. *al-laylih al-misaḥbalih*, this is the day of the festival after the month of Ramadan.

Of course, Ramadan is a complete month and during this month people are used to staying awake all night then sleeping at dawn. From dawn, they stay asleep until mid-morning when they go to work, or until the afternoon. Everyone according to their own nature: those who have a job [to do] get up early, and those who do not have a job continue sleeping until they get up to pray.

So, *al-laylih al-misaḥbalih* is the day of the festival, or [rather] the eve of the festival because the eve of the festival is still Ramadan and people will still be awake and full of sleep. They will not have gone to sleep in the evening because they will have only just woken up, so the next day comes and they are still awake. The day of the festival comes and they are still awake and tired. They go about their business when they are absolutely exhausted. The evening comes and they are tired. This tiredness [comes] from staying up all night on the first night. The next day they want to visit their women relatives and go and celebrate the festival and go to visit their friends. After lunch, they can't sleep because they want to chew. Okay? You can't sleep when you haven't yet chewed.

---

12 This description of *al-laylih al-misaḥbalih* differs from that of al-Ḥawālī in *Ṣafḥatun min Tārīxi al-Yamani al-Ijtimāʿī*. al-Ḥawālī describes *al-laylih al-misaḥbalih* (*laylat al-musaḥbalih*) as the second night after Ramadan [eve of the second of Shawwal], so called because *jāriyat al-bayt*, a benign jinni, *tusaḥbil* [drags] people from room to room, but they are so dead to the world that they don't wake up. It is also called *laylat al-yatīma* (al-Ḥawālī vol. 2, 121). According to Muhammad Abduh Ways of the silver market, people are taken by the jinni to the place of their birth. Until the time of the Revolution (1962), M. A. Ways says parents would carry their children to another room in the house after they had fallen asleep and in the morning claim they had been taken there by *jāriyat al-bayt*.

hāḏā[13] *akṯar an-nās yif^{c}alū hākaḏā wa-gadū ^{c}īd / mijābirih midrī māhū / f-tjī laylat al-^{c}īd*[14] *wa-l-wāḥid ^{c}ādū tā^{c}ib / bi-tsalḥab salḥabih / hāh / ya^{c}nī mā bi-yuxṭāš illā w-hū tā^{c}ib wa-hāḏā f-hī ysammawhā al-laylih al-misaḥbalih / hāḏā al-misaḥbalih / hāḏa l-kalimih an-nās gad nisiyūhā / mā ^{c}ād bī-staxdimūhāš al-ān ya^{c}nī mā ^{c}ād aḥadd bi-ḏkurhā hāḏa l-kalimih / lākin yisammawhā minn awwal al-laylih al-misaḥbalih bi-hāḏa l-uslūb / ḏaḥḥīn an-nās gad nisiyū / mā ^{c}ād yifakkirūš /*

hāḏā[15] *wa-^{c}ād bih kalimih ṯānīyih ḥakk al-wald / aṭ-ṭufl ^{c}inda-mā yūlad / wa-midrī māhū kān minn awwal yiddawhin ḏawlay al-iṯnayn lākin gad an-nās nisiyūhin / ḥakk awwal innū kān aṭ-ṭufl / awwal-mā tūlidih umm^{w}ih aw midrī māhū / ^{c}ādī bi-tuxṭā bi-l-magāmuḍ ḥakkih / wa-tlāḥigih wa-tmassiḥlih / wa-tġassilih wa-midrī māhū / law-mā: tūfī / wa-mā ^{c}ābiš ḏawlayyik wa-^{c}ādī jālisih ġayr bug^{c}athā wa-ḏawlayyik bi-ddawhin lā ^{c}indahā / tijirr ḥan*[16] *tūfī ḥakkaha l-wilād*[17] *tijirr turbuṭ ḏawlayyik al-ladāh ḥakkahā / ḥakk al-ṭufl u-midrī māhū / hāḏā ġarr min al-xurrāfāt aw min al-kalām yitkallamū ^{c}alayh an-nās / turbuṭhun kullahin / wa-tirjumhin / nisīt b-ismahā yisammūhā hāḏā al-^{c}ādih / illā lhā 'ism lākin anā māš dārī mā yisammaw al-^{c}ādih hāḏā / al-midrī /*

al-muhimm / hāḏa ṯ-ṯintayn hāḏawlā gad nisiyūhā an-nās min al-^{c}ādāt[18] *illī kān yi^{c}malūhin / al-laylih al-musaḥbilih mā ^{c}ād bi-ḏkurūš al-laylih al-musaḥbilih mā hum bi-ḏkurū 'illum*[19] *tā^{c}ibīn wa-midrī māhū lākin gadī tayyi l-kalimatayn / hāḏa llī 'anā fāhim ^{c}annahā / iḏā ^{c}ād bih ḥājih ṯāniyih māniš dārī bihā 'allāh a^{c}lam / fa-l-wāḥid / hānā kānayn bih ašyā yi^{c}rifhin gad tġayyarat / ^{c}ammā kānat zamān /*

---

[13] The demonstrative refers back to the preceding discussion. Cf. *Syntax* pp. 382-4.

[14] Verbal clause with inanimate subject. Cf. above.

[15] Use of demonstrative pronoun to signal introduction of new subject. Cf. above.

[16] From *ḥīn*.

[17] Inversion of attributed term–attribute. Cf. *Syntax* p. 224.

[18] Prepositional attribute *min al-^{c}ādāt* separated from attributed term by verb phrase.

[19] Simplification. From *illā 'innahum*.

Most people do this when it is the festival, visiting each other and whatever else, and then the evening of the festival comes and they are still tired. They just drag themselves around. Okay? I mean, they walk and they are really tired so they call this *al-laylih al-misaḥbalih*. This *misaḥbalih,* this word, people have forgotten it. They no longer use it now and no one can remember this word any more, but in the past they used to call it *al-laylih al-misaḥbalih* in this way. Now people have forgotten [it] and no longer think [of it].

There is another word used for babies. When a child is born. They used to use these two [terms] in the past, but now people have forgotten them. In the past, the child, when his mother had first given birth to him and whatever, she would walk around with his swaddling bands and go after him, wipe up after him and wash him and I don't know what until she had finished.[20] This no longer happens. She just stays in her place and they bring [things] to her.[21] She would take, when she had finished her birth period, she would take those things of hers and those for the baby and bind them up. This is just one of the folk customs or one of the sorts of things people talk about. She would bind them all up and throw them away. I have forgotten what they call this custom. It does have a name, but I don't know what they call this custom. I don't know.

Anyway, people have forgotten about these two customs which they used to follow: *al-laylih al-musaḥbalih,* they no longer remember *al-laylih al-musaḥbalih*, they just think that they are exhausted and I don't know what, but it is these two words. This is what I understand about them. If there is anything else then I don't know about it, God knows best. Here there used to be things [people] knew about, but they have changed from how they were in the past.

---

[20] i.e. until she has finished the forty-day period after birth.

[21] i.e. the women in the house help the new mother.

al-jahhāl fī ramaḍān

kān zamān / an-nās ^{c}alā busāḍathum wa-hāḏā / yiddaw amṯilih yiddaw ḥājāt / yitkallamū ^{c}annahā ašyā kaṯīrih / ḏaḥḥīn gad tġayyarat al-lumūr / fa-maṯalan fī ramaḍān law tšūfī ramaḍān / mā kān yijī ramaḍān li-l-jahhāl az-zuġār / illā bi-farḥah hākaḏāhā[22] / limih / ^{c}alā 'asās ^{c}a-ysīrū yimassaw / wa-l-masā hāḏā / hū ba^{c}d al-faḍūr / al-^{c}ašī / al-jahhāl az-zuġār / ba^{c}d al-faḍūr / mā yif^{c}alū / yisīrū yimassaw / hāḏā yisammā[23] al-masā / fa-l-masā hāḏā yisīrū lā ^{c}ind agāribhum aw al-jīrān ḥakkuhum / yištama^{c}ū[24] ṯalāṯih arba^{c}ah xamsih / lākin hī mā ^{c}ābiš hāḏa l-^{c}ādih bass ġarr anā bayn-aḏkurhā min zamān /

al-masā yisīrū / lā ^{c}ind al-bayt / ḥagg maṯalan / baythum / bayt wāḥid min al-jahhāl wa-ṯ-ṯānī xubratih / yiduggu l-bāb wa-yiṣayyuḥū / yā masā jīt amassī ^{c}indukum / wa-xubratih yiṣayyuḥū illī ma^{c}ih yigūlū limih limih / yā masā as^{c}ad allāh hal-masā / wa-hāḏawlā yijāwibū / limih limih / yā masā / gad lanā xayrāt fī bābukum limih limih / wa-yijissū yiddaw hāḏa l-lanāšīd al-gadīmih /

wa-ḏawlayyik ahl al-bayt bi-sma^{c}ū / mā kān biš taliviziyūn yišġalhum wa-yiddaw ḥagg al-latfāl wa-hāḏā / mā kān biš hāḏawlā kānu l-jahhāl yif^{c}alū hākaḏā wa-ḏayyik mixazzin / ṣāḥub al-bayt illī bī-massaw bābih / iḏā mā jāwabš mā yigūlu l-jahhāl / ḥarrig w-inḍug māšī xirīnā bāb al-bayt / hū ḏik sā^{c} yisma^{c} al-kalimih hāḏīk / gadū yirbuṭluhum bugših wallā bugšatayn wallā / hāḏā minn awwal / wallā xamsih bugaš wallā riyāl / ma^{c}nā ḥarrig w-unḍug innak tjirr hāḏā illī ^{c}a-ddīlanā[25] / w-if^{c}al gurṭāṣ ḥarrikhā[26] / w-irjumhālanā ^{c}alā mayd nidrā ayn ^{c}a-dinka^{c} / hāḏā ^{c}ādat al-masā / al-lawwalih / hāḏa l-liyyām mā ^{c}ābiš ḥagg al-masā hāḏā / gad al-jahhāl ġarr yitimmū ġarr yitġaddaw / aw yit^{c}aššaw / yiḥmilū ḥamlih yibsiru t-taliviziyūn / yibsirū ḥagg al-latfāl /

---

[22] Suffixation of *-hā* to emphasise indefinite demonstrative. Cf. texts 4, 9, 11, etc..

[23] Internal passive. Cf. text 7. Cf. *Syntax* pp. 91-2.

[24] Anticipatory devoicing of *j* before *t*.

[25] Elision of *t* of subject pronoun.

[26] Anticipatory devoicing of *g* to *k*.

Children in Ramadan

In the past, people used to do things simply. They would recite proverbs and talk about things, they would talk about things a lot. Now things have changed. So, during Ramadan, for instance, if you consider Ramadan. The children used to really look forward to Ramadan. Why? Because they would go and play *al-masā*.[27] This *al-masā* would be after breaking the fast in the evening. Young children, after breaking the fast, what would they do? They would go and play *al-masā*. This was called *al-masā*. For [the game] *al-masā*, they would go to their relatives or their neighbours. Three, four or five of them would get together. But there is no longer this custom, it is just that I can [still] remember it from the past.

For [the game] *al-masā*, they would go to someone's house, maybe their own house, the house of one of the children and the others would be his mates. They would knock at the door and cry out, '*Yā masā,* I have come to play *yā masā* at your house!' and his mates who were with him would shout out and say, 'Why! Why!' [He would say,] '*Yā masā*, may God bless this evening!' and the others would answer, 'Why! Why!' [He would say,] '*Yā masā*! We have been at your door for a long time!' 'Why! Why!' And they would keep on singing these old chants.

The people of the house would listen. There was no television to occupy them with children's programmes and the like. There was none of this. The children would do this while the person whose door they were singing at would be chewing. If he didn't answer, what would the children say? 'Light and throw, or we'll shit at your door!' Then he would hear what was said and wrap them up a coin or two. This was in the past – or five coins or a riyal. The meaning of 'Light and throw!' is fetch that which you are going to give us and put [it] in a bag, set it alight, and throw it for us so that we know where it is going to fall. This is the old custom of *al-masā*. These days, you no longer get *al-masā*. The children just finish having lunch or supper. Then they rush to watch television. They watch the children's programmes.

[27] AS points out that *al-masā* is similar to Halloween game of 'Trick or treat'. In al-Ḥawālī's description of this tradition, children usu. given piece of *malūj* or money. If they were given *malūj*, they would sell it in the bread market and buy sweets (al-Ḥawālī vol. 2, 113).

tammat ḥakk al-latfāl xarajū aš-šāriᶜ / jarrū yilᶜabū zurgayf wallā yilᶜabū rabal[28] / *wallā 'ayyi ḥāj*[29] /

ḏaḥḥīn gad maᶜānā hāḏi l-liyyām maᶜānā l-badal / wa-hāḏa l-badal bih / bī-bīᶜū šibz[30] / *šibz fī garāṭīṣ zuġayrih bi-ᶜišrīn riyāl ġālī bi-ḏ̣hakū ᶜala l-jahhāl / yifᶜalū fīhā ka-ḏayyahā ḥājih liᶜbih mudawwirih / argām / min wāḥid / lā miyih / ḍabᶜan fī kulla wāḥid gurṭāṣ yištaraw šibz bi-lgā wāḥid min hāḏā ḥakk al-badal / wa-hāḏā ḥakk al-badal ᶜalā sās innum ᶜa-yddaw jawāyiz / yištīlak tištarī miyat šibz al-wāḥid bi-ᶜišrīn / kam jahd al-jāhil yijiss yiwātī fa-yirjaᶜ yisīr yiddawlih jawāyiz* /

fa-ᶜindanā hānā l-jahhāl bi-lᶜabūbihin hāḏawlā / baynathum al-bayn / kulla wāḥid yiḍraḥ ḥakkih al-badal / lā šī wāḥid ṣāḥubuh[31] *yiḍraḥ badal wa-ḏayyik yiḍraḥ al-badal / wa-yixalfaᶜūhin man ᶜa-yxallī 'innin yigtalibayn / la ktalabayn yigmaših yaᶜnī 'innahū yišillahinlih / wa-yigmaš yaᶜnī yišillahinlih illī gallabhin / lā ma gdirš yilᶜab ṣāḥubuh / wa-man gimišhin šallahinlih*[32] /

hāḏa l-liᶜibāt illī bi-lᶜabū[33] *al-jahhāl / yijissū ġayr yitṣayyaḥū / ḥakkī / gāl ḥakkī / anā ġalabtak / gāl anā gimišthin / gāl anā / hāḏa llī bi-lᶜabū*[34] / *mā ᶜād biš sāᶜ awwal / al-misā hāḏāk wa-l-ḥalā wa-l-hāḏā / wallā yilᶜabū mulāḥagih wallā yilᶜabū rakḍ / tirtī / ayyi ḥāj gadum ġayr yilᶜabū hāḏa l-jahhāl hāḏa l-liyyām / hāḏa l-jahhāl az-zuġār / wa-l-kibār gadum ġarr yisīr*[35] *yixazzinū / wallā yilwaw / wa-ramaḍān hāḏā hū ramaḍān šahr al-xayr / wa-l-barakih* /

---

28 The use of the perfect in these asyndetically linked subordinate and main clauses is due to following (main) clause depending on fulfillment of action mentioned in initial clause and hence to *if ... then* nature of the sentence. Cf. *Syntax* p. 64-5. Cf. texts 8 and 22. Asyndetic linkage enhances a sense of speed in the narration. Cf. *Syntax* p. 306.

29 Underarticulation. From *ḥājih*.

30 Loan word. From *chips*.

31 Cf. *Syntax* p. 241 (cf. also Mörth 1997: 129-30 for use of *wāḥid* + noun with possessive pronoun in modern Arabic dialects).

32 Note the use of the perfect in the main clause to a universal-conditional-concession clause. Cf. *Syntax* p. 64-5. Cf. above.

33 Lack of anaphoric pronoun in attributive clause. Cf. *Syntax* pp. 234-5.

34 Lack of anaphoric pronoun in attributive clause. Cf. above.

35 Lack of number agreement on translocative verb.

When the children's [programmes] have finished, they go out into the street and start playing marbles or rubber bands or anything.

Now we have swaps these days. Swaps involves them selling crisps, crisps in small paper bags for twenty riyals – [it is] expensive, they cheat the children. They put a small round toy[36] in the bags with numbers from one to a hundred. Of course, in every one of the bags they buy crisps in they find one of these swaps. They have these swaps so that they can give out prizes. They want you to buy a hundred packets of crisps for twenty [riyals] each. What a lot of trouble for the child to keep on collecting [these swaps], then going back for them to give him prizes.

Here the children play with these among themselves. Each one puts his own swaps down. If one of his friends puts down a swap, he puts down a swap, and they [try to] flip them over; whoever is able to get them to flip over, if they are turned over, wins them, which means that he takes them for himself. *yigmaš* means that he takes those he has turned over. If he isn't able [to do this] his friend plays, and whoever wins them takes them for himself.

These are games which the children play. They keep on shouting, 'Mine!' [The other] says, 'Mine! I beat you!' [The other] says, 'I won them!' He says, 'Me!' This is what they play. It is not like the old days with *al-masā* and the pleasant things and that. Or they might play chase or kicking [*tirtī*]. Children will play anything these days. This is [just] the young children. The older ones just go and chew or wander around. Ramadan is Ramadan, the month of goodness and blessing.

---

[36] This small round toy which I translate here as 'swaps' probably corresponds to pogs used in Britain and found in crisp packets in the late nineties.

20 *Al-li^{c}ibāt ḥagg al-aṭfāl*

az-zurgayf

ḏā:ḥḥī:n ša-ktuble:š[1] *mā ma^{c}nā hāḏawlahā / gultī / tištay yā jānīt mā ma^{c}nā zurgayf / az-zurgayf / hāḏawlā hin li^{c}bih / yil^{c}abūbihin al-juhhāl az-zuġār / ḍab^{c}an bī-bī^{c}ūhin fi d-dakākīn / sā^c al-kurah*[2] */ li^{c}ab zuġār / zijāj zuġār / hin sā^c al-kurah / yijissū yil^{c}abū / yištarawhin al-jahhāl*[3] *wa-ba^{c}dā yil^{c}abū / al-li^{c}bi llī yil^{c}abūhā / maṯalan yil^{c}abū 'iṯnayn / yištaw yil^{c}abū / hāḏāk ma^{c}ih zurgayf / wa-hāḏāk ma^{c}ih zurgayf / maṯalan nigūl hayya ^{c}a-dlā^{c}ibnī / gāl hayy / min xamsih / gāl min xamsih / ḏayyik yiḍraḥ xamsih / wa-ḏayyik yiḍraḥ xamsih zurgayf / wa-yuḍruḥūhun wasṭ ad-dāyirih / dāyirih bi-masāfih / ya^{c}nī ^{c}alā gadr az-zurgayf ^{c}alā sās innahin yintašrayn*[4] */ yirjimūhin wasṭ ad-dāyirih mā yuxrujanš*[5] */ iḏā xaraj min ad-dāyirih / yuḥrum*[6] *yil^{c}ab aṯ-ṯānī /*

fa-[7]*l-li^{c}bih hāḏā yindišūhin*[8] */ ya^{c}nī yindišūhin / yinširūhin wa-yisīrū / yil^{c}abū min masāfat kam mitr / yijirr al-lā^{c}ib ḏayyik / bi-yadih hākaḏā yakfa^c*[9] */ miš yurjumih / b-aṣābu^{c}uh zayy illī bi-rkuḏū az-zurgayfī / wa-z-zurgayfī ysīr lā ^{c}ind az-zurgayfī / iḏā kfa^c wāḥid miš xayrāt / wa-xarajayn al-iṯnayn zayy al-makfa^c / w-allaḏī yikfa^c / yu^{c}tabar*[10] *gimišhin / iḏa gfa^c iṯnayn yu^{c}tabar kušš*[11] */ wa-hākaḏā yil^{c}abū min iṯnayn / min xamsih / min ^{c}ašarih / wallā yijirrū ġurgih / yil^{c}abū fīhā / ġurgih ba^{c}īdih wa-yil^{c}abū min ba^{c}īd / yirmawhā lā ^{c}ind al-ġurgih / lā daxal al-ġurgih / yil^{c}ab aṯ-ṯānī / wa-'ayn-mā ḍaraḥ ḏayyik az-zurgayfī yil^{c}abū min tayyik al-masāfih / law-mā 'āxir wāḥid hū 'allī gimiš / wa-yišillahinlih / hāḏa z-zurgayf /*

---

[1] Vowel lengthening and lowering due to hesitation. From *ša-ktubliš*. AS tells me he should have said *ša-tḥākāliš* 'I am going to talk to you'.

[2] Predicandless predicate. Cf. *Syntax* p. 124.

[3] Verbal clause with dynamic verb.

[4] Syncope. From *yintaširayn*.

[5] Asyndetic linkage of consequential clause. Cf. *Syntax* p. 311.

[6] Internal passive. Cf. text 7. Cf. *Syntax* pp. 91-2.

[7] Consequential use of *fa-*. Cf. *Syntax* pp. 299-300.

[8] According to AS, this verb is used only for games.

[9] Assimilatory devoicing of *g* to *k*.

[10] Internal passive. Cf. text 7. Cf. *Syntax* pp. 91-2.

[11] Loan word. From Persian *kish* 'check' (in chess). In SA, it is also used in chess.

20 Children's games

Marbles

Now I'm going to tell you what these [things] mean. Janet, you said that you wanted the meaning of *zurgayf* [marbles]. Marbles are a toy which young children play with. Of course, they sell them in the shops. [They are] like balls, small toys, small bits of glass. They are like balls. They sit and play. The children buy them and then they play. The game they play, for example, when they play, two want to play. One of them has [some] marbles and the other has marbles. For example, we would say, 'Come on, will you play with me!' [One] says, 'Yes, for five!' [The other] says, 'For five!' One puts down five, and the other puts down five marbles. They put them in the middle of the circle – a circle a little distance away – depending on [how many] marbles there are so that they scatter. They throw them into the circle so that they don't go out. If [one of them] goes out of the circle, [that player] is out[12] and the next one plays.

For this game, they spread them[13] out, I mean they spread them out. They spread them out and go and play from a distance of a few metres. One player takes hold of [one marble] like this in his hand and strikes. He doesn't throw it, he flicks the marble with his fingers. The [one] marble goes to the [other] marble. If he strikes one, not a lot, and both go out – the marble he hit with and the one he managed to hit – it is said that he wins them. If he hits two, it is considered a foul throw.[14] In this way, they play either for two, or five, or ten, or they make a hole which they play into, a hole which is far away and they play from a distance. They throw them[15] into the hole. If they go into the hole, the next one plays. Wherever that marble falls, they play from that distance. The last one[16] wins and he takes them for himself. That is marbles.

---

[12] i.e. misses a turn.

[13] i.e. the marbles.

[14] i.e. and the other ones takes his turn.

[15] i.e. the marbles.

[16] i.e. the one who puts the last marble into the hole.

al-gufaygif

wa-l-gufaygif / hāḏa l-li^{c}bi ṯāniyih / li^{c}bih yijirrū kurah / kān min awwal yif^{c}alu l-kurah mā kān biš kurāt zuġār / kān[17] *yijirrū šarābih / hāḏa š-šarābāt allī yilbasūhin / yidaxxilū wasṭahā xirag wallā mā kān*[18] */ wa-^{c}aṭṭafūhō*[19] */ wa-fi^{c}ilūhā sā^{c} kurah / yisīr wāḥid / yisannib hākaḏā / wa-hū mugaffī / wa-ṯ-ṯāniyīn gafāh kulluhum / wa-hū yiṣīḥ gufaygif / wa-ḏayyik yigūl mustalgif allī warāh*[20] */ wa-hū yirjum al-kurah / lā zigimūhā / ḏayyik yiṯnī / lā mā zigimūhāš tijiss bug^{c}athā / wa-ba^{c}dā ḏayy allī rajamhā / yisīr yilāḥighum / yilāḥig hāḏa llī hū bi-l^{c}abū m^{c}ih / wa-yigfa^{c} bi-l-kurah / iḏā gfa^{c}hum bi-l-kurah / man wuga^{c}at fīh / yuḥrum / wa-yiḍla^{c} badalih / wa-hākaḏa l-li^{c}bah ḥagg al-gufaygif /*

aš-šibrīzih

wa-š-šibrīzih / hāḏa l-li^{c}bi ṯ-ṯāliṯih / aš-šibrīzih mā hāḏawlā kulluhin nil^{c}ab miṯl al-gufaygif wa-š-šibrīzih mā ^{c}ad bi-l^{c}abūhinš / maṯalan aš-šibrīzih hāḏā / kayf yil^{c}abūhā[21] */ yiḍraḥ rijl fawg rijl / wāḥid yijlis / wa-yiḍraḥ rijl fawg rijl / wa-ba^{c}d ar-rijl yiṭla^{c} yad wa-yifrid al-yad hākaḏā / wa-ba^{c}dayn yiḍraḥ al-yad aṯ-ṯānī wa-yifrithā*[22] */ wa-ḏawlayyik illī bi-l^{c}abū ma^{c}ih / yinuṭṭū / min fawg aydiyih / law dakamū yadih / yu^{c}tabar ḥurimū*[23] */ lā mā dakamūš / yuwāṣul al-li^{c}bih / wa-ḏayyik yib^{c}id yad / wa-yinuṭṭū min jadīd / f-iḏā dakamū yadih / yiḥram / wa-yijiss ḏayyik makān illī dakam yadih / lā mā dakamš yadih / yib^{c}id al-yad aṯ-ṯāniyih / wa-ba^{c}dā 'arjilih / wa-yinuṭṭū fawg arjilih / wa-'in dakamū rijlih / yil^{c}ab illī dakam yijiss bug^{c}atih / wa-hākaḏā law-mā tinthī āxir rijl / wa-yiṯnī min jadīd ḏayyik*[24] */ hāḏa š-šibrīzih /*

[17] Lack of number agreement on the linking verb. Cf. *Syntax* pp. 154ff.

[18] Universal-conditional-concession clause. Cf. *Syntax* p. 353.

[19] *Imāla* accompanied by labialisation due to the preceding emphatic *ṭ*.

[20] Attributive clause separated from attributed term by verb phrase *yigūl mustalgif*.

[21] Rhetorical question.

[22] Anticipatory devoicing of *d* to *t*.

[23] Internal passive. Cf. text 7. Cf. *Syntax* pp. 91-2.

[24] *ḏayyik* functions here as afterthought, or tail (Dahlgren 1998: 36), outside the predication.

Gufaygif[25]

Gufaygif, this is the second game. A game where they take a ball. In the past, they used to make a ball – there weren't any small balls [then]. They would take a sock, the socks which they wear, and put rags or whatever there was into it, close it up, and make it like a ball. One goes and stands like that with his back turned. The others are all behind him, and he shouts, '*Gufaygif!*' The one[s] behind him call, '*Mustalgif!*'[26] and then he throws the ball. If they catch it, the one [who threw it] plays again. If they don't manage to catch it, it stays where it is.[27] Then, the one who threw it goes and chases them.[28] He chases those who are playing with him and hits [them] with the ball. If he hits them with the ball, whoever it lands on is out and takes his place. That is what the game of *gufaygif* is like.

Porcupine[29]

Porcupine, this is the third game. Porcupine, all of these we used to play, such as *gufaygif* and porcupine, but they don't play them anymore. For example, this porcupine, how do they play it? You put one leg on top of the other. One [person] sits down and puts one leg on top of the other. After the leg, he puts up a hand and extends the [fingers of his] hand like that. Then he puts the second hand on [the first] and extends it, and those who are playing with him jump over his hands. If they strike his hand, they are out. If they don't strike [it], [the one who is sitting] continues the game. He removes a hand, and they jump again. If they strike his hand, [the one who strikes it] is out and takes the place of the one whose hand he hit. If he doesn't strike his hand, [the one who is sitting] removes the other hand and then his legs, and they jump over his legs. If they strike his leg the one who struck takes his place, and [the game] is like that until the last leg, then that one does it again. That is porcupine.

---

25 Also described by Husayn al-Amri in Serjeant and Lewcock (1983: 525).

26 i.e. ready to catch!

27 i.e. the ball stays where it landed.

28 i.e. the others.

29 Also described by Husayn al-Amri in Serjeant and Lewcock (1983: 527).

at-tirtī

tištay nisajjil ᶜan at-tirtī / aw al-liᶜabāt fī l-yaman minnaha t-tirtī / at-tirtī hāḏā hū liᶜbih kun[30] *nilᶜabhā wa-ᶜād iḥna zuġār / kayf kunnā nilᶜabhā / kunnā nijirr iḥna*[31] *majmūᶜatayn niktisim*[32] *majmūᶜatayn*[33] */ wa-l-majmūᶜatayn hāḏā yaᶜnī yilᶜabū tirtī / at-tirtī hī rakḏ / yaᶜnī 'ayš*[34] *rakḏ inn iḥna nitrākaḏ / al-murākaḏuh hāḏā tijī / inna kulla wāḥid yirkaḏ bi-rijlih / allī hū min al-majmūᶜah aṯ-ṯāniyih / yirkuḏuh kayf-mā rakaḏuh*[35] *yaᶜnī / al-muhimm innū yirkuḏuh bi-gafāh / miš yirkuḏuh hākaḏā bi-tijāhah / sāᶜ-mā ḥīn yurkuḏ al-kurāh / māšī / yurkuḏuh ᶜalā gafāh / yijirr rijlih wa-yurkuḏuh sāᶜ-mā yurkuḏ al-ḥimār hākaḏā bi-rijlih / yirfis al-ḥimār*[36] */*

al-muimm[37] *inn iḥna nitrākaḏ / wayn-mā wugaᶜat*[38] *wugaᶜat fī l-wāḥid / yaᶜnī mā ᶜād nibālīš / inn iḥna nūjaᶜ aṯ-ṯānī wallā šī māšī / gadū nitrākaḏ murākaḏuh / kayf-ma wgaᶜ tūgaᶜ / fī wašših fī fummih fī lukfih fayn-mā wgaᶜat / ahamma šī 'innī tūgaᶜ rakḏuh / fī jism al-wāḥid sawā / muᶜawwaḏuh / wa-hāḏa r-rakḏ / baᶜḏ al-aḥyān bi-t'aṯṯar bi-nt'aṯṯar minnahā lākin mā bi-nḥuss*[39] */ ᶜād iḥna zuġār / nitrākaḏ / murākaḏuh xabīṯih / wa-hāḏa t-tirtī / mā ᶜād bi-lᶜabūhāš hāḏa l-iyyām / gad al-jahhāl nisiyūhā /*

baᶜḏuhum bi-yilᶜabū / aḏkur ann ibnī kān yilᶜab w-anā kunt aṣayyuḥ fawgih li'annī liᶜbih šūᶜah / yaᶜnī bayn-aḥissalahā al-ān / min awwal mā kunnāš niḥissahā hāḏā zayy-mā 'ibnī ḏalḥīn mā bī-ḥiss / al-muhimm yilᶜab / yurkuḏūh yurkuḏhum / al-muhimm innahū bī-ḥiss innahā mutᶜah / li'annī 'aḏkur anā min awwal innū / kun[40] *nilᶜab /*

---

30 Simplification. From *kunnā nilᶜabhā*.

31 Post-position of independent pronoun *iḥna* to emphasise subject. Cf. *Syntax* p. 251.

32 Anticipatory devoicing of *g* to *k*.

33 Adverbial noun complement. Cf. *Syntax* pp. 144-5.

34 Use of pan-Yemeni *ayš*.

35 Universal-conditional-concession clause. Cf. *Syntax* pp. 351-4.

36 Reformulative apposition of verb phrases. Cf. *Syntax* p. 245.

37 Underarticulation of *h*. From *al-muhimm*.

38 Universal-conditional-concession clause. Cf. *Syntax* p. 352.

39 Degemination of *ss* to *s* before negative suffix *-š* (cf. Watson 1999b: 504). Cf. also below.

40 Simplification. From *kunnā nilᶜabhā*.

Tirtī

You want us to record about *tirtī* or the games in Yemen including *tirtī*. This *tirtī* is a game which we used to play when we were young. How did we used to play it? We used to take two teams. We would divide up into two teams, and these two teams would play *tirtī*. *Tirtī* is kicking. That means what, kicking, we would kick each other. This kicking [game] would involve everyone kicking with their leg those who were from the other team. He would kick him however. The important thing was that he kicked out at him behind, and not that he kicked out at him like that in front as you do when you kick a ball. No. He would kick out at him behind. He would get his leg and kick him like donkeys[41] kick with their hindlegs. [Like] donkeys[42] kick.

Anyway, we would kick each other wherever it[43] landed on the person. We didn't care whether we hurt the other [person] or whatever, no. We would kick each other wherever: in his face, in his mouth, in his mouth, wherever [the kick] landed. The most important thing was that it was a proper kick on the body of the other person. Sometimes this kicking would affect us, we would be hurt by it, but we didn't realise that because we were still young. We would kick each other in a harmful way. This was *tirtī*. They don't play this anymore these days. The children have forgotten it.

Some of them play, [though]. I can remember that my son used to play and I used to shout at him because it is a bad game. I mean, I realise that now, but in the past we didn't realise it, just as my son doesn't realise now. The main thing was that he played and they kicked him and he kicked them [back]. The main thing was that he thought of it as a form of pleasure. I can remember that we used to play [it].

---

[41] Singular in Arabic.

[42] Singular in Arabic.

[43] i.e. the kick.

wa-ba^{c}dā buh wāḥid min aṣḥābanā / ya^{c}nī iḥna l-jahhāl ḥakk al-ḥārah / buh wāḥid rakaḍūh fī rijlih / wuja^{c}atih wa-ktasarat rijlih / wa-^{c}ālajūh / wuga^{c}at fīhā ṯalāṯ ^{c}amalīyāt / šallūh al-gāhirih ṯalāṯ marrāt wa-hum bi-šillūh yisabbirū rijlih tayyik li'annī xsi^{c}at wa-ktasarat / wa-midrī māhū / hāḏa t-tirtī lākin hī li^{c}bih xaṭīruh / hāḏā hī li^{c}bat at-tirtī /

ḍarab al-ḥudwī

wa-l-li^{c}bih aṯ-ṯāniyih allī hī gufaygif / miš gufaygif / ^{c}afwan / ḍarab al-ḥudwī / ḍarab al-ḥudwī hāḏā kayf bi-l^{c}abūbihā / nisammīhā ḍarab al-ḥudwī wa-ruju^c yudwī / kayf yil^{c}abū ḍarab al-ḥudwī / maṯalan yiktsimū[44] *iṯnayn*[45] */ iṯnayn wa-ṯnayn*[46] */ al-muhimm majmū^{c}ah fī majmū^{c}ah*[47] */*

wa:-hāḏa l-majmū^{c}atayn[48] */ nijirr ḥajar / ṯintayn ḥijār*[49] */ wa-nṭraḥḥun fī l-gā^c / mufāragāt šwayyih ^{c}an ba^{c}ḍathun al-ba^{c}ḍ / wa-ba^{c}d-mā njirr al-ḥajar nijirr ṯintayn ^{c}aṣī / ^{c}uṣīyuh ṭawīluh / wa-^{c}uṣīyuh zuġayruh / al-^{c}uṣīyu z-zuġayruh hāḏā tijī ġarr ṭūlahā zayy-mā tigūlī ṭūl bayn al-farg ḥakk aṯ-ṯintayn al-ḥajar / wa-ba^{c}dayn nijirr al-… al-^{c}uṣīyuh /*

awwal-ma yibdā li^{c}bat al-farīg al-awwal / hum / yijirrū yiṭraḥū al-^{c}ūdī az-zaġīr al-^{c}uṣī az-zuġayrih fawg al-ḥijār / wa-ba^{c}dā yijirr bi-l-^{c}uṣī al-kabīrih yijirrih yigfa^c / yirfa^c al-^{c}uṣīyu z-zuġayrih min bayn al-ḥijār la-l-hawā / wa-yikfa^{c}hā bi-l-^{c}uṣī al-kabīrih / ^{c}alā sās tisīr masāfih ba^{c}īdih /

al-majmū^{c}a ṯ-ṯāniyih gadī hānāk mirayya^{c}ah / tiḥāwil innahā timsak al-^{c}uṣīyu z-zuġayrih / innahā timsakhā bi-yadhā gabl-mā tṭraḥ la-l-arḍ / iḏā misikhā lā yadhā / ilā yadih[50] */ yu^{c}tabar / hāḏāk aš-šaxṣ allī bi-l^{c}ab aṯ-ṯānī yi^{c}tabarū ḥurimū*[51] */ yisīr*[52] *nil^{c}ab iḥna badalhum /*

---

44 Anticipatory devoicing of *g* to *k*. Syncope of stressed vowel. From *yigtasimū*.

45 Adverbial noun complement. Cf. *Syntax* pp. 144-5.

46 Repetition of *iṯnayn* conveys distributive sense (cf. Mörth 1997: 147).

47 Repetition of singular noun conveys distributive sense. Cf. above and earlier texts.

48 Noun phrase functions here as adverb. Cf. *dawl ar-rijāl* in text 17.

49 Dual used for nouns of time or measure. In most other cases, *iṯnayn* (fem. *ṯintayn*) heads apposition phrase. Cf. *Syntax* pp. 247-8, *Ṣbaḥtū!* pp. 93-4 (cf. Mörth 1997: 141-2).

50 Reformulative apposition of prepositional phrases. Cf. *Syntax* p. 244.

51 Internal passive. Cf. text 7. Change of number from singular to plural.

52 Mistake in person agreement.

Then there was one of our friends. I mean we were children from the neighbourhood, there was one who was kicked on his leg. It hurt him and his leg was broken. They treated him and three operations were carried out [on his leg]. They took him to Cairo three times to do his leg because it was damaged and broken and whatever. This is *tirtī*, but it is a dangerous game. This is the game of *tirtī*.

Ḍarab al-ḥudwī

And the second game which is *gufaygif*. Not *gufaygif*, sorry, *ḍarab al-ḥudwī*. This *ḍarab al-ḥudwī*, how do they play it? We call it *ḍarab al-ḥudwī wa-rujuᶜ yudwī*.[53] How do they play *ḍarab al-ḥudwī?* For example, they divide into two. Two and two. In any case, one group against [another] group.

For these two teams, we take a stone, two stones, and put them on the ground a little bit away from each other. Then after we take the stone, we fetch two sticks, a long stick and a short stick. The short stick will be the same length as the distance between the two stones. Then we take the ... the stick.

When the turn of the first team starts, they take the small stick, the small stick, and place it on the stones. Then they take the large stick, they take it and hit and raise the small stick from between the two stones into the air, and they hit it with the large stick so that it goes a long way.

The second team is ready waiting over there and tries to catch the small stick, to catch it in their hands before it hits the ground. If they catch it in their hands, it is said that the person who was playing, the other one, it is said that they are out, and we go to play instead of them.

---

53 AS suggests that *al-ḥudwī* may be a reference to a type of large dark-coloured bird. In this case, the game would translate as 'he hit the bird, and returned to pester, the Bedouin'.

lākin lā ma msakhāš nisīr nijirrahā min ḥayṯ-mā ṭaraḥat / al-^{c}uṣīyu z-zuġayrih / wa-njirrahā wa-nurjumhā / lā ^{c}ind aṯ-ṯintayn al-ḥijār / al-muhimm inn iḥna niḥāwil nuḍrub aṯ-ṯintayn al-ḥijār / iḏā mā ḍarabnāš aṯ-ṯintayn al-ḥijār nixallīhā 'agrab masāfih / jambahā / agalla šī /

allī hū bi-yil^{c}ab al-lawwal[54] */ hū bī-kūn jamb al-ḥijār / ^{c}inda-mā rjum lā ^{c}ind hānā al-^{c}uṣī az-zuġayrih / hū yiḥāwil innahū yiriddahā / yiriddahā / yib^{c}idhā bi-'akbar bu^{c}d ya^{c}nī yikfa^{c}hā bi-l-^{c}ūdī al-kabīr / al-^{c}uṣī al-kabīrih wa-yixallīhā tisīr ayyi masāfih ba^{c}idih / hāḏā hū 'asās al-li^{c}bih /*

fa:-^{c}inda-mā tūṣal / iḏā wuṣulat al-... iḏā wuṣul al-^{c}ūdī az-zaġīr hāḏā lā jamb al-ḥijār / wa-masāfatih agall min masāfat al-^{c}ūdī al-kabīr / allī al-^{c}uṣīy al-kabīrih / yu^{c}tabarū barḍū ḥurimū / ahamma šī inn al-^{c}uṣī az-zuġayrih tūṣal lā 'agrab bug^{c}ah / min al-ḥajar aw fi l-ḥajar / lākin iḏā wuṣulat fi l-ḥajar ya^{c}tabar ḥurim zayy-mā ka-'annana msakthā / wa-hāḏāk hū bī-ḥāwil an yiriddahā /

iḏā mā wuṣulatš wa-hī ba^{c}idih / bi-masāfat al-^{c}ūdī al-kabīr / fī hāḏīk al-laḥḏuh / ḏayya llī bi-l^{c}ab / yisīr lā ^{c}ind al-^{c}uṣī az-zuġayrih / w-iḍrubhā ma^{c} ṯalāṯ ḍarabāt / yiḍrubhā al-^{c}uṣī az-zuġayrih / wa-ṯ-ṯalāṯ aḍ-ḍarabāt hāḏā / kulla ḍarbuh / aḍ-ḍarbuh al-ūlā[55] *maṯalan / yigūl fīhā ḍarab al-ḥudwī / w-yuḍrub al-^{c}uṣī az-zuġayrih / bi-l-^{c}uṣī al-kabīrih / wa-l-^{c}uṣī az-zaġīrih hāḏī 'iḏā ṭulu^{c}at maṭla^{c} iḏā rtafa^{c}at hākaḏā / hū yizāyid yiḥāwil an yigfa^{c}hā yigarribhā kaḏāk / iḏā ma rtafa^{c}atš tibgā bug^{c}athā wa-hū yif^{c}al aḍ-ḍarbu ṯ-ṯāniyih / yigūl / wa-ruju^{c} yudwī / hāḏa ḍ-ḍarbu ṯ-ṯāniyih / wa-nafs aš-šī / yiḥāwil an yigfa^{c}hā wa-yigfa^{c}hā kaḏāk / wa-ḏā ma rtafa^{c}atš tibgā bug^{c}athā / wa-yjirr aḍ-ḍarbuh aṯ-ṯāliṯih wa-yigūl wa-ruju^{c} yudwī*[56] */ wa-yuḍrubhā aṯ-ṯāliṯih / ba^{c}d hāḏā / nibsir kam al-masāfih allī yibta^{c}id minnahā al-^{c}ūdī ḏayy al-^{c}uṣī az-zuġayrih /*

wa-^{c}ād bih ḥājih / iḏā gāl iḏā fi xilāl aṯ-ṯalāṯ aḍ-ḍarabāt hāḏawlā 'iḏā hū bi-yigfa^{c} bi-l-^{c}uṣī az-zuġayrih wa-mā kfa^{c}hāš / wuga^{c}at fi l-gā^{c} miš fi l-^{c}uṣīyuh az-zuġayrih / ya^{c}tabar ḥurim li'annū ba^{c}ḍ al-aḥyān hū yijī yuḍrub fi l-gurnih / ḥakk al-^{c}uṣīyu z-zuġayrih ^{c}alā 'asās yixallīhā tirtafi^{c} /

54 Exophoric pronominal use of definite clause. Cf. *Syntax* pp. 416-17.

55 Use of standard *ūlā* in place of SA *awwalih*.

56 i.e. *^{c}ind al-badwī*.

But if they don't manage to catch it, we take it from wherever it went, the small stick, we take it and throw it towards the two stones. The important thing is that we try to hit the two stones. If we don't manage to hit the two stones, we make it as close as possible next to them, the least thing.

The first one who plays, he will be beside the stones. When they throw the small stick over here, he tries to hit it back, to send it back and send it away as far as he can, I mean he hits it with the large stick, the large stick, and makes it go a long way away. This is the basis of the game.

When it lands, if the small stick lands next to the stones and the distance [between it and the two stones] is less than the length of the large stick, that of the large stick, they[57] are also considered to be out. The most important thing is that the stick gets as near as possible to the stones or [hits] the stones. However, if it lands on the stones he is said to be out just as if I had caught it. The other one tries to hit it back.

If it doesn't reach [the stones] and it is further away than the length of the large stick, at that moment the one who is playing goes to the small stick and hits it three times. He hits it, the small stick. At each of these three strikes, for instance the first strike, he says, '*Darab al-ḥudwī!*' and he hits the small stick with the large stick. The small stick, if it goes up [into the air], if it rises up like that, he tries to hit it again and get it over there. If it doesn't go up but stays in its place, he takes a second strike, and says, 'And he came back to pester!' This is on the second strike. And its the same thing. He tries to hit it and to hit it over there. If it doesn't go up but stays in its place, he takes a third strike, and says, 'And he came back to pester!' and hits it a third time. After this, we see what distance the stick, that small stick, has gone.

There is something else: if he said, if, during these three strikes, if he [tried] to hit the small stick and didn't hit it, but it[58] landed on the ground, not on the small stick, he is said to be out because sometimes he goes to hit the end[59] of the small stick so that he can get it to go up [into the air].

---

57 i.e. the person who was in.

58 i.e. the strike.

59 Lit: 'corner'.

fa-ḏā ma wga^{c}atš fī l-gurnih wuga^{c}at fī l-gā^{c} yu^{c}tabar ḥurim / al-muhimm[60] */ ba^{c}dā 'asīr absir al-^{c}uṣī az-zuġayrih hāḏā waynahī / min masāfat al-ḥijār / wa-nibda' ni^{c}idd / wa-ni^{c}idd wāḥid iṯnayn ṯalāṯih arba^{c}ah / ya^{c}nī kam al-masāfih allī bta^{c}adat minnahā al-^{c}uṣīy az-zuġayrih / wa-hākaḏā / nistamirr bi-l-li^{c}bih / ^{c}alā wāḥid wāḥid / law-mā nuḥrum / iḏā mā ḥurumnāš nibgā mistamirrīn wa-tibdā' lanā wāḥid iṯnayn ṯalāṯih tu^{c}tabar zayy an-nugaṭ / lanā / hāḏā hī ḍarab al-ḥudwī / wa-ruju^{c} yudwī /*

sab^{c}ah

wa-nil^{c}ab sab^{c}ah hāḏa l-li^{c}bih yil^{c}abūhā farīgayn / maṯalan al-farīg al-wāḥid min ṯalāṯih ašxāṣ / hāḏa s-sab^{c}ah / nijirr sab^{c} ḥājāt maṯalan al-ġiḍā ḥagg al-bibz[61] *aw ayya ḥājih / nijirr niṭruḥḥā / sab^{c} ^{c}alā šakl sab^{c} / hāh / wa-nruṣṣahā ^{c}arḍ al-jidār*[62] */ maṯalan hānā nruṣṣahā ^{c}arḍ al-jidār / wa-nāxuḏ kurah / lā mā biš kurah nijirr aš-šarābāt hākaḏā / hāh wa-ndaxxil lā dāxilhā xirag / ni^{c}mal xirag dāxil lā hānā / ba^{c}dā nṣallaḥḥā zayy al-kurah / wa-yrūḥ*[63] *min hānāk min ba^{c}īd / masāfat sab^{c} xaṭawāt / wi-ḍrub / ṯalāṯ ḍarabāt ma^{c} al-wāḥid / ṯalāṯ ḍarabāt / yuḍrub hāḏā as-sab^{c} al-ġuḍāyāt / iḏā ramāhā ^{c}ala l-arḍ min awwal ḍarbuh / yihrub / hū yihrub / anā fī hāḍāk*[64] *al-laḥḍuh aḥmil ajirr al-kurah / w-aḥāwil armīhā ^{c}arḍuh / iḏā ramayttā*[65] *^{c}arḍuh ya^{c}nī fust / fī hāḍīk al-laḥḍuh /*

^{c}alayy ad-dawr / innanā rūḥ aḍrub / iḏā ramaythin yibgaw yilāḥigūnī 'anā[66] */ anā hrub wa-hum yilāḥigūnī bi-l-kurah / yiḥāwil yikfa^{c}nī*[67] *ya^{c}nī yirmīnī ayy yikfa^{c}nī / hum yilāḥigūnī w-anā ḥāwil / atxallaṣ minnahum / wa-'awṣal ilā n-nugḍuh hānā / ḥayṯ-mā l-bibz allī bi-rāḥayn fī l-arḍ / ajamma^{c}hin wa-raṣṣahun ^{c}alā wāḥid wāḥid arajji^{c}hin makānhin /*

---

60 Underarticulation of *h* in *muhimm*. Not accepted by speaker.

61 Loan word. From *Pepsi*.

62 i.e. alongside the wall.

63 Use of non-SA *rāḥ*. Predicandless predicate. Cf. *Syntax* pp. 125-7.

64 Lack of agreement with the following feminine noun.

65 Complete perseverative assimilation of *h* of pronoun to *t*.

66 Post-position of independent pronoun *anā* to emphasise object. Cf. *Syntax* p. 251.

67 Anticipatory devoicing of *g* to *k*. Change of number from plural to singular.

But if it doesn't hit the end and hits the ground, he is said to be out. Anyway, then I go to see where the small stick is in relation to the stones, and we begin to count. We count one, two, three, four, I mean, the distance that the small stick is away from them.[68] We keep going with the game in this way, one by one, until we are out. If we don't go out, we continue and [this] one, two, three are considered to be points for us. This is *ḍarab al-ḥudwī, wa ruju^c yudwī*.

Seven

We also play seven. In this game, two teams play. For example, the one team will have three people. This is seven. We take seven things such as the top of a Pepsi bottle or anything. We take [them] and put them in the form of seven,[69] okay? And we arrange them along the side of the wall. For example, here we would arrange them alongside the wall. Then we take a ball. If there is no ball we take socks, okay, and put rags inside them.[70] We put rags inside here. Then we make it like a ball. [One] goes over there, a distance of seven paces, and he has three strikes with one, three strikes. He hits the seven tops. If he throws them to the ground with the first strike, he runs, he runs.[71] At that moment, I run to take the ball and try to hit him with it. If I hit him [as he runs], I win that time.

Then it is my turn. I go and hit [them]. If I throw them[72] down, they[73] start to chase me. I run, and they chase me with the ball. They try to hit me, I mean they throw [it] at me or hit me. They chase me and I try to get away from them and reach the spot over there, where the Pepsi [tops] are which have gone onto the ground. I gather them up and arrange them one on top of the other and put them back in their place.

[68] i.e. the stones.

[69] i.e. one on top of the other.

[70] Cf. text on *Gufaygif* for description of making a ball.

[71] i.e. with his friends.

[72] i.e. the bottle tops.

[73] i.e. people from the other team.

ṭabᶜan hum bī-ḥāwilū yimnaᶜūnī / min ann[74] *awṣal lā hāḏa l-munḍuguh / bi-l-kurah / yaᶜnī bi-ymsik al-kurah wa-yḏ̣rubhā ᶜarḏ̣ī / yiḥāwil an yikfaᶜnī / iḏa luḍaᶜatnī l-kurah iḏa lḍaᶜatnī yaᶜnī msikat fīnī aw ḏ̣arabat fīnī / aᶜtabar inna xsirt allī lāḥagūnī hum man bi-yijaw badalī / wa-yikūn majmūᶜāt / maṯalan iḥna ṯalāṯih arbaᶜah / tamām / iḏā ḥna ṯalāṯih wa-hum ṯalāṯih / hum aḏ̣-ḏ̣arūrī yuḏ̣rubū ṯ-ṯalāṯih hum*[75] *min aṣḥābī / aw anā bayn-xallīhum yiḥāwilū yuḏ̣rubūnī / wa-ṣāḥubī yirūḥ yiṣallaḥhun / wa-hākaḏā / yaᶜnī hī nawᶜ min al-liᶜabāt /*

[74] Gemination of *-n* of function word before vowel-initial word. Cf. texts 16 and 17.

[75] The pronoun, *hum*, refers back to *aṯ-ṯalāṯih* 'the three'.

Of course, they[76] try to stop me from reaching that place with the ball. I mean, he takes the ball and throws it towards me, he tries to strike me. If the ball touches me, if it touches me or hits me, I am considered to have lost and the ones who were chasing me, they are the ones who come [to play] in my place. They will be groups. For example, we [would] be three or four, okay? If we are three and they are three, then they must hit all three of my friends or I could let them try to hit me, while my friend goes to arrange them.[77] Like that. This is one type of game.

[76] i.e. the others.

[77] i.e. the seven things.

21 *Al-wagal*

ya^{c}nī tijirrī ḥajar zaġīrah / wa-tuṭraḥīhā fī ’awwal / yisammūh awwal ṯānī ṯāliṯ lā xamz / tutraḥī fī ’awwal wa-tudsa^{c}īhā ba-r-rijl / al-yusrā / ba-r-rijl aš-šimāl[1] *hāḏā / wa-titnabba^{c}ī / nibbā^{c}ah / hāḏā nisammī nibbā^{c} / tinba^{c}ī min al-lawwal lā ṯ-ṯānī lā l-xāmis / wa-ba^{c}dayn tijay / fī bayt aš-šayṭān / tinazzilī ’arjuliš aṯ-ṯintayn*[2] */ wa-ba^{c}dayn tiwāṣulī / w-iḏā nijuḥtī tif^{c}alī al-ḥajar fī ṯānī / ya^{c}nī law tidsa^{c}ī al-xaṭṭ hāḏā tibgā tuxrujī wa-tjī ṣaḥbatuš*[3] *xabīratiš*[4] *til^{c}ab / wa-hākaḏā / law-mā tikammilī xāmis wa-ba^{c}dā tirja^{c}ī sādis / ya^{c}nī bayt aš-šayṭān mā yaḥtasabš / tikammilī wa-ba^{c}dayn tiġammuḏī ^{c}uyūniš aṯ-ṯintayn*[5] */ wa-tugūlī laymū’n / yugūlū yes*[6] */*

– mišī hākaḏā / mišī hākaḏā /

– ya^{c}nī timšay tidsa^{c}ī dāxil al-murabba^{c} hāḏā / w-intī muġammaḏuh mā tibsirī wa-lā ḥājih[7] */ wa-tugūlī laymūn iḏā mā dasa^{c}tiš al-xaṭṭ hāḏā aw hāḏā / ya^{c}nī fī l-wasaṭ / yugūlū ‘yes’ / w-iḏā ġuluṭṭī dasa^{c}tī fī l-xaṭṭ hāḏā / aw xarajat rijliš hānā ’aw šī / yugūlū ‘no’ ya^{c}nī tuxrujī / lammā tijay bayt aš-šayṭān tiftaḥī ^{c}uyūniš tirtāḥī rāḥah / wa-ba^{c}dayn al-jihah hāḏī / iḏā nijuḥtī / wa-tšillī l-ḥajar hāḏīk az-zaġīrih wa-tugūlī dāxil wallā xārij ya^{c}nī ^{c}ala l-wara’ / ya^{c}nī al-murabba^{c} hāḏā bī-kūn warāya / w-anā musannibih hānā / nugūl dāxil wallā xārij wa-bi-rjimūhā yigūlū xārij aw dāxil ayyi šī /*

– lā / nugūl ^{c}alā-mā ’arād allāh /

---

1 Explanatory reformulative apposition. Cf. *Syntax* p. 244.

2 Dual not very productive in SA (cf. text 20). Where a noun takes a possessive pronoun, as here, the numeral *iṯnayn* (fem. *ṯintayn*) functions as appositive to plural noun.

3 Syncope of unstressed vowel. From *ṣāḥubatuš*.

4 Reformulative apposition. Cf. *Syntax* p. 244.

5 Where a noun takes a possessive pronoun, the numeral *iṯnayn* (fem. *ṯintayn*) functions as appositive to plural noun. Cf. above.

6 The words ‘yes’ and ‘no’ have been used by Yemeni children playing this game at least since the Revolution in 1962. AS does not know when this usage first started.

7 Asyndetic linkage of consequential clause. Cf. *Syntax* p. 311.

21 Hopscotch[8]

You take a small stone and put in on the first[9] [square]. They call it first, second, third to fifth. You put [it] on the first [square], then step on it with your left foot. With the left foot. Then you hop. We call this hopping. You hop from the first to the second to the fifth.[10] Then you come to 'the house of the devil' and you put down both your feet. Then you continue. If you succeed, you put the stone in the second[11] [square]. If you tread on that line, though, you go out, and your friend comes to play. It is like that until you complete the fifth,[12] and then you go back to the sixth.[13] 'The house of the devil' doesn't count. You finish, then you close both your eyes and say, 'Lemon!' They say, 'Yes!'

– It isn't like that! It isn't like that!

– I mean, you go and step into the square with your eyes closed so you can't see anything. Then you say, 'Lemon!' If you haven't trodden on this line or that, I mean, [you are] in the middle, they say, 'Yes!' But if you went wrong and trod on the line or your foot went outside here or whatever, they say, 'No!' That means that you are out. When you get to 'the house of the devil', you can open your eyes and relax. Then the next side, if you have managed. Then you take the little stone and say, 'Inside or outside!' from behind. I mean, this square will be behind me and I am standing here. We say, 'Inside or outside!' and they throw it saying, 'Outside or inside!' or whatever.

– No! We say, 'As God wishes!'

---

8 The speaker is a married woman in her late-teens or early-twenties living along the Ta'izz road. This text is more instructional than the descriptions of games given by AS. It was recorded in the yard while the speaker and her younger sister demonstrated the game. The interruptions are by her sister.

9 Indefinite in Arabic.

10 Definite in Arabic. Cp. note above and notes below.

11 Indefinite in Arabic.

12 Indefinite in Arabic.

13 Indefinite in Arabic.

– *ᶜalā-mā 'arād allāh / yallāh / wa-baᶜdayn iḏā jit al-ḥajar fī hāḏa l-murabbaᶜ / hāḏā yukūn baytiš antī / tirtāḥī fīh / yaᶜnī titnabbaᶜī lākin law-mā tudxulī hāḏa l-bayt / tirtāḥī bi-ṯ-ṯintayn al-arjul / miṯl bayt aš-šayṭān / wa-hākaḏā law-mā timsakī al-biyūt kullahā / baᶜd aṯ-ṯānī maṯalan aṯ-ṯānī llī yilᶜab*[14] *baᶜdiš / mā yiḥiggalih šī aw yijiss fī baytiš / yinbaᶜ min hānā lā hānā / min hānā lā hānāk / wa-law gad liš hāḏawl aṯ-ṯintayn yinbaᶜ min hānā lā hānā / illā 'iḏā samaḥtīlih bass / iḏā mā samaḥtīš lāzim yinbaᶜ min hānā lā hānāk / wa-hāḏa smahā wagal / la-l-banāt wa-l-ᶜiyyāl / kulluhum sawā / yilᶜabu l-banāt wa-l-ᶜiyyāl*[15] */*

---

14 The actual referent is a girl here. Here the unmarked masculine forms are used. Cf. texts 4, 12 and 24 where unmarked masc. gender is used when the actual referent is feminine.

15 Verbal clause with emphasis on subject. Verbal subject provides new information as if in answer to the question, 'Who plays the game?'

– 'As God wishes!' Okay! Then if the stone comes into that square, this will be your house and you can relax in it. I mean, you hop, but when you come into that house, you can put both feet down, like [in] 'the house of the devil'. It goes on like that until you have all the houses. Then the second one, I mean the next one who plays after you. He doesn't have the right over anything and he can't stay in your house. He has to hop from here to here, from here to there. If those two are yours, he has to hop from here to here, unless you have given him permission [to land on your house]. If you haven't given permission, he has to hop from here to there. This is called *wagal* [hopscotch]. [It] is for girls and boys alike. Girls and boys play.

22 *Ramaḍān*

asajjil mā bi-nif^c al fī ramaḍān / fī ramaḍā:n / maṯalan / min ḥīn nigūm min an-nawm / nisīr nitwaḍḍaf / nigūm min an-nawm as-sā^c ah ^c ašr[1] */ nitġassal wa-nitlabbas wa-midrī māhū wa-nsīr al-waḍīfuh / al-waḍīfuh ^c ašr ^c ašr wa-nuṣṣ / iḏa l-wāḥid yitwaḍḍaf yiwaggi^c / yjābir šwayyih yibsir mā ma^c ih min ^c amal / gām fi^c ilih*[2] */ wa-yijlis lā: wakt aḍ-ḍuhr / 'aḏḏan ḍuhr / yisīr yiṣallī / kull al-muwaḍḍafīn yisīr*[3] *yiṣallaw wakt ṣalāt aḍ-ḍuhr /*

wa-ba^c d ṣalāt aḍ-ḍuhr nirja^c nitwaḍḍaf / iḥna mā bi-nuxrujš niṣallī fi l-jāmi^c gad[4] *ma^c ānā jāmi^c fi l-^c amal*[5] */ ġurfi llī*[6] *nṣallī fīhā / wa:-ba^c dā: / niwāṣul al-^c amal / la-s-sā^c ah ṯalāṯ / wa-min as-sā^c ah ṯalāṯ / ba^c dayn kulla wāḥid yirūḥ yiwaggi^c / tawgī^c al-xurūj / wa-yiriḥlih*[7] */ nisīr niṣallī ^c aṣr fi l-jawāmi^c nidrislanā šwayyih / law-mā: yi'aḏḏin ^c aṣr / wa-ba^c dā: niṣallī ṣalāt al-^c aṣr /*

ba^c d ṣalāt al-^c aṣr / gad al-wāḥid yitxawwar / yā yisīr yištarīlih ḥājih min as-sūg / rawānīyih / wallā malābis / wallā gušmī / wallā 'ayy:i šī / yitwālah yiḏayyu^c al-wakt[8] */ wallā yisīr al-bayt yibizz al-jahhāl wa-yuxruj šwayyih hū wayhum*[9] *dawrih / ayn-mā lafī / maṯalan / al-gariyih / al-wādī / al-... ayyi maḥall al-muhimm innī dawrih / tūga^c dawrih la s-sā^c ah xams / xams wa-nuṣṣ /*

yuḏwī al-wāḥid gadū bī-zāwuṭ / hāḏā ḍab^c an iḏa štarā gāt ^c ala ṭ-ṭarīg / yuḏwī al-wāḥid u-gadū bī-zāwuṭ yūṣal la-l-bayt / ma^c l-jahhāl / yitwaḍḍu' / yitjahhiz nafsih / yisīr al-jāmi^c al-maġrib / yijirr al-faḍūr[10] */*

---

[1] When non-suffixed numeral *^c ašar* occurs at the end of phrase it usu. lacks ending *-ar* or is pronounced *^c ašr*. Cf. *Ṣbaḥtū!* p. 237.

[2] In sentences in which action of main verb dependent on the fulfillment of that mentioned in the subordinate clause, as here, the verb is often placed in the perfect. Cf. text 20.

[3] Lack of number agreement on translocative verb.

[4] Use of *gad* for emphasis.

[5] Asyndetic linkage of explanatory clause. Cf. *Syntax* p. 309.

[6] The clausal definite article *illī, allaḏī, allī* usu. follows definite nouns. It can occasionally, as here, follow indefinite nouns. Cf. *Syntax* p. 235.

[7] Reflexive verb. Cf. *Syntax* pp. 202-3.

[8] Asyndetic linkage of purpose clause. Cf. *Syntax* pp. 169-71.

[9] Cf. *Ṣbaḥtū!* pp. 217-18.

[10] String of asyndetically linked clauses conveys sense of speed and list of activities. Cf. *Syntax* p. 314. Cf. also end of para. 1.

22 Ramadan

I shall record what we do during Ramadan. During Ramadan, for example, from when we get up from sleeping to go to work. We get up at ten o'clock. We get washed and dressed and whatever else and go to work. Work is at ten or ten thirty. When you go to work, you sign on. You chat a little and see what work you have to do, you do it then stay until noon time. The noon prayer is called and you go to pray. All the employees go to pray at the time of the noon prayer.

After the noon prayer, we go back to work. We don't go out to pray in the mosque [because] we have a mosque at work, a room which we pray in. Then we carry on with work until three o'clock. And from three o'clock, then everyone goes to sign off and goes away. We go to pray the mid-afternoon prayer in the mosques. We recite the Qur'an a bit until the mid-afternoon prayer is called, then we pray the mid-afternoon prayer.

After the mid-afternoon prayer, you start to long for [certain types of food]. You may go to buy yourself something from the market – *rawānī* or clothes or long, white radish or whatever – you amuse yourself to use up time. Or you go home and take the children and go for a walk with them wherever you want, for example, the village, the valley, ... or anywhere. The important thing is that it is a walk. The walk will last until five o'clock, or five thirty.

Then you go home quickly. Of course, this is if you have bought gat on the way. You go home quickly. You arrive at the house with the children. You do your ablutions. You get yourself ready, then you go to the mosque at sunset taking your breakfast.

yūga^{c} al-faḍūr ḥāmuḍuh[11] */ wallā salaḍuh / wallā: zaḥāwug ^{c}ala s-salaḍuh / zġayrih tamrih / sambūsih / li'annum yiṣallaḥū fi l-bayt hāḏawlā / ma štarāš*[12] */ hāh / w-yiḥinn al-jāmi^{c} /*

al-jāmi^{c} zid nūṣal šwayyih gabl al-maġrib lā ^{c}ādū baḥīn / nitjābir šwayyih iḥna wa-man kān hānāk fi l-jāmi^{c} / nitjābir / al-muhimm niḏayyu^{c} al-wakt / wa:-law-mā yi'aḏḏin / wa-ḥīn yi'aḏḏin / ġayr yigūl allāh hū 'akbar / illa w-kulla wāḥid gadū al-lij^{c} fi yadih / yidaxxilih fumm^{w}ih / gadū ġayr muzāwaḍuh / wa-munātifih fi l-jāmi^{c} / ^{c}ād ma^{c} akṯarat al-jahhāl wa-l-hāḏā yiḥawwišu n-nās jamā^{c}ah / yinātifū ḏayyik al-lakl ma^{c} al-jū^{c} / minātifih / al-mu'aḏḏin bī-'aḏḏin w-hū bi-yākul / mā yitimm yi'aḏḏin illa / w-gadū bi-gḍub aṣ-ṣalāh / gām aṣ-ṣalāh / bi-nnātiflana[13] *l-lakl ḏayyik al-mawjūd hinayyik al-faḍūr / wallā šī ma tnātafnā / wa-nṣallī / niṣallī maġrib / wa-ba^{c}dā nṣallī s-sinnih /*

wa-ba^{c}dā / ba^{c}da-mā niṣallī nigūm niriḥlanā / nuḏwī al-bayt / wa-ḥīn nuḏwī al-bayt nuḏwī wa-gad iḥna / šābi^{c}īn šwayyih / mā ^{c}ābiš al-jaw^{c} ḏayyik / nūṣal ^{c}āḍušīn / nif^{c}al galaṣ mā' / galaṣayn[14] *mā' / bardag / gadīd / wa-l-baḍn mašbūjih / mā ^{c}a-nistirš nākul hāḏāk al-lakl al-mawjūd allī gad iḥna bi-nitxawwarih gabl al-maġrib / tif^{c}al al-marih ḏayyā wa-ḏayyā wa-ḏayyā wa-ḏayyā*[15] */ wa-min kulla šī bi-txawwar wāḥid / mā yijī fawg al-māyidih illā w-gadū šābi^{c} mā ^{c}ād yistirš yākul min šī / wa-niḥna miṯaggalīn buḍūnanā /*

nigūm nitfarraj at-taliviziyūn šwayyih / nitfarraj ḏayyā muḏī^{c} fi waraḍuh aw gad bi-ddī badalih māhū / ^{c}indī waḏīfuh / nigūm niḏḥak šwayyih nitfarrajih hāḏa l-musalsal yiddaw / kūmidī sa^{c}ūdī / wāḥid ismih ^{c}abdullāh ^{c}aṣīrī[16] */ wa-^{c}inda-mā yixalluṣ nuxruj /*

---

[11] Verbal clause with inanimate subject.

[12] No object pronoun.

[13] Reflexive verb. Cf. *Syntax* pp. 202-3.

[14] Dual used with noun of measure. Cf. *Ṣbaḥtū!* p. 93.

[15] Verbal clause with emphasis on object.

[16] String of asyndetically linked clauses conveys sense of speed and list of activities. Cf. *Syntax* p. 314, 315-6.

Breaking the fast will consist of soured fenugreek, or salad, or a spicy dip with salad, a few dates, or samosas, because they prepare these [things] at home. They don't buy [them]. Okay? Then you go to the mosque.

We get to the mosque shortly before sunset, if it is still early. We chat with whoever else is there at the mosque, we chat. In any case, we use up time. When prayer is called, when prayer is called he[17] simply says, 'God is the greatest!' and everyone puts the bit of food which is in his hand into his mouth. It is just a something quick or a snack in the mosque. With all the children and the like, people congregate and take a small bit of food for their hunger. A snack. The muezzin calls for prayer while he is eating. He has hardly finished the call for prayer before he is hurrying through the prayer. He starts the prayer. We snatch a morsel of the food which is there to break the fast with, then we pray. We pray the sunset prayer. Then we pray the Sunna.

Then, after we have prayed, we get up and go. We go back home. When we go home, we go home a bit full. There is no longer that same hunger. We arrive thirsty. We have a glass of water, two glasses of water, a glass of apricot syrup, then our stomachs are full. We can no longer eat the food which is there that we hankered after before sunset. Your wife makes this, that and the other, everything you have hankered after, but by the time it reaches the table you are already full, you can't eat a thing and our stomachs are full.

We start to watch a little television. We watch that 'Reporter in a scrape' or whatever they have in place of it, what is it? 'I have a job'. We laugh a little, we watch the serial. They put on a Saudi comedy, someone called Abdullah Asiri. When it finishes, we go out.

[17] i.e. the muezzin.

anā 'agūm axruj anā afᶜallī[18] *laffih ka-ḏayyahā / hiniyyih hiniyyih*[19] */ law-mā gadū wagt al-gāt w-anā gūm axazzin / hāh wa-hāḏā*[20] *kullih kulla yawm / wa-baᶜdā nxazzin al-ᶜašī / la-s-sāᶜah ṯintayn / la-s-sāᶜah iṯnᶜāš iṯnᶜāš wa-nuṣṣ / wāḥidih / ṯintayn / l-ayyaḥīn wugaᶜ / kullih ᶜalā ḍaᶜm al-gāt / afᶜal laffih šwayyih wa-baᶜd uḍwī al-bayt argud*[21] */ ṯintayn ṯintayn wa-nuṣṣ / argudlī*[22] *la-s-sāᶜah ṯalāṯ wa-nuṣṣ / w-agūm atsaḥḥar / tayyi l-yawmatayn*[23] *anā 'anaᶜᶜis mā 'astirš agūm aṣallī fajr / wa-l-mafrūḍ agūm aṣallī fajr / jamāᶜah / wa-kulla yawm hākaḏā' / hāḏā ramaḍān kayf b-ūgaᶜ hāḏa l-liyyām hāh / niᶜmih*[24] */*

18 Reflexive verb. Cp. use of this verb in phrases such as *afᶜallī bardag gahwih, afᶜallī ᶜargih ḥammām*. Cf. texts 9, 11, 18, 25, 27.

19 Repetition of locative pronoun conveys distributive sense.

20 The demonstrative pronoun acts as clausal anaphoric pronoun. Cf. *Syntax* pp. 382-4.

21 Asyndetic linkage of purpose clause. Cf. *Syntax* pp. 169-71.

22 Reflexive verb. Cf. *Syntax* pp. 202-3.

23 Dual used with noun of time. Cf. *Ṣbaḥtū!* p. 93.

24 Predicandless predicate. Cf. *Syntax* p. 125.

I get up and go for a walk, here or there, until it is time for gat. Then I start to chew, okay, and all this [happens] every single day. Then we chew in the evening until two o'clock, until twelve o'clock, twelve thirty, one, two, until whenever. It all depends on the taste of the gat. I take a short walk, then I go home to sleep at two or two thirty. I sleep until three thirty, then I get up to have the last meal before daybreak. These past couple of days I have overslept. I have not been able to get up to do the dawn prayer. I ought to get up to do the dawn prayer with the others. Every day it is like that. This is what Ramadan is like these days. [It's] a blessing.

23 *Al-akl ḥagg ramaḏ̣ān*

al-lakl ḥakka ramaḏ̣ān / fa-l-lakl ḥakk ramaḏ̣ā'n / yūgaᶜ xayrāt / wa-n-nās yitxawwarū ḥājāt kaṯīrih / fa-maṯalan / yisabbirū[1] */ mā yisawwaw / al-ḥāmuḏ̣uh hāḏā min al-lašyā' al-muhimmih / wa-l-salaḏuh*[2] */ wa-š-šfūṭ / wa-l-ḏ̣abīx / mā jamb aṭ-ṭabīx / wa-z-zaḥāwig / wa-z-zaḥāwig hāḏā min al-lakl / wa-baᶜḏ̣ al-aḥyān yifᶜalū bint ṣaḥn / bint ṣaḥn wallā / wa-š-širbih / aš-širbih muhimmih yaᶜnī / ḏ̣arūrī yākulū š-širbih gad*[3] *an-nās yifᶜalūhā dāyiman / wa-mā ᶜād bih jamb aš-širbih / wa-r-rizz / hāḏā la-l-lakl / yijayn / yaᶜnī yumkin yitwājidayn hāḏawlā kull:ahin / fī sufrih wāḥidih / wa-'ayḏ̣an yigarribū min al-mašrūbāt yifᶜalū al-gadīd / al-karkaday / ayyi ᶜaṣīr ḏ̣arūrī min šarāb aw ayyi ḥājih / wa-l-līm / yifᶜalū*[4] */*

wa-yiḥallaw baᶜd al-lakl yisabbirū ḥājāt xayrāt / yisabbirū al-jīlī / yisabbirū al-krīm karamallih / yisabbirū al-maḥallabī / hāḏawlā min al-maḥalliyāt / allī yiḥallawbhin / wa-ᶜad bih / al-ḥājāt al-yamanīyih maṯalan / hāḏā yamanī mā hīš mustawradih hī ar-rawānī / wa-š-šᶜūbīyāt / wa-l-baglawih / hāḏawlā kullahin ḥā:liyāt / yaᶜnī … wa-l-gaḏ̣āyuf / wa-hāḏawlā lā mā hinš musabbirāt fī l-bayt / nisīr ništarīhin min xārij li'ann yitwājidayn fī ramaḏ̣ān bi-kaṯrih wasṭ as-sūg / fī bāb as-sabaḥ / fī l-gāᶜ / fī taḥrīr / fī kulla bugᶜah[5] *yisabbirū hāḏa l-lašyā / wa-n-nās yitxawwarūhin wa-yisīr*[6] *yištarawhin /*

wa-ḥakk al-faḏ̣ūr / yaᶜnī hāḏa l-faḏ̣ūr hū gabl al-ᶜašā / yaᶜnī an-nās yištaraw ḥājāt kaṯīrih / allī yuxwar[7] */ ḏ̣abᶜan at-tamrih hāḏā hū min al-muhimm fī ramaḏ̣ān / yifṭurū bi-tamrih akṯarat an-nās*[8] */*

---

1 Verb in masc. pl., although activity carried out by women. Cf. texts 4, 12, 21, 24. Cf. *Syntax* p. 126.

2 Hesitation results in lack of assimilation of definite article to initial 'sun' letter of noun. Cf. also unassimilated *-l-* in *al-ḏ̣abīx* below.

3 Use of *gad* to emphasise predicate.

4 Post-position of verb. Verb given here as afterthought.

5 Asyndetic linkage of three prep. phrases with repetition in each case of *fī* conveys sense of incomplete list. Cf. *Syntax* pp. 316-17. The prep. phrases function as identificatory appositives to *wasṭ as-sūg*. Cf. *Syntax* pp. 241-3.

6 Lack of number agreement on translocative verb. Cf. *Syntax* pp. 169-71.

7 Internal passive. Cf. text 7. Cf. *Syntax* pp. 91-2.

8 Verbal clause with animate subject following prep. complement to emphasise subject.

23 Food during Ramadan

Food during Ramadan. There is a lot of food during Ramadan. People crave many things. For example, they make, what do they make, soured fenugreek. This is one of the important things, and salad, and *šafūṭ*, and mixed vegetables, what else is there besides mixed vegetables, and spicy dip. And spicy dip, these are types of food. Sometimes they make 'daughter of the plate', 'daughter of the plate', or, and broth. Broth is important. They have to eat broth. People always make it. What else is there besides broth? Rice, these are things to eat, all of these things may be present at a single table.[9] They also bring out drinks. They make apricot syrup, hibiscus juice, it is essential to have some type of juice from syrup or anything, and lime, they make.

They have a lot of sweet dishes after the meal. They make a lot of things. They make jelly. They make creme caramel. They make milk pudding. These are some of the sweet dishes they have. There are also Yemeni dishes, for example these are Yemeni and are not imported: they include *rawānī*, *šuᶜūbīyāt* and *baglawih*. All of these are sweet .... There are also small triangular doughnuts fried in melted butter and served with honey. If these are not made at home, we go and buy them from outside, because there are a lot in the marketplace during Ramadan – in Bab al-Sabah, in al-Ga', in Tahrir. They make these things everywhere. People crave them and go to buy them.

For breaking the fast, breaking the fast is before supper, people buy a lot of things which are craved; of course, dates are important during Ramadan. Most people break the fast with dates.

---

[9] i.e. at one meal.

lākin al-fuḍūr tūga^{c} xawarāt / al-basbūsih / as-sambūsih / mā yisammawhin hāḏawlahā[10] / al-kabāb allī yisabbirūhin / al-kabāb / al-kabdih[11] / ya^{c}nī yitxawwar wāḥid hāḏā ġarr yifṭurūbuh wa-bass / yifṭurūbuh / wa-ṭ-ṭa^{c}mīyuh / hāḏawlā / yā yisabbirūhin fi l-bayt / yā nuxruj[12] wakt ad-dawrih hāḏāk gabl al-maġrib yuxruj[13] wāḥid yilwī / wa-yištarīhin / wa-yiḏ̣wī al-bayt yufṭurūbuhun /

wa-fawg al-^{c}ašā ^{c}ādum yisabbirū ba^{c}ḏ̣ al-aḥyān al-futūt / ba^{c}ḏ̣ al-aḥyān yisabbirū l-ma^{c}ṣūbuh / ba^{c}ḏ̣ al-aḥyān yisabbirū s-sabāyā / wa-kulla ^{c}ala l-xawrih allī yixwarūhā fi l-bayt / fa-hāḏawlā' / akṯarattum[14] mijtama^{c}īn fī wajbih wāḥidih[15] / li'ann an-nās bi-txawwarū / yijīluhum[16] šahīyih la-l-lakl yitxayyalū midrī mā ya'kulū / lākin law-mā yijī wakt al-lakl / yallāh / ya'kulū min kulla ḥājih šwayyih / lannum bī-jaw yākulū wakt al-fuḍūr xayrāt / yifṭurū bi-z-zaḥāwug wallā bi-l-... salaḍuh wallā bi-l-kabāb wallā bi-l-kabdih wallā bi- ... / bi-hāḏa llī bi-txawwarūhin / sambūsih /

as-sambūsih fī hāḏi l-liyyām gad ištaharat ya^{c}nī gadī bi-kaṯrih mawjūdih fi l-laswāg / fi l-maḏ̣ā^{c}um / ya^{c}nī wāḥid yuxruj yibsir ġarr hāḏ̣āk min as-sā^{c}ah xams wallā min arba^{c} wa-maḏ̣la^{c} / gad yibsir ġayr al-maḏ̣ā^{c}um wa-maḥallāt al-ḥalawīyāt wa-l-hāḏā gadum ġarr yisabbirū / sambūsih / wa-yibī^{c}ū sambūsih / li'annī tu^{c}tabar faḍūr / an-nās yifṭurūbuhā / fa:-gadī mašhūrih / ba^{c}ḏ̣ al-aḥyān iḥna fi l-bayt bi-nsabbir wallā ništarī / li'annū gad al-^{c}ajīnih ḥakkahā / gadī mawjūdih fi s-sūg / mumkin an aštarī ^{c}ajīnat as-sambūsih /

ḏ̣ab^{c}an as-sambūsih hāḏī bi-tkawwan min / ^{c}ajīnih / ya^{c}nī ḥakk al-xubz / wa-'ayḏ̣an yijirrū daggih / ad-daggih hāḏī[17] yixalluṭūhā ma^{c} al-bagdūnis / ma^{c} aṭ-ṭarūḏuh / ma^{c} al-baṣal / wa-yi^{c}malūhā wa-yikšnūhā[18] /

---

[10] Suffixation of *-hā* to emphasise demonstrative. Cf. texts 4, 9, 11, etc.

[11] String of identificatory appositives to *xawarāt*. Cf. *Syntax* pp. 241-3.

[12] Change of person to first plural.

[13] Change of person from first plural to third masc. sing.

[14] Complete perseverative assimilation of *h* to *t*.

[15] *wāḥidih* functions as attribute to emphasise singularity of noun (cf. Mörth 1997: 118).

[16] Lack of gender agreement with following feminine subject.

[17] Topicalisation of object. Cf. *Syntax* p. 130.

[18] Degemination of medial radical *š* and syncope. From *yikaššinūhā*.

But breaking the fast is for the things you crave: basbusa, samosas, what do they call them those kebabs that they make, kebabs, liver. I mean you crave this. They simply break the fast with it, and that's it. They break the fast with it, and falafil. These [things] they either make at home or we go out when it is time for a stroll before sunset, you go out and wander round and buy them, then go home to break the fast with them.

For supper, they also sometimes make torn bread with ghee; sometimes they make hot bread shredded onto ghee and honey; sometimes they make *sabāyā*. It all depends on what you crave in the family. Most of these things are put together for a single meal because people crave [them]. They get an appetite for food and imagine what they want to eat, but when the time comes to eat, that's it, they eat a little of everything because they get to eat a lot at the time of breaking the fast: they break the fast with a spicy dip, or with ... salad, or with kebabs, or with liver or with ... with whatever they had a craving for – samosas.

Nowadays, samosas have become very well known and are found all over in the marketplace and in restaurants. I mean, you go out to see at that time from five o'clock or from four onwards. You just see the restaurants and the confectioners as they are preparing samosas and selling samosas because it is considered to be breakfast, people break the fast with them. They are well known. Sometimes we make [them] at home or we buy [them] because the dough you need for them is there in the marketplace. I can buy dough for samosas.

Of course, samosas are made from dough used for bread. They also take mince. They mix this mince together with parsley, with dill, with onion, then they make them and add fried vegetables to the meat.

wa-yisabbirūhā wa-yixallawhā jā:hizih muḥammarah hāḏā kullih / wa-yijirrū hāḏa l-^{c}ajīnih ba^{c}dā yidaxxilū wasṭahā as-sambūsih / yidaxxilū wasṭahā hāḏa al-… / hāḏa d-daggih wa-l-lašyā hāḏā / wa-ba^{c}dā yijirrū yigillawhā ^{c}ala z-zayt / wa-tuxrij miḥammarah / wa-tūga^{c} laḏīḏih / wakt al-faṭūr / hāḏā li-l-lakl ḥakk ramaḍān /

ḍab^{c}an al-ḥāmuḍuh wa-s-salaḍuh wa-l-hāḏā / al-ḥāmuḍuh / hī ḥulbuh / yisammawha ḥāmuḍuh / ḥulbuh / bayḍō / miš xaḍrā / ḥulbuh bayḍō / yijirr[19] *yif^{c}alūlahā šwayyih xall / wa-šwayyih sukkar / galīl sukkar wa-šwayyih xall / wa-yākulūhā bi-l-gušmī / al-gušmī hāḏā yištaraw*[20] *min al-magāšim / wallā min al-baggālāt / wallā min as-sūg / lākin akṯarat an-nās yif^{c}alū dawrih li-l-mikšāmih / wa-yštaraw / gušmī / bay^{c}ah wa-salaḍuh wa-yijaw yākulūh / hāḏā al-ḥāmuḍuh / tu^{c}tabar*[21] */ awwal wujbih yākulūhā / ^{c}inda-mā yit^{c}aššaw / yijirrū al-gušmī wa-yisk^{c}ū*[22] *^{c}alayh yisk^{c}ū al-ḥilbih allī hī ḏā*[23] *ḥāmuḍuh / fa-nsammīhā al-ḥāmuḍuh /*

hāḏawla l-lašyā llī ḏakartā[24] *'akṯarathā ya^{c}nī kullahā*[25] *ta^{c}tabar / ḥakk ramaḍān / mawjūdih / fī ramaḍān / ya^{c}nī miṯl al-gadīd / hāḏā min al-lašyā l-muhimmih fī ramaḍān yištarawha n-nās kulluhum / ḍab^{c}an fī ramaḍān tukṯar / širā' al-bahārāt / miṯl al-ḥawā'ij / miṯl al-milḥ / miṯl al-milḥī / miṯl as-sa^{c}tar / miṯl al-kammūn*[26] */ hāḏawlā kullahin yištarawn*[27] *xayrāt an-nās tibsir ^{c}alayhā zaḥ:mih*[28] *fī bidāyat ramaḍān / ya^{c}nī gabl ramaḍān bi-yawm wallā … / yisīru n-nās kulluhum yištaraw tixayyilak innum midrī mā gad*[29] *yif^{c}alū / hāḏā bi-nisbih lā hāḏa l-bahārāt ḥakk ramaḍān /*

---

[19] Lack of number agreement on linking verb.

[20] Inversion of verb–object to emphasise object. Cf. *Syntax* pp. 143-4.

[21] Internal passive. Cf. text 7. Cf. *Syntax* pp. 91-2.

[22] Syncope. From *yiska^{c}ū*.

[23] Presentational particle. Cf. *Syntax* pp. 422-3.

[24] Elision of *h* of the object pronoun *-hā*.

[25] Corrective, reformulative appositive preceded by *ya^{c}nī*. Cf. *Syntax* p. 246.

[26] Fivefold repetition of *miṯl al-* with asyndetic linkage conveys sense of incomplete list. Cf. *Syntax* pp. 316-17. The prep. phrases function as identificatory appositives to *al-bahārāt*. Cf. *Syntax* pp. 241-3.

[27] *h*-deletion and syncope. From *yištarawhin*.

[28] Lengthening of *ḥ* in the stressed syllable of a word which receives main sentence stress.

[29] Modal use of *gad* before imperfect verb.

They make them and leave them ready and fried. They take the dough, then they put the samosa [filling] inside it. They put this ... this mince and these [other] things inside it.[30] Then they start to fry them in oil, and they turn out brown and taste delicious when you break the fast [with them]. This is about food during Ramadan.

[31] Of course, [there is also] soured fenugreek and salad and the like. Soured fenugreek is fenugreek which they call *ḥāmuḍuh*. White fenugreek, not green,[32] white fenugreek. They add a little vinegar and a little sugar to it, a small amount of sugar and a little vinegar, then they eat it with long, white radish.[33] This radish they buy from the vegetable gardens or from the grocer's shops or from the marketplace, but most people will take a walk to the vegetable gardens and buy radish, leeks and lettuce and go and eat them. Soured fenugreek is considered to be the first dish you eat when you have supper. You take hold of a radish and dip it in. You dip in the fenugreek which is the soured fenugreek. We call it *ḥāmuḍuh*.

These things that I have mentioned, most of them, I mean all of them are considered to be for Ramadan. [They are] around in Ramadan. Such as apricot syrup. This is one of the important things in Ramadan which everyone buys. Of course, during Ramadan a lot of spices are bought such as salt, such as salt with wild thyme and chilli, such as wild thyme, such as cumin. People buy all these things in large amounts. You can see crowds around them at the beginning of Ramadan. I mean, the day before Ramadan or ... all the people are going to buy [things], it makes you wonder what on Earth they are doing. This is in relation to the spices for Ramadan.

---

[30] i.e. the middle of the dough.

[31] Compare the descriptive nature of this following part of the text with the instructional nature of recipes given in text 6. Cf. also AS's description of the preparation of *bint aṣ-ṣaḥn* in text 24.

[32] The fenugreek used for *saltih* is usu. whipped up with dried, crushed leeks which give it a green appearance.

[33] It is generally agreed that long, white radish should be eaten with soured fenugreek because the radish on its own causes foul-smelling burps (cf. al-Ḥawāli, vol. 2, 21).

wu-^{c}alā-mā gult / al-gadīd / hā̲dā min al-lašyā' al-muhimmih yištaraw[34] *an-nās / wa-l-gadīd hā̲dā hū ^{c}ibārih ^{c}an al-bargūg / ka-mā gadū / mā ya'kulūš an-nās wallā / allī bī-laggiḍūhun taḥt aš-šijar ^{c}inda-mā tjī al-^{c}aṣfūr tākulih bi-yinka^c gadū ṭayyub gawī / wa-yjirrū hā̲da l-bargūg / yijaffifūh / fī l-lajbī / ḥakk al-biyūt ḥakkum hā̲dawlā llī bi-zra^{c}ū 'ašjār al-bargūg / yijaffifūh / law-mā yijī ramaḏ̣ān gadū / yābis hāka̲dā / wa-ba^{c}dā yibī^{c}ūhā la-n-nās / wa-n-nās kayf yif^{c}alū hā̲da l-gadīd*[35] */ yifawwirū al-bargūg / ma^{c}a mā' / yiġassilūh awwal ḥājih wa-ba^{c}dayn yifawwirūh bayn al-mā' / wa-'aywih yifawwirūh / yif^{c}alū sukkar wa-hā̲dā ba^{c}dā yibarridūh / wa-yi^{c}tabar ya^{c}nī šarāb / bāhir / fī ramaḏ̣ān / anā ḥibb al-bargūg gawī / hā̲da l-gadīd /*

ah fī ramaḏ̣ān nākul law-mā nišba^c / ya^{c}nī yākul wāḥid xayrāt / wa-ya^{c}nī maṣārīf al-linsān hānā / tukṯar / fī ramaḏ̣ān / li'annū yištarī ḥājāt kaṯīrih mišū zayy al-liyyām al-^{c}ādiyih / yugaḏ̣ḏ̣ī bi-l-laḥmih wa-l-ḥulbuh wa-l-midrī[36] *māhū / hā̲dā fī ramaḏ̣ān kullahin yitwā:jidayn*[37] */ al-laḥmih ya^{c}nī min aḏ̣-ḏ̣urūrīyāt ^{c}alā mayd al-ḥilbih / yif^{c}alū šwayyih marag / hā̲dā bi-nisbih li-l-lakl ḥakk ramaḏ̣ān / w-anā ḏ̣alḥīn šā-'ašraḥ / kayf bi-f^{c}alū al-bint aṣ-ṣaḥn*[38] */ wa-^{c}ād ma^{c}ānā / ḏ̣ab^{c}an / as-sḥūr / as-sḥūr hā̲dā hū gabl / ya^{c}nī wakt al-fajr / iḥna bi-ntsaḥḥar fī l-bayt ḥakkanā /*

---

[34] Lack of object pronoun. Cf. *Syntax* pp. 234-5.

[35] Rhetorical question.

[36] Note use of definite article with the now almost lexicalised phrase *midrī* 'I don't know'.

[37] Vowel lengthening in stressed syllable of intonation phrase.

[38] Apposition phrase in place of annexion phrase *bint aṣ-ṣaḥn*. Cf. *Syntax* pp. 193-4.

And, as I said, apricot syrup. This is one of the important things that people buy. This syrup is from apricots which people don't eat. [People] gather them up beneath the trees when the birds come to eat them and they fall. They are very good. They[39] take these apricots and dry them on the roofs of their houses, of those who cultivate the apricot trees. They dry them, so that when Ramadan comes they are [completely] dried. Then they sell them to people. How do people make this syrup? They boil up the apricots with water. They wash them first thing, and then boil them in water and, yes, they boil them. They add sugar and then cool it down. This is thought to be an excellent syrup in Ramadan. I like apricots, this apricot syrup, very much.

Yes, in Ramadan we eat until we are full. I mean, you eat a lot and the amount people spend here during Ramadan goes up because they buy a lot of things, not like on normal days when they are content with meat and fenugreek and I don't know what. In Ramadan, all these things are available: meat is essential so that they can make a little broth for the fenugreek. This is about food for Ramadan. I am now going to explain how they make *bint aṣ-ṣaḥn*, and then we also have the last meal before daybreak. This last meal before daybreak is before dawn. We take this last meal in our house.

---

[39] i.e. the people who own the apricot trees.

24 *As-saḥūr wa-bint aṣ-ṣaḥn*

as-saḥūr

bi-nisbih la-s-sḥūr / hū b-ūga^{c} / ^{c}aṣīd / wa-maḏīṭ / wa-širbih / wa-ftūt ^{c}alā ḥalīb / wa-ḥulbih bayḏō / wa-ḏamū'l / ^{c}alā gahwih / hāḏawlā kullahin / ya^{c}nī yu^{c}tabarayn[1] *as-sḥūr / ḏab^{c}an / ya^{c}nī / yixtalif min bayt lā bayt*[2] */ miš ḏarūrī 'ann yikūnayn kull:ahin mawjūdāt / ^{c}ala s-sḥūr ya^{c}nī mumkin ḥājatayn ṯalāṯ min hāḏa l-ḥājāt / yākulū an-nās / wa-ḏ-ḏamū'l / yākulūhā hī zayy al-ka^{c}k awlā hākaḏā / yākulūhā / ^{c}alā gahwih / ya^{c}nī ba^{c}da-mā yitsaḥḥarū / yijlisū kaḏayyā yitgahwaw / wa-ya'kulū ḏamūl / yizīdū yirzimū*[3] *al-lakl / hāḏā as-sḥūr /*

bint aṣ-ṣaḥn

fa-ḏaḥḥīnih / šā-zīd ašraḥ ḥakk al-… mā yisammūhā / bint aṣ-ṣaḥn / kayf yisabbirūhā[4] */ al-bint aṣ-ṣaḥn kayf yif^{c}alū bint aṣ-ṣaḥn*[5] */ yijirrū ṯintayn*[6] *bayḏ / wa-ḥawālī / ṯalāṯih galaṣāt dagīg / wa-šwayyih mā' / šwayyih xamīrih / šwayyih milḥ / wa-mal^{c}agatayn samn / wa-kulla hāḏawlā / yuxluṭūhā hāḏā ma^{c}a hāḏā / wa-yi^{c}jinūhā xayrāt / wa-ba^{c}d-mā yi^{c}jinūhā xayrāt / ba^{c}da-mā yi^{c}jinūhā xayrāt gulnā / wa-ba^{c}dā yixarrijūhā / lā ṣaḥn / fīh šwayyih dagīg /*

ba^{c}dā yigaṭṭa^{c}ūhā ^{c}alā zuġayrih zuġayrih[7] */ ḥakk ḥawālī ṯn^{c}ašar*[8] *guḏa^{c} / iḏa ṣ-ṣaḥn kabīr aw ṯamān guḏa^{c} iḏa ṣ-ṣaḥn zaġīr / wa-ba^{c}d hāḏā kullih / yijirrū / yišnijūhā / ya^{c}nī yibrimūhā / wa-ḥīn yibrimūhā yixallawhā ba^{c}dā tiflit / wa-ba^{c}dā yimaddidūhā fi ṣ-ṣaḥn / yimaddidūhā fi ṣ-ṣaḥn bi-yadhum / wa-ba^{c}da-mā yimaddidūhā fi ṣ-ṣaḥn yijirrūhā min aṣ-ṣaḥn / wa-yfattiḥūhā 'akṯar / bi-yadhum / min yad lā yad law-mā gadī xafīfih sā^{c} al-warag /*

---

1 Internal passive. Cf. text 7. Cf. *Syntax* pp. 91-2.

2 Repetition of singular noun *bayt* conveys distributive sense.

3 By eating something with coffee this helps to settle the food. The verb *razam - yirzim* is used in a variety of contexts, but has the basic sense of 'to push s.th. down'.

4 Speaker uses unmarked masc. pl. form throughout this text to describe work which is done by women. Cf. texts 12, 21, 23. Cp. text 4 in which the specific fem. plural mainly used.

5 Annexion phrase *bint aṣ-ṣaḥn* follows apposition phrase *al-bint aṣ-ṣaḥn*.

6 Stress shift to initial syllable of numeral (**ṯintayn* not *ṯin*tayn*) to avoid stress clash.

7 Repetition of *zuġayrih* to convey distributive sense. Cf. *Syntax* p. 251-2.

8 Pronunciation of *-ar* of ^{c}*ašar* before noun. Cf. *Sbaḥtū!* p. 237. Cp. *as-sā^{c}ah ^{c}ašr* text 22.

24 The last meal before daybreak and bint aṣ-ṣaḥn

The last meal before daybreak[9]

The last meal before daybreak consists of dhurah porridge, barley gruel, broth, bread broken with milk, white fenugreek and cake with coffee.[10] All of these are considered to be part of the meal before daybreak. Of course, it does differ from one household to another. It isn't necessary for them to all be available for the meal before daybreak. People could eat two or three of these things, and cake. They eat this cake which is like ordinary cake, they eat it with coffee. After they have eaten this meal, they sit there and drink coffee and eat cake to help the food to settle. This is the last meal before daybreak.

Bint aṣ-ṣaḥn[11]

Now I am going to explain about, ... what do they call it, *bint aṣ-ṣaḥn*, how they make it, *bint aṣ-ṣaḥn*, how they make *bint aṣ-ṣaḥn*. They take two eggs, approximately three cups of flour and a little water, a little yeast, a little salt and two spoons of ghee. They mix all of these [ingredients] together and knead it a lot. After they have kneaded it a lot, after they have kneaded it a lot, I said, then they take it out onto a [metal] plate with a little flour on.

Then they cut it into small pieces, into around twelve pieces, if the plate is large, or eight pieces if the plate is small. After all this, they begin to work it between the fingers and the palm, that is to say they knead it. When they knead it, they then leave it to rise. Then they spread it out on the plate. They spread it out on the plate with their hands.[12] After they have spread it out on the plate, they take it from the plate and open it out more, with their hand[s], [passing it] from one hand to the other until it is as thin as paper.

---

9 The meal *saḥūr* is often referred to as *ġadā* 'lunch' in San'a.

10 A drink made from coffee husks and spices. For translation fluency, I translate it simply as 'coffee' since there is otherwise no acceptable single-word translation of *gahwih*.

11 Cp. the descriptive nature of this text with the instructional nature of recipes given in text 6. Cf. AS's description of the preparation of soured fenugreek in text 23.

12 Singular in Arabic.

wa-ba^{c}dā yijirrū aṣ-ṣaḥn / yif^{c}alūlih samn fī gā^{c}atih / wa-ḥīn yif^{c}alūlih samn fi l-gā^{c}ah ḥakk aṣ-ṣaḥn[13] */ yijirrū hāḏa l-^{c}ajīnih wa-gadī xafīfih gawī / yiḍruḥūhā fawg ḏayyik as-samn / wa-ba^{c}dā yif^{c}alū mal^{c}agih samn*[14] */ fawg tayyik illī gad ḍaraḥūhā / wa-yjirru ṯ-ṯāniyih / wa-yif^{c}alūlahā ya^{c}nī yiḍraḥūhā fawg tayyik wa-yif^{c}alūlahā samn / wa-hākaḏā / ^{c}alā wāḥidih wāḥidih*[15] */ law-mā yitimmūhin kull:ahin*[16] */ wa-yistamirru l-^{c}amalīyih ^{c}inda-mā yitimmūhin / gad al-guḍa^{c} kullahin gadin jāhizāt / yirja^{c}ū yif^{c}alū fī l-laxīr mal^{c}agih samn min ḍālu^{c} / fī l-wajh / wa-šwayyih guḥṭuh / wa-šwayyih jiljilān / wa-yixallawhā tuxmar / hinayyik /*

wa-law-mā gadī xāmirih / yidaxxilūha l-firn / titḥammar wasṭ al-firn / ya^{c}nī middih mi^{c}ayyinih hum yijissū yilāḥiḏūhā yibsirūhā gadī ḥamrā wallā mā gadīš muḥammarih / ba^{c}da[17] *hāḏā kullih / yigarribūhā' / ^{c}inda-mā yixarrijūhā min al-firn ḍab^{c}an / yigarribūhā ^{c}ala l-māyidih / min šān ya'kulūhā' / yif^{c}alū fawgahā ḍālu^{c} / šwayyih samn / wa-šwayyih ^{c}asal / wa-^{c}ād yūga^{c} ^{c}asal lā hū ^{c}asal baladī yūga^{c} ḥālī / wa-hāḏā / wa-ba^{c}dā yākulūhā /*

---

[13] Use of annexion phrase *gā^{c}atih* followed by attribution phrase *al-gā^{c}ah ḥakk as-samn* for stylistic variation. The longer attribution phrase carries more emphasis.

[14] Apposition. Cp. *šwayyih dagīg*, etc. Cf. *Syntax* p. 243.

[15] Repetition of *wāḥidih* to convey distributive sense. Cf. above.

[16] Lengthening of sonorant in stressed syllable of intonation phrase.

[17] Epenthesis.

Then, they take the plate and put some ghee on the base of it. When they have put ghee on the base of the plate, they take the dough which is now very thin and place it on the ghee. Then they put a spoonful of ghee on the top of that which they have [just] put down, and they take the second. They put on this, I mean they put it on top of the other, and put ghee on that, and it is like that one by one until they have finished them all. They continue this process until they have finished them and all of the pieces are ready. They then put a spoon of ghee on top, on the face[18] of the last one, and a little black cumin seed and some sesame seeds, and they leave it there to rise.

When it has risen, they put it into the oven so that it browns in the middle of the oven. For a certain length of time, they stay and watch it to see whether it has browned or whether it is not yet brown. After all this, they bring it over. When they take it out of the oven, of course, they bring it over to the table so that they can eat it. They put a little ghee and a little honey on the top of it. Honey is nice[st] if it is local honey.[19] Then they eat it.

[18] i.e. the upper-part. Metaphor in Arabic carried over in the English translation.

[19] Local [*baladī*] products are considered to be purer than imported products and are hence valued (and priced) more highly.

25 *Ifṭār*

b-ism illāh ar-raḥmān ar-raḥīm / al-yawm šā-sajjil / mā faḏarna l-yawm / wa-kayf yūga^c al-fuḏūr / gabl al-maġrib / štarayna l-gāt / al-yawm ba^{c}d al-ġadā / an-nahārih / wa-ḏawayna l-bayt / ba^{c}da-mā ḏawaynō / gadū bi-dris / twaḏḏaynō / wa-sirna l-jāmi^c / mā gad sirtš ana[1] *l-jāmi^c li'ann gad al-wakt kulla wāḥid yisīr al-jāmi^c / anā sirt bayt ^{c}ammī nufṭur / w-an agullukum mā faḏarna l-yawm / fī bayt ^{c}ammī faḏarnō / iḥna wa-l-jahhāl / iḥna wa-^{c}ammī wa-jahhālih / kullanā*[2] */*

al-yawm yūga^c al-fuḏūr ḥakkanā / hū sā^c kulla yawm mišū yawm kaḏā wa-yawm kaḏā[3] */ yūga^c al-fuḏūr basbūsih / ya^{c}nī sambūsih / wa:-kubaybā't / salaḏuh / ^{c}ala z-zaḥāwig / wa-ḥāmuḏuh / hāḏa l-yawm wuga^c al-fuḏūr / wa-zid iddawlanā šwayyih fūl min baynahin / kunnā mirayya^{c}īn la-l-maġrib ayyaḥīn ^{c}a-ygraḥ / wa-kān al-yawm awwal yawm ibnī 'ibrāhīm ṣā:m*[4] */ li-'awwal yawm yiṣūm fī ḥayātih ya^{c}nī kān al-yawm ṣām li'annu l-jum^{c}ah / mrayya^{c}īn la-l-maġrib wa-hū bi-dris / al-^{c}ādih ḥīn an-nās*[5] *yisīru l-jāmi^c / allī*[6] *yibizzalih ma^{c}ih šwayyih ḥāmuḏuh / w-allī yibizzalih tamrih w-allī yibizzalih / zaḥāwug wa-lugmih / wa-hākaḏā / w-iḥnā garaḥ al-madfa^c / basmalnā / akalnā ḏayyik al-fuḏūr kull:ih / wa-širibnā bardag mā' / wa-širibnā bardag ^{c}aṣīr / wa-sirna l-jāmi^c /*

wuṣulna l-jāmi^c wa-^{c}ādū bi-gūm aṣ-ṣalāh / wa-hū bi-gūm aṣ-ṣalāh / tibsir fī ṣawḥ ḥakk al-jāmi^c / an-nās jālisīn ^{c}alā šakl ḥalagāt ḥalagāt[7] */ ya^{c}nī l-^{c}ādih inna law-mā yijī wāḥid bi-ḥakkih al-fuḏūr / yuḏraḥuh aṯ-ṯānī yuḏraḥuh jambih wa-jambih / wa-hākaḏā / wa-hākaḏā / wa-yifṭurū majmū^{c}āt / wa-yūga^c ḥālī / yūga^{c}lih ḏa^{c}m wa-liḏḏih / yitnātifū / al-lakl minātifih / min kuṯr aṭ-ṭa^{c}m allī fīh /*

---

1 Post-position of independent pronoun to emphasise subject pronoun. Cf. *Syntax* p. 251. Change of subject from first plural to first sing.

2 Serial apposition, from *iḥna wa-l-jahhāl* to *kullanā*. Such serial apposition is common in Arabic, but does not translate comfortably into English.

3 Repetition of *yawm kaḏā* to convey distributive sense.

4 Lack of anaphoric pronoun in attributive clause to *awwal yawm*. Cf. *Syntax* pp. 234-5.

5 Noun of general significance, *an-nās*, comes between adjunction and verb. Cf. *Syntax* pp. 112, 116-17.

6 Exophoric pronominal use of definite clause. Cf. *Syntax* pp. 416-17.

7 Repetition of *ḥalagāt* to convey distributive sense. Cf. repetition of *jambih* below.

25 Breaking the fast

In the name of God, the Compassionate, the Merciful. Today, I am going to record what we broke the fast with today, and what breaking the fast consists of. Before sunset, I bought gat, today, after lunch in the afternoon, then I went home. After I went home, it was time to recite the Qur'an. I did my ablutions and went to the mosque. I didn't go to the mosque because it was the time when everyone was going to the mosque. I went to my [paternal] uncle's house to break the fast. I am going to tell you what we broke the fast with today. We broke the fast at my uncle's house, with the children, me and my uncle and his children, all of us.

Today breaking the fast was, it was the same as every day, it isn't one day like this and another day like that, breaking the fast consisted of basbusa, I mean samosas, small kebabs, salad with a spicy dip, and soured fenugreek. This is what breaking the fast was today. They also gave us a little foul with all of this. We were waiting for sunset for when [the cannon] is fired. Today was the first day that my son Ibrahim fasted. The first day that he has fasted in his life. I mean, it was today he fasted because it was Friday. Waiting for sunset, the Qur'an was recited. Usually, when people go to the mosque, some take a little sour fenugreek with them, some take dates, some take a spicy dip and bread, like that. When the cannon was fired, we said, 'In the name of God, the Compassionate, the Merciful!' We ate all that breakfast and drank a glass of water, we drank a glass of juice, then we went off to the mosque.

We arrived at the mosque while he[8] was just calling for prayer. While he was calling for prayer, in the courtyard of the mosque you could see everyone sitting in lots of circles. It is customary that when someone brings his own breakfast he puts it down and the next one puts his down next to him and so on, and like that, they break the fast in groups. It is really nice like that. It is tasty and nice. They take small amounts of the food there with all the taste that it has.

---

[8] i.e. the muezzin.

daxalnā wa-gām aṣ-ṣalāh / ṣalaynō[9] */ tammayna ṣ-ṣalāh sallam*[10] *baᶜd aṣ-ṣalāh / xarajnā min al-jāmiᶜ / riḥnālanā / kulla wāḥid raḥlih baytum / yisīr yifṭur / anā ḍawayt al-bayt / ḍawayt w-abī ᶜādū dāxilī / jay min al-jāmiᶜ / jalast anā w-abī nufṭur / garrabna l-faḍūr / al-ᶜašā yaᶜnī hāḏā / baᶜd al-faḍūr yūgaᶜ ᶜašā' /*

kān al-ᶜašā: laḥmih[11] */ wa-ḥulbih / wa-širbih / u-mā ᶜad bih / wa-marag wa-ᶜaṣī'r / ᶜaṣīr al-gadī'd / hāḏa l-ᶜaṣīr al-gadīd*[12] *fiᶜilatih al-marih ḥakkī*[13] *'ams / w-iḥna bi-nufṭur wa-jā' axī ᶜabd al-laṭīf / jā' ᶜabd al-laṭīf laḥaglih*[14] *lijᶜ maᶜānā wa-nnātif iḥna wa-hū al-lakl bi-nākul / šibiᶜnā / wa-l-ḥamdulillāh / ḍuluᶜt anā bazzayt ġarr al-ḥawlī ḥakkī / wa-sirt ṣalā bayt ᶜammī /*

fī bayt ᶜammī ligīt bayt ᶜammī kulluhum / w-ibnī wa-maratī wa-kulluhum an-nās hānāk / iddawlī bardag gahwih / itgahwayt baᶜd al-ᶜašā / tgahwayt fiᶜiltalī bardag gahwih[15] */ wa-ᶜammī gad ᶜammar at-titin / gad al-būrī mujahhaz gadū bi-šrab madāᶜah / ddālī naxs wa-bi-nitfarraj at-talaviziyūn / kānū bi-ddaw waḏīfuh / hāḏā musalsal kūmidī bi-ddaw min al-MBC fī ramaḏān / yaᶜnī muḏḥuk / yijī yiddīlak nās wa-yijiss yixallum*[16] *yifᶜalū ḥarakāt / yāsᶜam innum yištaw waḏīfuh aw midrī māhū / yijissū yifᶜalū ḥarakāt wa-hāḏā / wa-yirjaᶜ yigulluhum fī l-laxīr hayyā bsir al-mirāyih tayka / wa-yigullih al-kāmira xafiyih /*

ja:last hānāk šwayyih / wa-tgahwayt / wa-xarajt / sirt al-ḥammām / gult afᶜallī[17] *ᶜargih ḥammām / wuṣult la-l-ḥammām wa-ᶜādū muġallag mā gad biš wallā maxlūg / muġallag min xārij / iftaḥt al-ḥammām / wa-daxalt / waḥdī / mā bih ḥadd ill anā / daxalt / xalaṣt al-ladāh ḥakkī / wa-daxaltalī /*

---

9 *Imāla* and labialisation of *-ē* due to emphatic *ṣ*.

10 Uninflected verb.

11 Verbal clause with initial linking verb and emphasis on post-subject complement.

12 Annexion phrase *ᶜaṣīr al-gadīd* followed by apposition phrase *al-ᶜaṣīr al-gadīd*. Cf. *Syntax* pp. 193-4. Topicalisation of object. Cf. *Syntax* p. 130.

13 Emphatic use of *ḥagg* phrase with noun of human relationship. Cp. *Syntax* p. 179.

14 Reflexive verb. Cf. *Syntax* pp. 202-3.

15 *fiᶜiltalī bardag gahwih* functions as a reformulative appositive to *tgahwayt*.

16 From *yixallīhum*.

17 Reflexive verb. Cf. *Syntax* pp. 202-3. Cf. use of this verb in texts 9, 11, 18, 22, 27.

We went in[to the mosque] and prayer was being called. We prayed. We finished praying then greeted[18] after praying. We went out of the mosque and left. Everyone went home,[19] going to break the fast.[20] I went home. I went home and my father was just coming in from the mosque. My father and I sat down and broke the fast. We laid out the [breakfast], supper, I mean. After breaking the fast, it is supper.

Supper consisted of meat, fenugreek, soup and, what else is there, broth, juice, apricot syrup – my wife made this apricot syrup yesterday. We were eating when my brother Abd al-Latif came. Abd al-Latif caught up with us and found himself something to eat. We ate with him until we were full, thanks be to God. I got up and just took my towel and went off to my uncle's house.

At my uncle's house, I found the whole of my uncle's family including my son and my wife and everyone was there. They gave me a cup of coffee. I drank coffee after supper. I drank coffee, I had a cup of coffee. My uncle had prepared the bowl of the water-pipe. The clay bowl [of the water-pipe] had been prepared and he was smoking the water-pipe.[21] He gave me a puff [of the water-pipe] while we watched television. They were showing 'a job'. This is a comedy series they broadcast from the MBC during Ramadan. A comedian brings on people and makes them do things, as if they wanted a job or I don't know what. They keep doing things and at the end he says to them, 'Come on, look at that mirror!' and he tells them that the camera was hidden.

I stayed there for a while, I had coffee and went out. I went to the bath-house. I said I would have a bath sweat. I arrived at the bath-house and it was still locked. There wasn't a soul there. Locked from the outside. I opened the bath-house and went in on my own. There was no one there but me. I went in. I took off my clothes and took myself in.

---

18 Muslims conclude the prayer by saying, 'Peace be upon you!' to either side of them. AS describes this as greeting the angels around him.

19 Lit: 'everyone [s.] went to their [i.e. pl.] house'.

20 In fact, for supper.

21 Indefinite in Arabic.

ᶜa:ragt šwayyih / baᶜd-mā ᶜarakt[22] */ gumt atġassal / tlayyaft wa-tṣabbant wa-bayn-asakkiblī*[23] *mā' / law-mā: gadanā ḥāmī /*

jā' al-ḥammāmī[24] */ jay ydawwir man gad fī l-ḥammām / aha xarajt / wa-baᶜda-mā xarajt ṣallaytalī*[25] *al-ᶜišā hinayyik fī l-ḥammām / li'annū bih bugᶜah hānāk yiṣallaw fīhā / ayš*[26] *agūl / yaᶜnī bugᶜah yiṣallaw fīhā / xarajt min al-ḥammām / wa-jīt kaḏā ṣalā l-bayt /*

---

[22] Anticipatory devoicing of *g* to *k*.

[23] Reflexive verb. Cf. *Syntax* pp. 202-3. This form II verb has an intensive, repetitive sense additional to the sense of the corresponding form I verb *sakab* 'to pour s.th.'

[24] Verbal clause with dynamic verb.

[25] Reflexive verb. Cf. *Syntax* pp. 202-3.

[26] Use of pan-Yemeni *ayš*.

I sweated a little. After I had sweated, I began to wash myself. I used the loofa and soaped myself, throwing water over myself until I became hot.

The bath-man came. He was coming to see who was in the bath-house. Then I came out, and after I came out I did the evening prayer there in the bath-house, because there is a place where they can pray. What [else] should I say? I mean, a place which they can pray in. I came out of the bath-house and set off for home.

aywih / ḏaḥḥīn antī dārī[1] *mā šā-gulliš / mā ᶜa-nifᶜal la-l-ᶜīd / wa-mā yifᶜalū: an-nās kull:uhum la-l-ᶜīd / ḍabᶜan gad kullu bayt bī-fakkir fī l-ᶜīd / al-ᶜīd hāḏā bī-fakkirūbih kayfih*[2] */ yištaw kswuh*[3] *la-l-jahhāl / lā šī wāḥid maᶜih ṯalāṯih arbaᶜah*[4] *jahhāl / bī-fakkir kayf yiksī al-jahhāl hāḏawlā / wa-kswat al-jahhāl mā hīš raxīṣuh wallā šī / yallāh al-murattab al-yawm hāḏā mā ᶜad yikfīš ḥakk*[5] *kiswat jāhil walla ṯnayn /*

ḍabᶜan al-kswih[6] *māhī*[7] */ al-kswih*[8] *tištī tištarīlih banḍalūn*[9] */ wa-tištarī šamīz*[10] */ wa-tištarīlih gunḍuruh jadīd*[11] */ tištarīlih šarābāt / wa-jākitt*[12] */ wallā badlih / kāmilih badal hāḏawlā kulluhin / wa-zinnih / hāḏā la-l-wāḥid / min al-jahhāl / wa-'iḏā hī bint / tštī fustān / wa-jazmih jadīd*[13] */ walla ṯnayn fasātīn*[14] *agalla šī / wa-banṭalūn / wa-l-malābis ad-dāxilīyih fanilliyih wa-kalasūn /*

hāḏawlā bi-nisbih la-l-jahhāl kayf al-wāḥid bī-jiss yifakkir mā yištarīhin la-l-jahhāl / hāḏā la-l-jahhāl / wa-l-bint wa-l-kull yištarawlahā gabbāḏāt / wa-yištarūlahā ṭawg / yitḥaylawlahā yiddawlahā al-ḥājih ᶜalā gadr al-ḥālih mā lafīyū[15] */ wa-l-wald / nafs aš-šī yiddaw ᶜalā gadr al-ḥālih / hāḏā bi-nisbih la-l-jahhāl min at-tajhīzāt ḥakk al-ᶜīd /*

wa-ᶜād iḥna ništī / li-yawm al-ᶜīd / ḥājāt al-ᶜīd / maṯalan ḥājāt al-ᶜīd iḥna bi-ništarī hānā fī l-bayt / anā bayn-aštarī la-l-bayt ajirr ad-daxiš /

---

1 Underarticulation of feminine ending *-yih*. Cf. texts 5, 10.

2 Rhetorical question.

3 Syncope of initial stressed vowel with stress migration to final syllable. Cf. Introduction.

4 Asyndetic linkage of alternative numerical phrases. Cf. *Syntax* p. 312.

5 Here *ḥagg* heads an annexion phrase and is used in the sense of 'for'. Cf. *Syntax* p. 224.

6 Syncope. From *kiswih* 'clothes'.

7 Rhetorical question.

8 The noun functions here as an adverb. Cf. *dawl ar-rijāl* in text 17.

9 Loan word. From French *bantalon*.

10 Loan word. From French *chemise*.

11 Lack of gender agreement with the preceding feminine noun.

12 Loan word. From *jacket*.

13 Lack of gender agreement with attributed term.

14 Non-use of dual for nouns indicating other than time or measure. Cf. *Ṣbaḥtū!* pp. 93-4.

15 Cf. text 10 for use of *lafī* in universal-conditional-concession clauses.

26 Festivals

Yes, now you know what I am going to tell you about, what we do for the festival, and what all the people do for the festival. Of course, every household is thinking about the festival. This festival, what do people think about? They want to buy outfits for the children. If there is someone who has three or four children, he will wonder how he can clothe these children. Children's outfits are not cheap or anything. Wages today are not enough for the outfits for one or two children.

Of course, what are outfits? For outfits, you will need to buy him trousers, you will buy a shirt; you will buy him new shoes; you will buy him socks, and a jacket, or a complete suit instead of all these [things], and a full-length robe. This is for one of the children. If she is a girl, she will want a dress, new shoes, or two dresses at least, trousers, and underclothes – a vest and pants.

This is as far as the children are concerned. How he[16] keeps thinking what he is going to buy for the children. This is for children. For a girl,[17] he will also buy her hairclips, and he will buy her an alice-band. He thinks the world of her and will buy her whatever he can afford, whatever he can find. For a boy,[18] it is the same thing: he will give him whatever he can afford. These are some of the festival preparations they do for the children.

We also need festival things for the day of the festival. For instance, the festival things we buy here for the household, I will buy black peas for the household.

---

[16] The 3 m.pl. pronoun used to refer to fathers in general in this passage is translated by the English 3 m.sg. 'he'. This is because of the conceptual difficulties associated with literal translations of later phrases such as 'they m. think the world of her and give her whatever they can afford and whatever they can find' where fathers are described in the plural, but daughters in the singular.

[17] Definite in Arabic.

[18] Definite in Arabic.

w-aštarī zabīb / wa-lawz / lawz baladī / al-lawz al-baladī al-yaw:m gadū ġālī hānā / gadū[19] *ba^{c}ḍ an-nās yištaraw baladī / ba^{c}ḍ an-nās yištaraw / xārijī / al-xārijī hū yijan*[20] *ḍuwāl wa-l-baladī hū yijī zaġīr wa-ḍa^{c}īm / ništī fustu:g / wa-ništī: mḥabb al-^{c}azīz / wa-ništī: milayyam / wallā šiklīt / šukalātih / min hāḏawlā kull:ahin hāḏawla llī ništī ništarīhin / wa-^{c}ūdih ^{c}alā mayd ni^{c}awwid al-musallimīn / wa-^{c}uḍr / ni^{c}aṭṭurhum / hāḏawla l-ḥājāt allī ništīhin li-yawm al-^{c}īd /*

wa-'iḍāfuh ilā ḏā:lik[21] */ ^{c}ād ya^{c}nī an-niswān fī kulla bayt / yit^{c}abayn wa-yišgayn wa-yizīd*[22] *yisabbirayn / al-ka^{c}k ḥakk al-^{c}īd / ka^{c}k al-^{c}īd*[23] *hāḏā yisabbirū*[24] *ka^{c}k / kulla bayt yif^{c}al iṯnayn ṯalāṯih ṣuḥū'n / ġayr illī hum xayrāt al-lahl yif^{c}alū 'akṯar min arba^{c}ah / min xamsih ṣuḥūn / wa-l-ka^{c}k illī yisabbirūh / ka^{c}k ^{c}ādī wa-ka^{c}k musamman / al-ka^{c}k al-musamman hāḏā / yif^{c}alūlih sukkar / yūga^{c} misakkar / sā^{c} al-biskut / wa-ka^{c}k yif^{c}alūh bi-tamr / yif^{c}alū dāxilih tamr / wa:-hāḏa llī yif^{c}alayn*[25] *an-niswān / li-yawm al-^{c}īd /*

wa-^{c}inda-mā yijī al-^{c}īd / yijirr[26] *ya^{c}nī an-niswān fī l-bayt laylat al-^{c}īd hāḏawlā gadin yinaḍḍufayn al-bayt wa-yinaffuḍayn gabl al-^{c}īd bi-yawm bi-yawmayn / wa-yijahhizayn aṣ-ṣuḥūn ḥakk al-… / ḥakk al-ka^{c}k / wa-ḥakk ja^{c}ālat al-^{c}īd nisammīhā ja^{c}ālat al-^{c}īd / yijahhizannahā / tif^{c}al*[27] *fī ḏayya ṣ-ṣaḥn šwayyat daxiš*[28] *wa-tif^{c}al fī ḏayya ṣ-ṣaḥn šwayyih lawz wa-tif^{c}al fī ḏayya ṣ-ṣaḥn / šwayy*[29] *zabīb / wa-ḏayya ṣ-ṣaḥn tif^{c}al fīh šwayyih miḥabb al-^{c}azīz / wa-šwayyih fustug fī ṣaḥn / šwayyih gar^{c} fī ṣaḥn /*

---

19 *gadū* is analysed as the copula *gad* + dummy pronoun *(h)ū*. Cf. *Syntax* p. 413.

20 Diphthong simplification of *-ayn* from *yijayn*. Note use of fem. pl. verb and pl. adjective while subject pronoun is *hū*. This indicates speaker was thinking of referent (*lawz*) as a plural entity. Cp. following clause. Cf. fem. pl. agreement for collectives in texts 4, 5, 12.

21 Classicism.

22 Lack of number agreement on the linking verb.

23 Attribution phrase *al-ka^{c}k ḥakk al-^{c}īd* followed by annexion phrase *ka^{c}k al-^{c}īd* for stylistic variation.

24 Switch from specific fem. pl. to general masc. pl. agreement. Cf. texts 4, 12, 21, 23, 24.

25 Switch back to fem. plural subject with explicit noun subject.

26 Lack of agreement with following fem. plural subject. Probably due to hesitation.

27 Change of subject from fem. plural to fem. singular.

28 Annexion phrase. Cp. following apposition phrase *šwayyih lawz*.

29 Underarticulation. From *šwayyih*.

I will buy raisins, almonds, local almonds. Local almonds today are very expensive here. Some people buy local, some people buy imported [ones]. The imported [ones] are long, while the local [ones] are small and tasty. We want pistachios, we want peanuts, we want boiled sweets or soft wrapped sweets, or chocolate. We want to buy some of all of these things, and sandlewood so that we can incense those who come to greet [us], and perfume to perfume them. These are the things that we want for the day of the festival.

In addition to that, the women in every house are going to a lot of effort, working hard and also making cakes for the festival. For festival cakes, they make cake. Every household will make two or three plates, unless there are a lot in the family and then they will make more than four or five plates. The cake they make is normal cake and cake with fat. For the cake with fat, they add sugar. It is sugary, like biscuits, and there's a cake they put dates in. They put dates inside it. This is what the women do for the day of the festival.

When the festival comes they take, I mean, the women of the house on the eve of the festival, they clean the house and dust one or two days before the festival. They prepare the plates for the ... for the cakes and for the festival sweets, we call them *ja^{c}ālat al-^{c}īd*. They prepare them. She[30] will put a few black peas on this plate and she will put a few almonds on that plate and she will put a few raisins on that plate, and on that plate she will put some peanuts, some pistachios on a plate, some pumpkin seeds on a plate.

---

30 i.e. the woman of the house.

hāḏawlā kullahin tifᶜalhin fī l-maᶜšarih / wa-fī ṣ-ṣuḥūn / wa-ṣ-ṣḥūn fīhin hākaḏā / min hāḏa llī gad atḥākayt ᶜanhin gabl šwayyih / wa-yawm al-ᶜīd / gad al-marih tijahhiz ḥakkahā / al-mabxarih / wa-tjahhiz an-nār / wa-tjahhiz al-gahwih / wa-tjahhiz al-ᶜaṣīr / walla l-fīmtū / wa-l-mā' al-bārid / hāḏawlā tijahhizhin kull:ahin / tijī wa-gadī jāhizih /

iḥna yawm al-ᶜīd aṣ-ṣubḥ / nisīr niṣallī 'awwal ḥājih fī l-jāmiᶜ / niṣallī ṣalāt al-ᶜīd / al-ᶜīd ᶜindanā hānā hū 'akṯarathā / la-l-laṭfāl / walla l-makālif / al-makālif hin / yaᶜnī al-wāḥid lammā maᶜih min makālif miṯl uxtih / ummʷih / ᶜammatih / xālatih / hāḏawlā al-agārib / yisammūhin makālif / baᶜd-ma ntimm niṣallī / ṣalāt al-ᶜīd / nirjaᶜ al-bayt / nibaddil / wa-nsallim salām al-ᶜīd ᶜalā / 'ahlana llī fī l-bayt /

wa-baᶜdā gad kullu wāḥid gadū muwakkaf lā fī jaybih šwayyih zalaṭ / li'ann al-ᶜīd ᶜindanā hānā / law-mā: yaᶜnī ᶜinda-mā jay axruj min al-bayt gadanā mubaddal wa-jāhiz anā wa-jahhālī / yaᶜnī kullu wāḥid hū wa-jahhāluh wa-hāḏā / yibda' yisīr yizūr ahlih / hāḏa llī yizūr ummʷih / yizūr uxtih / yizūr ᶜammatih / hākaḏā / yijirr maᶜih zalaṭ / az-zalaṭ hāḏā gadū ᶜinda-mā yisīr yisallim ᶜala l-marih / yiᶜsibhā / wa-l-ᶜasb[31] */ ᶜibārih ᶜan innū yiddīlahā / maṯalan / hāḏa l-liyyām yiššī yiddī min miyatayn / illī maᶜih zalaṭ*[32] *yiddī min miyatayn allī maᶜih mā biš maᶜih zalaṭ yiddī min xamsīn yiddī min ᶜišrīn / yiddī min miyih / al-lawwalīn mā yiddaw zalaṭ illā galīlih / yaᶜnī mā yitᶜaddawš al-miyih / al-miyih gadī xayrāt hāḏa l-lawwalīn / illā manū ġanī maᶜih zalaṭ xayrāt gadū yiddī / aš-šabāb gadum yizayyidū šwayyih / allī yiddī al-miyatayn / allī yiddī al-xamsamiyih allī yiddī 'alf / allī yiddī ṯalāṯamiyih*[33] */ kulla wāḥid ᶜalā gadrih /*

ḍabᶜan anā maṯalan miṯlī 'anā / 'aštī ᶜala l-lagall fī l-ᶜīd al-wāḥid[34] */ ᶜasb / fī ḥudūd xamsatᶜāš*[35]*. lā ᶜišrīn alf / li'annanī bayn-azūr xawātī bayn-azūr ᶜammātī bayn-azūr ahlī /*

---

[31] According to al-Ḥawālī, *ᶜasb* originally meant a stud fee (al-Ḥawālī vol. 2, 121).

[32] Exophoric pronominal use of definite clause. Cf. *Syntax* pp. 416-17.

[33] Four asyndetically linked definite clauses functioning as exophoric pronominals. Repetition of clausal definite article conveys sense of incomplete list. Cf. below.

[34] Attribution of *al-wāḥid* to emphasise singularity of noun (cf. Mörth 1997: 116-17).

[35] Non-pronunciation of *-ar* ending of *ᶜašar* when numeral occurs at end of phrase. Cf. text 22. Cp. *ṯnᶜašar guḍaᶜ* in text 24.

All of these she puts on a large round copper tray and on plates, and these plates will have those things I have just spoken about. On the day of the festival, the woman will prepare her incense burner, and prepare the charcoal, and prepare the coffee and prepare the juice or the Vimto, and the cold water. She will prepare all these things. She will come and be ready.

On the morning of the festival, we go to pray first thing in the mosque. We do the festival prayer. Here the festival is mainly for the children or the women. The women are, I mean, if you have women relatives such as your sister, your mother, your [paternal] aunt,[36] your [maternal] aunt, these are relatives, and they call them *makālif* [women relatives]. After we finish the festival prayer, we go back to the house and get changed and we give festival greetings to our family who are at home.

Then everyone makes sure that he has a little money in his pocket because for the festival here, when I come to go out of my house and me and my children are changed and ready, everyone begins to go with his children to visit his family. Those who visit their mother, their sister or their [paternal] aunt,[37] like that, take money with them. This money is so that when he goes to greet the woman he can give her some festival money. The festival money that he gives to her these days, he will want to give around 200; those who have [a lot of] money will give around 200; those who do not have [much] money will give around 50 or give around 20, or give around 100. Older people only give a little money – that is, they won't give more than a hundred. A hundred would be a lot for older people, except for those who are rich who have a lot of money, then they will maybe give [more]. Young people give a bit more: some give 200, some give 500, some give 1,000, some give 300. Everyone [gives] what they can afford.

Of course, me, for instance, [someone] like me needs at least around fifteen to twenty thousand to give as festival money for the one festival because I go to visit my sisters, I visit my [paternal] aunts, I visit my family.

---

[36] Or mother-in-law.

[37] Or mother-in-law.

bayn-azūr ahlī kull:uhum[38] */ wa-'ayḏ̣an ^{c}inda-mā lgā jahhāl / min agāribī hāḏawlā kulluhum / aššī 'a^{c}subhum / ḏayya ddīlih ^{c}išrīn / ḏayya ddīlih xamsīn / ḏayya ddīlih miyih*[39] */ wa-hākaḏā l-kull /*

fa-l-jahhāl gadī farḥathum yawm al-^{c}īd / gadum ġarr yi^{c}jibhum yisīrū min bayt lā bayt fī ^{c}ind ahluhum / min šān yisallimū / nisammīh salām al-^{c}īd / wa-ḥīn yisīr al-jāhil yisallim lā bayt ^{c}ammih wallā lā bayt xālih wallā lā bayt ^{c}ammatih wallā lā ^{c}ind umm^{w}ih / wallā ^{c}ind jaddatih wallā lā ^{c}ind bayt sīdih / mā yisīr illā w-hū mrā^{c}ī 'ayyaḥīn-mā yu^{c}subūh[40] */ gadū ġarr yudxul sā^{c} al-malg^{w}ūṣ / law-mā ġarrih yi^{c}assibūh wa-gā'm*[41] */ 'ayn ^{c}a-tsīr gāl yisīr yisallim / yisīr al-bayt aṯ-ṯānī bayt ^{c}ammih wallā bayt xālatih wallā / wa-hākaḏā / hāḏā ḥakk al-^{c}īd /*

an-niswān fī l-biyūt / gad kulla marih dintaḏur / maṯalan allī bint ḏayyā ^{c}al abūhā / ^{c}a-yjaw ahlahā / li'annī fī bayt zawjahā ḍab^{c}an / ^{c}a-jaw ahlahā / ^{c}a-yjaw axwathā[42] */ fa-tgarribluhum / aṣ-ṣuḥūn hāḏīk illī fīhā az-zabīb wa-l-lawz wa-d-dixiš wa-hāḏā / wa-ḥīn yūṣalū 'ahlahā / yūṣalū ^{c}indahā yijissū šwayyih / yākulū dixiš wa-zabīb wa-lawz wa-ḏayyā / yākulū min ja^{c}ālat al-^{c}īd / ba^{c}da-mā yākulū min ja^{c}ālat al-^{c}īd / yugūmū / yugūlū ^{c}a-yruḥūluhum / wa-hī / al-marih gadī tigūl jissū šwayyih / ^{c}ādū ḥīn / bayna-mā gadī yallāh tiruḥūlukum ^{c}a-yjaw aṯ-ṯāniyīn*[43] */ wa-yigūm*[44] *yi^{c}assibūhā /*

gad kullu wāḥid ya^{c}sib ^{c}alā gadr isṭṭā^{c}atuh[45] */ wa-hākaḏā / fī kulla bayt / wa-^{c}inda kulla 'usrih / hāḏā fī ṣan^{c}ā bi-ḏāt ya^{c}nī / salām al-^{c}īd / ^{c}ind an-nās kull:uhum ya^{c}nī fī l-yaman / lākin salām al-^{c}īd fī ṣan^{c}ā 'akṯarathum mā bu-xruj illā bi-^{c}asb / gad iḥna nisīr min bayt lā bayt ^{c}ind agāribnā /*

---

38 Fourfold repetition of *bayn-azūr* with asyndetic linkage of clauses conveys sense of incomplete list. Cf. *Syntax* pp. 316-17.

39 Repetition of *ḏayyā* with asyndetic linkage of clauses. Cf. above. Note *ḏayyā* functions similarly to *allī* in asyndetically linked definite clauses above.

40 Universal-conditional-concession clause with imperfect verb in place of perfect.

41 Use of perfect in syndetically linked main clause which depends on fulfillment of action stated in initial subordinate clause. Cp. text 19 . Cf. *Syntax* p. 65.

42 Asyndetically linked verbal clauses with repetition of verb and emphasis on contrastive subjects.

43 Asyndetic linkage of explanatory clause. Cf. *Syntax* p. 309.

44 Lack of number agreement on linking verb.

45 Syncope of unstressed vowel and assimilation of emphasis. From *istiṭā^{c}uh* 'ability'.

I visit the whole of my family. Also, when I meet one of all my child relatives, I will want to give them festival money. One I will give 20, another I will give 50, another I will give 100, like that.

The day of the festival is for the children's enjoyment. They just like to go from house to house among their relatives to greet. We call it festival greetings. When children[46] go to greet their [paternal] uncle's family or their [maternal] uncle's family or their [paternal] aunt's family, or [when they go] to their mother's or their grandmother's or to their grandfather's house, they only go so that they can wait to be given festival money. They just go in like someone who's been stung, and they have hardly been given their festival money when they get up. 'Where are you going?' They will say they are going to greet, they are going on to the next house, their [paternal] uncle's house or their [maternal] aunt's house or wherever. This is for the festival.

Women in the houses, every woman waits, for example, so-and-so's daughter waits for her father. Her family will come because, of course, she is in her husband's house. Her family will come; her brothers will come, and she will offer them the plates with raisins, almonds and black peas and the like. When her family arrive, they will come to her and stay a short while eating black peas, raisins and almonds and the like, eating the festival sweets. After eating the festival sweets, they will get up and say they are going. The woman will say, 'Stay a little! It is still early!' But really she [means], 'Okay, you can go, [because] the others are coming.' Then they will give her the festival money.

Everyone gives as much festival money as they can, and it is like that in every house with every family. This is particularly so in San'a. I mean, there are festival greetings with everyone in Yemen, but festival greetings in San'a for most of them have to involve festival money. We go from house to house among our relatives.

[46] Singular in Arabic.

wa-nmakkinhā[47] */ dixiš / wallā ka^{c}k / wallā … wa-nmakkinhā min hāḏawlā kullahin / wuga^{c} wa-hāḏā mā yijī ḍ-ḍuhr illā wa-gadiḥna mašbūjīn / min kuṯrat mā bi-nākul min bayt lā bayt / hāḏā salām al-^{c}īd /*

wa-ba^{c}dā / ba^{c}da-ma nkammil nisallim ^{c}ala l-makālif ku:llahin / nisīr nidawwir al-gāt / ništarīlanā gāt / ba^{c}da-mā ništarī l-gāt / nuḍwī al-bayt nitġaddā / ḍab^{c}an gadiḥna nitlāgā / iḥna w-ahlanā wa-ya^{c}nī llī yilgā 'axwatih wa-'agāribih wa-^{c}iyyāl ^{c}ammih wa-hāḏā / wa-nittafig / ^{c}alā 'inn aḥna nixazzin ma^{c} ba^{c}ḍ / kullanā fī bayt wāḥid / ammā nixazzin fī baytanā / wallā nixazzin fī bayt ^{c}ammatī / wallā nixazzin fī bayt ^{c}ammī / gadū 'iḥna mittafigīn ya^{c}nī / w-iḏā ttafagnā ^{c}ind bayt wāḥid gad kullanā / kulla wāḥid[48] *yikallim aṯ-ṯānī / wa-niltagī fī l-bayt hāḏāk / wa-nsīr nixazzin /*

hāḏā bi-nisbih lanā / bi-nisbih la-l-jahhāl / gadum ġarr yinabbaw ^{c}alā-mā gultališ min bayt lā bayt / yilaflifū hāḏa l-^{c}asb ḥakkuhum / wa-fāriḥ[49] *bi-z-zalaṭ / kam ūgi^{c}lak / gāl kam ūgi^{c}lak / kulla jāhil yuṣayyuḥ kam ūgi^{c}lak / gāl kam ūgi^{c}lak / yisīr*[50] *yištarawluhum li^{c}ib min hāḏawla l-girrīḥ wallā yijirrūluhum musaddasāt min ḥakk al-mā'*[51] */ li'anna hāḏawlā ^{c}a-yuxrujayn / fī l-^{c}īd / yuxrujayn la-l-jahhāl az-zuġār wa-l-jahhāl az-zuġār yi^{c}jibhum hāḏa l-ḥājāt / yištarawhin / w-innū*[52] *ma wgi^{c}lih min ^{c}asb sār ištarā hāḏa l-li^{c}ib / ammā ḏayyik al-yawm wi-ksirhā /*

hāḏā bi-nisbih lan iḥna[53] *wa-bi-nisbih la-l-jahhāl / wa-n-niswān gadin / ba^{c}da-mā yijaw ahlahin kull:ahin*[54] *yisallimū ^{c}alayhin / tijahhiz*[55] *al-ġadā wa-hāḏā wa-yitġaddaw / wa-ba^{c}dā tisīr ba^{c}d al-ġadā tisallim ^{c}al ahlahā / wa-tsallim ^{c}alā 'agāribhā 'illī garībīn min ^{c}indahā / wa-yisīrayn yijlisayn / salām al-^{c}īd / ^{c}indahin / yijissayn ma^{c}a ba^{c}ḍ an-niswān fī biyūt /*

---

47 Idiomatic phrase meaning 'we have' or 'we take'. *-hā* functions as dummy object pronoun. Cf. *Syntax* pp. 413-14.

48 *kulla wāḥid* acts here as an appositive to *kullanā*.

49 Lack of number agreement with plural referent.

50 Lack of number agreement on linking verb. Cf. note above.

51 Lit: 'pistols for water'. Cf. *Syntax* p. 222 for other descriptive uses of *ḥagg* phrase.

52 Consequential marker.

53 Post-position of pronoun to emphasise annex of preposition. Cf. *Syntax* p. 251.

54 Lack of gender agreement on verb.

55 Change of subject from fem. plural to fem. singular.

We keep eating black peas or cake or ... we eat some of all these things, and by the time noon comes we are full from all we have been eating at one house and the other. This is the festival greeting.

Then, after we have finished greeting all our female relatives, we go to look for gat. We buy ourselves gat. After we have bought gat, we go home to have lunch. Of course, we meet up with our family; some meet their brothers, their relatives, their [paternal] cousins and the like; then we agree to chew all together in one house. Either we chew in our house, or we chew in my [paternal] aunt's house, or we chew in my [paternal] uncle's house. We come to an agreement, and if we have agreed [to chew] at someone's house, everyone will talk to the next [person] and we will meet up in that house and go and chew.

This is as far as we are concerned. As far as the children are concerned, they just call, as I said, from one house to the other collecting this festival money of theirs and delighting in the money. 'How much have you got?' [One] says, 'How much have you got?' Every child yells out, 'How much have you got? How much have you got?' They go to buy themselves toys such as those firecrackers, or they get themselves water pistols because these [things] come out for the festivals. They come out for the young children and young children love these things and they buy them. So with whatever festival money they have, they go out and buy these things, but they break them on the same day.

This is as far as we and the children are concerned. With the women, after all their family has been to greet them, they prepare lunch and have lunch. Then, after lunch, she will go to greet her family and greet her relatives who live close by. They will go and sit. Festival greetings for them involves the women sitting together in [their] houses.

yaᶜnī lā sārat al-marih lā bayt ahlahā / tijlis ᶜindahum wa-yjayn xawāthā wa-yijī[56] *'axwathā*[57] */ yaᶜnī / kullahin an-niswān*[58] *illī hin agārib yijayn yijissayn maᶜa baᶜḍ / wa-nafs aṭ-ṭarīguh / salām al-ᶜīd ᶜindahin hākaḏā / hāḏā bi-nisbih lā salām al-ᶜīd ᶜindanā fi l-yaman / yirayyaᶜūlih mirāᶜah /*

ḍabᶜan anā maṭalan ᶜādanā / nisīt mā gūl ḥājih / iḥna l-ᶜīd ᶜindanā hū yawm al-ᶜīd maṭalan / āxir yawm fī ramaḍān / hāḏā / nitimm ramaḍān wa-baᶜdā nᶜayyid / anā maṭalan law sirt azūr ahlī kull:uhum wa-bigyat marih wallā ṯintayn min ahlī mā zurtahinš / mumkin an[59] *asīr al-yawm aṯ-ṯānī / allī yisammawh ṯānī al-ᶜīd / yawm ṯānī al-ᶜīd yisīr*[60] *yisallimū / wa-hāḏā gadū 'āxir yawm minnak tisīr lā ᶜind agāribak / tsīr tisallim ᶜalayhum wa-tsīr ḏayyā tsallim ᶜalayhum salām al-ᶜīd / lā t'axxart akṯar min hāḏā mā gadū ᶜayb / wallā 'iḏā sirt al-yawm ma startš tisīr / tsīr al-yawm aṯ-ṯānī / hāḏā bi-nisbih lā salām al-ᶜīd /*

wa-ᶜād baᶜḍ an-nās / fi l-ᶜīd / yiḍayyufū / makāliffum[61] */ yidᶜawhin / yijayn yitġaddayn ᶜindahum / wa-yiᶜmalūlahin ḍīfuh / yisammūhā ḍīfuh inn al-ġadā yidᶜawhin kullahin daᶜwih wa-yitġaddaw maᶜa baᶜḍ / wa-hāḏā ḥālī / iḥna bi-nsabbir hāḏā fi l-bayt ḥakkanā / ᶜa-nidᶜī xawātī / wa-nḍayyufhun fi l-bayt / yijayn yitḍayyifayn / gadin / lā gadin muḍayyafāt gad iḥna nisabbir al-ġadā /*

nisīr niḏbaḥ / yawm al-ᶜīd / nijirr aṭ-ṭalī / ništarī ḍalī wa-nisīr niḏbaḥih fi l-mazḥaṭ / wallā nidᶜī jazzār / yijī yiḏbaḥih fi l-bayt / baᶜda-mā yiḏbaḥih / ḏik sāᶜ yūgaᶜ ḥālī al-jahhāl yirtāḥū yibsirū aḏ-ḏibāḥah wa-l-midrī mā hū / w-iḥna nijirr al-kabdih / aṣ-ṣubḥ hāḏāk / wa-ᶜādū ḥīn / nisīr nifᶜallih ṣabūḥ / nigaṭṭaᶜhā ġayr zuġār zuġār[62] */ zuġār zuġār sāᶜ al-laḥmi z-zuġār / wa-nifᶜalhā ṣabūḥ / tūgaᶜ ṣabūḥ ḥālī / bi-s-samn wa-l-bahārāt wa-l-hāḏā min arwaᶜ mā yikūn /*

---

56 Lack of number agreement on verb.

57 Syndetically linked verbal clauses with repetition of verb and emphasis on contrastive subjects. Cf. above.

58 Inversion of apposed term–appositive for emphasis. Cf. *Syntax* p. 251.

59 Deletion of final vowel *-ā*. From *anā* 'I'.

60 Lack of agreement on initial translocative verb.

61 Total perseverative assimilation of *h* to *f*.

62 Repetition of *zuġār* conveys distributive sense. Cf. *Syntax* pp. 251-2.

I mean, if a woman goes to her family's house, she will sit with them and her sisters will come and her brothers will come. I mean, all the women who are related will come and sit together, and festival greetings are the same with them. This is with regard to our festival greetings here in Yemen. They wait for [the festival] in anticipation.

Of course, I have still forgotten to mention something. The festival here is the day of the festival, for example. The last day of Ramadan, we finish Ramadan and then we celebrate. For example, if I went to visit all my family and there were one or two women left in my family who I hadn't been able to visit, I could go the next day, which they call the second day of the festival. The second day of the festival they go to greet. This is the last day that you can go to your relatives. You go to greet them and go to give them festival greetings. If you are any later than that it is shameful, or if you went today then you can't go the next day. This is as far as festival greetings are concerned.

Also, some people entertain their female relatives during the festival. They invite them over to have lunch with them. They hold a lunch party for them. They call it a lunch party [*ḍīfuh*] because they invite them all for lunch and they have lunch together. This is nice. We do this in our household. We will invite my sisters and entertain them in the house. They come as guests. If they are guests, we make the lunch.

We go and slaughter on the day of the festival. We get the goat. We buy a goat and go to slaughter it in the abattoir, or we call a butcher who comes to slaughter it at the house. After he slaughters it, at that time it is nice, the children are happy to see the slaughter and whatever. We take the liver that morning while it is still early, and go and make breakfast from it. We chop it up into lots of small pieces like chopped meat and have it for breakfast. It makes a really nice breakfast with ghee and spices and the most delightful things there are.

baᶜdā yijayn xawātī ᶜindanā[63] */ nijlis maᶜa baᶜḍ / nitġaddā / baᶜda-mā nitġaddā 'iḥna nuxruj nixazzin / wa-hin yijlisayn fī l-bayt / yisallimayn ᶜal ummī wa-ᶜalā baᶜḍahun wa-zid yijaw baᶜḍ al-lahl ᶜindanā / yaᶜnī hākaḏā / hāḏā fī l-ᶜīd /*

wa-baᶜd al-yawmayn aṯ-ṯānī maṯalan[64] *al-ᶜīd ᶜindanā maᶜānā 'ijāzih ṯalāṯih iyyām wallā / arbaᶜ iyyām / fī l-ᶜīd al-kabīr wallā / baᶜda-ma nhī salām al-ᶜīd wa-ᶜād maᶜānā 'ijāzih / nuxruj dawrih / al-yawm aṯ-ṯānī iḏ iḥna nuxruj dawrih aṣ-ṣubḥ fawg as-sayyārih wallā šī / nisīr al-gariyih / nisīr al-wādī / ayyi bugᶜah wallā nisīr jidirr / wallā nisīr / ḏarawān / gadiḥna nifᶜal dawratnā lā hānāk / wa-ništarī gāt min hānāk li'ann hāḏa l-manāḍug tuᶜtabar*[65] *manāḍug / la-l-gāt / yaᶜnī zirāᶜat al-gāt hānāk / wa-yūgaᶜ al-gāt hānāk arxaṣ min hānā*[66] */ ḍabᶜan maᶜ kuṯrat an-nās allī bi-sīr*[67] *yištaraw gāt min hānāk wa-hāḏā / bi-yiġlaw al-gāt / wa-'inn*[68] *al-mugāwitih wa-l-mufāwidīn / bi-yūgaᶜ akṯar law-mā 'inn al-gāt yūgaᶜ ġālī / fa-yawm al-ᶜīd wa-ṯānī al-ᶜīd al-gāṭ hāḏā bi-yūgaᶜ ġālī nār*[69] */ fa-l-mugāwitih hinyatluhum*[70] */ bī-jirrū zalaṭ xayrāt / hāḏā ᶜan al-ᶜīd wa-bi-salāmih /*

---

[63] Verbal clause with dynamic verb.

[64] *maṯalan* functions as filler here.

[65] Internal passive. Cf. text 7. Cf. *Syntax* pp. 91-2.

[66] Verbal clause with initial linking verb and emphasis on following complement.

[67] Lack of number agreement on translocative verb.

[68] Presentational particle. Cf. *Syntax* p. 425.

[69] *nār* used as an adverb. *ġālī nār* lit: 'expensive Hell' = 'hellishly expensive'.

[70] This verb usu. occurs with an implicit dummy subject pronoun. Cf. *Syntax* p. 413.

Then my sisters come over to us, and we sit together and have lunch. After having lunch, we go out to chew and they stay in the house to greet my mother and each other, and some more people come over to us from the family. This is during the festival.

After the two days, the second, for the festival we have a three-day or four-day holiday for the big festival. After the festival greetings are over, and while we are still on holiday, we go on a trip. The second day if we go out in the morning in the car or whatever, we will go to the village or we go to the valley,[71] any place, or we go to Jidirr[72] or we go to Dharawan.[73] We make a trip over there and buy our gat from there because these areas are said to be areas for gat. I mean, gat is cultivated there, and gat is cheaper there than it is here. Of course, with the large number of people going to buy gat from there, gat is becoming expensive. And there are the gat growers and middle-men increasing so that gat becomes [even more] expensive. On the day of the festival and the second [day] of the festival gat becomes hellishly expensive. The lucky gat sellers! They make loads of money! This is about the festival with peace.

[71] i.e. Wadi Dhahr.

[72] A place 15 kilometres from San'a on the Amran road.

[73] A place half-way between San'a and Amran.

27 *Al-ᶜiris*

d̲aḥḥīn asajjil / d̲aḥḥīn asajjil ḥakk al-ᶜiris ḥakk axī / yimkin anā ġuluṭṭ aw midrī mā / al-muhimm asajjil ḥakk al-ᶜiris ḥakk axī / ḥakk axī al-ᶜiri:s[1] *xālid maṯalan / ad̲akkir ᶜannih / ᶜan al-ᶜiris ḥakk xālid / xālid axī / ḥīn zawwajnāh / hū gadū 'aṣġar wāḥidnā*[2] *fi l-bayt / kayf ḥikāyat zawājatih / šā-gulliš kayfih /*

awwal ḥājih / fakkar innū yitzawwaj / ixtā:r al-marih allī yištī[3] */ iḥna sirnā lā ᶜind ahlahā / ṭalabnāhā minnahum / wāfagū / kayf bī-timm ṭalab al-marih / yaᶜnī bi-dwassaḍū al-lahl / bi-nās ṯāniyīn*[4] */ yigūlūluhum ništī bint fulān / yis'alū 'ahlahā luhum*[5] */ ᶜa-ywāfagū / hum yisīrū lā ᶜind al-ahl d̲awlayya / yigūlūluhum ibn fulān yištī bintkum fulānih / mā ra'yukum / midrī māhū / yigūlū xallīnā ᶜa-nnabbīkum*[6] */ wa-baᶜdā hum yāxad̲ū fatrih / wa-baᶜdayn yinabbaw / bi-l-muwāfagih wallā bi-r-rafḍ / hād̲ā ᶜinda-mā yinabbaw / ḥakk al-ᶜiris / wa-baᶜdā: / ittafagnā / ᶜalā yawm miᶜayyan /*

al-yawm al-miᶜayyan hād̲ā kān / yawm xamīs / sirnā lā hānāk / nuxṭub al-bint ḥakkahum[7] */ ᶜinda-mā sirnā nuxṭubhō / sirnā majmūᶜah min al-ahl / anā w-abī w-axwatī / wa-ᶜammī / wa-ᶜammī aṯ-ṯānī wa-kullanā sirnā / bazzaynā maᶜānā ḥakk al-xuṭbuh*[8] */ ḥakk al-xuṭbuh hī yiddaw badlih d̲ahab wallā sāᶜah wallā 'ayya ḥājih yixtārūha l-ahl / ahl al-ḥarīw*[9] */ wa-yisīrū / bih marbaṭ gāt yaᶜnī / bih kīs fīh gāt xayrāt / wa-yisīrū kulluhum ᶜalā 'asās lā ᶜind bayt ahl al-ḥarīwih / hād̲a llī ᶜa-yuxṭubūhā la-l-wāḥid /*

iḥna sirnā lā hānāk kullanā hād̲awlā / wa-baᶜd-mā wuṣulnā lā hānāk / istagbalūnā fi l-bāb / wa-daxalnā /

---

1 Inversion of attributed term-attribute to emphasise annex of attribute. Cf. *Syntax* p. 224.

2 *wāḥid* often functions as annex to elative or ordinal (cf. Mörth 1997: 124).

3 Lack of anaphoric pronoun in attributive clause. Cf. *Syntax* pp. 234-5.

4 Verbal clause with emphasis placed on the following complement *bi-nās ṯāniyīn*.

5 Unusual placement of explicit noun object before prep. phrase with pronoun annex. Cf. *Syntax* p. 150.

6 Up to this point in the narrative, all clauses are linked asyndetically, conveying sense of speed and brevity. Cf. *Syntax* pp. 315-16.

7 *ḥagg* not usu. used to describe family relations. Cf. *Syntax* pp. 179-80. When used, as here, it may imply a degree of impersonality. Cp. *al-marih ḥakkī* in text 25.

8 Annexion phrase with *ḥagg* functioning as independent noun phrase. Cf. *Syntax* p. 224.

9 Identificatory apposition. Cf. *Syntax* p. 243.

27 Weddings

Now I'm going to record, now I'm going to record about my brother's wedding. Maybe I have made some mistakes or whatever. Anyway, I'm going to record my brother's wedding, about my brother Khalid's wedding, for example. I can remember it, Khalid's wedding, Khalid my brother when we married him off. He is the youngest one of us in the family. What is the story of his wedding? I shall tell you about it.

The first thing was he thought he would get married. He chose the woman he wanted. We went to her family and asked for her from them. They agreed. How do you ask for a woman's hand? The family choose other people to act on their behalf. They say to them, 'We want so-and-so's daughter.' They ask her family for them. When they agree, they go to those people and say to them, 'So-and-so's son wants the hand of your daughter so-and-so. What do you think?' and I don't know what. They say, 'Leave us to get in touch with you.' They take a little while, then they give their consent or refusal. This is when they tell them about the wedding. Then we agreed on a specific day.

That certain day was a Thursday. We went over there to engage their daughter. When we went to engage her, we went as a group from the family: me, my father, my brothers, my [paternal] uncle, my other [paternal] uncle, all of us went. We took things for the engagement with us. For engagement things they give a gold set[10] or a watch or anything that the family, the groom's family, choose. Then they go. There will be a bunch of gat, a bag with lots of gat, then they will all go to the house of the bride's family, the one they are going to engage for someone.

We all went over there. When[11] we arrived there, they met us at the door and then we went in.

[10] Principally a gold collar which covers much of the upper chest, but may also include bracelet, earrings, etc.

[11] Lit: 'after'.

wa-gadū 'ahlahā mawjūdīn hānāk / axwatha l-kibār / li'ann abūhā maṯalan gad māt hāḏā / allī xaṭabnāhā l-axī / axwatha l-mawjūdīn al-kubār / wa-'a^{c}mūmahā wa-xālahā / wa-min agāribhā majmū^{c}ah / daxalnā ^{c}indahum / nixazzin / jalasnā hānāk / fī l-makān / w-iḥna bi-nxazzin wa-nitjābar / wa-hum bī-raḥḥibūbinā /

ba^{c}d-mā raḥḥabūbinā ṭab^{c}an / ba^{c}d-mā wuṣulnā sallamnāhum / nūṣal niddī al-gāt lā ^{c}indahum / nimakkinhum[12] */ w-iḥna kulla wāḥid minnanā ma^{c}ih gātih fī yadih / wa-hum al-mawjūdīn hānāk gad kullu wāḥid ma^{c}ih gāt fī yadih / allī makkannā al-gāt*[13] *hū gadū 'agrab wāḥid*[14] *ya^{c}nī 'ammā al-ax al-kabīr walla l-ab walla l-xāl walla l-... ayyi wāḥid garīb / iḥna makkannāhum al-gāt wa-hum jarrū al-gāt wa-ba^{c}dā bad'ū yigassimū al-gāt / la-l-mawjūdīn / yiddawluhum gāt / w-iḥna yiddawlanā gāt minnih / ^{c}alā sās inn gadum bī-gassimūh lā n-nās al-mawjūdīn kull:uhum /*

jalasnā / xazzannā / wa-ttafagnā / iḥna wa-l-ahl ba^{c}da-mā gad ya^{c}nī ba^{c}d-mā gad xazzannā ḥawālī sā^{c}ah wallā sā^{c}atayn / w-iḥna jālisīn bi-nitjābar wa-bī-raḥḥibūbinā w-iḥna niraḥḥibhum / wa-ḏayyā bī-jābir ḏayyā wa-ḏayyā bī-jābir ḏayyā ba^{c}d hāḏā kullih / iftaḥna l-ḥadīṯ / fī l-mawḏū^{c} allī jīnā min ajlih / wa-hum gālūlanā ahlan wa-sahlan irḥabū ^{c}ala r-rās wa-l-^{c}ayn / ittafagnā 'iḥna w-iyyāhum[15] */ kam hū al-mahr / ḥakk al-^{c}iris / ba^{c}d-ma ttafagnā iḥna w-iyyāhum / makkannāhum ḏayyik ḥakk al-xuṭbuh / lā ^{c}indahum / wa-jalasnā muxazzinīn lā maġrib / lā ba^{c}d al-maġrib*[16] *wa-riḥnālana l-bayt / hāḏā 'awwal mā fi^{c}ilnā fī l-^{c}iris / hāḏā gabl al-^{c}iris /*

ba^{c}d fatrih / jalasnā / gulnā nisīr ni^{c}gid / ya^{c}nī / gadū yizawwijūhum hākaḏa l-^{c}agd / yisammū hākaḏā / sirnā ^{c}induhum nixazzin / nafs aš-šī[17] */ xazzannā / šallaynā ma^{c}ānā gāt / wa-šallaynā zabīb / wa-lawz / wa-šallaynā: al-mahr / bagiyat al-mahr al-mawjūd ^{c}indanā*[18] */*

---

[12] *nimakkinhum* functions as a partial synonym for the clause *niddī al-gāt lā ^{c}induhum*.

[13] Exophoric pronominal use of definite clause. Cf. *Syntax* pp. 416-17.

[14] Use of *wāḥid* as annex to elative. Cf. above.

[15] Cf. *Ṣbaḥtū!* pp. 217-18.

[16] Corrective reformulative apposition. Cf. *Syntax* p. 246.

[17] Predicandless predicate. Cf. *Syntax* pp. 123-7.

[18] Identificatory apposition. Cf. *Syntax* p. 243.

Her family were already there, her older brothers – because the father of the one we engaged for my brother had already died – her older brothers, her [paternal] uncles and her [maternal] uncle. There were a group of her relatives. We went in with them to chew. We stayed there in the room chewing and chatting while they welcomed us.

Of course, after they had welcomed us, after we arrived we greeted them. When we arrive, we give them the gat, we give [it] to them. Each one of us had their gat in their hand. Everyone of those who were there [also] had gat in their hand. The one we gave the gat to was the closest one,[19] [it could be] either the elder brother, or the father, or the [maternal] uncle, or ... anyone close. We gave them the gat and they took the gat, then they began to divide the gat out to those present, to give them gat. They also gave us some gat from it because they were dividing it out to all the people who were there.

We sat and chewed and came to an agreement with the family after we had been chewing for around one or two hours. We were sitting and chewing and they welcomed us and we welcomed them. Someone would be talking to someone else, and someone else would be talking to someone else. After all this, we started to talk about the matter we had come for. They said to us, 'You are welcome!' and, 'Welcome on the head and the eye!' We came to an agreement with them about how much the dowry should be for the wedding. After we had come to an agreement with them, we gave them the engagement items and stayed chewing until sunset, until after sunset, then we went home. This is the first thing we did for the wedding. This was before the wedding.

After we had waited a little while, we said, 'Let's go and complete the marriage contract!' This means they get them married through a contract. This is what they call it. We went to their house to chew. [It was] the same thing, we chewed, we took gat with us, we took raisins and almonds and we took the dowry, the remainder of the dowry that we had with us.

---

[19] i.e. the closest male relative to the woman they went to engage. The man who was going to give her away.

wuṣulnā lā hānāk wa-hum hādawlāk al-lahl mirayyaᶜīn / raḥḥabūbinā / wa-jalasnā iḥna w-iyyāhum / ahlan wa-sahlan / yā marḥabā wa-yā mashalā[20] *ḥayyākum allāh*[21] *wa-midrī māhū / min hādawlā / jalasnā lā hānāk / ṭabᶜan axī gadū maᶜānā hāda l-marrih / jalasnā / wa-šallaynā maᶜānā gāḍī / ᶜalā mayd yiᶜgid az-zawāj /*

law-mā gadiḥna jālisīn la-n-nahārih hākadā / gālū yiᶜgidū az-zawāj / gām la-l-makān at-tānī / al-gāḍī zigim bi-yad axī / wa-zigim bi-yad / axʷ al-ḥarīwih allī yaᶜtabir hū walī 'amraha l-kabīr wa-muwakkilhā / hī gadī tiwakkil man ištat / yaᶜnī / misik al-gāḍī yad axī / wa-yad ḍayyik[22] */ wa-yigullih / yō kadā nisītih / wa-yigullih / innī gabiltuka zawjan li-muwakkalatī bi-š-šarṭ wa-l-mahr al-musammā baynanā*[23] */ wa-hāḍāk yigullih anā gabiltu z-zawāj minnahā*[24] *wa-midrī māhū / al-muhimm yiraddid baᶜda-mā yigullih al-gāḍī / xalāṣ / yigūl baᶜdahā al-gāḍī al-fātiḥah*[25] */ yigraw al-fātiḥah / kulluhum allī kānū mawjūdīn hānāk /*

baᶜd-mā yitimmū girāyat al-fātiḥah / yixarrijū az-zabīb wa-l-lawz / wa-hādawlāk gadum mawjūdīn hinayyik muḥawwišīn mirāᶜiyīn / yijirrū az-zabīb wa-l-lawz wa-yirjimūhin fawguhum / wa-dik sāᶜ / minātifih[26] */ kullu wāḥid yištī yišġatlih*[27] *šwayyih wa-yibizzalih*[28] */ lā ḥudnuh / w-iḥna ġarr bi-nhāzir az-zabīb wa-l-lawz / la-ḥdānanā / kull wāḥid yištī yibizzalih / yibizzalih šwayyih zabīb wa-šwayyih lawz wa-dayyā yibizzalih xayrāt wa-dayyā yibizzalih šwayyih / wa-dayyā yigūl yiriḥlih mā yištīš*[29] */ lākin ḥālī hākadā / yaᶜnī midrī kayfū yaᶜnī / ḥilwah*[30] */*

---

[20] Set greeting.

[21] Set greeting.

[22] Verbal clause with dynamic verb and emphasis placed on the object.

[23] This set phrase is spoken in Standard Arabic.

[24] This set phrase is spoken in Standard Arabic. These phrases are usu. spoken in the reverse order given here.

[25] Verbal clause with dynamic verb and emphasis placed on the object.

[26] Predicandless predicate. Cf. *Syntax* p. 125.

[27] Reflexive verb. Cf. *Syntax* pp. 202-3.

[28] Reflexive verb. Cf. above.

[29] Asyndetic linkage of consequential clause. Cf. *Syntax* p. 311.

[30] Use of non-SA *ḥilwah*.

We arrived there and the family were waiting. They welcomed us and we sat down with them, 'Welcome! Welcome! May God give you life!' and whatever else. This type of thing. We stayed there. Of course, this time my brother was with us. We stayed and we brought a judge with us so that he could draw up the marriage contract.

When we had been sitting there until late afternoon, they said they would draw up the marriage contract. The judge went to the other room and took hold of my brother's hand, then he took the hand of the bride's brother who was considered to be her legal guardian and her representative. She can appoint whoever she wants as a representative. The judge took my brother's hand and the hand of the other one and said to him. Oh, I've forgotten it! He says to him, 'I accept you as a husband for my charge for the bridal sum and dowry named between us.' The other [person] says to him, 'I agree to marry her.' and whatever else. Anyway, he repeats after the judge tells him. That's it. After that, the judge recites the opening chapter of the Qur'an. All of those who were there recite the opening chapter.

After they have finished reciting the opening chapter of the Qur'an, they take out the raisins and almonds. They are all there gathered together and waiting. They take the raisins and almonds and throw them over themselves. At that moment, [it is] snatching, everyone wants to grab a little and take it into the folds of his sarong. We are just scooping up raisins and almonds into the folds of our clothes. Everyone wants to take [some]. Some take a few raisins and a few almonds, one takes a lot and another takes a little, and another says he is going so he doesn't want [any]. But it is nice like that. I don't know. [It's] nice.

ba^cd-ma ntimm / hāḏā kullih / nirja^c al-makān / nitimm al-gāt ḥakkanā / wa-nxazzin / wa-ngūm niriḥlanā / ṭab^can / w-iḥna hānāk gad ḥaddadnā / 'ayyaḥīn al-^ciris / ḏalḥīn gad zawwajnāhum / fi^cilna l-^cagd az-zawāj[31] / *lākin niḥaddid al-^ciris ayyaḥīnih / gulnā ^calā yawm mi^cayyin / xalāṣ /*

hum / fī hāḏīk al-laḥḏuh / ba^cd-mā riḥnā / yibdū yijahhizū li-binthum / w-iḥna nibdā nijahhiz l-ibnanā al-^ciris / mā 'illī bi-yi^cmalū hum[32] / *bī-sīr*[33] *yiksaw al-ḥarīwih / yiksawhā ya^cnī yištarawlahā al-malābis / wa-yištarawlahā kulla ḥājāt ḥakk al-^ciris / yizīd*[34] *yištarawlahā ḏahab / hinayyik bi-l-mahr ḥakkahā / yibda'ū yijahhizū / fī l-^ciris / w-aḥna nsīr / nibda' nijahhiz fī l-^ciris /*

aḥna mā fi^cilnā / sirnā / fi^cilnā allāhumma ṣallā wa-sallam ^calayh[35] / *ad-da^cawāt / fi^cilna d-da^cawāt / ṭab^can l-illī hum xārij / wa-ba^cdā jīnā fī yawm min al-ayyām hākaḏā / jalasnā mixazzinīn / nuktub ad-da^cawāt man hum illī bi-nuktubluhum / bada'nā nisajjil asāmī / allī niddīluhum ad-da^cawāt / bada'nā bi-l-asāmī ḥakk al-ahl / al-ahl hum xayrāt*[36] / *iktabnāluhum ad-da^cawāt li-l-ahl / ba^cda-mā tammaynā ḥakk al-ahl*[37] *fī waragih / jarraynā katabnā ḥakk al-jīrān wa-l-ma^cārīf wa-l-xubrih / w-aṣḥābanā / kulluhum / bada'nā nuktub ad-da^cawāt / hāḏā 'awwal ḥājih aktabnāhum fī warag / wa-ba^cdā min warag / bada'nā nuktub ad-da^cawāt/*

ṭab^can mā fi^cilnāš ṭawālī la-d-da^cwih / li'annū gad rubba-mā tikarrir wāḥidih wallā ṯintayn / ^ca-tkarrarayn kaṯīr law katabnā ^calā ḍūl fī d-da^cawāt / fa-hāḏā[38] *bada'nāhin fī warag / wa-t'akkadnā 'innū al-asāmī mā tkarraranš walla l-hāḏā / fi^cilnā fī ḥakk axī xālid yimkin miyih wa-sab^cīn da^cwih / hāḏā ḥakk xālid / wa-ba^cdā bada'nā niwazzi^c ad-da^cawāt / ^calā 'asās / wazza^cna d-da^cawāt ḥakk axī gabl al-^ciris bi-'usbū^c /*

---

[31] Apposition phrase in place of annexion phrase. Cf. *Syntax* pp. 193-4.

[32] Rhetorical question. Post-position of pronoun to emphasise subject. Cf. *Syntax* p. 251.

[33] Lack of number agreement on the translocative verb.

[34] Lack of number agreement on the linking verb.

[35] Speaker inserts this religious filler phrase while thinking what to say next.

[36] Asyndetic linkage of explanatory clause. Cf. *Syntax* p. 309.

[37] Annexion phrase with *ḥagg* functioning as independent noun phrase. Cf. *Syntax* p. 224.

[38] Consequential use of *fa-*. Cf. *Syntax* pp. 299-300. Demonstrative pronoun refers back to clauses from *bada'nā nuktub ad-da^cawāt*. Cf. *Syntax* pp. 382-4.

After we have finished all that, we go back to the room,[39] and finish our gat. We chew, then we get up to go. Of course, while we were there, we decided when the wedding would be. Now we had married them, we had drawn up the marriage contract, but we [still had to] determine when the wedding would be. We settled on a certain day, and that was that.

That moment, after we had left, they began to get their daughter ready, and we began to get our son ready for the wedding. What is it that they do? They go and buy clothes for the bride. *yiksawhā* means that they buy her clothes and buy her all the things needed for the wedding. They go and buy her some more gold there with her dowry. They begin to prepare for the wedding, and we go to begin to get ready for the wedding.

What did we do? We went and did, God bless [the Prophet] and grant him salvation, the invitations. We did the invitations, of course, for those who were outside.[40] Then we came in one day, and sat chewing and writing the invitations, who there were we should write to. We began to write down names of those we should give invitations to. We began with the names of family members, because there are a large number in the family. We wrote invitations to the family. After we had finished the family on one piece of paper, we began to write down the neighbours, acquaintances and friends, and our friends, all of them. We began to write the invitations. For this, the first thing [we did] was to write them[41] down on paper, and then from the paper we began to write the invitations.

Of course, we didn't do the invitations straight away, because one or two may have been duplicated. A lot would have been duplicated, if we had written the invitations straight away. So we started them on paper and we made sure that the names weren't repeated or whatever. For my brother Khalid, we did around 170 invitations. This was for Khalid. Then we began to distribute the invitations, so that we had the invitations for my brother distributed a week before the wedding.

---

[39] i.e. where we were chewing gat.

[40] i.e. those outside the immediate family.

[41] i.e. their names.

wa-mā fiᶜilnā fi l-ᶜiris / zakkannā ᶜalā / n-naššād gabl al-ᶜiris bi-šahrayn / an-naššād[42] *nisīr lā ᶜindih / tigullih*[43] *maᶜānā ᶜiris yawm abū fulān / ništīk tijī / yigullak iṭruḥ ᶜarbūn / tiḍruḥ lih ᶜarbūn xamsamiyih wallā alf girš wallā kam-mā kān*[44] */ ḥasb-ma ttafagt ant wayh*[45] */ iḏā hū ṣāḥubak ᶜa-ygullak xalāṣ anā šā-jī / wa-hū gadū musajjal ᶜindahum hinayyik innū fī yawm kaḏā / ᶜa-yūgaᶜ al-ᶜiris ḥakk fulān / xalāṣ anā muᶜarban ᶜinduhum / wa-nsīr niᶜarbin / al-fannān / innū al-ᶜiris ḥakkanā yūgaᶜ yawm abū fulān / ᶜarbanna l-fannān wa-ᶜarbanna n-naššād / wa-wazzaᶜna d-daᶜawāt hāḏīk al-ayyām /*

an-niswān min ṣalayhun bī-jahhizayn la-l-ᶜiris / fiᶜilayn la-ṯ-ṯāliṯ / la-ṯ-ṯāliṯ sārayn dawwarayn al-muġanniyih / tijī tiġannī fi ṯ-ṯāliṯ / ᶜarbanannahā ᶜalā 'asās yawm kaḏā li'ann al-muġanniyih barḏū / maᶜāhā ᶜirisāt wa-hāḏā / fa-ḍarūrī kulla ᶜiris yijaw yiᶜarbanūlahā lā yištawhā / ᶜala l-yawm allī ᶜa-tijī fīh / hāh /

wa-gabl al-ᶜiris iḥna fiᶜilna l-ᶜiris ḥakk axī fī bugᶜah hākaḏāhā[46] *nisammīhā mafraj / fi l-bistān ḥakkanā / absarnā hī gadī 'aḥsan bugᶜah fīhā / fiᶜilna l-mafraj / al-mafraj hū fīh barik hākaḏā fī l-wasaṭ / kayf fiᶜilnā / wa-l-ḥawš hū kabīr kaḏayyā / sirnā ddaynā ġarr wāḥid ṣāḥubnā*[47] */ jā' sagaf al-barik hāḏīk bi-l-xašab / kullahin / sagafhā bi-l-xašab kullahā*[48] */ wa-xallāhā misāwiyih la-l-'arḍ / wa-baᶜdā jarraynā fiᶜilnā xaymih min ḍāluᶜ / ġaṭṭaynā al-... ḏayyik al-mafraj allī maftūḥ*[49] */*

wa-baᶜdā ddaynā firiš / farrašnā al-mafraj / farrašnā xārij al-mafraj hāḏā ku:llih / fiᶜilnā farš wāḥid / wa-baᶜdā gassamnāh lā majālis /

---

42 Topicalisation of prepositional annex. Cf. *Syntax* pp. 131-2.

43 Change of subject from specific 1 pl. to general 2 m.s.

44 Universal-conditional-concession clause. Cf. *Syntax* pp. 351-3.

45 Cf. *Ṣbaḥtū!* pp. 217-18.

46 Suffixation of *-hā* to emphasise indefinite demonstrative. Demonstrative separates attributive clause from attributed term. Cf. *Syntax* p. 217.

47 After *wāḥid*, noun with pronoun annex functions as indefinite. Cf. *Syntax* pp. 175, 241 (cf. also Mörth 1997: 129-30).

48 *kullahā* is a correction for earlier *kullahin*.

49 Adjectival attributive clause *allī maftūḥ* in place of attributive phrase *al-maftūḥ*. Cf. *Syntax* pp. 236-7.

What did we do for the wedding? We made sure about the reciter two months before the wedding. For the reciter, we went to his house. You say to him, 'We are having a wedding on such-and-such a day, and we would like you to come.' He will say to you, 'Put down a deposit.' You give him a deposit of 500 or 1,000 riyals or however much depending on what you have agreed with him. If he is your friend, he will say to you, 'That's okay, I will come.' Then he is booked for them there, because [he will say], 'On such-and-such a day, so-and-so's wedding will take place and I am booked for them.' Then we go and pay a deposit for the singer. Our wedding was to take place on such-and-such a day. We paid a deposit for the reciter and paid a deposit for the singer, and distributed the invitations during this time.

For their part, the women had been getting ready for the wedding. They did the third [day].[50] For the third [day], they went and looked for a woman singer who could come and sing on the third [day]. They paid a deposit for her for that day because the woman singer also had [other] weddings, so for every wedding it is essential that they go and pay a deposit for her if they want her for the day on which she is to come. Okay?

Before the wedding – we had my brother's wedding in a place which we call a *mafraj* [reception room], in our garden. We saw that it was the best place. We did up the reception room. The reception room has a pool in the centre. How did we do it? The yard is large like that. We went and just brought one of our friends over who came and laid wood over the whole pool. He laid wood over the whole of it, and made it level with the ground. Then we put a tent over the top and covered … that part of the reception room which was open.

Then we brought furnishings and furnished the reception room and furnished the whole area outside the reception room. We furnished it all in one. Then we divided it up into smaller sitting areas.

---

[50] The third day after the nuptial night, i.e. the Sunday.

ūgi^{c} rāyi^{c} jidd:an / ya^{c}nī ḥālī gawī / wa-l-mafraj iftaḥnāh wa-ba^{c}adna l-abwāb wa-xallaynāh maftūḥ / baytanā kān barḏ̣ū 'ayḏ̣an maftūḥ / farrašnāh ū-jahhaznāh la-l-^{c}iris / bayt ^{c}ammatī wa-ḏāk jāhiz / li'annum ^{c}a-yjaw nās xayrāt /

yawm al-^{c}iris / jaw an-nās xayrāt / aṣ-ṣubḥ w-iḥna bi-njahhiz gabl al-... / hāh[51] *miš gabl aṣ-ṣubḥ / al-yawmayn gabl al-^{c}iris gad iḥna bi-njahhiz al-ganādīl wa-nisabbir az-zīnih / xārij / sirna ddayna l-makrafūnāt / wa-ddayna s-sammā^{c}āt / wa-ddaynā / al-jihāz ḥakk mikabbir aṣ-ṣawt / wa-ddaynā hāḏawlā kullahin / ya^{c}nī maṯalan az-zīnih / bi-nsīr ni^{c}arbinhā wa-l-kull zayy-mā ni^{c}arbin al-fannān wa-ni^{c}arbin an-naššād / ya^{c}nī al-^{c}irbān hāḏā hū 'inn nidfa^{c} fulūs lā wāḥid nizakkin ^{c}alayh innū yjī fī yawm kaḏā /*

fa-[52]*jaw aṣḥāb az-zīnih*[53] */ rakkabū zīnathum / wa-jā' ṣāḥub al-mikrafūn rakkab al-makrafūnāt / wa-rakkab as-sammā^{c}āt / wa-rakkab kulla šī / al-makrafūnāt ba^{c}ḏ̣ al-aḥyān bī-jayn ma^{c} an-naššād wa-ba^{c}ḏ̣ al-aḥyān bi-niddīhin min ^{c}ind wāḥid mutxaṣṣaṣ bihin / rakkabna z-zīnih yawm ... gabl al-^{c}iris bi-yawmayn / yijaw xubrat axī wa-ḥna ya^{c}nī / hāḏā gadī ^{c}ādih / innū lā gad šī ^{c}iris ma^{c} wāḥid aṣḥābuh yijaw / ^{c}indih gabl al-^{c}iris yawmayn ṯalāṯ usbū^{c} / yibsirū lā hū yištī ḥājih / yisā^{c}idūh fīhā / yi^{c}āwinūh fī 'ayy ḥājih yištī*[54] */ yirakkibū zīnih / yirakkibū makrafūnāt / yisīr*[55] *yiddaw fīriš / yifarrišū al-bayt yiddaw ḥājāt / sabbarna z-zīnih / sabbarna l-makrafūnāt*[56] */ yawm al-^{c}iris jahhaznā al-mafraj hāḏāk / bi-l-madākī wa-l-madāfil wa-l-ṯalājāt al-mā' wa-l-mā' / ddayna l-karātīn / al-gawārīr al-mā'*[57] */*

jalasnā xazzannā / al-ḥarīw libis / libs al-^{c}iris / libis al-magḏ̣ab / wa-libis as-sumāḏ̣uh / ya^{c}nī / libishin hāḏawlā kullahin / wa:-jā' wakt al-gāt /

---

51 *hāh* is used here to signal correction.

52 Sequential use of *fa-*. Cf. *Syntax* pp. 299.

53 Verbal clause with dynamic verb and emphasis on subject. Cf. further examples below.

54 Lack of anaphoric pronoun in attributive clause. Cf. *Syntax* pp. 234-5.

55 Lack of number agreement on translocative verb. Cp. *Syntax* pp. 154-5.

56 From *wa-ḥna ya^{c}nī hāḏā gadī ^{c}ādih* there is a string of asyndetically linked clauses which convey a sense of brevity and speed. Cf. above. Cf. *Syntax* pp. 315-16.

57 Identificatory apposition phrase. Cf. *Syntax* pp. 242-3.

It was very beautiful! [It was] really lovely! The reception room we opened up, we removed the doors and left it open. Our house was also open. We furnished it and made it ready for the wedding. My [paternal] aunt's house and that was [also] ready because a lot of people were going to come.

On the day of the wedding, a lot of people came in the morning while we were preparing ... Sorry! Not before the morning, two days before the wedding, we were preparing the lights and setting up the decorations outside. We went and brought the microphones, we brought the loudspeakers and we brought the amplifier. When we brought all of these things, for instance the decorations, we went to pay a deposit for them just like we paid a deposit for the singer and paid a deposit for the reciter. Paying a deposit means that we pay money to someone to make sure that he will come on such-and-such a day.

Then the people with the decorations came and put up their decorations. The person with the microphone came and set up the microphones and set up the loudspeakers and set up everything. The microphones sometimes come with the reciter and sometimes we get them from someone who specialises in them. We set up the decorations one day ... two days before the wedding. My brother's friends came. With us, it is customary that if someone has a wedding, his friends come to his house two or three days or a week before the wedding. They see if he needs anything they can help him with. They help him in anything he wants: they set up decorations; they set up microphones; they go and fetch furnishings; they furnish the house; they bring things. We did the decorations and did the microphones. On the day of the wedding, we got the reception room ready with arm-rests, spittoons, water flasks and water. We brought boxes with bottles of water.

We sat and chewed. The bridegroom put on wedding clothes. He put on a sarong[58] and put on a large coloured turban.[59] He put all of these things on, then came the time for gat.

[58] Definite in Arabic.

[59] Definite in Arabic.

iḥna mā nibarra^{c}š ^{c}indanā / mā nif^{c}alš al-bara^{c} fī 'usratnā / aw iḥna nsīr niddī bara^{c} wa-ḍumbuluh wa-ḏayyā iḥna mā niddīhinš lākin fī bīr al-^{c}azab / hum mašhūrīn bi-l-bara^{c} / al-bara^{c} hāḏā yiddaw nās yiḍambul wāḥid yidugg ^{c}alā ṭāsuh / aṭ-ṭāsuh wa-ṭ-ṭumbuluh / wa-yiḍumbulū / wa-n-nās yurguṣū / ^{c}alayhā ya^{c}nī yiḥibbu r-rakṣ[60] *^{c}ala l-bara^{c} hāḏā li'ann an-nās lā gad šī ragṣat bara^{c} yi^{c}jibhum / iḥna ^{c}indanā fī 'usratnā mā niddīš al-bara^{c} hāḏā gad iḥna ṯānī /*

al-muhimm / jalasnā fī l-makān hāḏāk jaw al-xubrih / ^{c}alā wāḥid wāḥid / imtala l-makān / wa-jaw nās xayrāt / kān ^{c}indanā wāḥid James[61] *hāḏā jā' ^{c}indanā / fī l-^{c}iris kān hū 'awwal yawm lih fī l-yaman / zawjiš yā Janet / jā' wa-šāf al-^{c}iris ḥakk axī wa-xazzan ma^{c}ānā wa-l-kull wa-xallaynāh jamb al-fannān / jaw ba^{c}d ṯalāṯih fannānīn badal-mā hū wāḥid / jaw ṯalāṯih fannānīn / xubrat axī wa-ḏayyā / jaw xayrāt / ba^{c}d al-ġadā hāḏāk wa-n-nās mixazzinīn w-iḥna sāyirīn jāyiyīn / ḏayyā yištī ḥājih niddīlih / ḏayyā yištī madā^{c}ah niddīlih / ḏayyā yištī ni^{c}ammir ya^{c}nī / nuxdum an-nās / ahl al-ḥarīw wa-gadum hinayyik yuxdumu n-nās / wa-nijiss šwayyih nif^{c}allanā*[62] *^{c}ūdī gāt / yibda' ba^{c}d al-ġadā hāḏāk ba-n-našīd bi-ṣalāt ^{c}ala n-nabī wa-hāḏā yibda' an-naššād yiddī / yinšid / wa-yiṣallī ^{c}ala n-nabī šwayyih wa-bi-yimdaḥ fī l-^{c}arūs wa-hāḏā / wa-gaḏḏā*[63] *law-mā yitimm / nijlis šwayyih / nitjābar wa-midrī māhū /*

wa-ba^{c}dā yijirr al-fannān al-^{c}ūd[64] *wa-yiddī 'uġniyih ḥāliyih / yimdaḥ fī l-^{c}arūs / ya^{c}nī wa-kalām ḥālī w-allāh yā ^{c}arūs allāh yihannīk wa-hāḏā / yiddī al-kalām ḥakk al-^{c}iris / wa-hākaḏā ḍūl ba^{c}d al-ġadā / an-naššād yiddī yinšid nišūdih / wa-l-fannān yiddī 'uġniyih / wa-ḏayyik al-fannān yiddī 'uġniyih ṯāniyih wa-ḏayyik al-fannān aṯ-ṯāliṯ yiddī 'uġniyih ṯāliṯih / ṯalāṯih fannānīn wa-naššād wa-hum bi-ġannaw wa-yinšidū ḍūl ba^{c}d al-ġadā / law-mā gadū ḏayyik ba^{c}d al-maġrib / al-^{c}ašī /*

---

60 Anticipatory devoicing of *g* to *k*.

61 After *wāḥid*, and in a few other cases, a proper noun may function as indefinite. (Cf. *wāḥid ṣāḥubnā* above).

62 Cf. use of this verb in different contexts in texts 9, 11, 18, 22, 25.

63 i.e. *gadū hākaḏā* 'it is like that'.

64 Verbal clause with dynamic verb.

We don't do the *bara*^{c} dance at our house. We don't do the *bara*^{c} dance in our family, nor do we go and fetch drums and the like. We don't do this, but in Bir al-Azab they are famous for their *bara*^{c} dancing. For the *bara*^{c}, they bring on people who drum, someone bangs on a plate, a plate and a drum and they drum, and people dance to it. They love dancing to the *bara*^{c} because people enjoy it if there is a *bara*^{c} dance. In our family, we don't have *bara*^{c} dancing. We are different.

Anyway, we sat in that room, and friends came one by one, and the room filled up. Lots of people came. There was this James who came to us for the wedding. It was his first day in Yemen, your husband, Janet. He came and watched my brother's wedding and chewed with us too. We put him beside the singer. Then three singers came rather than one. Three singers came. Friends of my brother and the like, a lot came after lunch and people were chewing with us coming and going. One wanted us to give him something; another wanted us to give him the water-pipe; another wanted us to prepare the bowl of the water-pipe, I mean we served the people. The groom's family, when they are there, they serve the people. Then we sat a little and had a branch of gat. After lunch, they started with recitations and prayers for the Prophet and the like. The reciter would begin to recite and pray for the Prophet a little, then praise the groom. It was like that until he finished. We sat for a while and chatted and I don't know what.

Then the singer took the lute and sang a nice song praising the groom with nice words [such as], 'By God, oh groom, may God congratulate you!' and the like. He would talk about the wedding. It was like that the whole afternoon: the reciter would give his recitations and the singer would sing a song. Then the next singer would sing another song and the third singer would sing a third song. [There were] three singers and a reciter and they sang and recited the whole afternoon until it was after sunset in the evening.

ḍab^c^an al-ḥarīw jālis bug^c^atih gadū yigūm / min al-makān ḏayyā lā ḏayya l-makān / iḥna l-mafraj hū kān gā^c^ah wāḥidih[65] *w-innum*[66] *kulluhum bi-bsirūh / lākin gām sār al-bayt ḥakkanā li'ann kān bih nās ṯāniyīn / wa-sār lā bayt ^c^ammatī lannū bih nās ṯāniyīn / nās hum jaw xayrāt /*

nijlis lā: l-^c^ašī / al-^c^ašī yuxrujū an-nās yiṣallaw / wa-ysīr[67] *yiḏbilū al-gāt akṯarattum*[68] */ ba^c^ḏathum ġarr galīlih ya^c^nī yibgā l-gāt fī 'algāffum / wa-yijissū yitgahwaw šwayyih / wa-yitjamma^c^ū an-nās kulluhum*[69] *allī mā jawš yixazzinū ba^c^d aḏ-ḏuhr*[70] *gadum bī-jaw al-^c^ašī / hāḏa l-^c^ašī kull an-nās yitwājidū fīh / yijaw yiziffū / law-mā gad an-nās mitwādīn*[71] *kull:uhum / gadī la s-sā^c^ah tis^c^ tis^c^ wa-nuṣṣ hākaḏā jalasnā / wa-ba^c^dā bada'nā xarajna š-šāri^c^ kull:anā / fī xārij aš-šāri^c^ ḥayṯ-ma l-ganādīl / gadū ġallagnā ġarr aš-šāri^c^ / wa-bada'na z-zaffih /*

az-zaffih hāḏā / an-naššād hāḏā bi-bda' yinšid / wa-yddī kalimāt / du^c^ā 'ilā llāh wa-yiddī kalimāt / yinšum fīha l-ḥarīw / wa-yimdaḥih bi-l-waṣf al-jamīl / wa-n-nās hānāk yiraddidū ba^c^dih / kalimāt mu^c^ayyinih titraddad / wa-hū yiddī 'abyāt min aš-ši^c^r hākaḏā / bi-ḏarīgat anāšīd wa-ṣalāt ^c^ala n-nabī / wa-madḥ la-l-ḥarīw / wa-ba^c^ḏ al-aḥyān yigūl … / wa-zaġridayn wa-l-muḥjirāt yizaġridayn / an-niswān fī l-ajbī yitfarrajayn an-nās / yijirrayn / yuḥjirayn / wa-hākaḏā ḥakk sā^c^ah[72] *ḥakk sā^c^atayn w-iḥna ġarr jālisīn fī š-šāri^c^ / ḥawālī sā^c^atayn w-iḥna jālisīn fī š-šāri^c^ bi-nziff / bī-ziffū al-ḥarīw / law-mā yūṣalū lā bāb al-bayt /*

wuṣulnā lā bāb al-bayt / bad'ū šwayyih min an-nās yidxilū / hāḏīk az-zaffih / jalasnā 'awwal ḥājih hānāk šwayyih fī š-šāri^c^ / ba^c^d-mā tammaynā z-zaffih kullahā / ba^c^d-ma ntimm az-zaffih jalasnā fī š-šāri^c^ / fi^c^ilnā ḥilgih kabīrih / wa-jaw al-fannānīn yiġannaw /

---

[65] *wāḥidih* functions as attribute emphasising singularity of noun. Cf. earlier texts.

[66] Presentational particle. Cf. *Syntax* p. 425.

[67] Lack of number agreement on translocative verb.

[68] Total perseverative assimilation of *h* to *t*. Cf. perseverative assimilation of *h* to *f* below.

[69] Verbal clause with emphasis on subject further enhanced by emphatic appositive *kulluhum*. Cf. *Syntax* p. 249.

[70] Exophoric pronominal use of definite clause. Cf. *Syntax* pp. 416-17.

[71] Intervocalic voicing of *t* to *d*.

[72] Annexion phrase with *ḥagg* often used independently with following time annex.

Of course, the groom was sitting in his place, then he got up from one room to the other room. For us, the reception room [area] was a single floor so they could all see him, but he got up and went to our house because there were other people there. Then he went to my [paternal] aunt's house because more people were there. Lots of people came.

We sat until the evening. In the evening, people went out to pray and most of them went to spit out their gat. A very few of them kept the gat in their mouths, then they stayed and had some tea. All the people gathered together; those who hadn't been able to come to chew in the afternoon came in the evening. On this evening, all the people are there. They come for the wedding procession. When all the people had congregated – until around nine o'clock or half past nine we waited – then all of us began to go out into the street, outside in the street where the lights were. We closed off the street totally and began the wedding procession.

During this procession, the reciter begins to recite and say some words, invocations to God and words with which he praises the groom. He praises him using beautiful descriptions and the people there repeat after him. Certain words are repeated and he recites verses of poetry in the way of recitations and prayer for the Prophet and praise to the groom. Sometimes he says ... And they ululate, the women[73] utter shrill ululations. The women on the roofs watch the people. They start to ululate. [It was] like that for one or two hours while we were on the street, we did the wedding procession for around two hours on the street, they do the wedding procession for the groom, until they reach the door of the house.

When we reached the door of the house, a few of the people began to go in. For this wedding procession, the first thing we did was stay on the street for a short while after we had finished the whole wedding procession. After we had finished the wedding procession, we stayed on the street. We formed a large circle and the singers began to sing.

[73] Lit: 'ululators'.

bad'ū al-fannānīn yiġannaw[74] *yiddaw aġānī / ṣan^{c}ānīyuh / al-šabāb*[75] *gāmū yurguṣū / allī bi-yurguṣ hū wa-xubratih / w-aṣḥābuh wa-hāḏā / w-allī yištī yurguṣ / bad'ū yurguṣū ^{c}ala l-aġānī hāḏīk aṣ-ṣan^{c}ānīyuh al-jamīlih allī fīhā daggat ar-ragṣuh aṣ-ṣan^{c}ānīyuh al-ḥāliyih / ragaṣū / ḥakk yijī sā^{c}ah / wa-ṭab^{c}an hāḏā bi-tijḏib aš-šabāb kaṯīr / tixallīhum yijaw min kulli bug^{c}ah / yijaw yurguṣū yibsirū al-ḥarīw / li'annū al-ġunā / bi-kūn ^{c}abr al-makrafūnāt / wa-l-makrafūnāt bi-tudxul li-s-sammā^{c}āt wa-s-sammā^{c}āt fi l-ajbī / tinda^{c} aṣ-ṣawt sawā 'an hū ba^{c}īd wa-l-garīb wa-l-hāḏā / ya^{c}nī hāḏa l-^{c}ašī / ragaṣū / wa-šibi^{c}ū ragṣuh /*

gumnā zaffayna l-ḥarīw / allī hū 'axī / lā wasṭ al-bayt min jadīd / daxalna l-mafraj hānāk / daxalu n-nās kulluhum / daxalū hū wa-xubratih kulluhum / wa-l-mad^{c}ūwīn wa-l-hāḏā[76] */ lā ḥaflat aš-šahay / ba^{c}ḏuhum rāḥūluhum / w-akṯarathum daxalū / daxalna l-makān / bada'nā niwazza^{c} / ya^{c}nī garāḏīṣ gadhin mujahhazāt hāḏā / ḥakk ḥaflat aš-šahay / fīhā biskut wa-fīhā kīk wa-fīhā šikalīt yō wa-kaḏā / wazza^{c}nāhin la-l-mawjūdīn kulluhum wa-la l-jahhāl wa-l-hāḏā / wa-šahay / wa-jalasū / an-nās akalū wa-yitsāmarū wa-l-ḥarīw baynahum / wa-bi-ḏḥakū wa-yiddaw nukat / wa-hum jālisīn / ba^{c}ḏuhum bī-gūm yiruḥūluhum / ba^{c}ḏ aš-šabāb ya^{c}nī llī hum xubrat axī gawī / w-ahl al-ḥarīw / yijlisū /*

gabl hāḏā kullih šā-zīd atimm ḥakk al-ḥarīw[77] */ al-ḥarīw jālis / ma^{c}ānā w-iḥna kullanā jālisīn hānāk / fi hāḏīk al-laḥḏuh / an-niswān fi l-bayt / mirayya^{c}āt / fā^{c}ilāt ḥaflih / ṭawīluh ^{c}arīḏuh*[78] */ dā^{c}iyāt an-niswān aṯ-ṯāniyāt al-jīrān wa-l-hāḏā yijayn yibsirayn al-ḥarīwih / ba^{c}dā yigūmū min ahl al-ḥarīw / amman abūh / wallā ^{c}amūmih / wallā 'axwatih / gāmū majmū^{c}ah / min usrat al-ḥarīw / sārū / fawg as-sayyārāt / yiddaw al-ḥarīwih / ṭab^{c}an as-sayyārāt gadhum yisarrajūhin al-^{c}ašī al-aḏwā fīhā malān min kulla jihah /*

[74] Verbal clause with initial linking verb.

[75] Hesitation results in unassimilated *-l-* of definite article.

[76] Verbal clause with dynamic verb and complex subject. Provides identity of subject in preceding clause (*n-nās kulluhum*).

[77] Annexion phrase with *ḥagg* functioning as independent noun phrase. Cf. *Syntax* p. 224.

[78] Cp. use of this phrase *ṭawīluh ^{c}arīḏuh* in text 1 to describe large market areas.

The singers began to sing and sing San'ani songs. The young men began to dance: those who danced with their friends, and those who wanted to dance began dancing to those beautiful San'ani songs which have the lovely San'ani dance rhythm. They danced for about an hour. Of course, this really brought the young men along: it got them to come from everywhere. They came to dance and to see the groom because the singing came through microphones, and the microphones were attached to loudspeakers, and the loudspeakers were on the roofs sending out the sound near and far. This evening, they danced until they tired of dancing.

We got up and took the groom, who was my brother, back into the house again. We went into the reception room there. Everyone came in. He[79] came in with all his friends and the guests for the tea party. Some of them left, but most of them came in. We went into the room. We began to distribute paper bags which had been prepared for the tea party. They had biscuits and cake and chocolate and the like in them. We distributed them to all those who were there and to the children, etc. and [gave them] tea. The people sat and ate and stayed up with the groom among them laughing and telling jokes while they were sitting. Some of them got up to leave. Some of the young men who were very close friends of my brother and the groom's family stayed.

Before all this, I am going to finish [telling you] about the groom. The groom was sitting with us and we were all sitting there. At that moment, the women were in the house waiting, having a big party. [They had] invited other women, the neighbours and the like to come to see the bride. Then some of the groom's family, either his father or his [paternal] uncles or his brothers, a group of the groom's family got up and went in cars to fetch the bride. Of course, they had put lights all over the cars in the evening. There were lights in every direction.

---

[79] i.e. the groom.

al-ġammāzāt ġarr bi-tġammiz ḏayyā wa-ṭarragū ġarr yisammū an-nās innum xāḏiyīn yisīr[80] *yiddaw ḥarīwih / yūṣalū lā bayt al-ḥarīwih /*

fī bayt al-ḥarīwih / wa-l-kull fi^{c}ilayn ḥaflih / ḥaflat niswān / šahay wa-ġunā wa-kull šī / hāḏā fī bayt al-ḥarīwih / ^{c}inda-mā wuṣulū lā bayt al-ḥarīwih ahl al-ḥarīw gadum ġarr yisma^{c}ū aṭ-ṭarrīgāt ḥakk as-sayyārāt wa-l-hāḏā gadum mirayya^{c}īn fī l-bāb / yistagbilūhum / ahlan wa-sahlan / ḥayy allāh man jī'[81] */ irḥabū / ^{c}ala l-^{c}ayn wa-r-rās / daxalnā / anā sirt ma^{c}āhum / daxalnā bayt al-ḥarīwih / jalasnā hānāk / gaddamūlanā l-kīk wa-l-ka^{c}k wa-z-zabīb wa-d-dixiš wa-l-hāḏā / wa-š-šahay / garrabūlanā hāḏāk wa-nikūn jālisīn ^{c}induhum wa-hum bī-jahhizū ḥarīwathum / bī-yijahhizū ladāthā wa-yijahhizū 'anfushum wa-yixṭaw ma^{c}āhā / šiiribnā hāḏawlā kullahin / w-iḥna mirayya^{c}īn lahum law-mā yijahhizu l-ḥarīwih / wa-fī baytanā hū ḏakka*[82] *'axī mirayya^{c} / w-ahlī mirayya^{c}īn law-mā nūṣal /*

law-mā gad al-ḥarīwih jāhizih / xarajat fawg as-sayyārih / wa-s-sayyārih gadī mizahnagih bi-l-garāḏīṣ al-jamīlih wa-l-ḥalā wa-l-hāḏā / wa-tkūn sayyārih jadīdih āxir mūdīl / hāḏā ṭabī^{c}ah hāḏa l-iyyām / wa-xarajnā / min baythum / wa-bi-njūb aš-šawāri^{c} hākaḏā / nisammī an-nās inn ma^{c}ānā ḥarīwih / law-mā gadiḥna garīb min al-bayt / garīb min al-bayt gad abī hānāk mirāyi^{c} / wa-ba^{c}ḏ ^{c}umūmī mirayya^{c}īn wa-min al-ahl / yistagbilū ahl al-ḥarīwih / awwal-mā wuṣulnā waṣṣalna l-ḥarīwih lā bāb al-bayt gadum yigūlū 'ahlan wa-sahlan yiraḥḥibū bi-ahlan wa-sahlan wa-miš ^{c}ārif ayš /

yitxilū ba^{c}ḏ ahl al-ḥarīwih ma^{c} al-ḥarīwih[83] *yidaxxilū binthum lā wasṭ makānahā / wa-yisallimū ^{c}alayhā wa-yākulū šwayyih ka^{c}k wa-l-kīk wa-z-zabīb wa-l-lawz allī gaddamūluhum ahl al-ḥarīw / wa-yigūm*[84] *yigūlū ma^{c} as-salāmih xāṭurkum*[85] *yigūm yiruḥūluhum /*

[80] Lack of number agreement on translocative verb.

[81] Pausal *imāla* raising final vowel from *-ā* to *-ī*.

[82] Distal presentational particle. Cf. *Syntax* p. 424.

[83] Verbal clause with dynamic verb. Cf. examples above.

[84] Lack of number agreement on linking verb.

[85] Bride's farewell (Piamenta 1990-1: 132).

The indicators were flashing and they peeped the horns just to let the people know that they were going to fetch a bride. They arrived at the bride's house.

At the bride's house, they also held a party, a women's party [with] tea and singing and everything. This was at the bride's house. When the groom's family arrived at the bride's house, they[86] just heard the peeping of the car horns and they were waiting at the door to meet them [with], 'Welcome! May God make live the one who has come! Welcome on the eye and head!' We went in. I had gone with them. We entered the bride's house and sat there. They offered us cake and biscuits, raisins and roasted chickpeas, etc. and tea. They offered us these things while we sat with them and they were getting their bride ready, getting her clothes ready and getting themselves ready to go with her. We drank all this[87] while we were waiting for them to prepare the bride. Meanwhile, at our house, my brother and my family were there waiting for us to arrive.

When the bride was ready, she went out into the car. The car had been decorated with beautiful strips of paper and pretty things, etc. It was a new car, the latest model. This is usual these days. We went out from their house and went through the streets. We let the people know that we had a bride with us, until we approached the house. Near to the house, my father was there waiting along with some of my [paternal] uncles and others from the family to meet the bride's family. As soon as we arrived and delivered the bride to the door of the house, they were saying, 'Welcome!' and welcoming [them] saying, 'Welcome!' and whatever else.

Some of the bride's family came in with the bride so they could bring their daughter into her room and greet her and eat some biscuits and a little cake and raisins and almonds which were offered to them by the groom's family. Then they started to say, 'Goodbye!' and got up to leave.

---

[86] i.e. the bride's family.

[87] Plural in Arabic.

an-niswān ḏik sā^{c} *yijirrayn yistajlayn*[88] *al-ḥarīwih / kullahin yuxrujayn yištayn yibsirayn al-ḥarīwih al-mawjūdāt kull:ahin hānāk mirayya*^{c}*āt ḍūl al-yawm / law-ma tji l-ḥarīwih yibsirannahā / awwal-mā tūṣal al-ḥarīwih kullahin yihibbayn yibsirayn al-ḥarīwih / wa-man absarhā gāmat rāḥatlahā*[89] */*

ar-rijāl ^{c}*inda-mā wuṣulū / ḏik sā*^{c} *gad al-ḥarīw yidrā 'innum gad wuṣulū / ba*^{c}*d-mā tūṣal šwayyih al-ḥarīwih bayt al-ḥarīw / yigūmū ar-rijāl / ba*^{c}*dahā bi-šwayyih / yigūlū la-l-ḥarīw yallāh axṭā / txul al-bayt* ^{c}*ind al-ḥarīwih / da*^{c}*aynā 'axī / fi*^{c}*ilnālih zaffih zuġayrih / wa-daxxalnāh al-bayt / xalāṣ iḥna riji*^{c}*nā riḥnālanā /*

bigī al-fannān hānāk wa-l-fannānīn wa-hāḏā / ^{c}*ādum ḥakk samrih xubrat axī* ^{c}*ādum ḥakk samrih /* ^{c}*ādum mixazzinīn / yištaw yijissū yurguṣū / wa-fi*^{c}*lan / jalasū / hānāk ragaṣū wa-ġannaw / lā fajr wa-hum bi-yurguṣū wa-bī-ġannaw / al-ḥarīw daxal* ^{c}*ind ḥarīwatih / w-akṯarat an-nās rāḥūluhum / mā bigī 'illā l-agārib wa-l-ma*^{c}*ārīf wa-l-xubrih allī yištaw yijissū yurguṣū / hāḏā laylat al-*^{c}*iris/*

gumna l-yawm aṯ-ṯānī allī hū ysammaw aṣ-ṣabāḥ / aṣ-ṣabāḥ gām al-ḥarīw / gaddamūlih aṣ-ṣabūḥ / ṣṭabaḥ / w-iḥna ṣṭabaḥnō / wa-xarajnā gadiḥna / iḥna ṭab^{c}*an sāmirīn ḍūl al-layl wa-gad iḥna tā*^{c}*ibīn lākin gad iḥna nitḥammil laylat* ^{c}*iris / farḥah*[90] */ gumna l-yawm aṯ-ṯānī / ṣṭabaḥnō / wa-gulnā* ^{c}*a-nuxruj dawrih / xarajnā dawrih / ba-s-sayyārāt ḥawālī* ^{c}*išrīn sayyārih ma*^{c}*ānā / wa-kull sayyārih fīhā 'arba*^{c}*ah xamsih sittih wa-ḏayyā wa-jahhāl [wa-]malān /*

xarajnā sirnā dawrih / sirnā wādī ḍahr / sirnā hānāk kullanā ḥna wa-l-ḥarīw wa-l-xubrih hāḏawlā kulluhum / wuṣulnā fawg jabal hākaḏā / wa-fawg al-jabal / law-mā wuṣulnā hānāk jarrū al-banādig / wa-fi^{c}*ilūluhum*[91] ^{c}*alāmāt hākaḏā / wa-bi-tnaṣṣa*^{c}*ū* ^{c}*ala l-*^{c}*alāmāt hāḏī / yibsirū manū 'aḥsan wāḥid /*

---

[88] *istajlā* has the sense of to see and examine the bride when she comes into the women's section of the groom's house.

[89] Switch from masc. sing. in subordinate clause to fem. sing. agreement in main clause.

[90] Predicandless predicate. Cf. *Syntax* pp. 123-7.

[91] Reflexive verb. Cf. *Syntax* pp. 202-3. Cf. use of this verb in texts 9, 11, 17, 22, 25.

The women at that time were going to see the bride. All of them went out because they wanted to see the bride. They were all there and had been waiting all day until the bride came so that they could see her. As soon as the bride arrived, they all jumped up to see her. When someone had seen her, they got up and left.

When the men arrived, the groom realised straight away that they had arrived. After the bride arrived at the groom's house, the men came a short time after her and said to the groom, 'Come on, go into the house to the bride!' We called my brother. We had a small procession for him and took him into the house. Then we returned and left.

The singer and the [other] singers stayed there. They were still there for the evening party; my brother's friends were still there for the evening party. They were still chewing and wanted to stay and dance. And indeed they did stay there and danced and sang, until dawn they were dancing and singing. The groom went to his bride and most of the people went away. The only people left were relatives and acquaintances and friends who wanted to stay and dance. That was the night of the wedding.

We got up the next day which they call the *ṣabāḥ*.[92] The morning after the nuptial night, the groom got up and they offered him breakfast. He had breakfast and we had breakfast, then we went out. Of course, we had been up all night and we were tired, but we could stand [staying up all night] on a wedding night. [It's a time of] rejoicing. We got up the next day and had breakfast and said we would go on a trip. We went on a trip with cars, we had around twenty cars. Each car had around four, five or six [people], and was full of children.

We went out and had a trip. We went to Wadi Dhahr. We all went there with the groom and his friends. We arrived on top of a mountain and when we got to the mountain, they took out the guns and made themselves targets, then aimed at these targets to see who was the best one.[93]

---

[92] i.e. the morning after the nuptial night.

[93] i.e. the best shot.

wa-minnuhum al-ḥarīw w-anā wa-kullanā wa-bi-nunṣa^c / nuḏrub aw man yinṣa^c an-naṣa^c hāḏā / gambarnā hānāk yimkin sā^cah aw sā^catayn / wa-riji^cnā /

hāḏāk al-yawm / iḥna gad ^cazzamnā ahl al-ḥarīwih / innum yikūnū[94] *yitġaddaw ^cindanā fī nafs … / fī ṯānī yawm / wa-hum wāfagū / hāḏā min al-^cādāt innak ba^cḏ al-aḥyān tid^cī ahl al-ḥarīwih yijaw yitġaddaw ^cindak yawm aṣ-ṣabāḥ / ba^cḏ al-aḥyān gadak tigulluhum u^cḏirūnā min kulla šay / wa-hum yigūlūlak i^cḏirnā kulla šay ya^cnī / gad kulla wāḥid / yista'ḏin min aṯ-ṯānī / ahl al-ḥarīw yista'ḏinū min ahl al-ḥarīwih w-ahl al-ḥarīwih yista'ḏinū min ahl al-ḥarīw / innū mā biš baynahum šī /*

riji^cna l-bayt / sirnā ṣallaynō / jum^cah / wa-ba^cd-mā ṣallaynā l-jum^cah riji^cnā rayya^cnāluhum / l-ahl al-ḥarīwih yijaw / law-mā jaw / wa-zid da^caynā 'ahlanā kulluhum / al-mawjūdīn ḥawlanā / wāḥid aw iṯnayn min al-jīrān al-garībīn allī gadum jambanā / aw ba^cḏ xubrat axī / tġaddaynā / hāḏāk al-yawm / ba^cda-ma tġaddaynā / ṭab^can fī l-yawmayn al-lawwalih allī gabl al-jum^cah wa-gabl al-^ciris / ^cādatan innū al-ḥarīw / yikūn / mā biš ^calayh yi^cmal ayyi šay / hāḏā gabl laylat al-^ciris / aṣḥābuh w-ahlih yuxdimūh wa-yif^calū kulla šay wa-hū mā ^calayh illā yijlis mu^cazzaz mukarram / lākin yawm ṯānī aṣ-ṣabāḥ[95] */ xalāṣ gad tamm al-^ciris ḥakkih*[96] *mā ^cād ma^cih illā yisīr wa-yijī / gadum yiddaw hāḏā bi-ḏarīg aḏ-ḏuḥk wa-z-zabj ya^cnī ḥājih ḥāliyih / yigūm yinfa^c yistagbil ansābih al-jidād / ḥīn yijaw / law-mā yijaw yistagbilhum / wa-yigarribluhum wa-yif^calluhum / ya^cnī yiddīluhum al-bug^cah al-ḥāliyih / hākaḏāhā / ya^cnī hū al-mustagbil luhum li'annum ḏuyūfuh /*

wa-ntġaddā / wa-ba^cd-mā nitġaddā nigūm nutxul al-makān ḥakk al-gāt / yitxulū yif^calūluhum bardag gahwih / ba^cd-mā yif^calū bardag gahwih / yijlisū / kulla wāḥid yixarrij al-gāt ḥakkih / iḥna xarrajnā l-gāt / wa-ddaynāh la-ḏ-ḏuyūf ḥakkanā / ddaynāluhum marbaṭ gāt lannī[97] *hāḏī ^cādih /*

---

94 *yikūn* used to indicate future tense here. Cf. *Syntax* p. 75.

95 Identificatory apposition. Cf. *Syntax* p. 241.

96 Verbal clause with definite inanimate subject.

97 From *li'annī*.

They included the groom, me and all of us. We aimed to hit or [to see] who could hit the target. We stayed there for about one or two hours, then we went back.

That day, we had invited the bride's family to come and have lunch with us on the same ..., on the second day, and they had agreed. This is one of the customs that sometimes you invite the bride's family to come and have lunch on the day after the nuptial night. Sometimes you say to them, 'Excuse us for everything!' Then they say to you, 'Excuse us for everything!' I mean everyone excuses themselves in front of the other. The groom's family ask the bride's family to accept their apologies, and the bride's family ask the groom's family to accept their apologies so that there is nothing [bad] between them.

We returned to the house. We went and did the Friday [prayer]. After we had done the Friday [prayer] we came back and waited for them, for the bride's family to come, until they came. We had also invited all of our family who were around, one or two close neighbours who are next door to us or [and] some of my brother's friends. We had lunch on that day. After having lunch – of course, on the couple of days before the Friday and before the wedding it is normal that the groom has nothing to do. This is before the nuptial night. His friends and family serve him and do everything so that all he has to do is sit and be honoured and exalted. However, the next day, the day after the nuptial night, that is the end of his wedding, so he has to come and go. They talk about this in a laughing and joking way and it [is felt to be] something nice. He [now] has to be useful and meet his new in-laws when they come. When they come, he meets them and serves them and does things for them. For instance, he will give them the nicest place[98] in that way. He is the person who meets them because they are his guests.

We have lunch. After having lunch, we get up and go into the room for gat. They go in and have a glass of coffee. After they have had coffee, they sit down and everyone gets out his own gat. We got out the gat and gave it to our guests. We gave them a bunch of gat because this is customary.

---

[98] i.e. to sit.

hāḏā lā ḍuyūfak tiddīluhum gāt lā ᶜinduhum xayrāt[99] / *ddaynāluhum gāt xayrāt xazzanū* / *wa-zid gassamnā lā baᶜḍ al-xubrih al-gāt* / *hum al-gāt allī ᶜinduhum hāḏāk kullih* / *yijirrūluhum*[100] / *gāt xayrāt wa-yisīr*[101] *yigassimūh* / *l-allī jambuhum* / *min aṣḥābuhum aw minnanā aw hāḏā* / *xazzannā* / *wa-hum xazzanū lā s-sāᶜah xams* / *wa-gāmū gālū nista'ḏinkum kfītū wa-silimtū*[102] *wa-midrī māhū* / *wa-gāmū rāḥūluhum* /

gabl hāḏā kullih / *al-ḥarīw bi-jlis maᶜānā mixazzin* / *lā s-sāᶜah arbaᶜ* / *wa-yigūlūlih gūm riḥlak* / *yisammūh yiḍarrūh* / *yiḍarrūh min baynhum yigūlūlih yigūm yiriḥlih ᶜind maratih* / *yaᶜnī mā yismaḥūliš innū yijiss xayrāt wa-l-ḥarīwih ḥakkih*[103] *jālisih hānāk waḥdahā* / *māšī* / *mā bilā yigūm yiriḥlih ᶜindahā hāḏā hī al-ᶜādih* / *gāmū rāḥūluhum* / *iḥna bigīnā nixazzin mixazzinīn hānāk* / *hāh w-inthā al-ᶜiris ḥakkanā hākaḏā* /

bigīnā ḥawālī / *'usbūᶜ* / *w-iḥna bi-nxazzin ġarr al-ahl al-garībīn maᶜa baᶜḍ* / *baᶜd al-ġadā ᶜalā sās innū yijī nitjābar iḥna wa-l-ḥarīw wa-hāḏā* / *wa-l-ḥarīw yijiss ᶜindanā lā 'arbaᶜ wallā xams* / *nigullih gūm riḥlak* / *ᶜind al-ḥarīwih ḥakkak* / *hākaḏā* / *li-middat usbūᶜ w-iḥna bi-nxazzin wa-nitjābar* / *hāḏa l-ᶜiris bī-kūn bi-hāḏa ṭ-ṭarīguh* /

wa-ṭabᶜan / *fī bayt al-ḥarīw* / *ᶜād bih ḥakk an-niswān* / *allī hū baᶜd al-ġadā yijayn yibsirayn al-ḥarīwih wa-yistagbilannahā wa-yifᶜalayn ġadā lā niswān wa-ḍīfuh* / *wa-hidār wa-dāwiyih*[104] / *wa-ᶜād bih yawm ṯāliṯ al-ᶜiris yawm ṯānī al-ᶜiris wa-l-kull wa-hin fāriḥāt* / *baᶜdā ᶜād an-niswān yifᶜalayn yawm ṯāliṯ* / *yawm aṯ-ṯāliṯ hāḏā yifᶜalayn ġunā* / *yijayn niswān akṯar min ar-rijāl allī yijaw* / *yijayn niswān zaḥmih*[105] *lā gad ġarr fīh ġunā wa-simiᶜayn innū bih ġunā xalāṣ* / *yijayn min kulla bugᶜah* /

---

99 Attribute separated from attributed term by prep. phrase. Cf. *Syntax* p. 217.

100 Reflexive verb. Cf. *Syntax* pp. 202-3.

101 Lack of number agreement on translocative verb.

102 Set phrase.

103 Unusual use of *ḥagg* phrase with noun of human relationship probably to convey degree of impersonality here. Cp. *Syntax* pp. 179-80. Cf. above.

104 The idiomatic phrase *hidār wa-dāwiyih* is used in a slightly derogatory way.

105 Adverbial noun complement. Cf. *Syntax* pp. 144-5.

This is for your guests. You give them a lot of gat. We gave them a lot of gat and they chewed, and we also divided the gat out to some of our friends. All this gat that they had, they took a lot of gat and then shared it out to those sitting next to them – their friends or us or whoever. We chewed and they chewed until five o'clock. Then they got up and said, 'Excuse us. You have done enough [in your hospitality] and may God keep you free from harm!' and whatever else. Then they got up and left.

Before all of this, the groom was sitting with us chewing until four o'clock and then they said to him, 'Get up and go!' They call this sending him out. They send him out from them and tell him to go to his wife. I mean, he isn't allowed to sit for a long time while his bride is sitting there on her own. No. He has to go to her. This is the custom. They[106] got up and left. We stayed chewing there. Okay, and that is how our wedding ended.

For around a week, we chewed with just close family members after lunch so that we could chat with the groom. The groom would stay with us until four or five. [Then] we would say to him, 'Get up and go to your bride!' [It was] like that for a week, with us chewing and chatting. Weddings are done in this way.

Of course, at the groom's house, there were also women's [parties] which were after lunch when they would come to see the bride and meet her. They[107] would make lunch for women guests with a lot of talk. There is also the third day after the wedding. On the second day of the wedding, they are also rejoicing. Then there are some women who celebrate the third day [after the wedding]; on the third day, they have singing. More women come than men. Women come in crowds: they only have to hear that there is singing and that's it, they come from everywhere.

[106] i.e. the guests.

[107] i.e. the women of the house.

yūga^{c} al-ġunā wa-yiġannayn / wa-yurguṣayn / zayy ar-rijāl ya^{c}nī bass ġarr muġallag ^{c}ala n-niswān li-waḥdahin / mā biš baynahin rijāl abadan / hāḏā ma^{c}āhin aṯ-ṯāliṯ / wa-yawm al-ḥaflih an-niswān /

wa-ba^{c}ḏ̣ an-nās ^{c}ādum yif^{c}alū sābi^{c} / iḥna gadū aṯ-ṯāliṯ / ya^{c}nī ba^{c}ḏ̣uhum yigūlū gadū ṯāliṯ wa-sābi^{c}[108] */ hāḏā hū al-ḥaflih / hāḏa l-^{c}iris ḥakkanā llī hū wuga^{c} ḥakk axī / mumkin anā zāyadt / mā zāyadt māšī li'annā gaṣṣart fī ḥājih wallā šī 'inna-mā / bayn-addīhā bi-šakl ^{c}āmm aw hākaḏā kayf bi-tuḥṣal / wa-bi-tuḥṣal ^{c}ind akṯarat an-nās hākaḏā / lākin ba^{c}ḏ̣ an-nās bī-jaw yif^{c}alū al-^{c}iris ḥakkum ṯāniyih /*

kayf bī-jaw yif^{c}alū al-^{c}iris ḥakkuhum hāḏawlā / al-gabāyil / fī bīr al-^{c}azab[109] */ yijī yif^{c}al ^{c}iris / wa-gabl al-^{c}iris yif^{c}al al-^{c}iris hū b-ūga^{c} al-xamīs wa-l-jum^{c}ah / aw yikūn aḥadd wa-ṯnayn / lākin ba^{c}ḏ̣uhum bī-jī yif^{c}al gabl al-xamīs yif^{c}al ṭarḥ / al-ḥinnā yisammawh / hāḏā*[110] *yi^{c}zim an-nās ^{c}indih yijaw yawm ar-rabū^{c} / yisammīhā laylat al-ḥinnā / al-magīl wa-l-ḥinnā / wa-s-samrih / wa-yijaw yixazzinū yawm ar-rabū^{c} ba^{c}d al-ġadā / la-l-^{c}ašī lā nuṣṣ al-layl / yigūm wa-yiḥannaw al-ḥarīw / yif^{c}alūlih šwayyih ḥinnā fī yadih / wa-yiḏ̣rabū bi-ṭāsuh / allī al-bara^{c} / yiḏ̣rubū bi-ṭāsuh / wa-yisammaw an-nās /*

wa-ba^{c}ḏ̣ an-nās bī-jaw allī hum mit'axxirīn wallā šī wallā l-garībīn allī mā gadumš hānāk yijaw / yibdaw yiṭraḥū la-l-ḥarīw / ṭarḥ yisammaw / ṭarḥ la-l-ḥarīw / ya^{c}nī misā^{c}adih la-l-ḥarīw hāḏī gadī ^{c}ādih ya^{c}nī w-iḏā hū jā ḥadd fī l-^{c}iris ḥakkih gadanā[111] *^{c}ārif min šān asīr agḏ̣ī fī ^{c}irisih aw fī ^{c}iris ibnih hākaḏā*[112] */ wa-hākaḏā wa-ragṣat bara^{c} yawmayn ṯalāṯ / hāḏā l-^{c}iris fī ba^{c}ḏ̣ aṯ-ṯāniyīn / w-iḥna ^{c}irisnā hū hākaḏāk / hāḏa llī gadart ^{c}alayh / ah wa-ma^{c} as-salāmih /*

---

[108] i.e. the parties of the third and seventh day are combined on the third day.

[109] Rhetorical question.

[110] Demonstrative pronoun functions as clausal anaphoric pronoun. Cf. *Syntax* pp. 382-4.

[111] Change of subject referent.

[112] i.e. if someone comes to your wedding and gives you a gift of money you have to attend their wedding or the wedding of one of their close relatives and give them a gift of money. Reference to proverb *ḥagg an-nās fī ṭ-ṭāguh* 'people's belongings [stay] on the window'. Cf. text 28.

There is singing and they sing and dance like the men [do], but it is confined to women on their own. There are never any men among them. The women have the third [day after the wedding] and the party day.[113]

Some people also [have a party] on the seventh [day after the wedding]. With us, it is the third [day]. Some of them say that it is the third and the seventh [in one party]. This is the party. This is how our wedding was for my brother. I may have said too much, I didn't say too much, no, I may have missed some things out or whatever, but I am just telling [you] in a general way how it happens. It happens like this for most people, but some people conduct their weddings in a different way.

How do they, the tribesmen, have their weddings in Bir al-Azab? They have a wedding, and before the wedding they make the wedding to be on the Thursday and Friday, or it could be a Sunday and Monday, but some of them give money gifts the day before the Thursday. They call it the henna [day]. For this, he[114] invites people to come over to him on the Wednesday. They call it the night of henna, chewing and henna, and the evening party. They come and chew on the Wednesday after lunch until the evening, until halfway through the night. He[115] gets up and they henna the groom putting a little henna in his hand, and they bang on a plate which is [for] the *bara*^{c} dance. They bang on a plate and call people.

Some people come who are late or whatever, or relatives who were not yet there come. They begin to give presents of money to the groom. They call it *ṭarḥ* [giving money gifts], money gifts to the groom. This is help for the groom. This is a custom. And if someone comes to his wedding,[116] I need to know [who came] so that I can go to his wedding or to his son's wedding to repay him, like that. The *bara*^{c} dancing goes on for two or three days. This is what weddings are like for some other people, and our wedding was like that.[117] This is as much as I can tell you. Good-bye.

113 This is the day of the wedding, i.e. Thursday.

114 i.e. the groom.

115 i.e. the groom.

116 i.e. the wedding of someone in the speaker's close family.

117 i.e. as I have just explained.

lammā fi l-wilā'd / lammā nsīr nifraḥ li-l-wālidih / nisammīhā ṭabᶜan al-farḥah / wa-nsīr niddīlhā / miyih / aw xamsī'n / yaᶜnī kullu wāḥid ᶜalā / ᶜalā-mā yištī / ᶜalā kayfih / yaᶜnī lāzim innū yiddīlhā farḥah / yā 'immā zalaṭ / aw hadiyih la-n-nīnī / niddīlahā šāl aw baṭānīyuh aw / ayyi ḥājah min hāḏa l-ḥājāt / w-iḏā hī bint niddīlha xrāṣ aw xātam / aywih / la-n-nīnī / aw niddī zinnih la-l-lumm / al-muhimm inn iḥna lāzim inn iḥna nddīlhā ḥājah / yaᶜnī nsammī hāḏa l-farḥah /

fa:-law-mā tkammil ḥīn tūlad wāḥidih tūlad ṯāniyih / min allaḏi dditlahā / lāzim innī yaᶜnī tiriddalhā / tiriddalhā l-farḥah / hāḏā[1] *'iḏā jābatlahā miyih tirajjiᶜlhā miyih / w-iḏā jābatlahā zinnih tiddīlhā zinnih / wa-'iḏā ddit lā bint axrāṣ tirajjiᶜ lā bint axrāṣ / maṯalan additlahā ḥīn wilidat lāzim tirajjiᶜhālhā fi l-wilā'd / yaᶜnī fī wilād aṯ-ṯāniyih / maṯalan antī wlidtī / antī wlidtī / addīliš hadīyih / wa-law-ma ntī tkammilī w-ana wham w-awlad intī tirajjiᶜī nafs al-hadīyih / lāzim yikūn nafs al-hadīyih / aywih hū mugāribih / w-iḏā hī filūs yaᶜnī lāzim inn intī tirajjiᶜī nafs al-filūs allaḏī jābatliš / hāḏā fī l-wilād /*

wa-fī al-ᶜiris hākaḏā wa-l-kull / yaᶜnī lāzim / fī al-ᶜiris / fī al-ᶜiris nisammīhā ṭarḥ / mā al-farḥah iḥna nxallīhā fī l-wilād / nigūlhā fī l-wilād / wa-fī al-ᶜiris lāzim nigūl / lāzim nijīb maᶜānā ṭarḥ / miṯl maṯalan jaw fī ᶜirisī wa-ḍaraḥūlī zinnih / aw ṣarmīyuh / aw xātam / wa-law-mā yiᶜarrisū lā ḥadd min ahlahā 'aw min bint hāḏ allaḏī ṭaraḥatlī aw ibnhā aw uxthā lāzim nirūḥ[2] *wa-njībalahā nafs allaḏī jābatlanā / fī hāḏā nigūl yaᶜnī yigūlū ḥagg an-nās fī aṭ-ṭāguh / yaᶜnī 'intī jibtīlī ḥājah axallīhā fī aṭ-ṭāguh / law-mā yūgaᶜliš ḥājah ajirrahā w-arijjaᶜhā lā ᶜindiš / dirītey*[3] */ ḥagg an-nās fī ṭ-ṭāguh / dirītey /*

hāḏā fī al-wilād u-fī al-ᶜiris / wa-bih nās bī-jībū ḍalī / yaᶜnī fī l-ᶜiris / wa-bih bī-jībū dagīg wa-gamḥ wa-sukkar / yaᶜnī ayyi ḥājah lāzim innī tirjaᶜ bi-nafs aš-šī / iḏā ddawliš ayyi ḥājah lāzim tiriddīhā bi-nafs aš-šī / yaᶜnī nafs an-nawᶜ / agūlliš lāzim tiriddīlhum / hāḏā fī al-ᶜiris /

---

1 *hāḏā* refers back to preceding clauses from *fa-*. Cf. *Syntax* pp. 382-4.

2 Switch from first sing. to first plural. Switch back to first sing. below (*jibtīlī*).

3 Pre-pausal diphthongisation of *-ī*. *dirītī* is used here in the same sense as AS uses *hāh*.

28 Births and weddings

At a birth. When we go to visit a new mother, we call it, of course, the *farḥah* [congratulatory visit]. We go and give her 100 or 50 [riyals]. Everyone [gives] what they want, as they wish. I mean, you have to give her a gift whether it is money or a present for the baby. We may give her a shawl or a blanket or any of these things. If it's a girl, we give her earrings or a ring. Yes, for the baby. Or we give the mother a dress. Anyway, we have to give her something, and we call that the congratulatory gift.

When she has finished [the forty-day birth period], when someone else has a baby, someone who has given her something, she has to give back to her, she has to give her back the gift. So, if she has given her 100 [riyals], she gives her back 100; and if she gave her a dress, she gives her back a dress; and if she gave a [baby] girl earrings, she has to give a girl earrings. For instance, if she gave her something, when she gives birth she has to return it on the birth, when the other [woman] gives birth. For example, if you gave birth, if you gave birth, I give you a present, and when you have finished [the birth period] and I get pregnant and give birth, you give back the same present. It has to be the same present. Yes, it's similar. And if it is money, you have to give back the same [amount of] money that she gave you. This is for births.

And for weddings it's like that too. You have to. For weddings, for weddings we call it a wedding gift. The birth gift we leave for births, we say it for births. For weddings, we have to say we have to bring a wedding gift with us. For example, if they came to my wedding and gave me a dress or a woman's head covering or a ring, when someone from their family or the daughter of someone who gave me a gift, or her son or her sister gets married, I have to go and give her the same as she gave me. For this we say, they say, 'Other people's possessions [stay] in the window.' I mean, you gave me something, I leave it in the window and then, when anything happens to you, I take it and give it back to you. Do you understand? 'Other people's possessions [stay] in the window'. Do you understand?

This is at births and weddings. Some people bring a sheep, I mean at a wedding, some bring flour, wheat or sugar, whatever it is she has to return the same thing. If they gave you something, you have to give back the same thing, I mean the same type. I am saying you have to give it back to them. That is [what happens] at weddings.

GLOSSARY

The alphabetical order for listing the words in this glossary is as follows:
a, ᶜ, b, d, ḏ, ḍ, f, g, ġ, h, ḥ, i, j, k, l, m, n, r, s, ṣ, š, t, ṭ, ṯ, u, w, x, y, z.

a

aᶜād – yiᶜīd	to return s.th.; to bring s.th. back
aᶜjab – yiᶜjib	to please s.o.
aᶜjam pl. *ᶜijmān*	dumb
aᶜlam	more learned
ab pl. *ābāh*	father
abᶜad	further
abadan	ever [in neg.]
abrahā	Abraha [male name]
absar – yibsir	to see s.th.
abyaḍ f. *bayḍā*	white
adāh f., pl. *adawāt*	clothes; things
aḏā – yi'ḏī	to bother s.o.; to annoy s.o.
aḏā'	excrement
aḏḏan – yi'aḏḏin	to call for prayer; to be called [prayer]
afḍal	preferable
afḍalīyuh f.	preferential treatment
aftaḥ – yiftaḥ	to open s.th.
agall	less
agrab	closer
aġlaḍ	thicker
aġlā	more expensive
ahamm	more important
ahl pl. *ahālī*	people; family
ahla[n] wa-sahla[n]	welcome!
aḥmā	hotter
aḥmar f. *ḥamrā*	red; brown
aḥsan	better
ajmal	more beautiful
akal – yākul	to eat s.th.
akbar	larger; older
akl	food
aktab / iktab – yiktib	to write s.th.
akṯar	more
akṯarat + noun	most of ...
akṯarat-mā	most commonly; mainly
al-ān	now
al-awwalīn	1. people of the past. 2. the older generation
al-ᶜašī	the evening; in the evening
al-bayḍā f.	al-Bayda [place in Yemen]
alf pl. *ulūf*	thousand
al-fātiḥah f.	[title of opening chapter of the Qur'an]
al-gāhirih f.	Cairo
al-gur'ān	the Qur'an
al-hind f.	India
al-ḥabaših f.	Ethiopia

al-ḥāḍur	the present
al-ḥudaydih f.	Hudayda [place in Yemen]
al-ḥujarīyih f.	the Hugariyya [area in Yemen]
ālif	used to s.th.; knowing s.th.
ālih f., pl. *–āt*	machine
al-kāmira xafīyih	candid camera [the camera is hidden]
allaḏī / allī / illī	that; which
allāh	God
allāh yiḥayyīk	[reply to *ḥayyāk* …]
al-māḍī	the past
al-muhimm	the important thing; the main thing; anyway
alṭaf	nicer; prettier
al-xalīj	the Gulf
al-yaman m./f.	Yemen
al-yamanīyih f.	Yemenia [airline]
al-yawm	today
a^c*lā*	higher
amām	in front of; before
ammā / mā	as for
ammā … aw	either … or
amr pl. *umūr*	matter; thing
ams	yesterday
anā	I
an^c*am – yin*^{c}*im [+* ^{c}*alā]*	to bless; to bestow blessing [on s.o.]
ant	you m.s.
antayn	you f.pl.
antī	you f.s.
antū	you m.pl.
arba^c*ah*	four
arba^c*īn*	forty
arḍ f., pl. *arāḍī*	ground; land; territory
arḍīyuh f.	flooring
ar-rub^c *al-xālī*	the Empty Quarter
arwa^c	more beautiful; more wonderful; more delightful
arxaṣ	cheaper
asās pl. *usus*	basis
as^c*ad*	to make s.o. happy; to bless s.o.
ashal	easier
āsif	sorry
asmar f. *samrā*	brown
as-sābig	the past
aswad f. *sawdā*	black
aṣbaḥ – yuṣbaḥ	to become
aṣfar f. *ṣafrā*	yellow
aṣġar	smaller; younger
aṣl pl. *uṣūl*	origin
aṣlan	originally; in fact
aṣlī	original

aṣ-ṣīn f. — China
ašbīh — similarity
at-turk / al-atrāk — the Turks
aṭ^{c}am — tastier
āṯārī — historical; archaeological
aṯ-ṯānī — the next
aw — or
awfā – yūfī — to complete s.th.
awlā — or
awlā'ik — those
awlāk — those
awwal — first
[min] awwal / al-awwal — at first; in the past
awwalīyih f. — priority
awwal-mā — 1. the first thing. 2. as soon as; when first [adjt.]
awwal šī — the first thing
ax pl. *axwih* — brother
axaḏ – yāxuḏ — to take s.th.
axḍar f. *xaḍrā* — 1. green. 2. wet
axīr — end
āxir — last
axraj — more profitable
ayḍan — also
āyih f., pl. *–āt* — verse of the Qur'an
ayn — where
ayn-mā — wherever
ayš — what
ayy — any
ayyaḥīn — when
ayyaḥīn-mā — whenever
ayyan / ayyin — which
aywā / aywih — yes
azrag f. *zargā* — blue

c

^{c}abr — through; across
^{c}ad- — [future particle for 1 p.s. only]
^{c}adad pl. *a^{c}dād* — number
^{c}adanī — south; south-facing [i.e. facing Aden]
^{c}ādatan — usually [class.]
^{c}add – yi^{c}idd — to count s.th.
^{c}addad – yi^{c}addid — to count s.th.
^{c}addil — [name of mosque]
^{c}ādī — 1. normal. 2. that's okay
^{c}adīd — many; a number of
^{c}ādih f., pl. *–āt* — custom; habit
^{c}aḏar – yi^{c}ḏir — to excuse s.o.
^{c}afš — baggage
^{c}afwan — sorry; excuse me

^{c}agad – yi^{c}gid	to draw up [a marriage contract]
^{c}agb	after
^{c}agd pl. *^{c}ugūd*	1. upper arched window, now with coloured glass. 2. contract
^{c}agd zawāj	marriage contract
^{c}agīg	semi-precious stone; gem stone
^{c}agl pl. *^{c}ugūl*	mind
^{c}ajan – yu^{c}jin	to knead s.th.
^{c}ajīnih f., coll. *^{c}ajīn*	dough
^{c}akas – yi^{c}kis	to reflect s.th.
^{c}alā	on; against
^{c}alā gadr	according to
^{c}ālaj – yi^{c}ālij	to treat s.o.
^{c}alā jamb	to the side!
^{c}alā kayfih	as he likes
^{c}ālam	world
^{c}alā-mā	as [adjt.]
^{c}alā mā 'arād allāh	as God wishes
^{c}alā mayd	so that; in order that
^{c}alāmih f., pl. *–āt*	target
^{c}alā sās	so that
^{c}alā sibb / ^{c}asibb	for; because of
^{c}alā šakl	in the form of
^{c}alā šigg	to the side!
^{c}alā ṭ-ṭalab	on demand
^{c}alā ṭūl	straight ahead; straight away
^{c}alayy ad-dawr	it is my turn
^{c}ālī	high
^{c}allag – yi^{c}allig	to hang s.th. up
^{c}allāgīyih f., pl. *–āt*	bag; box
^{c}allam – yi^{c}allim	to teach s.o. s.th.
^{c}ām pl. *a^{c}wām*	year
^{c}amal – yi^{c}mal	to do s.th.
^{c}amal pl. *a^{c}māl*	work
^{c}āmal – yi^{c}āmil	to treat s.o.; to deal with s.o.
^{c}amalīyih f., pl. *–āt*	operation; process
^{c}āmil pl. *^{c}ummāl*	worker
^{c}amm pl. *a^{c}mūm*	[paternal] uncle; father-in-law
^{c}āmm	general
^{c}ammar – yi^{c}ammir	to prepare bowl of water-pipe with tobacco and charcoal
^{c}ammih f., pl. *–āt*	[paternal] aunt; mother-in-law
^{c}ammal – yi^{c}ammil + lā	to do s.th. to s.o.
^{c}amrān f.	Amran [place in Yemen]
^{c}an	about
^{c}an ṭarīg	via; by way of
^{c}arabīyih f., pl. *–āt*	barrow; wheelbarrow
^{c}araḍ – yu^{c}ruḍ	to display s.th.
^{c}araf – yi^{c}raf	to know s.th.

^{c}*arag*	sweat
^{c}*arag – yu*^{c}*rug / yi*^{c}*rag*	to sweat
^{c}*araṭ – yu*^{c}*raṭ*	to gnaw s.th.; to chew s.th.
^{c}*arban – yi*^{c}*arbin*	to pay s.o. a deposit
^{c}*arbūn* pl. ^{c}*arābīn*	deposit
^{c}*arḍ*	1. breadth; side. 2. display
^{c}*arḍ* + noun	across; on the side of
^{c}*argih* f.	sweating; a sweat
^{c}*arīḍ*	wide; broad
^{c}*ārif*	knowing
^{c}*arraf – yi*^{c}*arrif*	to let s.o. know s.th.
^{c}*arras – yi*^{c}*arris + lā*	to marry s.o. off
^{c}*arūs* pl. ^{c}*irsān*	bridegroom
^{c}*asab – yi*^{c}*sib / yu*^{c}*sub*	to give ^{c}*asb* to s.o.
^{c}*asal*	honey
^{c}*asb*	festival money [given to women and children]
^{c}*asīb* pl. ^{c}*uswab*	scabbard
^{c}*askar* pl. ^{c}*asākir*	soldier
^{c}*assab – yi*^{c}*assib*	to give ^{c}*asb* to s.o.
^{c}*aswab – yi*^{c}*aswib*	to give ^{c}*asb* as a present
^{c}*aṣab – yi*^{c}*ṣub*	to bind s.th.; to tie s.th. up
^{c}*aṣar – yu*^{c}*ṣur*	1. to twist; to bend; to turn [e.g. road]. 2. to press oil
^{c}*aṣfūr* pl. ^{c}*aṣāfīr*	bird
^{c}*aṣīduh* f., coll. ^{c}*aṣīd*	porridge [from wheat or sorghum]
^{c}*aṣīr* pl. *–āt*	juice
^{c}*aṣr*	mid-afternoon
^{c}*aṣruh* f., pl. ^{c}*aṣarāt*	twist in the road; hairpin bend; turn
^{c}*aṣṣab – yi*^{c}*aṣṣub*	1. to bind s.th. 2. to put on a headband
^{c}*āṣumuh* f., pl. ^{c}*awāṣum*	capital
^{c}*ašā*	evening meal
^{c}*ašān*	so that; because
^{c}*ašarih*	ten
^{c}*ašī* / ^{c}*ašīyih* f.	evening
^{c}*aṭṭaf – yi*^{c}*aṭṭuf*	to fold s.th. up
^{c}*aṭṭar – yi*^{c}*aṭṭur*	to perfume s.o.
^{c}*āṭuš*	thirsty
^{c}*āwan – yi*^{c}*āwin*	to help s.o.
^{c}*awwad – yi*^{c}*awwid*	to perfume s.o. with sandlewood
^{c}*ayb*	shame
^{c}*ayn* f. pl. ^{c}*uyūn*	eye
^{c}*aynih* f., pl. *–āt*	type
^{c}*ayš*	bread
^{c}*ayyad – yi*^{c}*ayyid*	to celebrate the festival
^{c}*ayyinih* f., pl. *–āt*	type
^{c}*azūmih* f.	invitation
^{c}*azam – yi*^{c}*zim*	to invite s.o.
^{c}*azzam – yi*^{c}*azzim*	to invite s.o.
^{c}*ibārih* ^{c}*an*	consisting of; constituting
^{c}*īd* pl. *a*^{c}*yād*	festival; holiday

^{c}*iddih* f., pl. ^{c}*idad*	number
^{c}*iddat* + noun	a number of ...
^{c}*ilāj* / ^{c}*ulāj* pl. *–āt*	treatment
^{c}*ilbih* f., pl. ^{c}*ilab*	tin; box
^{c}*ilm*	knowledge
^{c}*inab*	grapes
^{c}*ind*	with; at the house of; at
^{c}*ind-mā*	when [adjt.]
^{c}*irbān*	paying a deposit
^{c}*irif – yi*^{c}*raf*	to know s.th.
^{c}*irig – yi*^{c}*rag*	to sweat
^{c}*iris* pl. *a*^{c}*rās*	wedding
^{c}*irj*	lameness
^{c}*īs*	very good
^{c}*išā*	evening prayer
^{c}*išrīn*	twenty
^{c}*iyyāl* m.pl.	children; boys
^{c}*tabar – yi*^{c}*tabir*	to consider s.th. [to be] s.th.
^{c}*tagad – yi*^{c}*tagid*	to believe s.th.
^{c}*tamad – yi*^{c}*tamid* + ^{c}*alā*	to depend on s.th.
^{c}*ūd* pl. *a*^{c}*wād*	lute; oud
^{c}*ūdih* f., coll. ^{c}*ūd*	sandlewood
^{c}*ūdī* pl. ^{c}*īdān*	twig; stick
^{c}*uḏmī* pl. ^{c}*uḏmān*	bone
^{c}*umlih* f., pl. ^{c}*umal*	currency
^{c}*umurhā*	it f. is still as it was
^{c}*uṣī* / ^{c}*uṣīyuh* f., pl. *a*^{c}*ṣī*	stick
^{c}*uṭr*	perfume
^{c}*uṭūr* pl. *–āt*	perfume

b

bā^{c} *– yibī*^{c}	to sell s.th.
ba^{c}*ad – yib*^{c}*ad* / *yib*^{c}*id*	to remove s.th.
ba^{cc}*ad – yiba*^{cc}*id*	to remove s.th.
ba^{c}*d*	after
ba^{c}*dā*	then; afterwards
ba^{c}*d-mā*	after [adjt.]
ba^{c}*ḏ*	some
ba^{c}*ḏ al-aḥyān*	sometimes
ba^{c}*īd*	far; distant
bāb pl. *abwāb*	gate; door
badā – yibdī	to appear
bada' – yibda'	to start; to begin [doing s.th.]
badal	instead of; in the place of; swaps [game]
baddal – yibaddil	to change s.th.
badlih f., pl. *badalāt*	suit; outfit
badlih ḏahab f.	wide gold collar; gold set
badrī	early

badrūm pl. *–āt*	cellar
badwī pl. *badū*	bedouin
bagarih f., coll. *bagar*	cow
bagdanūs	parsley
baggālih f., pl. *–āt*	grocery shop; grocer's shop
bāgī	remaining
bagiyih f., pl. *–āt*	remainder
baglawih f.	cake made from shredded wheat and syrup
baġl pl. *baġāl*	mule
bahār pl. *āt*	spice
bāhiḍ	excessive; exhorbitant; expensive
bahīmih f., pl. *bahāyim*	cow; she-donkey
bāhir	very good
baḥīn	early
baḥr pl. *baḥār*	sea
bakā – yibkī	to cry
bakkar – yibakkir	to do s.th. early; to get up early
bākir	early
bālā – yibālī + bi-	to care about s.th.
baladī	local
balāš	for nothing
ball – yibill	to wet s.th.
ballaġ – yiballiġ	to inform s.o.
bāmiyih f.	lady's fingers; okra
banā – yibnī	to build s.th.
bank pl. *bunūk*	bank
banṭalūn pl. *–āt*	trousers
barac	men's dance
barad – yibrid	to become cool; to cool off
barakih f.	blessing
baram – yibrim	to knead s.th. [e.g. dough] in the hand
bard	cold
bardag pl. *barādig*	glass; cup
bardih f., pl. *baradāt*	curtain
barḍū	also
[bargaṭ] pl. *barāguṭ*	lump
bargūg	apricots
bārid	1. cold; cold drink. 2. water carrier
bāridī pl. *bawārid*	bin
barik f., pl. *birkān*	pool; pond
barrac – yibarrac	to perform the *barac*
barrad – yibarrid	to cool s.th.
basbūsih f.	cake made from flour, eggs, sugar, coconut with sugar syrup
basīṭ	simple
basmal – yibasmil	to say *b-ism illāh …*
bass	but; only
bāṣ pl. *–āt*	bus
baṣal	large spring onions

bašmag pl. *bašāmig*	shoe
bāt – yibīt / yibāt	to go off; to be from the previous day
baṭāṭuh f., coll. *baṭāṭ*	potato
baṭn f., pl. *buṭūn*	belly
baṭāniyuh f., pl. *–āt*	blanket
baxūr	incense
bawl	urine
bāya^{c} *– yibāyi*^{c}	to bargain; to negotiate
bay^{c}*ah* f.	leeks
bayḍuh f., coll. *bayḍ*	egg
bayḍānī	of/from al-Bayda
bāyi^{c} pl. *–īn*	seller
bāyit	off; stale; from the previous day
bayn	between; in
bayn-mā	while
bayt pl. *biyūt*	1. house. 2. family; household 3. verse
bayt aš-šayṭān	'safe place' in hopscotch; 'house of the devil'
bayya^{c} *– yibayya*^{c}	to sell s.th.
bayyā^{c} pl. *–īn*	seller
bayyan – yibayyin	to appear
bayyat – yibayyit	to leave s.th. until the next day
bazz	cloth; material
bazz – yibizz / yibuzz	to take s.th.
bazzaġ – yibazziġ	to pick s.th. in sprigs
bī^{c}	selling
bi^{c}*lālī* pl. *ba*^{c}*ālil*	blob of dirt; dead, dirty skin
bibs / bibz	Pepsi
bidāyih f., pl. *–āt*	beginning
bi-dūn	without
biḏā^{c}*ah* f.	goods
bi-ḏāt	especially
bi-ḍabṭ	exactly
bigī – yibgā	to remain
bih	there is
bi-hāḏa l-ḥudūd	in this region; about this amount
bījū f., pl. *–āt*	Peugeot [taxi]
bi-kam	how much/many?
bi-kaṯrih	a lot
bilād f., pl. *balāyid*	village; home town
bilād f., pl. *buldān*	country
bilzigī pl. *balayzig*	bracelet
bināyih f., pl. *–āt*	building
bi-nisbih + lā	in relation to s.th.
binn	coffee
bint f., pl. *banāt*	girl; daughter
bint aṣ-ṣaḥn f.	sweet dish of layered pastry with honey and black cumin seed; 'daughter of the plate'
bīr f., pl. *abyār*	well

bi-raġm inn / ann…	despite the fact that…
birmih f., pl. *biram*	deep clay cooking pot
birr	wheat
bi-sā^{c}at + pronoun	quickly; straight away
bisbās	chilli peppers
biskut	biscuit
bistān pl. *basātīn*	garden
bi-stimrār	continually
bi-sur^{c}ah	quickly
bi-xayr	well
bizzāġ	picking in sprigs [verbal noun of *bazzaġ*]
bristaw f.	pressure-cooker [from Presto]
btā^{c} – yibtā^{c}	to buy; to sell
bta^{c}ad – yibta^{c}id	to go far; to go away; to leave; to be removed
bu^{c}d	distance
bug^{c}ah f., pl. *buga^{c}*	place; spot
bugših f., pl. *bugaš*	bundle
bundug pl. *banādig*	gun
būrī pl. *bawārī*	clay bowl of water-pipe
busāṭuh f.	simplicity
buṣṣālūh f.	round onions
būtāgāz f.	Butagaz
d	
da^{c}ā – yid^{c}ī	to call s.o.; to invite s.o.
dā^{c}ī	inviting [adj.]; inviter; caller
da^{c}wih f., pl. *da^{c}awāt*	invitation
dafa^{c} – yidfa^{c}	to pay s.th. [a price]
daffā – yidaffī	to heat s.th. up
dagdag – yidagdig	to knock
dagg – yidugg [+ ^{c}alā]	to knock [on] s.th.; to bang [on] s.th.; to hit s.th.
daggat al-^{c}ūd f.	music on the oud or lute
daggih f.	1. mince. 2. knocking. 3. musical beat
dagīg	imported white flour
dagīgih f., pl. *dagāyig*	minute
dahan – yidhan	to grease s.th.; to butter s.th.
dakam – yidkim	to hit s.th.; to strike against s.th.
dakkih f., pl. *dikak*	stone slab for sitting on
dalhaf – yidalhif	to push s.th.
dalw pl. *adliyih*	bucket
damm	blood
dār f., pl. *dūr*	house
dār – yidūr	to circulate; to go round
darab – yidrib	to fall
darajih f., coll. *daraj* pl. *darājīn*	stair; step
daras – yudrus / yidris	1. to learn; to study. 2. to recite [e.g. the Qur'an]
darīs	recital [of the Qur'an]
darrā – yidarrī	to make s.th. known to s.o.
dasa^{c} – yidsa^{c}	to tread on s.th.; to step on s.th.

dast pl. *dusūt*	cauldron
dawā – yidwī	to bother; to annoy; to pester
dawā pl. *adwiyih*	medicine; liquid medicine
[sāᶜāt] dawām f.pl.	working hours; opening hours
dawarān	turning; going round
dāwiyih f.	a lot of talk; noise
dawl pl. *adwāl*	turn
dawlih f., pl. *duwal*	state; country
dawmih f., coll. *dawm*	doum fruit
dawr pl. *adwār*	1. floor [e.g. first floor]; level. 2. go; turn
dawrih f., pl. *dawarāt*	trip; walk; tour
dawwar – yidawwir	to look for s.th.; to go round
dawwax – yidawwax	1. to make s.o. dizzy. 2. to become dizzy
daxal – yudxul	to enter s.th.; to go into s.th.
dāxil	in; inside
dāxilī	1. inner. 2. about to go in; going inside
daxiš / daxišš	roast chickpeas; black peas
daxl	income
daxxal – yidaxxil [+ fī]	to put s.th. [into s.th.]; to import s.th.
daxxan – yidaxxin	to smoke [s.th.]
dāyiman	always [class.]
dāyirih f., pl. *dawāyir*	circle
daymih f., pl. *diyam*	traditional kitchen
dayzal	diesel
ddā – yiddī	to give s.th.
ddarab – yiddarib	to fall
diblūmāsī	diplomatic
dif'	warmth
difi – yidfi	to become warm
dihlīz pl. *dahālīz*	hall; place
dijājih f., coll. *dijāj*	chicken
dīk pl. *adyāk*	cockerel
dirāsih f.	learning
dirī – yidrā	to know s.th.
dīwān pl. *dawāwīn*	sitting room [often best room]
duᶜā	invocation [to God]
dublih f.	ring
duggih f., pl. *dugag*	necklace with [usu. eight] large silver spheres
duġrī	straight ahead
dukkān pl. *dakākīn*	shop; store
dūlāb pl. *dawālīb*	drawer; cupboard
dūlār pl. *–āt*	dollar
dunyā f.	world
dūš	shower
duwā pl. *adwiyih*	medicine
duxūl	entering; bringing in
duxxān	smoke

ḏ	
ḏā	[proximal presentational particle]
ḏabaḥ – yiḏbaḥ	to slaughter [s.th.]
ḏabal – yiḏbil	1. to spit out s.th. [usually gat]. 2. to put ashes where clay oven to be placed
ḏahab	gold
ḏāk	that m.; [distal presentational particle] m.
ḏakar – yiḏkur	to remember s.th.; to mention s.th.
ḏakkar – yiḏakkir	to remember s.th.; to remind s.o. of s.th.
ḏalḥīn / ḏaḥḥīn / ḏalḥīnih	now
ḏamūlih f., coll. *ḏamūl*	cake made from wheat flour, butter and eggs
ḏarrā – yiḏarrī	to sprinkle s.th.
ḏawlāk	those
ḏawlayya	these
ḏawlayyak	those
ḏayyā	this m.
ḏayyik	that m.
ḏibāḥah f.	slaughter
ḏiḥlih f.	[small type of gat with rust-coloured leaves]
ḏīk	[distal presentational particle] f.
ḏiksāᶜ / ḏīk sāᶜ	at that time; straight away
ḍ	
ḍaᶜf pl. *aḍᶜāf*	double
ḍaᶜīf pl. *ḍuᶜāf*	weak; thin
ḍaġṭ	pressure; gravity
ḍahak – yiḍḥak (+ ᶜalā)	to laugh; (to laugh at s.o.; to cheat s.o.)
ḍaḥk / ḍuḥk	laughter
ḍahr pl. *ḍuhūr*	back
ḍaḥḥā – yiḍaḥḥī	to dry s.th. in the sun; to hang s.th. out to dry in the sun
ḍall – yiḍull + min	to shade s.th. from s.th.
ḍarab – yuḍrub	to hit s.th.; to bang s.th.
ḍarab al-ḥudwī	[name of a game]
ḍarbuh f., pl. *ḍarabāt*	hit
ḍarūrī	necessary; essential
ḍarūrīyih f., pl. *–āt*	essential thing
ḍawā – yuḍwī	to go home
ḍaww pl. *aḍwā'*	light
ḍawwā – yiḍawwī	to take s.o./s.th. home
ḍaxm	enormous; vast
ḍayf pl. *ḍuyūf*	guest
ḍayyaᶜ – yiḍayyuᶜ	to lose s.th.; to use up s.th. [e.g. time]
ḍayyaf – yiḍayyuf	to entertain s.o.; to receive s.o. hospitably
ḍīfuh f.	women's party; lunch
ḍuhr	noon
ḍulāᶜī	from Dulāᶜ [area in Hamdān]
ḍulᶜī pl. *ḍulāᶜī*	rib
ḍulmī	dark

ḍulmīyuh f.	dark room
f	
fa-	so; then [clausal conj.]
fā^{c}*il*	doing; making
faḍḍal – yifaḍḍul	to prefer s.th.
fāḍī	empty; free
fagaṭ	only [class.]
fagīr pl. *fugarā*	poor
fāhim	understand
faḥas – yifḥas	to rub s.th.; to rub off dirt; to sharpen s.th.
faḥaṣ – yifḥaṣ	to grind s.th.; to burnish s.th. [e.g. a stone]
faḥḥ / fiḥḥ	hot and spicy
fajar – yifjir	to unblock s.th.
fajja^{c} *– yifajji*^{c}	to frighten s.o.; surprise s.o.
fajr	dawn
fākih pl. *fawākih*	fruit
fakkar – yifakkir	to think
falat – yiflit	to be soft; to be weak [e.g. dough]
fallat – yifallit	to leave s.th.; to let go of s.th.
fanilliyih f., pl. *–āt*	vest; jumper
fann	good time; fun
fannān pl. *–īn*	1. artist. 2. singer and oud player
fār – yifūr	to boil [intr.]
farad – yifrid	to extend s.th.; to unfold s.th. [e.g. fingers of the hand]
farag – yifrig / yifrug	to divide s.th. out; to share s.th.
faransī	French
fard pl. *afrād*	person
farg pl. *furūgāt*	difference
farḥah f., pl. *faraḥāt*	1. joy; pleasure. 2. congratulatory visit to a new mother; congratulatory gift
farīg pl. *firag / firwag*	team
fāriġ	empty
fāriḥ	happy; rejoicing
farraš – yifarriš	to furnish s.th.; to cover s.th. [e.g. the floor]
farš	furnishing
fās pl. *fu'ūs / fisān*	axe
fasax – yifsax	to remove the taste of s.th. [e.g. gat]
fāṣul	gap
faṣūliyuh f.	common beans
fataḥ – yiftaḥ	to open s.th.
fatḥah f., pl. *fataḥ*	opening
fatrih f., pl. *fatarāt*	while; time span
fattaḥ – yifattiḥ	to open s.th. up [e.g. dough]
fatūt	dish of torn bread and ghee
faṭar – yufṭur	to break the fast
faṭūr / fuṭūr	breaking the fast
fawg	on; on top of

fawwar – yifawwir	to boil s.th.
fāyir	boiling [water]
fāyiz pl. *–īn*	winner
fāz – yifūz	to win
fī	in
fi^{c}il – yif^{c}al	to do s.th.; to make s.th.; to put s.th.
fi^{c}lan	indeed [class.]
fidiyū pl. *–āt*	video
fiḍī – yifḍā	to make time
figh	jurisprudence
fihim – yifham	to understand [s.th.]
fī ḥudūd	around; in the region of
fikrih f., pl. *afkār*	thought
filim pl. *aflām*	film
filūs	money
fimtū	Vimto
firāš pl. *firiš*	mattress; covering [e.g. carpet, blanket]
firiḥ – yifraḥ [+ lā]	1. to be happy [for s.o.] 2. to pay a congratulatory visit to a new mother
firn pl. *afrān*	modern oven with stove; baker's oven; oven
firzih f., pl. *firaz*	taxi rank
fi-sā^c	quickly
fisaḥ	wide; roomy
fī sinn …	at the age of …
fī s-sābig	in the past
ftahan – yiftahin	to be relaxed; to relax
ftaja^c – yiftaja^c	to be shocked; to be scared
ftaxar – yiftaxir + bi-	to brag about s.th.; to show off with s.th.
ftilih f., pl. *fatāyil*	thread
fuḍḍuh f.	silver
fuj^{c}ah	suddenly
fūl	horse beans; broad beans
fulān	so-and-so
fulānī	such-and-such [adj.]
fumm pl. *afmām*	mouth
fundug pl. *fanādig*	hotel
furṣuh f., pl. *furaṣ*	chance
fustān pl. *fasātīn*	dress
fustug	pistachios
fuṣṣ pl. *afṣāṣ*	gem; semi-precious stone
fūṭuh f., pl. *fuwaṭ*	sarong

g

gā^c pl. *gī^{c}ān*	ground; floor; valley; plain
gā^{c}ah f., pl. *–^{c}āt / gī^{c}ān*	floor; base; bottom
gā^{c}at al-afrāḥ f.	wedding floor
gaba^c – yigba^c	to take s.th.
gabbāḍuh f., pl. *–āt*	hairclip
gabil – yigbal	to accept s.o./s.th.

gabīlī pl. *gabāyil*	tribesman
gabl	before
gabl-mā	before [adjt.]
gadam – yugdim / yigdim	to welcome s.o.
gadar – yigdir	to be able; can
gadar – yigdir + ^{c}*alā*	to be capable of [doing] s.th.
gaddam – yigaddim	to give s.th.; to offer s.th.
gadīd	apricot syrup
gadīm pl. *gudamā*	old
gādim	next
gadr	ability [e.g. to afford s.th.]
gaḍā – yigḍī	to pay a debt
gaḍāḍ	native cement to plaster containers
gaḍḍā – yugaḍḍī (+ bi-)	to carry on with s.th.; to do s.th.; (to be content with s.th.)
gāḍī pl. *guḍāh*	judge
gafā	behind
gafa^{c} *– yigfa*^{c}	to hit s.th.; to strike s.th.
gaflih f.	best part of gat at top of the branch
gafū^{c} *bilsin*	lentil bread
gafū^{c} *ḏirrih*	sorghum bread
gafū^{c} *rūmī*	corn bread
gahwih f.	spicy coffee husk drink
gahwih pl. *gahāwī*	1. coffee. 2. coffee shop; coffee house; house where meals are served
gāl – yugūl / yigūl	to say s.th.
gala^{c} *– yigla*^{c}	to pick s.th.; to uproot s.th.
galam pl. *aglām*	pen
galaṣ pl. *–āt*	cup; glass
galb pl. *gulūb*	heart
galīl	few; a little
gallā – yigallī	to fry s.th.
gallab – yigallib	to turn s.th. over
galla^{c} *– yigalla*^{c}	to pick s.th.; to uproot s.th.
gām – yigūm	1. to get up. 2. to begin [to do s.th.]
gamarīyih f., pl. *–āt*	moon-shaped window usu. made in alabaster
gambar – yigambir	to sit; to stay
gamḥ	wheat
gamīṣ pl. *gumṣān*	loose dress; dress worn by a bride
garab – yugrub + lā	to be related to
garābih f.	relationship
garaḥ – yigraḥ	to fire; to go off [e.g. cannon]
gar^{c}*ah* f., coll. *gar*^{c}	pumpkin seeds
garīb	close; near
garīb pl. *agārib*	relative
gāriḥ	strong and fast-acting
gariyih f., pl. *gurā*	village
garn pl. *gurūn*	1. horn. 2. century

garrā – yigarrī	to teach s.o. s.th.
garrab – yigarrib	to bring s.th. close; to set out s.th.; to lay the table; to offer s.th.
garraḥ – yigarraḥ	to crack s.th.; to make a cracking sound from s.th.
garṭaṭuh f.	being fed up; feeling malicious
gārūrih f., pl. *gawārīr*	bottle
gāsī	thick
gassam – yigassim	to divide [out] s.th.
gaṣabuh f., pl. *gaṣīb*	pipe
gaṣad – yugṣud	to intend s.th.; to mean s.th.
gaṣad – yugṣud [allāh]	to make a living
gaṣd	intention
gaṣr pl. *guṣūr*	palace
gaṣṣar – yigaṣṣar	to skimp; to fall short; to trim
gaššām pl. *–īn*	*gušmī*-patch worker
gāt	Catha edulis Forskal [known as] gat
gatal – yugtul	to kill s.o./s.th.
gaṭa^{c} *– yigṭa*^{c}	1. to cut s.th. 2. to cross s.th. [e.g. bridge, road]. 3. to buy [a ticket]
gaṭab – yigṭub	to hurry s.th.; to do s.th. quickly
gaṭal	pickings
gaṭār pl. *–āt*	train
gaṭīfuh f., pl. *gaṭāyuf*	small, triangular doughnuts fried in melted butter and served with honey
gaṭṭa^{c} *– yigaṭṭu*^{c}	to cut s.th. [up]
gaṭṭaf – yigaṭṭuf	to pick s.th. [e.g. *gāt*]; to harvest s.th.
gawī	1. strong; thick. 2. very
gawlathum	as they say
gidim – yigdam	to be/become old
gīmih f., pl. *giyam*	price; cost
gimiš – yigmaš	1. to collect s.th.; to gather up s.th. 2. to win s.th.
gindīl pl. *ganādīl*	light; lightbulb
girāyih f.	1. reading. 2. learning; studying
girī – yigrā	1. to study. 2. to read s.th.
girrīḥah f., pl. *girrīḥ*	rocket; firework; firecracker
girš pl. *gurūš*	Riyal
girših f., pl. *giraš*	husk; shell; peel; outer leaves; skin
gišr	spicy coffee husk drink also known as *gahwih*
gišrih f., coll. *gišr* pl. *gišar*	husk [e.g. of coffee beans]
gtalab – yigtalib	to turn around; to change
gtasam – yigtasim	to divide up into
gubbih f., pl. *gubab*	arch; vaulted building
gudrih f.	capability; ability
gufaygif	[name of a game]
gufl pl. *gufal*	lock
guḥṭuh	black cumin seed
gumgumī pl. *gamāgim*	tin can
gummāš	cloth
gunṭurih f., pl. *ganāṭur*	shoe

gurāš pl.	grazing animals; livestock
gurnih f., pl. *guran*	corner
gurṭāṣ / *garṭāṣ* pl. *garāṭīṣ*	paper [bag]
guṣṣ	goss; gypsum
guṣṣuh f., pl. *guṣuṣ*	story
gušmī f., coll. *gušm*	long white radish
guṭᶜah f., pl. *guṭaᶜ*	piece
guṭb pl. *agṭāb*	pipe-stem
guṭn	cotton
guwih f.	strength
guwwārih f., pl. *gawāwīr*	bread cover made from cloth

ġ

ġadā	lunch
ġaddā – yiġaddī	to give s.o. lunch
ġalā	high cost
ġalab – yiġlib	to beat s.o. [e.g. in a game]
ġālī	expensive
ġalīḏ	thick
ġallag – yiġallig	to lock s.th.; to close s.th.
ġamaz – yiġmiz	to indicate
ġammaḏ – yiġammuḏ	to close [the eyes]
ġammaz – yiġammiz	to indicate
ġammāz pl. *–āt*	indicator
ġanam	sheep
ġanī pl. *aġniyih*	rich
ġannā – yiġannī	to sing [s.th.]
ġaraf – yiġrif	to scoop up s.th.
ġarb	west
ġarīb pl. *ġurabā*	strange; stranger
ġasīl	washing
ġassal – yiġassil	to wash s.th./s.o.
ġaṣb	force; coercion; compulsion
ġaṭṭā – yiġaṭṭī	to cover s.th.
ġayr / *ġarr*	1. only. 2. apart from; unless
ġāz	gas
ġiḏā pl. *aġḏiyih*	food; nutrition
ġilī – yiġlī	to be/become expensive
ġubār	dust
ġudwuh	tomorrow
ġuluṭ – yuġluṭ	to be wrong; to make a mistake
ġummāḏuh f.	blind man's buff
ġunā	singing
ġurāb pl. *ġirbān*	crow
ġurfih f., pl. *ġuraf*	room
ġurgih f., pl. *ġurag*	cistern; hole; pit
ġuṭā / *ġiṭā*	1. top; cover. 2. open basket
ġuṭāyā f., pl. *–āt*	cover; top

h

hā	[proximal presentational particle]
habb – yihibb	to jump up; to get up
hādi'	low [e.g fire, gas]; quiet
hadīyih f., pl. *hadāyā*	present; gift
hāḏā	this m.
hāḏāk	that m.
hāḏawlā	these
hāḏawlāk	those
hāḏī	this f.
hāḏīk	that f.
hāḍāk	that m.
hāḍīk	that f.
hākaḏā	like this; like that
hānā	here
hānāk	there
handasī	geometrical; engineering [adj.]
hannā – yihannī	to congratulate s.o.
harab – yuhrub	to escape
hararī	from Harara [in Ethiopia]
harwas – yiharwis + fī	to shove s.th. into s.th.
hawā f.	air
hawir	greedy
hayl	cardamon
hayy / hayyā	come on!
hazar – yihzir	to snatch s.th. [up]; to pull s.th.
hāzar – yihāzir	to snatch s.th. [up]; to pull s.th.
hī	she
hidār	talk
hin	they f.
hinayyih	here
hinayyik	there
hinyatluhum	how lucky they m. are!
hizzih f.	shaking
htamm – yihtamm + bi-	to be interested in s.th.; to care about s.th.
hū	he
hum	they m.

ḥ

ḥabas – yiḥbis	to imprison s.o.
ḥabaš [sawdā] f.	[type of black stone]
ḥabašī	Ethiopian
ḥabaših f.	Ethiopia
ḥabb – yiḥibb	1. to like s.th.; to love s.th./s.o. 2. to want [to do s.th.]
ḥabb pl. *ḥubūb*	grain; pip; berry
ḥabbih f., pl. *–āt*	a unit; one
ḥabbih f., pl. *ḥubūb*	tablet
ḥabbih sawdā f.	black cumin seed
ḥabl pl. *ḥibāl*	rope

ḥabs pl. *ḥubūs*	prison
ḥadd	someone; anyone; no one [in neg.]
ḥadd pl. *ḥudūd*	limit; extent; border
ḥaddad – yiḥaddid	to establish s.th.; to determine s.th.
ḥadīd	iron
ḥadīgih f., pl. *ḥadāyig*	garden
ḥadīṯ	modern; new
ḥadīṯ pl. *aḥādīṯ*	1. discussion. 2. Prophetic tradition
ḥaḍar – yaḥḍur	1. to bring s.th. 2. to prepare s.th.
ḥafaḍ – yuḥfuḍ	to store s.th.; to retain s.th.; to keep s.th.
ḥāfaḍ – yiḥāfiḍ	to preserve s.th.
ḥafar – yiḥfar	to dig s.th.; to bore s.th.; to scoop s.th. out
ḥaflat ᶜiris f.	wedding party
ḥaflih f., pl. *–āt*	party
ḥagg – yiḥigg + lā	to have a right to do s.th.; to be the right of s.o.
ḥagīgī	real; true
ḥajar f., pl. *ḥijār*	stone; mortar
ḥajar – yiḥjir	to utter a shrill cry for joy; to ululate
ḥajarīyih f.	stonework
ḥajaz – yiḥjiz	to make a reservation; to confirm
ḥājih f., pl. *–āt*	thing
ḥajz	reservation
ḥākā – yiḥākī	to talk to s.o.
ḥakam – yiḥkim	to secure s.th.
ḥākim pl. *ḥukkām*	judge
ḥakkam – yiḥakkim	to secure s.th.
ḥalā f.	nice things; pleasantness; good thing
ḥalāwā f.	sweetness
ḥālī	nice; beautiful; good; sweet
ḥalīb	milk
ḥālih f., pl. *–āt*	condition; state; situation
ḥallā – yiḥallī	to make sweet things; to eat s.th. sweet
ḥamal – yiḥmil	to run; to hurry; to go fast; to rush [to do s.th.]
ḥamd	praise
ḥamī – yiḥmī	to become hot
ḥāmī	hot
ḥāmil	pregnant
ḥamlih f.	rushing
ḥammā – yiḥammī	to heat s.th.
ḥammam – yiḥammim	to bathe s.o.; to wash s.o.
ḥammām pl. *–āt*	modern-style bathroom; bath; public bath
ḥammāmī pl. *–īn*	man who works in Turkish bath; bath-man
ḥammas – yiḥammis	to press s.th. down; to massage s.o.
ḥāmuḍuh f.	whipped fenugreek soured with vinegar and sugar
ḥanafī / ḥanafīyih f., pl. *–āt*	tap
ḥanaš pl. *ḥinšān*	snake
ḥann – yiḥinn	to go [somewhere at a specific time or at time of speaking]; to do s.th. quickly

ḥannā – yiḥannī	to put henna on s.o.
ḥānūt pl. *ḥawānīt*	shop
ḥarag – yiḥrag	to set light to s.th.; to burn s.th.
ḥārah f., pl. *–āt*	area
ḥarakih f., pl. *–āt*	movement
ḥarām	unlawful
ḥarārih f.	heat
ḥarīw pl. *ḥarāwih*	bridegroom
ḥarīwih f., pl. *ḥarāwī*	bride
ḥārr	hot
ḥarrag – yiḥarrig	to set light to s.th.; to burn s.th.
ḥarrak – yiḥarrik	to move s.th.
ḥasab / ḥasb	according to
ḥasab – yiḥsub	to work s.th. out
ḥāsab – yiḥāsib	to pay s.o. for s.th.
ḥass – yiḥiss	to feel s.th.
ḥašīš	grass; hashish
ḥašwaš – yiḥašwiš	to stir [meat] with tomatoes, oil and onions
ḥaṣal – yuḥṣul	to happen; to take place
ḥaṣal – yiḥṣul + ᶜalā	to receive s.th.; to get s.th.
ḥaṣṣal – yiḥaṣṣul	to receive s.th.; to get s.th.
ḥattā	1. until; up to. 2. even
ḥaṭab	wood
ḥaṭṭ – yiḥuṭṭ	to put s.th.
ḥawā – yiḥwī	to contain s.th.
ḥawā'ij pl.	spices; black pepper
ḥāwal – yiḥāwil	to try
ḥawālī	around; about
ḥawḍ pl. *aḥwāḍ*	basin; trough
ḥawī pl. *ḥawāyā*	yard
ḥawl	around
ḥawlī pl. *–āt*	towel
ḥawš pl. *aḥwāš*	yard
ḥawwaš – yiḥawwiš	to gather together; to congregate
ḥayāh f., pl. *–āt*	life
ḥayawān pl. *–āt*	animal
ḥayd pl. *ḥiyūd*	mountain; mountain face; peak; cliff;
ḥayṯ-mā	where; wherever [adjt.]
ḥayy pl. *aḥyā'*	area; quarter
ḥayyāk allāh	thank you! [Lit: may God give you life!]
ḥijrih f., pl. *ḥijar*	hall; landing [in a house]; yard
ḥikāyih f., pl. *–āt*	story
ḥilbih / ḥulbuh f.	fenugreek
ḥilgih f., pl. *ḥalagāt*	circle
ḥilim – yiḥlam	to dream s.th.
ḥilw	beautiful
ḥimār pl. *aḥmirih*	donkey
ḥimī – yiḥmā	to become hot
ḥimil – yiḥmal	to carry s.th.

ḥīn	1. when. 2. because; since [adjt.]
(wa-ᶜādū) ḥīn	early
ḥinnā	henna
ḥirfih f., pl. *ḥiraf*	craft
ḥirig – yiḥrig	to burn; to blacken [intr.]; to become black [e.g. gat]
ḥirrāg	burning
ḥisāb pl. *–āt*	bill; fee
ḥiss	mind
ḥizām pl. *aḥzimih*	belt
ḥtasab – yaḥtasib + lā	to count for s.o.; to be taken into account for s.o.
ḥuḏn pl. *aḥḏān*	lap; folds of sarong or robe
ḥulm pl. *aḥlām*	dream
ḥurim – yuḥrum	to be out [in a game]
ḥuṣamuh f., pl. *ḥuṣam*	pebble; grit
ḥuṣān coll. *xayl*	horse
i	
ibb f.	Ibb [place in Yemen]
ibn pl. *abnā*	son
ibrih f., pl. *ibar*	needle
ibrat [al-ḥammām] f.	long rod for unblocking pipes
iḏā	if
iḏāfuh ilā	in addition to
igtiṣād pl. *–āt*	economy
iḥkām	securing
iḥna	we
iḥtilāl	occupation
ījār pl. *–āt*	rent
ijāzih f., pl. *–āt*	holiday
ilayn	to where
illā	1. but yes! [neg. response to neg. question]. 2. but, except
in	if
inn / ann	1. that. 2. [presentational particle]
inna-mā	however; but [adjt.]
in šā' allāh	God willing; hopefully
insān pl. *nās*	person
irtifāᶜ pl. *–āt*	height
ism pl. *asāmī*	name
istiṭāᶜah f.	ability
iṣlāḥ	making [e.g. bread]
itṣal – yitṣul + bi-	to telephone s.o.; to call s.o.
ittifāg pl. *–āt*	agreement
ittijāh pl. *–āt*	direction
iṯiyūbī	Ethiopian
iṯiyūbīyā f.	Ethiopia
iṯnā-mā / aṯnā-mā	while [adjt.]
iṯnayn	two

j

jā' – yijī	1. to come. 2. to turn out
ja^{c}al – yij^{c}al	1. to make s.th. 2. to buy sweets [children]
ja^{c}ālih f.	sweets
ja^{c}far – yija^{c}fir	to billow [e.g. smoke, sand]
jāb – yijīb + lā	to bring s.th. to s.o.
jāb – yijūb	to go through, round [e.g. streets]
jabal pl. *jibāl*	mountain
jabalī	mountainous
jābar – yijābir	to talk to s.o.; to pay condolences to s.o.
jadd pl. *ajdād*	[maternal] grandfather
jaddad – yijaddid	to renew s.th.
jaddih f., pl. *–āt*	[maternal] grandmother
jadīd pl. *judud*	new
jadr pl. *jidār*	wall
jaḏab – yijḏib	to attract s.o.
jaffaf – yijaffif	to dry s.th.
jahd pl. *juhūd*	effort
jahhaz – yijahhiz	to prepare s.th.
jāhil pl. *jahhāl*	child
jāhiz	ready
jākitt pl. *–āt*	jacket
jalas – yijlis	1. to sit; to stay; to wait. 2. to keep [doing s.th.]
jālis	sitting; staying; waiting
jallās pl. *jalālīs*	stand [e.g. for water-pipe]
jalsih f., pl. *jalasāt*	sitting
jama^{c} – yijma^{c}	to gather s.th.; to collect s.th.
jamā^{c}ah	together
jamal pl. *jimāl*	camel
jamā^{c}ah f., pl. *–āt*	group
jam^{c}ah	together
jambiyih f., pl. *janābī*	curved dagger; jambiya
jamī^{c} + noun	all
jāmi^{c} pl. *jawāmi^{c}*	mosque
jamīl	beautiful
jamma^{c} – yijamma^{c}	to collect s.th.
janb [pron. *jamb*]	beside; next to
janb pl. *junūb*	side
jannih f.	paradise; heaven
janūb	south
janūbī	southern
jār pl. *jīrān*	neighbour
jarā – yijrī	to run; to flow [e.g. water]
jārih f., pl. *–āt*	[female] neighbour
jarr – yijirr	1. to take s.th.; to bring s.th. 2. to set to [doing s.th.]
jarr pl. *jurūr*	coil; spring
jarrab – yijarrib	to try s.th.
jass – yijiss	1. to sit; to stay; to wait. 2. to keep [doing s.th.]
jāwab – yijāwib	to answer s.o.

jawāz pl. *–āt*	passport
jaw^{c} / *jū*^{c}	hunger
jawharih f., pl. *jawāhir*	jewel
jāwi^{c}	hungry
jaww	weather
jawz al-hind	coconut
jawzih f.	coconut
jayb pl. *juyūb*	pocket
jāyī	coming
jāyizih f., pl. *jawāyiz*	prize; reward
jazmih f., pl. *jazamāt*	shoe
jazzār pl. *–īn*	butcher
jiddan	very [class.]
jihah f., pl. *–āt*	direction
jild pl. *julūd*	skin; leather
jīlī	jelly
jiljilān	sesame seeds
jism pl. *ajsām*	body
jisr pl. *jusūr*	bridge
jtama^{c} – *yijtama*^{c}	to get together; to meet
jubā / *jūbā* f., pl. *ajbīyih*	roof
k	
ka-	like [prep.] [class.]
ka^{cc}*ak* – *yika*^{cc}*ik*	to make cake
ka^{c}*k*	biscuit-like cake made from flour, eggs and ghee; type of biscuit
kabāb	kebab
kābar – *yikābir*	to seek to surpass; to strive to outdo; to show off
kabdih f.	liver
kabīr pl. *kubār*	1. large; big. 2. grown-up; adult
kaḏā	this way
ka-ḏayyā	like that
kaḏāk	over there
kafā – *yikfī*	to be enough
kafat – *yikfit*	to bind; to wear s.th.
kalām	speech; s.th. said; talk
kalasūn pl. *–āt*	underpants
kalimih f., pl. *–āt*	word
kallaf – *yikallaf*	to cost s.o. s.th.; to ask s.o. to do s.th.
kallam – *yikallim*	to talk to s.o.
kam	how many/much? so many; a few
ka-mā	as [adjt.]
kāmil	whole; complete
kam-mā	as many as; however much [adjt.]
kammal – *yikammil*	to finish s.th.; to complete s.th.
kammīyih f., pl. *–āt*	amount
kammūn	cumin

kān – yikūn	[past]; to be
karkaday	hibiscus [juice]
karrar – yikarrir	to repeat s.th.; to do s.th. twice
kartūn pl. *karātīn*	box
kasā – yiksī	to buy clothes for s.o. [i.e. for festival or wedding]
kasar – yiksir	to break s.th.
kaššan – yikaššin	to add fried vegetables to meat
katab – yuktub	to write [s.th.]
kaṯīr pl. *kuṯār*	a lot; many
kawā – yikwī	to cauterise s.o.
kawb pl. *akwāb*	cup
kawkabān f.	Kawkaban [place in Yemen]
kawwā – yikawwī	to iron s.th.
kayf	how
kayf-mā	however
kayyas – yikayyis	to wash s.o. with a *kīs*
kibrīt	matches
kidmih f., pl. *kidam*	bap of mixed grains
kīkih f., coll. *kīk*	cake
kīlū	kilo
kīs pl. *akyās*	1. bag. 2. bath-bag; wash-mit
kiswih f.	clothes; outfit; bride's trousseau
kitlī pl. *katālī*	kettle
kiṯir – yikṯar	to be many, a lot
krīm karamallih	creme caramel
ktasar – yiktsir	to break
kubānih f., pl. *kubān*	maize cake
kubaybih f., pl. *–āt*	kebab
kūfiyih f., pl. *kawāfī*	hat; cap
kull	each; every; all
kull-mā	whenever; the more
kūmidī f., pl. *–āt*	comedy
kurah f., pl. *–āt / akrāt*	ball
kursī pl. *karāsī*	chair; seat
kušš	check [in chess]; foul move [in a game]
kūt pl. *akwāt*	jacket
kuṯr	many; large number; abundance
kuṯrih f.	many; large number; abundance
kwayyis	good

l

lā	1. to; for. 2. if. 3. no
lā^cab – yilā^cib	to play with s.o.
lā^cib pl. *–īn*	player
laban	milk
labbas – yilabbis	to dress s.o. in s.th.
labbih f., pl. *libab*	necklace which covers most of chest
lada^c – yilda^c	to strike s.th. lightly
ladāh pl.	clothes

lad̲īd̲	delicious
laff – yiliff / yiluff	to turn; to wrap s.th. up
laffih f.	walk round; circuit
laflaf – yilaflif	to collect s.th.
laggam – yilaggim	to feed s.o. s.th.
laggaṭ – yilaggiṭ	to gather s.th.; to pick s.th. [up]
lahabih f.	blazing fire
lā ḥadd	up to
lāḥaḍ – yilāḥiḍ	to see s.th.; to observe s.th.; to watch s.th.
lāḥag – yilāḥig	to chase s.o.; to go after s.o.
laḥḍuh f., pl. *laḥaḍāt*	moment
laḥḥ – yiluḥḥ	to make *laḥūḥ* [pancakes]
laḥmih f.	meat
laḥūḥah f., coll. *laḥūḥ*	pancake
lajan pl. *aljān*	large, shallow, metal bowl
lākin	but
lammā	when [adjt.]
laṣā – yilṣu'	to burn [intr.]
laṣṣā – yilaṣṣī	to set light to s.th.
laṭīf	nice
law	if
lawā – yilwī	to go around; to wander about
law-mā	when; until [adjt.]
lawn pl. *alwān*	colour
lawz	almonds
laxbaṭ – yulaxbaṭ	to mix up
layl f. *laylih* pl. *layālī*	night
laylat al-gubūl f.	wedding night
laylat al-ḥilfih f.	wedding night
laymūn	lemon
lā zāl	still
li'ann	because
li^{c}*bih* f., pl. *li*^{c}*ibāt / al*^{c}*āb*	1. game. 2. toy
li^{c}*bih* f., pl. *li*^{c}*ib*	toy
li^{c}*ib – yil*^{c}*ab*	to play s.th.
libb	edible seeds
libis – yilbas	to put on s.th.; to wear s.th.
libn	clay or mud brick
libs pl. *malābis*	clothes
liddih f.	delight; delectation
līfih f.	loofa
ligī – yilgā	to find s.th.
lihib – yilhab	to become very hot
lij^{c} pl. *aljā*^{c}	mouthful
lilmā	why
līm	lime
limi'/ limih	why
limi^{c} *– yilma*^{c}	to shine

lisān pl. *alsinih*	tongue
lisī – yilsā	to stick [intr.]
ltafat – yiltafit	to turn round
ltagā – yiltagī	to meet o.a.
lugf pl. *algāf*	mouth
lugmih f.	bread; small loaf or roll
lūkandih f., pl. *–āt*	small, generally low-class hotel
luṣwuh f.	kindling
luṭa^{c} – yilṭa^{c}	to strike s.th.; to hit s.th.

m

mā	what
mā'	water
ma^{c}	with
mā ^{c}adā	except for
ma^{c}āš pl. *–āt*	salary
ma^{c} ba^{c}ḍ	together
ma^{c}had pl. *ma^{c}āhid*	institute
ma^{c} hāḏā	despite this
ma^{c}idih f., pl. *mi^{c}ad*	stomach
ma^{c}īših f.	living; way of living
ma^{c}janih f., pl. *ma^{c}ājin*	kneading trough
ma^{c}lagih f., pl. *ma^{c}ālig*	hook
ma^{c}mūl	made
ma^{c}mūr	built
ma^{c}nā pl. *ma^{c}ānī*	meaning
ma^{c}rūf	known; well known
ma^{c}rūf pl. *ma^{c}ārif*	acquaintance
ma^{c}ṣaruh f., pl. *ma^{c}āṣur*	oil press
ma^{c}ṣūbuh f.	hot bread shredded onto ghee and honey
ma^{c}šarih f., pl. *ma^{c}āšir*	round brass or iron tray
ma^{c}zūm pl. *ma^{c}āzīm*	guest
mā … baṭātan	never; not at all
mā bilā	only
mablaġ pl. *mabāliġ*	amount
mablūl	wet
mabnī	built
mabsam pl. *mabāsim*	lip
madā^{c}ah f., pl. *madāyi^{c}*	water-pipe
madagg pl. *–āt*	pestle
madaḥ – yimdaḥ	to praise s.o. [usu. in poetry or song]
madallih f., pl. *–āt*	large water jar
mad^{c}ū	invited
madd – yimudd	1. to stretch s.th. out; to reach out. 2. to give s.th.
maddad – yimaddid	to stretch s.th.; to spread s.th. out
madfa^{c} pl. *madāfi^{c}*	cannon
madfal pl. *madāfil*	spittoon
madḥ	praise
madīnih f., pl. *mudun*	town

madrasih f., pl. *madāris*	school
maḏāg	taste
maḏaġ – yimḏaġ	to chew s.th.
maḏall pl. *–āt*	shade
mafraših f., pl. *mafāriš*	rug; carpet
mafraj pl. *mafārij*	room with a view [in which gat chews are held]; reception room
mafrūḍ	supposed; ought
mafrūš	furnished
maftūḥ	open
magaṣṣ pl. *–āt*	scissors
magfa^{c} pl. *magāfi*^{c}	the [e.g. stone, stick, marble] the player hits with
magīl	gat chew
maglā pl. *magālī*	stone or clay cooking pot
magmaṭuh f., pl. *magāmuṭ*	swaddling bands; nappy
magṭab pl. *magāṭub*	sarong
maġraf pl. *maġārif*	scoop
maġrib	sunset
maġsal pl. *maġāsil*	modern-style sink
maġṭaṣ pl. *maġāṭuṣ*	bath; Jewish ritual bath
mahr pl. *muhūr*	dowry; bride-price
maḥall pl. *–āt*	1. place. 2. shop
maḥallabīyih f.	ground rice or semolina pudding
maḥallī	local
maḥallīyan	locally
maḥallīyih f., pl. *–āt*	sweet food; pudding
maḥaṭṭuh f., pl. *–āt*	station
mā … illā	only
majḥaf pl. *majāḥif*	shovel
majlis pl. *majālis*	sitting place
majmū^{c}	collected together; grouped
majmū^{c}*ah* f., pl. *–āt*	group
majrā pl. *majārī*	course [e.g. for water]; drain
makān pl. *amkinih*	1. place. 2. [main living] room
m'akkad	certain
makkan – yimakkin + lā	to hand over s.th. to s.o.; to give s.o. s.th.
maklaf f., pl. *makālif*	woman
makrafūn pl. *–āt*	microphone
maksūr	broken
maktab pl. *makātib*	office
maktabih f., pl. *makātib*	library; bookshop
malak – yimlik + lā	to conduct the wedding contract for s.o.
malān	full
malatt pl. *–āt / amlāt*	wooden tobacco-box
mal^{c}*agih* f., pl. *malā*^{c}*ig*	spoon
malgūṣ	stung
mallā – yimallī	to fill s.th.
malūjih f., coll. *malūj*	large, flat bread; *malūj*

mamdūd	stretched
mamnū^c	prohibited
mamsak pl. *mamāsik*	handle
man	who; someone
mana^c – yimna^c + min	to prevent s.o. from doing s.th.; to prohibit s.o. from doing s.th.
manḍar pl. *manāḍur*	1. view. 2. top-floor room
manḍaruh f., pl. *manāḍur*	top-floor room
manṭaguh f., pl. *manāṭug*	region; area
manxul pl. *manāxul*	sieve
manzal	down
maraḍ pl. *amrāḍ*	sickness; illness
marag	broth; stock
maraysī	sugar
marbaṭ pl. *marābuṭ*	bunch [e.g. of gat]
marbūṭ	attached; tied
marḥabā	welcome!
mārib f.	Marib [place in Yemen]
marīḍ pl. *–īn / amrāḍ*	patient; sick person
marih f., pl. *niswān / nisā*	woman
markaz pl. *marākiz*	centre [e.g. of a *nāḥiyih*]
markūz + ^{c}alā	supported by; centred on
marr – yimurr + bi-	to pass by s.th.
marrih f., pl. *–āt*	time; once
martabih f., pl. *marātib*	bench
marwaḥah f., pl. *marāwiḥ*	fan
[al-]masā	1. evening. 2. the game *al-masā*
masāfih f., pl. *–āt*	distance
masaḥ – yimsaḥ	to wipe s.th.
masāj	massage
masdūd	blocked; sealed
[yā marḥabā yā] mashalā	welcome!
masjid pl. *masājid*	mosque
masjūn	imprisoned
masmūḥ	permitted
masra^c	early; soon; how soon!
massā – yimassī	1. to announce the curfew. 2. to play *al-masā*
massaḥ – yimassiḥ + lā	to wipe up after s.o.
maṣnū^c	made
maṣrūf pl. *maṣārif*	provisions
maṣrūf al-bayt	housekeeping money
maṣṣ – yimuṣṣ	to suck [s.th.]
mašā – yimšī	to walk; to go
mā šā' allāh	[expression of approval esp. of s.th. extraordinary]
mašbūj	swollen; bulging; stuffed
mašbūk	interlinked
mašġūl	busy
mašhūr	famous
māšī	1. no. 2. otherwise; or else

mašrab / mišrab pl. *mašārib*	mouthpiece; end-piece
mašrūbih f., pl. *–āt*	drink
māt – yimūt	to die
matā	when
matḥaf pl. *matāḥif*	museum
matkā pl. *madākī*	arm-rest
maṭar pl. *amṭār*	rain
maṭār pl. *–āt*	airport
maṭ^{c}*am* pl. *maṭā*^{c}*um*	restaurant
maṭbax pl. *maṭābux*	[modern-style] kitchen
maṭbū^{c}	stamped; manufactured [by machine]
maṭḥūn	ground [adj.]
maṭīṭ	thin wheat or barley gruel prepared with water, yoghurt, butter, green herbs, salt and chillies
maṭla^{c}	up; upwards
maṭlūb	required
maṭraguh f., pl. *maṭārug*	hammer
maṭrūḥ	put; placed
maṯal pl. *amṯāl*	proverb
maṯalan	for example; for instance
maw^{c}*id* pl. *mawā*^{c}*id*	appointment
mawḏ̣ū^{c} pl. *mawāḏ̣ī*^{c}	matter; subject
mawgad pl. *mawāgid*	brazier; stove
mawgi^{c} pl. *mawāgi*^{c}	place; position
mawgif pl. *mawāgif*	stop; stopping place
mawjūd	present; available
mawla^{c}*ī* pl. *mawāla*^{c}	addict [esp. to water-pipe]
mawsim pl. *mawāsim*	season
mawt	death
mawtar pl. *mawātir*	motor vehicle; car
mawzūn	correctly proportioned; balanced
maxbaših f., pl. *maxābiš*	long, wooden, bowlless spoon
maxbazih f., pl. *maxābiz*	padded mushroom-shaped pillow used to press bread onto sides of hot clay oven
maxdar pl. *maxādir*	drill
maxḏ̣ūb	beaten; stirred
maxlūg	creature; soul
maxlūṭ	mixed
maxraj	outside
maxṣūṣ + bi-	specially for; specialised in
maxṭā pl. *maxāṭī*	1. passage; channel [for water]. 2. bridge
maxzan pl. *maxāzin*	store
maxzūg	perforated; having a hole
māyidih f., pl. *–āt*	dining table or area
mā zāl	still
mazgam pl. *mazāgim*	handle
mazharih f., pl. *mazāhir*	vase
mazḥagih f., pl. *mazāḥig*	stone for crushing herbs, vegetables or salt

mazḥaṭ pl. *mazāḥiṭ*	abattoir
mazrū^{c}	cultivated
mi'ajjir	renting out
mi^{c}*ayyan*	particular; certain
mīdān / maydān pl. *mayādīn*	square
mīdān at-taḥrīr	Liberation Square
midawwir	rounded
middih / muddih f., pl. *–āt*	period of time
midrī	I don't know
miftahin	relaxed
migḥaf pl. *magāḥif*	shovel; scoop
migšāmih f., pl. *magāšim*	vegetable garden
miġsālih f., pl. *maġāsil*	laundry
mihrih f., pl. *mihar*	profession; work
miḥabb al-^{c}*azīz*	peanuts
miḥammar / muḥammar	browned
mijābirih	1. conversation. 2. gathering; visiting. 3. consolation [e.g. at funeral]
mijahhiz	preparing
mikabbir aṣ-ṣawt	amplifier
mikayyis pl. *–īn*	masseur
milawwaḥ	large thin flaky bread
milawwan	coloured
milḥ	salt
milḥī	1. small amount of salt. 2. salt with wild thyme and chilli
milja^{c} pl. *malāji*^{c}	cheek
milkih f.	wedding contract
min	from
min ajl	in order to; so that; for the sake of
minayn	whence; from where
min ḍumn	within
min gabil	by; on the part of
min jadīd	again [lit: from new]
min jayz	exactly like; like
min nāḥiyih	on the one hand
min šān	so that
minz^{c}*ij*	annoyed
mirāyih f., pl. *–āt*	mirror
mirayya^{c}	waiting
mirna^{c} pl. *marāni*^{c}	ramp of irrigation well
mirtifa^{c}	raised
misāfir pl. *–īn*	travelling [adj.]; traveller
misaḥbal	slow in work
misajjilih f., pl. *–āt*	tape recorder
misakkar	sugary; sweet
misāwī [la-l-arḍ]	level [with the ground]
misiḥ – yimsaḥ	to wipe s.th.
misik – yimsak	to have s.th.; to grab s.th.; to take hold of s.th.

mistadīr	round
mistagbil / mustagbil pl. *–īn*	person who meets s.o. else
mista'jir / musta'jir pl. *–īn*	tenant
mistalim pl. *–īn*	guard; s.o. in charge of s.th.; on duty
mistamirr	continuing
mistarāḥ pl. *–āt*	[traditional] bathroom; toilet
miṣayfan	well patinated [jambiya handle]
miš …	not
mišābah	similar
mišakkal	mixed [e.g. fruit drink; food]
*mišamma*ᶜ pl. *–āt*	plastic sheet
miškilih f., pl. *mašākil*	problem
mištarī pl. *–īn*	buyer
mišwār pl. *mašāwir*	business; errand; s.th. to do
mit'aṣṣal	deep-rooted; established
mit'axxir	late
*mit*ᶜ*addid*	many
*mit*ᶜ*awwad +* ᶜ*alā*	used to s.th.
*mitfarra*ᶜ	branching off
mitġayyar	changed
mitmayyiz	particular; distinguished
mitr pl. *amtār*	metre
mittafig	in agreement; agreed
mitwājid	available; very common
mitwātī	congregated; convened; gathered
mitzawwij	married
miṯaggal	heavy; full [e.g. of the stomach]
miṯāl pl. *amṯilih*	example
miṯgilih	heavily pregnant
miṯl	like
miwarrim	swelling; bulging
mixbāzih f., pl. *maxābiz*	bakery
miyih f., pl. *–āt*	hundred
mizahnag	decorated in a loud manner; dressed well
mizaflat	paved; asphalted
mīzān pl. *mayāzīn*	scales
mizhir	in flower; blooming; blossoming
mizmār pl. *mazāmīr*	pipe [oft. played at weddings]
mtadd – yimtadd	to lie down; to stretch out
mtalā – yimtalī	to fill up; to become full
*mu*ᶜ*allab* pl. *–āt*	tinned goods
*mu*ᶜ*allag*	suspended
*mu*ᶜ*arban*	booked through payment of a deposit
*mu*ᶜ*aṣwar*	with many turns; twisty [e.g. road]
*mu*ᶜ*aṭṭar*	perfumed
*mu*ᶜ*āwin* pl. *–īn*	assistant
*mu*ᶜ*awwaḍ*	in exchange
mubaddal	changed

mubargaṭ	lumpy
mubāšaratan	immediately [class.]
mubāšarih	immediately
mudawwar	round
mūdīl pl. *–āt*	model
mudīr pl. *mudarā*	manager
*muḏī*ᶜ pl. *–īn*	reporter
muḍayyaf	invited as a guest
muḍḥuk	comedian ; funny
mufārag	separated
mufargaš	lumpy
mufattaḥ	opened
mufāwid pl. *–īn*	middle-man
mugaffal	locked
mugaffī	having the back turned
mugahwī pl. *–īn*	landlord of *gahwih*
mugahwīyih f., pl. *–āt*	landlady of *gahwih*
mugārib	similar
mugāwit pl. *mugāwitih*	gat grower who sells to middle-man
mugawwit pl. *–īn*	gat trader
muġallaf	covered; wrapped
muġallag [+ ᶜalā]	locked; closed; confined [to s.o.]
muġammaḍ	with eyes closed
muġannī pl. *–īn*	singer
muġanniyih f., pl. *–āt*	[female] singer
muġtarib pl. *–īn*	emigrant [usu. worker]
muhaddam	destroyed
muhimm	important
muhtamm + bi-	concerned about
muḥabbab	good; desirable
muḥaddad	determined; certain
muḥāfaḍuh f., pl. *–āt*	governorate
muḥarram pl. *–āt*	forbidden thing
muḥawwiš	gathered together
muḥjirih f., pl. *–āt*	ululator [woman]
mujahhaz	prepared
mujaḥḥif pl. *–īn*	lavatory cleaner
*mujtama*ᶜ *[-īn]*	gathered; collected [usu. in plural]
mukaṯṯaf	thickly
mukawwan / mikawwan	made up of
mulāḥagih f.	chase
mulayyam	hard-boiled sweets
mulgāṭ pl. *malāgīṭ*	tongs
mumkin	[it is] possible
munātifih / minātifih f.	1. snatch. 2. snack; morsel
munfallit	left; isolated
muntaḍur	waiting
*murā*ᶜ*ī + lā*	waiting for s.o.
*murabba*ᶜ	square [adj.]

murabba^{c} pl. *–āt*	square
murākaḏuh	kicking o.a.
murakkab	set up; arranged
murattab pl. *–āt*	wage
muraṣṣa^{c}	decorated; inlaid
murhag	exhausted
murtafa^{c}	raised; hilly
murtāḥ	comfortable; well off
musaddas pl. *–āt*	pistol
musajjal / musajjil	booked; recorded in a book [e.g. singer]; registered
musallim pl. *–īn*	someone who greets
musalsal pl. *–āt*	serial
musammā	named
musamman	with fat [e.g. cake, biscuit]
musannib	standing
mustalgif	ready to catch
mustaṭīl	long
mustawrad	imported
muṣallaḥ	made
mut'akkid / muta'akkid	sure; certain
mut^{c}*ah* f.	enjoyment; pleasure
mut^{c}*ib*	tiresome
muttajah	facing
mutwassaṭ	medium; average; reasonable
muṭabbag	thin pastry pocket fried with egg, onion and tomato inside
muṭannun	meditating
muṭḥār pl. *maṭāḥīr*	[traditional] bathroom; toilet; basin for ablutions
muṯallaṯ	triangular
muwaḏḏaf pl. *–īn*	employee
muwāfagih f., pl. *–āt*	agreement
muwaggaṣ	dressed; trimmed [stone]
muwakkaf	prepared; always ready
muwakkalih f., pl. *–āt*	[female] charge; client
muwakkil pl. *–īn*	representative
muwāṣalāt f.pl.	means of communication or travel
muxaddar	doped-up
muxaddir pl. *–āt*	narcotic
muxalfa^{c}	worn; knocked; trimmed [e.g. stone]
muxarraj + ^{c}*an*	extension to
muxaṣṣaṣ	specialised
muxāṭab + bi-	responsible [for s.o.]; obliged [to s.o.]
muxazzag	perforated
muxazzin pl. *–īn*	[gat] chewer
muxlāṣ	silver
muxtalif	different
muxtaṣṣ	experienced
muzāwaṭuh f.	hurrying

n	
na^{cc}as – yina^{cc}is	1. to be drowsy; to be sleepy. 2. to doze; to oversleep
na^{c}īm	pleasure; happiness
na^{c}īm ^{c}alayk	the grace [of God] be upon you m.s.
naba^{c} – yinba^{c}	to jump; to hop; to leap
nabbā – yinabbī	to tell s.o.; to inform s.o.; to announce s.th.
nabbā – yinabbī + bi-	to tell s.o. s.th.
nabī pl. *anbiyih*	prophet
nada^{c} – yinda^{c}	1. to send out [e.g. sound]. 2. to do s.th.
nadaš – yindiš	to fling s.th. about; to spread s.th. out
naḏ̣ag – yunḏ̣ug	to throw s.th.
naḏ̣aj – yunḏ̣uj	to become ready; to be cooked
naḏ̣ar – yunḏ̣ur + ^{c}alā	to look at s.th.
naḏ̣ḏ̣af – yinaḏ̣ḏ̣uf	to clean s.th.
naḏ̣ḏ̣aj – yinaḏ̣ḏ̣uj	to make s.th. ready or cooked
naḏ̣ḏ̣am – yinaḏ̣ḏ̣um	1. to tidy s.th. up; to put s.th. in order. 2. to organise s.th.
nafa^{c} – yinfa^{c}	to be useful; to be of use; to benefit; to work
nafar pl. *anfār*	person
naffaḍ – yinaffiḍ	to dust
nafīs	precious
nafs + noun	[the] same …
nafs f., pl. *anfus*	self
nagaḏ – yingiḏ	to rescue s.o.
nagal – yungul	to move [s.th.]
nāgaš – yināgiš	to discuss s.th.; to chat
naggā – yinaggī	to clean s.th.; to pick out dirt from s.th.
nagīl pl. *nigwal*	mountain pass
nāgiṣ	lacking; too little
nagl	transport
nahā – yinhī	to come to an end
nahārih / nihārih f.	[late] afternoon
nāhī	yes; okay; good
naḥās	copper; brass
naḥat – yinḥat	to carve s.th.; to sculpture s.th.; to plane s.th.
nāḥiyih f., pl. *nawāḥī*	district
naḥt	carving; sculpting
nār f., pl. *nīrān*	1. fire; burning [e.g. charcoal]. 2. Hell. 3. hellishly; extremely [adv.]
nārih f.	a piece of fire [e.g. burning charcoal]
nasīb pl. *ansāb*	in-law
naṣa^{c} – yunṣa^{c} [+ ^{c}alā]	to aim [at a target]
naṣa^{c} pl. *anṣa^{c}ah*	target
našad – yinšid	to chant; to recite
našam – yinšum	to praise s.o.
našar – yinšir	to spread s.th. [out]
našīd pl. *anšidih / anāšīd / nišūd*	[type of song]; chant; recitation
naššād pl. *–īn*	reciter
nātaf – yinātif	to snatch s.th. [e.g. food]

naṭṭ – yinuṭṭ	to jump
nāwal – yināwil	to hand over s.th.
naw^{c} pl. *anwā*^{c}	type; kind
nawm	sleep
naxal – yunxul	to sieve s.th.
naxs pl. *anxās*	puff; breath; smoke
nazal – yinzil	to come down; to go down; to get out
nāzil	below; downstairs
nazzal – yinazzil	to lower s.th.; to take s.th. down; to put s.th. down
ni^{c}*mih* f.	boon; blessing
ni^{c}*ni*^{c}*ah* f.	mint
nibbā^{c}	jumping; hopping; leaping
nibbā^{c}*ah* f.	jumping; hopping; leaping
nigābih f., pl. *–āt*	guild; union
nihāyih f., pl. *–āt*	end
nijārih f.	carpentry
nijiḥ – yinjaḥ	to succeed
niki^{c} *– yinka*^{c}	to fall
nīnī pl. *nayānī*	baby
nisbih f., pl. *nisab*	relation
nisī – yinsā	to forget s.th.
nišārih f.	sawdust; shavings or dust [e.g. from wood or animal horn]
nšaġal – yinšaġil + bi-	to be occupied with s.th.; to be busy with s.th.
ntahā – yintahī	to be finished; to end; to come to an end
ntašar – yintašir	to be spread about; to become widespread
nugrih f., pl. *nugar*	drain; sewer; hole
nugṭuh f., pl. *nugaṭ*	point; spot
nuktih f., pl. *nukat*	joke
nuṣṣ	half
nušṭuh f.	activity; energy
nuxrih f., pl. *nuxar*	nostril

r

rabal	rubber bands; game played with rubber bands
rabaṭ – yurbuṭ / yirbiṭ	to tie s.th.; to bind s.th.
rabbaṭ – yirabbaṭ	to bind s.th.; to tie s.th.
rābi^{c} */ rāba*^{c} */ rābu*^{c}	fourth
radd – yiridd	to return s.th.
raddad – yiraddid	to repeat s.th.
rafa^{c} *– yirfa*^{c}	to raise s.th.
rafas – yirfis	to kick [e.g. donkey; horse]
rafḍ	refusal
ragabih f., pl. *–āt*	neck
ragad – yurgud	to sleep
ragaṣ – yurguṣ	to dance
ragga^{c} *– yiragga*^{c}	to sew s.th.
rāgī	refined; high

rāgid	sleeping; lying down
ragīg	thin
ragm pl. *argām*	number
ragṣuh f., pl. *ragaṣāt*	dance
rāḥ – yirūḥ	to go
rāḥ – yirīḥ + *lā* + pronoun	to go
raḥab – yirḥab	to be welcome
raḥag – yirḥig	to exhaust s.o.
rāḥah f.	rest
raḥḥab – yiraḥḥib + bi-	to welcome s.o.
raḥḥam – yiraḥḥam	to have pity
ra'īsī	principal; main
rajam – yirjum	to throw s.th.
rājam – yirājim	to throw s.th.
rajja^{c} *– yirijji*^{c}	to give s.th. back; to return s.th.
rajjāl pl. *rijāl*	man
rakaḍ – yirkuḍ	1. to kick s.th.; to flick [with finger]. 2. to run
rakan / rikin – yirkan	to reckon; to think
rakḍ	kicking; running
rākib pl. *rukkāb*	passenger
rakkab – yirakkib	1. to take s.o. as a passenger. 2. to set s.th. up; to erect s.th.
ramā – yirmī	to throw s.th.
ramaḍān	Ramadan [Islamic month of fasting]
ramzī	token [adj.]
rann – yirinn	to be relaxed
rās / ra's pl. *ru'ūs*	1. head. 2. top
rasam – yirsim	to draw s.th.; to draw on s.th.
rasmī	official [adj.]
raṣduh f., pl. *–āt*	main, asphalted road
raṣṣ – yiruṣṣ	to arrange s.th.; to set s.th. in order; to pave s.th.
rašš – yirišš	to spread s.th. out
raṭab	1. softness; juiciness. 2. bread layered with fat and baked in *tannūr* oven
rawānī / rawānīyih f.	cake to which sugar and water syrup [*šurūb*] is added
raw^{c}*ah* f.	charm; beauty
rawwā – yirawwī	to show s.o. s.th.
rāxī	smooth; thin
raxīṣ / ruxīṣ	cheap
ra'y	view; opinion
rāyaḥah f.	scent; smell
rayḥān pl. *rayāḥīn*	parsley
rāyi^{c}	wonderful; marvellous; charming; beautiful
rayya^{c} *– yirayya*^{c} + *lā*	to wait for s.o./s.th.
razam – yirzim	to press down on s.th.
razzam – yirazzim	to press down on s.o./s.th.
rīf pl. *aryāf*	countryside
rīḥ f., pl. *riyāḥ*	wind
rīḥah f.	smell

riḥlah f., pl. *riḥalāt*	trip; journey
riji^{c} – *yirja*^{c}	to return
rijl f., pl. *arjul*	leg; foot
rikib – *yirkab*	to ride s.th.
rizg	boon; blessing
rizz	rice
rtafa^{c} – *yirtafa*^{c}	to go up [e.g. in value or physically]
rtāḥ – *yirtāḥ [+ bi-]*	1. to rest; to take a rest. 2. to be happy [with s.o.]
rtakaz – *yirtakiz*	to stand [or be] in the centre of s.th.
rubba-mā	maybe
rubṭuh f., pl. *rubaṭ*	bunch [e.g. of gat]
ruḍī – *yurḍā*	1. to agree [to do s.th.]. 2. to want
rūḥ [al-gāt] f.	the best [of the gat]; the essence [of something]
rukbih f., pl. *rukab*	knee
rūmī	maize; corn
rūtī	loaf-shaped white bread

s

sa'al – *yis'al*	to ask s.o. s.th.
sā^{c}	like
sā^{c}*ad* – *yisā*^{c}*id*	to help s.o.
sa^{c}*ah* f.	size; extent; shape; form
sā^{c}*ah* f., pl. *–āt*	watch; hour
sa^{c}*am*	i.e.; that is to say
sa^{c}*lih* f.	cough
sā^{c}*-mā*	like; as [adjt.]
sa^{c}*tar*	wild thyme
sa^{c}*y*	effort; endeavour
sabab pl. *asbāb*	reason
sabāyā f.	layered wheat bread with eggs, honey and ghee
sab^{c}*ah*	seven
sab^{c}*īn*	seventy
sabbar – *yisabbir*	to make s.th.; to prepare s.th.
sābig	previous
sadd pl. *sudūd*	dam
safar	travel; journey
sāfar – *yisāfir*	to travel
sagaf – *yisgif*	to make a roof over s.th.
saggā – *yisaggī*	to water; to irrigate s.th.
sahar – *yishar*	to stay awake at night
sāhir	staying awake at night
sahl	easy; [it's] okay
saḥab – *yisḥab*	to take away s.th.; to remove s.th.
sāḥil pl. *sawāḥil*	1. [traditional] sink; washing floor; scullery. 2. coastal plain
saḥūr	last meal in Ramadan before daybreak
sā'il	liquid [adj.]
sajjal – *yisajjil*	to record s.th.

saka^c – yiska^c	to dip s.th. into e.g. *saltih*, soured fenugreek or soup
sakab – yuskub	to pour s.th.
sakan – yuskun	to live; to inhabit
sākin	living
sākit	silent; quiet
sakkab – yisakkib	to pour s.th. [repeatedly]
salabih f., coll. *salab*	rope
salaṭuh f.	salad
salām	peace
salḥabih f.	dragging o.s. around
salīṭ	oil
sallam – yisallim + ^calā	to greet s.o.
sallih f., pl. *–āt / silal*	basket
saltih f.	hot dish of meat broth topped with whipped fenugreek; *saltih*
samaḥ – yismaḥ + lā	to allow s.o. to do s.th.
sāmaḥ – yisāmiḥ	to forgive s.o.
sambūsih f.	small triangular-shaped pie of flaky pastry stuffed with cheese or meat and served hot; samosa
samḥ	straight; fixed
sāmir	staying awake at night
sammā – yisammī	to call s.o. s.th.
sammā^cah f., pl. *–āt*	1. loudspeaker. 2. earphones
samn	clarified butter; ghee
samn baladī	local clarified butter; ghee
samrih f.	1. staying awake at night. 2. evening party
samsarih f., pl. *samāsir*	caravanserai
sani	drawing water from a well or cistern
sānī	straight
sanih f., pl. *sinīn / sanawāt*	year
sannab – yisannib	to stand; to stand up
sār – yisīr	to go [s.where]
sarab – yisrab	to queue up
sārab – yisārib	to queue up
sarayān	diffusion
sarḥah f., pl. *saraḥāt*	open square or space
sarīr pl. *sirwar*	bed
sarraj – yisarrij	to put the light on; to put lights on s.th. [e.g. car]
sarsarī pl. *–īn*	tramp; vagabond
satar – yistir / yistur	to be able; can
saṭḥ pl. *suṭūḥ*	level; surface
sawā	1. good; proper. 2. together. 3. properly [adv.]
sawā – yiswā	to be equal to s.th.
sawā 'ann ... aw	whether ... or
sawd	charcoal
sawwāg pl. *–īn*	driver
sawwāḥ pl. *–īn*	tourist
sāyiḥ pl. *suwwāḥ*	tourist
sāyilih f.	river-bed; water course

sāyir	going
saykal pl. *–āt*[1] / *sayākil*	bicycle
sayl pl. *suyūl*	water [in water course]; rain; flash flood;
sayyab – yisayyib	1. to pour s.th. 2. to carry s.th.
sayyārih f., pl. *–āt*	car
sfinj	foam; sponge
si^{c}r pl. *as^{c}ār*	price
sīd pl. *asyād*	[paternal] grandfather
sijn pl. *sijūn*	prison
sikkīnih f., pl. *sakākīn*	knife
silim – yislam	to be safe; to be free from harm
simi^c – yisma^c	to hear s.th.
sinnih f.	Sunna
sirwāl pl. *sarāwīl*	underpants; loose trousers
sittih	six
sittīn	sixty
siyāḥī	touristic
siyāsih f.	politics
snī – yisnā	to draw water from a well or cistern
sta^{c}mal – yista^{c}mil	to use s.th.
sta'ḏan – yista'ḏin	to excuse o.s.
stagbal – yistagbil	to meet s.o.; to receive s.o.
staḥagg – yistaḥagg	to be worthy; to deserve
sta'jar – yista'jir	to rent s.th.
stajlā – yistajlā	to see [the bride]
stamarr – yistamirr	to continue; to persist
starih f., pl. *star*	jacket
staṭā^c – yistaṭī^c	to be able
stawā – yistawī	to be ready [e.g. food]
staxdam – yistaxdim	to use s.th.
sufrih f., pl. *sufar*	dining place; table
sūg pl. *aswāg*	market
sūg al-^{c}irj	lame [donkey] market
sukkar	sugar
sūr coll. *aswār*	wall [e.g. of city]; fence
surūr	delight

ṣ

ṣa^{c}duh f.	Sa^{c}da [place in Yemen]
ṣabāḥ	morning
ṣabar – yiṣbur	[in neg.] can't be; can't do
ṣabb – yiṣubb	to fill s.th.; to pour in s.th.
ṣabbar – yiṣabbur	[God] to grant forbearance
ṣābūn pl. *ṣawābīn*	soap
ṣadīg pl. *aṣdugā'*	friend
ṣadr pl. *ṣudūr*	1. chest. 2. hot room in bath-house

[1] According to AS, children use the plural *saykalāt*, whereas adults tend to use plural *sayākil*.

ṣaff pl. *ṣufūf*	line
ṣaffā / ṣfā – yuṣaffī / yuṣfī	to wash s.th.; to rinse s.th.
ṣāfī	pure
ṣafīf pl. *ṣufwaf*	shelf
ṣāḥ – yiṣīḥ	to shout; to cry out
ṣaḥḥ	true; that's right!
ṣaḥḥī	healthy
ṣāḥī	awake; woken up
ṣaḥn pl. *ṣuḥūn*	plate
ṣāḥub pl. *aṣḥāb*	friend; mate
ṣāḥub al-bayt	house-owner; head of the household; landlord
ṣāḥubuh f., pl. *–āt*	[female] friend
ṣāj pl. *ṣījān*	frying pan
ṣalā	towards; in the direction of; to
ṣalaḥ – yiṣluḥ [+ bayn]	1. to be right; to be fine. 2. to negotiate [between two parties]
ṣalāh f., pl. *ṣalawāt*	prayer
ṣalaṭuh f.	salad
ṣalfā – yiṣalfī	to rinse s.th.
ṣallā – yiṣallī	to pray
ṣallaḥ – yiṣalluḥ	to set s.th. up; to prepare s.th.; to make s.th.
ṣalṣuh f.	sauce
ṣām – yiṣūm	to fast
*ṣan*ᶜ*ā* f.	San'a [capital of Yemen]
*ṣan*ᶜ*ānī*	San'ani
*ṣara*ᶜ *– yuṣra*ᶜ	to benumb s.o.; to make s.o. dizzy
ṣaraf – yiṣraf	1. to change money. 2. to spend
ṣarf	1. spending. 2. money-changing; exchange
ṣarmīyuh f., pl. *–āt*	women's head covering
ṣarrāf pl. *–īn*	money changer
ṣawḥ pl. *aṣwāḥ*	courtyard of a mosque
*ṣawma*ᶜ*ah* f., pl. *–āt / ṣawāmu*ᶜ	minaret
ṣawt pl. *aṣwāt*	1. noise; sound. 2. voice
ṣayfānī	well patinated [jambiya handle]
ṣāyum	fasting
ṣayyaḥ – yiṣayyuḥ	to shout
ṣīnī	Chinese
ṣīṭ	[name which is well known and has a] reputation
ṣṭabaḥ – yiṣṭabuḥ	to have breakfast
ṣṭafā – yiṣṭafī	to rinse o.s. off; to bathe
*ṣṭara*ᶜ *– yiṣṭara*ᶜ	to become dizzy
ṣubḥ	morning
ṣubī pl. *ṣubyān*	boy; youth
ṣubūḥ	breakfast
ṣudg	1. truth; necessity. 2. real; true; proper. 3. really!
ṣūf	wool
ṣullā' pl. *ṣulayl*	wide stone pot for making pancakes
ṣumāṭuh f., pl. *ṣamāyuṭ*	men's turban
ṣundūg pl. *ṣanādīg*	box

ṣurruh f., pl. *ṣurur*	bundle
ṣūruh f., pl. *ṣuwar*	picture; image

š

šā-	[future particle for 1 p.s. only]
ša^{c}bī	popular; people's; public
ša^{c}īr	barley
ša^{c}rih f., coll. *ša^{c}r*	hair
šābb pl. *šabāb*	youth; young man
šābi^{c}	full; satiated
šabk pl. *šibāk*	luggage rack; screen; net
šadd – yišidd	to tighten s.th.
šaḏarawān pl. *–āt*	fountain
šāf – yišūf	to see s.th.
šaffaṭ – yišaffiṭ	to make *šafūṭ*
šafūṭ	sour pancake mixed with yoghurt, milk and chilli peppers; *šafūṭ*
šagā – yišgā	to labour; to do physical work
šagā	work; wage
šāgūṣ pl. *šawāgīṣ*	small rectangular or square window which opens fully for ventilation. Sometimes in the middle of a *gamarīyih*
šagwar – yišagwir	to smoke a cigarette
šaġal – yišġal	to bother s.o.; to trouble s.o.; to occupy [e.g. s.o.'s mind]
šaġaṯ – yišġaṯ	to take a handful of s.th.; to snatch s.th. up
šāhad – yišāhid	to see s.th.; to watch s.th.
šahay / šāy	tea
šāhig	high; tall; lofty; towering
šahīyih f.	appetite
šahr pl. *šuhūr*	month
šaḥan – yišḥan	to load s.th.; to transport s.th.
šajarih f., pl. *šijar / šijarāt / ašjār*	tree
šakīyih / šakwih f.	complaint
šakl pl. *aškāl*	shape; form
šāl pl. *šīlān*	shawl
šāl – yišīl	to take s.th.
šall – yišill	to take s.th.
šambū	shampoo
šamīz pl. *–āt*	shirt
šamm	smell
šams f.	sun
šanaj – yišnij	to knead [dough] between the palm and the fingers
šanṭuh f., pl. *šanaṭāt*	bag; case
šarāb	syrup; drink
šarābih f., pl. *–āt*	sock
šaraḥ – yišraḥ	to explain s.th.; to describe s.th.
šarākih f.	partnership

šāri^{c} pl. *šawāri^{c}*	street
šarī^{c}ah f.	[Islamic] law; Sharia
šarikih f., pl. *–āt*	company
šarṭ pl. *šurūṭ*	1. condition. 2. bridal sum
šāš pl. *šīšān*	cloth
šāših f., pl. *–āt*	women's head-cover of very thin fabric
šāṭur	clever
šaxṣ pl. *ašxāṣ*	person
šaybih pl. *šayabāt*	old man
šayx pl. *šuyūx*	Shaikh; learned man
šī	there is [in cond. clauses and questions]
šī / šay pl. *ašyā*	thing
ši^{c}r	poetry
šibām f.	Shibam [place in Yemen]
šibi^{c} – yišba^{c}	to become full
šibiḥ – yišbaḥ	to take hold of s.th.; to grasp s.th.
šibrīzih f.	porcupine [name of a game]
šibz	crisps
šigārih f., pl. *šagāyir*	cigarette
šigg	beside; next to
šijnī pl. *ašjān*	branch
šiklīt	soft, wrapped sweets
šimāl	1. left. 2. north
širā f.	purchase
širb	drink
širbih f.	broth
širib – yišrab	to drink s.th.; to smoke s.th.
širkih f.	meat
šiwāl pl. *–āt*	large sack
štā – yištī	to want s.th.
štagg – yištagg	to be split; to branch off
štaġal – yištaġil	to work
štahar – yištahir	to be well known, famous
štakā – yištakī	to complain; to make a complaint
štarā – yištarī	to buy s.th.
šṭāṭ – yišṭāṭ	to sell cereals or grains
štawā – yištawī	to be grilled
šū^{c}	bad
šu^{c}ūbīyāt f.pl.	thin pastry with syrup
šuġl	work
šuġlih f.	troublesome; hard work
šukalātih f.	chocolate
šukr	thanks
šurūb / šrub	sugar syrup [used for *rawānī*]
šuwāl pl. *–āt*	sack
šuwāx	urine
šwayyih	a little

t	
ta^{c}ab	tiredness
tā^{c}ib	tired; unwell
taba^{c} – yitba^{c}	to follow s.th.; to belong to s.th.
tabdīl	changing; replacement
tabsī pl. *tabāsī*	metal tray
tad̠kirih f., pl. *tad̠ākir*	ticket
tadxīn	smoking
tafkīr	thought
taglīd pl. *tagālīd*	tradition
taġīr pl. *–āt*	change
taḥkīm	1. arbitration. 2. securing
taḥt	below; beneath
tajhīz pl. *–āt*	preparation
tājir pl. *tujjār*	trader; merchant
tajwīd	Qur'an reading
tāk	that f.
t'akkad – yit'akkad	to ensure; to make sure
taks / taksī m./f., pl. *takāsī*	taxi
talaviziyūn pl. *–āt*	television
tamām	okay; good
tamm – yitimm	to finish s.th.; to finish [doing s.th.]
tamrih f., coll. *tamr* pl. *tumūr*	date [bot.]
tanak pl. *atnāk / tinīk*	water tank; tin
tannūr f., pl. *tanāwīr*	[traditional] round oven
tannūr ġāz f.	[modern] round, gas oven
tannūr ḥaṭab f.	[traditional] round, wood-burning oven
tarzīm	pressing down
tasjīl pl. *–āt*	recording
t'at̠t̠ar – yit'at̠t̠ar + min	to be affected by s.th.
taṭwīr pl. *–āt*	development
tawgī^{c}	signing; signature
t'axxar – yit'axxar	to be late
taxzīn pl. *–āt [al-gāt]*	gat chew
tayyih	this f.
tayyik	that f.
t^{c}addā – yit^{c}addā	to go beyond s.th.; not to be limited to s.th.
t^{c}ālaj – yit^{c}ālaj	to be treated
t^{c}allam – yit^{c}allam	to learn s.th.
t^{c}āmal – yit^{c}āmal + ^{c}alā	to deal with s.o.
t^{c}aššā – yit^{c}aššā	to have supper
t^{c}ayyan – yit^{c}ayyan	to see s.th.
tbāya^{c} – yitbāya^{c}	to bargain with o.a.
tbaḍḍa^{c} – yitbaḍḍa^{c}	to purchase things
tbaxxar – yitbaxxar	to recover
tdaxxal – yitdaxxil + bayn	to interfere; to come between [two parties]
tḍallal – yitḍallal	to be/sit in the shade
tḍayyaf – yitḍayyaf	to be a guest

tfarraj – yitfarraj to watch s.th. [e.g. television]
tfattaḥ – yitfattaḥ to be opened up; to be spread out [e.g. dough]
tgahwā – yitgahwā to drink coffee or tea
tgarṭaṭ – yitgarṭaṭ to be fed up
tgaṭṭa^{c} – yitgaṭṭa^{c} to be cut up
tġaddā – yitġaddā to have lunch
tġassal – yitġassil to wash o.s.
tġayyar – yitġayyar to change
tḥākā – yitḥākā [+ ^{c}an] to talk [about s.th.]
tḥallam – yitḥallam to dream [s.th.]
tḥammal – yitḥammal to carry s.th.; to bear s.th.; to be able to stand s.th.
tḥammam – yitḥammam to take a bath; to bathe
tḥammar – yitḥammar to brown; to become brown
tḥargag – yitḥargag to burn up inside; to be angry
tḥarrak – yitḥarrak to move
tḥaylā – yitḥaylā + lā to find s.o./s.th. attractive; to think the world of s.o.
ti^{c}ib – yit^{c}ab to tire; to get tired
ti^{c}izz f. Ta^{c}izz [place in Yemen]
tiḥirrāk movement
tijāh before; in front of; towards
tijāh pl. *–āt* direction
tilāwih f. recitation
tilifūn pl. *–āt* telephone
timiššā walking; going for a walk
tirtī kicking game; Tirti
tis^{c}ah nine
tis^{c}īn ninety
titin tobacco
tjābar – yitjābar / yitjābir to chat
tjahhaz – yitjahhaz to get ready; to prepare o.s.
tjamma^{c} – yitjamma^{c} to gather together
tkallam – yitkallim [+ ^{c}an] to talk [about s.th.]
tkarrar – yitkarrar to be repeated; to be duplicated
tkawwan – yitkawwan + min to consist of s.th.
tkayyas – yitkayyas to wash o.s. with a *kīs*
tlabbas – yitlabbas to get dressed
tlāgā – yitlāgā to meet up with o.a.
tlawwā – yitlawwā to go around; to wander around
tlayyaf – yitlayyaf to wash o.s. with a loofa
tmaddad –yitmaddid to spread out; to be spread
tmaššā – yitmaššā to go for a walk
tmaššaṭ – yitmaššaṭ to comb o.s.
tnabba^{c} – yitnabba^{c} to jump; to hop; to leap
tnaṣṣa^{c} – yitnaṣṣa^{c} to aim [at a target]
tnaššaf – yitnaššaf to dry o.s.
tnātaf – yitnātaf to grab; to snatch
trākaḍ – yitrākaḍ to kick o.a.
trawwaḥ – yitrawwaḥ to go home
trayyā – yitrayyā to dream; to have a dream

tsā^{c}ad – yitsā^{c}ad	to help o.a.
tsa^{cc}al – yitsa^{cc}al	to cough
tsabbar – yitsabbar	to be made; to be prepared
tsaḥḥar – yitsaḥḥar	to eat *saḥūr*
tsalḥab – yitsalḥab	to drag o.s. around
tsāmar – yitsāmar	to stay up all night
tsamma^{c} – yitsamma^{c}	to listen
tṣabban – yitṣabban	to soap o.s.
tṣallaḥ – yitṣallaḥ	to be made
tṣarraf – yitṣarraf	to spend
tṣayyaḥ – yitṣayyaḥ	to shout out
ttafag – yittafig [+ ^{c}alā]	to agree [on s.th.]
ttakā – yitkī + ^{c}alā	to lean on s.th.
turāb	dust; dirt; soil
turkī	Turkish
tuṣfī	rinsing
twaḍḍā – yitwaḍḍā	to perform the ablutions
twaḍḍaf – yitwaḍḍaf	to gain employment; to be employed; to go to work
twājad – yitwājad	to be available; to be present [in abundance]
twālah – yitwālah	to amuse o.s.; to have fun; to spend time
twassaṭ – yitwassaṭ + bi-	to get s.o. to mediate on o's behalf
twāṭā – yitwāṭā	to gather; to collect [intr.]
txallaṣ – yitxallaṣ + min	to get away from s.o./s.th.
txammar – yitxammar	to rise [e.g. dough]
txarrab – yitxarrab	to be destroyed; to be demolished
txaṣṣaṣ – yitxaṣṣaṣ + bi-	to specialise in s.th.
txawwar – yitxawwar	to desire s.th.; to crave s.th.
txayyal – yitxayyal	to appear; to seem; to imagine s.th.
tzawwaj – yitzawwaj	to get married

ṭ

ṭa^{cc}am – yiṭa^{cc}um	to let s.o. taste s.th.; to feed s.o. s.th.
ṭa^{c}īm	tasty; delicious
ṭa^{c}m	taste
ṭa^{c}mīyuh f.	patty made of beans, onions, garlic and parsley; falafil
ṭabaguh f., pl. *–āt*	layer
ṭabax – yuṭbux	to cook s.th.
ṭabāxuh f.	cooking
ṭab^{c}	stamp; impression
ṭab^{c}an	of course
ṭabī^{c}ah f.	nature; s.th. natural
ṭabīx	mixed vegetables
ṭābu^{c}	habit; custom
ṭaffā – yiṭuffī	to turn s.th. off [e.g. light, gas]
ṭāguh f., pl. *ṭīgān*	[opening] window
ṭaḥan – yiṭḥan	to grind s.th. [usu. grain]
ṭahāruh f.	ritual purity
ṭaḥḥan – yiṭaḥḥun	to grind s.th. [usu. grain]

ṭaḥīn	[ground] flour
ṭāḥūn pl. *ṭawāḥīn*	mill
ṭalab pl. *–āt*	call; demand
ṭalab – yuṭlub	to ask for s.th.; to demand s.th.
ṭal^{c}ah f., pl. *–āt*	hill; bank; slope
ṭalī pl. *aṭlā'*	goat; lamb
ṭall – yuṭull + ^{c}alā	to look out or down on s.th.
ṭalla^c – yiṭallu^c	to put s.o. in [e.g. a taxi]; to take s.th. up
ṭālu^c	top; upstairs; above
ṭālu^{c}ī	upper; going up
ṭamāṭīs	tomatoes
ṭambal – yiṭambul	to beat the drum
ṭannan – yiṭannun	to be distracted; to meditate
ṭaraf pl. *aṭrāf*	1. edge [of a place]; extremity. 2. anywhere
ṭaraḥ – yiṭraḥ [+ lā]	to put s.th.; to give s.th. [to s.o.]
ṭarḥ	giving wedding presents; wedding present
ṭarḥah f., pl. *ṭaraḥāt*	1. wedding present. 2. floor; level
ṭarī	fresh
ṭarīg f., pl. *ṭurwag / ṭurug*	road
ṭarīguh f., pl. *ṭurug*	way
ṭarr – yiṭarr	to send s.o. away; to kick s.o. out
ṭarrag – yiṭarrug	to sound the horn
ṭarrīguh f., pl. *–āt*	horn; noise of a horn
ṭāruf	1. [s.th.] at the end; at the extremity; on the edge. 2. anyone convenient
ṭarūṭuh f.	dill
ṭāsuh f., pl. *ṭīsān*	bowl; metal container; pan; plate
ṭawālī	1. straight on. 2. all the time. 3. straight away
ṭawīl pl. *ṭuwāl*	long; tall
ṭawwal – yiṭawwul	to spend a long time; to tarry
ṭawwar – yiṭawwur	to develop s.th.; to change s.th.
ṭayyub	good
ṭayramānuh f., pl. *–āt*	small room at top of house; watch-out room
ṭayyāruh f., pl. *–āt*	aeroplane
ṭīn	clay
ṭṭawwar – yiṭṭawwar	to develop; to go forward
ṭufāyuh pl. *–āt*	ashtray
ṭufl pl. *aṭfāl*	child
ṭuḥuṣ – yiṭḥaṣ	to fall; to slip
ṭūl	length
ṭūl al-wagt	the whole time
ṭulu^c – yiṭla^c	to go up
ṭumbuluh f., pl. *ṭanābul*	drum
ṭunnānuh f.	wonder; distraction; meditation
ṭunnānī	distraction; meditation
ṭurāz pl. *ṭuruz*	type; model; sort

ṯ

ṯalājih f., pl. *–āt*	1. fridge. 2. thermos flask

ṯalāṯih	three
ṯalāṯīn	thirty
ṯāliṯ	third
ṯaman pl. *aṯmān*	price; fare
ṯamān pl. *ṯawāmin*	week
ṯamānīn	eighty
ṯamāniyih	eight
ṯanā – yiṯnī	to do s.th. again
ṯānī	1. other; next. 2. second
ṯawmih / ṯūmih f., coll. *ṯawm / ṯūm*	garlic
ṯawrih f., pl. *–āt*	revolution
ṯulāṯī	triangular

u

uḏn f., pl. *āḏān*	ear
uḍāfi	additional
uġniyih f., pl. *aġānī*	song
umm f., pl. *ummahāt*	mother
usbū^{c} pl. *asābī*^{c}	week
uslūb pl. *asālīb*	method; way; means
usrih f., pl. *usar*	family
ustāḏ pl. *asātiḏih*	professor; sir
uṣbu^{c} pl. *aṣābu*^{c}	finger
uxt f., pl. *xawāt*	sister

w

wa-	and
wa^{c}*ā* pl. *aw*^{c}*iyih*	container; vessel
wa^{c}*y*	awareness
waḍīfuh f., pl. *waḍāyuf*	employment; job
wafā – yūfi	to come to an end
wāfag – yiwāfig	to agree
wagaf – yūgaf	to stop
wagal	hopscotch
wagf pl. *awgāf*	religious endowment; *wakf*
[al-]awgāf	*Wakf* Ministry
wagfih f., pl. *wagafāt*	stop
wagga^{c} *– yiwaggi*^{c}	to sign [s.th.]
waggaf – yiwaggif	to stop s.th.; to park s.th.
waggaṣ – yiwaggaṣ	to trim s.th. [usu. stone]
wāgi^{c}	real
wāgif	standing
wagīṣ	dressed stone
wagt pl. *awgāt*	time
waġd pl. *awġād*	scoundrel
wahhaf – yiwahhif + lā	to fan s.th. [e.g. a fire]
wāhimih	pregnant
waḥdih	on his own

wāḥid	one
waḥīd al-garn	rhinoceros
waja^c	pain
waja^c *– yūja*^{c}	to hurt s.o.
wajbih f., pl. *wajabāt*	meal
wajh / wašš pl. *wujūh*	face; front; upper side
wakkal – yiwakkil	to appoint s.o. [as a representative]
wald pl. *awlād*	boy; child
walī 'amr pl. *awliyih umūr*	legal guardian
wālidih f., pl. *–āt*	mother; new mother
wālif	used to; accustomed to
wallā	or
w-allāh / w-allāhi	by God!
warā / wara'	behind
waragat al-milkih f.	wedding contract
waragih f., pl. *–āt / warag*	leaf; paper
waraṭuh f.	scrape; dilemma
wardih f., coll. *ward*	flower
warrā – yiwarrī	to show s.o. s.th.
wasaṭ / wasṭ	middle
wasax	dirt
wāsi^c	wide; broad
wassa^c *– yiwassa*^{c}	to expand s.th.; to extend s.th.; to spread s.th. out
wāṣal – yiwāṣul	to continue s.th.
waṣf	description
waṣṣal – yiwaṣṣul + lā	to take s.th. to s.o./s.where
wāṭā – yiwāṭī	to collect s.th.; to gather s.th.
wāṭī	low
wazan – yūzin	to weigh s.th.
wazīr pl. *wuzarā*	minister
wazza^c *– yiwazzi*^{c}	to distribute s.th.
wazzan – yiwazzin	to weigh s.th.
wihimat – tawham	to become pregnant
wilād	birth; time after birth during which women visit the new mother
wilādih f.	birth
wilid – yūlad	1. to be born. 2. to give birth
wisi^c *– yisa*^{c}	to occupy [an area]
wuḍū'	ablutions
wuga^c *– yūga*^{c}	1. to become; to turn out; to be. 2. to happen; to fall
wulid – yūlad	to give birth; to be born
wusādih f., pl. *wasāyid*	back cushion
wuṣul – yūṣal [+ lā]	to arrive s.where; to reach [a place]

x

xabar	information
xābar – yixābir	to talk to s.o.
xabaš – yixbaš	to stir s.th.; to beat s.th.
xabaṭ – yuxbuṭ	1. to go around. 2. to hit s.o./s.th.

xabaz – yuxbiz / yixbiz	to make bread; to bake
xabbāz pl. *–īn*	baker
xabīr pl. *xubrih*	friend
xabīrih f., pl. *–āt*	[female] friend
xabīṯ	harmful; bad
xadam – yixdam	to serve s.o.
xadar – yixdir	to bore a hole in s.th.; to perforate s.th.
xaddar – yixaddir	to be doped up; to dope s.o.
xaḏḏ – yixiḏḏ	to be relaxed
xaḏ̣ab – yuxḏ̣ub	to beat s.th.; to mix s.th. [e.g. fenugreek, yoghurt]
xāf – yixāf	to be afraid
xafī	hidden; concealed
xafīf	light (of weight); thin
xāl pl. *axwāl*	[maternal] uncle
xalag – yuxlug	to create s.th.
xalaṣ – yuxliṣ	to take off [clothes]
xalāṣ	that's it! okay; well
xalaṭ – yuxluṭ	to mix s.th.
xalfa^c – yixalfa^c	to flip s.th. over
xālih f., pl. *–āt*	[maternal] aunt
xāliṣ	taking off [clothes]; having taken off [clothes]
xall	vinegar
xallā – yixallī	1. to leave s.th. 2. to make s.th. 3. to let s.o.
xallāb	fascinating
xallaṣ – yixalliṣ	1. to take off s.th. 2. to finish s.th.
xallaṭ – yixalluṭ	to mix s.th.
xamar – yuxmar	to rise [e.g. dough]
xāmir	risen
xamīrih f.	yeast; rising agent
xamsih	five
xamsīn	fifty
xānih f., pl. *–āt*	boot of a car
xarā	faeces
xaraj – yuxruj	to go out
xardal	mustard seeds
xārij	outside
xārijī	1. outer. 2. imported. 3. about to go outside; going outside
xarrab – yixarrib	to demolish s.th.
xarraj – yixarrij	to take s.th. out; to remove s.th.
xarṣ pl. *axrāṣ*	earring
xāsir pl. *–īn*	loser
xaṣm pl. *xuṣūm*	opponent
xāṣṣ	1. special; particular. 2. round, white pitta bread
xāṣṣatan	especially [class.]
xašabih f., coll. *xašab*	wood
xātam pl. *xawātim*	ring
xaṭab – yuxṭub	to engage [a woman]

xāṭī	going; walking
xaṭīr	dangerous
xaṭiyuh f.	walk
xaṭṭ / xuṭṭ pl. *xuṭūṭ*	line; road; way
xāṭur	sake; mind
xāṭur[kum]	goodbye! [bride's farewell]
xaṭwuh f., pl. *xaṭawāt*	step; pace
xawar – yixwar	to crave s.th.; to desire s.th.
xawrih f., pl. *xawarāt*	craving
xawwal – yixawwil	to save money; to economise
xayl coll., pl. *xiyūl*	horses
xaymih f., pl. *xiyam*	tent
xayr	goodness; blessing
xayrāt	a lot
xayṭ pl. *xuyūṭ*	string; rope
xayyaṭ – yixayyiṭ	to sew s.th.
xazag – yuxzug	to bore a hole in s.th.; to perforate s.th.
xazan – yixzin	to hold s.th. [e.g. heat]
xazwag – yixazwig	to make holes
xazzag – yixazzig	to bore a hole in s.th.; to perforate s.th.
xazzan – yixazzin	1. to chew gat. 2. to store s.th.
xibrih f.	experience
xiddār	numbing; narcotising [e.g. effect of gat]
[min] xilāl	through
xirgih f., pl. *xirag*	rag
xirī – yixrā	to defecate
xisārih f.	loss; payment
xisiᶜ – yixsaᶜ	to be damaged; to rot; to go bad
xisir – yixsar	to lose s.th.
xiyyāṭ	sewing
xizānih f., pl. *xazāyin*	1. safe [for money]. 2. room in bath-house with large water tank
xizzān	1. chewing [gat]. 2. storing
xtalaf – yixtalif [+ ᶜan]	to differ [from s.th.]
xtār – yixtār	to choose s.th.
xubzih f., coll. *xubz*	bread
xuḍruh f.	greenery
xulab	mud
xurrāfih f., pl. *–āt*	story; folktale; folk custom
xurūj	going out; exit
xuṭbuh f.	engagement
xuṭī – yuxṭā	to walk [person]; to go [e.g. car]
xuṭūbuh f.	engagement
xuzgī pl. *xizgān*	hole

y

yā	hey! [vocative particle]
yā … yā	either … or
yābis	dry

yad f., pl. *aydī / ayādī*	hand
yadawī	handmade; hand [adj.]
yā 'immā / yimmā … aw	either … or
yājūrih f., coll. *yājūr*	baked brick
y-allāh	come on! that's it!
yamanī	Yemeni
yamīn	right
*ya*ᶜ*nī*	i.e.; that is to say
*yā s*ᶜ*am*	i.e.; that is to say
yawm pl. *iyyām*	day
yawm al-aḥadd	Sunday
yawm al-iṯnayn	Monday
*yawm al-jum*ᶜ*ah*	Friday
yawm al-xamīs	Thursday
*yawm ar-rabū*ᶜ	Wednesday
yawm as-sabt	Saturday
yawm aṣ-ṣabāḥ[īyuh]	the day after the nuptial night
yawm aṯ-ṯalūṯ	Tuesday
yawmīyih / yawmī	daily
yibis – yības	to become dry; to dry out
yimkin	perhaps
yusrā f.	left

z

zabādī	yoghurt
zabaj – yizbij	to jest; to joke
zabal	weariness; annoyance
zabīb	raisins
zabj	joking
zād – yizīd + imperf.	1. to do s.th. again, more. 2. to keep doing s.th. 3. furthermore; also
zaff – yiziff	to accompany [a bride or bridegroom]; to conduct [the bride] in a solemn procession to her husband's house
zaffih f.	wedding; wedding procession
zāgim + bi-	holding s.th.; keeping s.th.
zaġbar – yizaġbir	to spout forth [e.g. water]
zaġbirih f.	spouting forth [e.g. water]
zaġīr pl. *zuġār*	small; young
zaġrad – yizaġrid	to ululate; to trill [e.g. bird]
zahrih f., coll. *zahr*	flower
zaḥag – yizḥag	to crush s.th.
zaḥāwug	spicy dip of chilli pepper, tomato, garlic and salt; *zaḥāwug*
zaḥmih f.	crowd; rush[ing]; shoving
zaḥwag – yizaḥwag / yizaḥwug	to make a spicy dip; to make *zaḥāwug*
zakkan – yizakkin + ᶜ*alā*	to inform s.o.; to verify s.th.
zalaṭ	money
zamān	time

zamīl pl. *zumalā*	colleague; friend
zamīlih f., pl. *–āt*	[female] colleague; [female] friend
zār – yizūr	to visit s.o./s.where
zara^{c} *– yizra*^{c}	to grow s.th.; to cultivate s.th.
zārat + noun	some …
zāratḥīn	sometimes
zārat wāḥid	the odd one
zawāj f. *zawājih* pl. *–āt*	wedding
zāwaṭ – yizāwuṭ	1. to be in a hurry; to hurry. 2. to panic
zawj pl. *azwāj*	husband
zawwaj – yizawwij	to marry s.o.
zaxraf – yizaxraf	to decorate s.th.
zāyad – yizāyid	to do too much
zāyid	1. increase. 2. too much
zayt	oil
zayy	like
zayyad – yizayyid	to overdo s.th.; to add more to s.th.; to increase s.th.
zayyaġ – yizayyiġ	to cause s.th. to deviate; to confuse s.o.
zayyan – yizayyin	to decorate s.th.; to make s.th. attractive
zayy-mā	as; like [adjt.]
zibādī	yoghurt
zibdih f.	butter
zid	1. also. 2. again. 3. else. 4. anymore [in neg.]
zifāf	wedding; wedding procession to take bride to bridegroom
zigim – yizgam	to take hold of s.th.; to grab s.th.; to grasp s.th.
zijāj / zujāj	glass
zijājī / zujājī	glass [adj.]
zīnih f.	decorations [usu. lights for weddings]
zinnih f., pl. *zinan*	fitted dress [women]; full-length robe [men]
zirā^{c}*ah* f., pl. *–āt*	cultivation
ziri^{c} *– yizra*^{c}	to be grown; to be cultivated
zirr	cloves
ziyādih	a lot; too much
ziyārih f., pl. *–āt*	visit
zugāg pl. *azgāg*	alley; lane
zugzugī pl. *zagāzig*	alley; lane
zuġayrī	small
zurgayfī coll. *zurgayf*	marble
zuwwih f., pl. *zuwaw*	corner

REFERENCES

Agius, Dionisius A. "Precedence of VOS over VSO in Modern Standard Arabic", 39-55 in Alan S. Kaye (ed.), *Semitic Studies in Honor of Wolf Leslau: On the occasion of his eighty-fifth birthday November 14th, 1991*. Wiesbaden, 1991.

Al-Akwa^c, Ismā^{c}īl ibn ^{c}Alī *Al-Amṯāl al-Yamānīyah*, 2 volumes. San'a/ Beirut, 1984.

Al-Azraqi, Munira *Aspects of the Syntax of the Dialect of Abha (south-west Saudi Arabia)*, PhD thesis. University of Durham, 1998.

Al-Ḥawālī, Muḥammad ibn ^{c}Alī al-Ḥusayn al-Akwa^c *Ṣafḥatun min Tārīx al-Yamani al-Ijtimā^{c}ī wa-Qiṣṣat Ḥayātī*, 3 volumes. No place/date.

Al-Šahārī, Jamāl al-Dīn ^{c}Alī ibn ^{c}Abd Allāh ibn al-Qāsim ibn al-Mu^{c}ayyad bi-llāh Muḥammad ibn al-Qāsim ibn Muḥammad al-Šahārī *Waṣf Ṣan^{c}ā': Mustall min al-manšūrāt al-jalīyah* (ed. ^{c}Abd Allāh Muḥammad al-Ḥibšī). San'a, 1993.

Dahlgren, Sven-Olof *Word Order in Arabic*. Göteborg, 1998.

Eksell Harning, Kerstin *The Analytic Genitive in the Modern Arabic Dialects*. Göteborg, 1980.

Hinds, Martin and El-Said Badawi *A Dictionary of Egyptian Arabic: Arabic-English*. Beirut, 1986.

Holes, Clive *Gulf Arabic*. London and New York, 1990.

Holes, Clive *Modern Arabic: Structures, Functions and Varieties*. London and New York, 1995.

Holes, Clive "Retention and loss of the passive verb in the Arabic dialects of Northern Oman and Eastern Arabic", 347-362 in *Journal of Semitic Studies* 43, 1998.

Jastrow, Otto — "Zur Phonologie und Phonetik des Ṣanᶜānischen", 289-304 in H. Kopp and G. Schweizer (eds.), *Entwicklungsprozesse in der Arabischen Republik Jemen*. Wiesbaden, 1984.

Johnstone, T.M. — *Eastern Arabian Dialect Studies*. Oxford, 1967.

Serjeant, R.B. and Ronald Lewcock (eds.) — *Ṣanᶜā': An Arabian Islamic City*. London, 1983.

Mackintosh-Smith, Tim — *Yemen: Travels in Dictionary Land*. London, 1997.

Mörth, Karlheinz — *Die Kardinalzahlwörter von Eins bis Zehn in den Neuarabischen Dialekte*. Wien, 1997.

Muḥammad, Asmā' — *Amṯāl Ṣanᶜānīyah: Jamᶜ wa-'iᶜdād*. San'a, no date.

Näim-Sanbar, Samia — "L'Habitat traditionnel a Ṣanᶜā': sémantique de la maison", 79-113 in *Journal Asiatique* 275, 1987.

Näim-Sanbar, Samia — "Contribution a l'étude de l'accent yéménite: Le parler des femmes de l'ancienne génération", 67-89 in *Zeitschrift für Arabische Linguistik* 26, 1994.

Piamenta, Moshe — *Dictionary of Post-Classical Yemeni Arabic*. Leiden, 1990-1991.

Reichmuth, Stefan — *Der arabische Dialekt der Šukriyya im Ostsudan*. Hildesheim/New York, 1983.

Retsö, Jan — *The Finite Passive Voice in Modern Arabic Dialects*. Göteborg, 1983.

Rossi, Ettore — *L'Arabo Parlato a Ṣanᶜā'*. Rome, 1939.

Rushby, Kevin — *Eating the Flowers of Paradise: A Journey Through the Drug Fields of Ethiopia and Yemen*. London, 1998.

Versteegh, Kees — *Pidginization and Creolization: The Case of Arabic*. Amsterdam/Philadelphia, 1984.

Versteegh, Kees — Review of Watson, *A Syntax of Ṣanᶜānī Arabic*, 795-799 in *Bibliotheca Orientalis LIV*, 1997.

Watson, Janet C.E. — *A Syntax of Ṣanᶜānī Arabic*. Wiesbaden, 1993.

Watson, Janet C.E. — "Emphasis in San'ani Arabic", 253-258 in *Proceedings of the Second Aïda Conference*, University of Cambridge, 1995.

Watson, Janet C.E. — *Ṣbaḥtū! A Course in Ṣanᶜānī Arabic*. Wiesbaden, 1996a.

Watson, Janet C.E. — "Emphasis in San'ani Arabic", 45-52 in *Three Topics in Arabic Phonology*, CMEIS Occasional Papers, 1996b.

Watson, Janet C.E. — "The directionality of emphasis spread in Arabic", 289-300 in *Linguistic Inquiry* 30, 1999a.

Watson, Janet C.E. — "Syllable structure and syllabification in Cairene and San'ani Arabic", 501-525 in Harry van der Hulst and Nancy A. Ritter (eds.), *The Syllable: Views and Facts*. Berlin, 1999b.

Watson, Janet C.E. — *Phonology and Morphology of Modern Spoken Arabic*. Oxford, (forthcoming)

Weir, Shelagh — *Qat in Yemen: Consumption and Social Change*. London, 1985.